Animals as Religious Subjects

Animals as Religious Subjects

Transdisciplinary Perspectives

Edited by Celia Deane-Drummond,
David L. Clough & Rebecca Artinian-Kaiser

B L O O M S B U R Y

LONDON • NEW DELHI • NEW YORK • SYDNEY

Bloomsbury T&T Clark

An imprint of Bloomsbury Publishing Plc

50 Bedford Square
London
WC1B 3DP
UK

1385 Broadway
New York
NY 10018
USA

www.bloomsbury.com

Bloomsbury is a registered trade mark of Bloomsbury Publishing Plc

First published 2013
Paperback edition first published 2014

British Library Cataloguing-in-Publication Data
A catalogue record for this books is available from the British Library.

ISBN: HB: 978-0-567-01564-8
PB: 978-0-567-65976-7
ePUB: 978-0-567-44521-6
ePDF: 978-0-567-57189-2

Library of Congress Cataloging-in-Publication Data
Deane-Drummond, Celia; Clough, David L; and
Artinian-Kaiser, Rebecca
Animals as Religious Subjects/Celia Deane-Drummond, David L. Clough,
Rebecca Artinian-Kaiser
p.cm
Includes bibliographic references and index.
ISBN 978–0–567–01564–8 (hardcover) – ISBN 978–0–567–19228–8 (pbk.)
2012045678

Typeset by Fakenham Prepress Solutions, Fakenham, Norfolk NR21 8NN

Contents

Acknowledgements

This book could not have been published without a great deal of support from many parties. In the first place, we acknowledge financial support from the Centre for Religion and Biosciences at the University of Chester, directed by Celia Deane-Drummond, which hosted the European Forum for the Study of Religion and Environment's third biennial meeting in May 2011. A substantial portion of the papers published in this book originated as plenary or short papers presented at this conference. We are grateful to the leadership of Professor Sigurd Bergmann, University of Trondheim, Norway, who was acting Chair of the European Forum for the Study of Religion and Environment. Celia Deane-Drummond was elected Chair of the Forum on a two-year term at the meeting. Second, we acknowledge the support of Gladstone's Library, Hawarden, where the meeting was held, and the extraordinary hospitality, the congenial atmosphere for intense academic discussion, and the provision of library facilities and other conference resources. This was a discussion across disciplines, and the library is extremely well placed to host such a conversation. We are also grateful to Kris Hiuser for his help with the conference arrangements. Soon after this conference, one of us, Celia Deane-Drummond, relocated to the University of Notre Dame. We would also like to acknowledge support for indexing and copyediting from the Institute for Scholarship in the Liberal Arts, College of Arts and Letters, University of Notre Dame. Finally, we would like to thank our publishers T&T Clark, and Jan-Peter Wissink and Anna Turton in particular, for their encouragement, support, and enthusiasm for this project.

Contributors

Rebecca Artinian-Kaiser is a doctoral student in theology at the University of Chester and a visiting graduate student at the University of Notre Dame. She holds post-graduate degrees in theology from the University of Edinburgh and from Duke Divinity School. She works at the boundary of theological ethics and environmental ethics and her current research aims to construct a theological and ethical framework for the environmental practice of ecological restoration. Rebecca lives in South Bend, Indiana with her husband and cat and enjoys working in her garden, expanding its variety of native species, and growing some of her own food.

Charles Camosy is Assistant Professor of Christian Ethics at Fordham University. He received his Ph.D. in theology from the University of Notre Dame in 2008 and has published articles in the *American Journal of Bioethics*, *Journal of Medicine and Philosophy*, *Journal of the Catholic Health Association*, *San Francisco Chronicle*, *Washington Post*, and *Commonweal* magazine. He has also authored *Too Expensive to Treat?: Finitude, Tragedy, and the Neonatal ICU* (2010), which won second place in the 2011 Catholic Media Association awards in the 'social issues' category, and *Peter Singer and Christian Ethics: Beyond Polarization* (2012). He is also the founder and co-director of the Catholic Conversation Project and a member of the ethics committee at the Children's Hospital of New York. Camosy regularly contributes to the website catholicmoraltheology.com.

Stephen R. L. Clark, formerly a Fellow of All Souls College, Oxford (1968–75), Lecturer in Moral Philosophy at the University of Glasgow (1974–83), and Professor of Philosophy at the University of Liverpool (1984–2009), is now retired from paid employment. He continues to manage an international e-list for philosophers, and to serve as Associate Editor of the *British Journal for the History of Philosophy*. His books include *Aristotle's Man* (1975), *The Moral Status of Animals* (1977), *From Athens to Jerusalem* (1984), *The Mysteries of Religion* (1986), *Civil Peace and Sacred Order* (1989), *How to Live Forever* (1995), *Biology and Christian Ethics* (2000), *G. K. Chesterton: Thinking Backwards, Looking Forwards* (2006), *Understanding Faith* (2009), *Philosophical Futures* (2011) and *Ancient Mediterranean Philosophy* (2012). He is married to Professor Gillian Clark of Bristol University, with three adult children and one grandson. His current interests are in the philosophy of Plotinus, the understanding and treatment of non-human animals, and science fiction.

Forrest Clingerman is Associate Professor of Philosophy and Religion at Ohio Northern University, where he teaches courses in theology, ethics, and the history of religious thought. Much of his work lies at the intersection of philosophy and religious thought. Throughout his work, the concept of place is taken as an important object of interpretation for environmental thought. He has published in the journals *Ethics, Place and Environment, Worldviews, Environmental Values, Environmental Philosophy, The Journal for the Study of Religion, Nature, and Culture*, and *Literature and Theology*, as well as in edited collections. He is co-editor of *Placing Nature on the Borders of Religion, Philosophy and Ethics* (with Mark H. Dixon, 2011), and the forthcoming *Interpreting Nature: The Emerging Field of Environmental Hermeneutics* (with Brian Treanor, Martin Drenthen, and David Utsler). He is also co-editor (with Brian Treanor) of a new book series, entitled *Groundworks*, to be published by Fordham University Press beginning in 2013, that will be devoted to fostering a deeper conversation between theology and philosophy on ecological issues.

David Clough is Professor of Theological Ethics and Head of the Department of Theology and Religious Studies at the University of Chester. He has recently published the first systematic theology of animals, *On Animals: Volume 1: Systematic Theology* (2012), which will soon be followed by a second volume on theological ethics. Previously, he co-edited with Celia Deane-Drummond *Creaturely Theology: On God, Humans and Animals* (2009). Other publications include *Faith and Force: A Christian Debate about War* (2007), co-authored with Brian Stiltner, and *Ethics in Crisis: Interpreting Barth's Ethics* (2005). Most of his journal articles and book chapters are available in Chester's open-access repository <http://bit.ly/dlclough> and he can be followed on Twitter using @DLClough. He is a Methodist lay preacher and lives next door to the zoo in Chester with his wife, three children, and a cat.

Celia Deane-Drummond is Professor of Theology at the University of Notre Dame with a concurrent appointment in the College of Science and a Fellow of the Eck Institute for Global Health at the University of Notre Dame. Previously, she held a professorial chair in theology and the biological sciences at the University of Chester (2000–11), and was Director of the Centre for Religion and the Biosciences launched in 2002. She was elected Chair of the European Forum for the Study of Religion and Environment in 2011 and has served as the editor of the international journal *Ecotheology* (2000–6). From 2009–10, she was seconded to the spirituality team at the Catholic Fund for Overseas Development (CAFOD), working explicitly in the area of environmental justice and climate change. Her more recent books include *Creation through Wisdom* (2000), *Brave New World* (2003), *ReOrdering Nature* (2003), *The Ethics of Nature* (2004), *Wonder and Wisdom: Conversations in Science, Spirituality and Theology* (2006), *Genetics and Christian Ethics* (2006), *Future Perfect: God, Medicine and Human Identity*, edited with Peter Scott (2006, 2nd edn, 2010), *Ecotheology* (2008), *Christ and Evolution: Wonder and Wisdom* (2009), *Creaturely Theology: On God, Humans and Other Animals*, edited with David Clough (2009), *Seeds of Hope: Facing the Challenge of Climate Justice* (2010), and *Religion and Ecology in the Public Sphere*, edited with Heinrich Bedford-Strohm (2011).

Adam Dodd received his Ph.D. in Media and Culture from the School of English, Media Studies and Art History, at the University of Queensland in 2009. From 2010 to 2012, he was Postdoctoral Research Fellow at the Department of Culture Studies and Oriental Languages, University of Oslo. His research interests are focused on the role that visioning technologies and representational conventions have played in developing conceptions of insects from the early modern period onward. He is the author of *Beetle* (Reaktion, forthcoming) and numerous articles on insects and culture.

Ingvild Sælid Gilhus is Professor of Religion at the University of Bergen, Norway. She is Vice-President of the International Association for the History of Religions (until 2015). She works in the areas of religion in late antiquity and new religious movements. Her main publications include *Laughing Gods, Weeping Virgins: Laughter in the History of Religions* (1997) and *Animals, Gods and Humans: Changing Attitudes to Animals in Greek, Roman and Early Christian Ideas* (2006). She is the book review editor of *Numen* and an editorial board member of *Temenos*.

Aaron S. Gross is an Assistant Professor of Theology and Religious Studies at the University of San Diego. He holds a Masters of Theological Studies from Harvard Divinity School and a Ph.D. in religious studies with a specialization in Jewish traditions from the University of California, Santa Barbara. Gross has lectured internationally at academic conferences and universities on issues related to animals and religion, and food and religion. He co-chairs the American Academy of Religion Consultation on Animals and Religion, serves on the board of the Society of Jewish Ethics, and is the founder and CEO of the nonprofit Farm Forward. Gross co-edited *Animal Others and the Human Imagination* (2012) and collaborated with novelist Jonathan Safran Foer on Foer's international bestseller, *Eating Animals* (2009). His essays have appeared in *The Central Conference of American Rabbis Journal, The Encyclopedia of Film and Religion, The Encyclopedia of Global Religion, The Huffington Post, The Oxford Handbook of Jewish Ethics, Shofar: An Interdisciplinary Journal of Jewish Studies,* and *Tikkun Magazine.*

Tim Ingold is Professor of Social Anthropology at the University of Aberdeen, and a Fellow of both the British Academy and the Royal Society of Edinburgh. Following 25 years at the University of Manchester, Ingold moved in 1999 to Aberdeen, where he went on to establish the UK's newest Department of Anthropology. Ingold has carried out ethnographic fieldwork among Saami and Finnish people in Lapland, and has written on comparative questions of environment, technology, and social organization in the circumpolar North, as well as on the role of animals in human society, on issues in human ecology, and on evolutionary theory in anthropology, biology, and history. More recently, he has been exploring the links between environmental perception and skilled practice, with a view to replacing traditional models of genetic and cultural transmission with a relational approach focusing on the growth of skills of perception and action within socio-environmental contexts of development. These ideas are presented in his book *The Perception of the Environment* (2000). Ingold's latest research pursues three lines of inquiry that emerged from his earlier work, concerning the dynamics of pedestrian movement, the creativity of practice, and the linearity of writing. These all came together in his book *Lines* (2007), along with three edited collections: *Creativity and Cultural Improvisation* (with Elizabeth Hallam, 2007), *Ways of Walking* (with Jo Lee Vergunst, 2008) and *Redrawing Anthropology* (2011). Ingold is currently writing and teaching on issues on the interface between anthropology, archaeology, art, and architecture. His latest book is entitled *Being Alive* (2011).

Eric Daryl Meyer is currently a doctoral candidate at Fordham University, in New York City. His research focuses on theological constructions of the human-animal distinction, and the role that they play in validating patterns of ecological degradation. He teaches courses in Early Christian history and contemporary Christian theology. He is an advocate for Wilderness and wild places and has been a backpacking/mountaineering guide in California and Colorado for more than a decade.

Sabine Obermaier is Associate Professor of Medieval German Literature in the German Department at the Johannes Gutenberg University of Mainz. Her research interests are in Middle High German 'poetry on poetry' (see her dissertation *Von Nachtigallen und Handwerkern. Dichtung über Dichtung in Minnesang und Sangspruchdichtung*), in medieval fables (notably of Indian origin with specific interests to narratological questions – see her habilitation treatise *Das Fabelbuch als Rahmenerzählung*) and, finally, in animal lore (see her recent miscellany volume *Tiere und Fabelwesen im Mittelalter*). She initiated the international and interdisciplinary *animaliter*-project 'Animals in Medieval European Literature' (www.animaliter.info) and published a variety of papers on this subject, for instance on the elephants in the Alexander romance or on the hippopotamus in classical and medieval encyclopaedic and narrative literature.

Raymond F. Person, Jr. is Professor of Religion and Chair of the Department of Philosophy and Religion at Ohio Northern University. His most recent book is *The Deuteronomic History and the Book of Chronicles: Scribal Works in an Oral World* (2010) and he is current working on a commentary on Deuteronomy for the Earth Bible Commentary series. He and his wife, Elizabeth, live on a 20-acre organic farm, which is run by a cooperative that he founded consisting of more than 20 families.

Robert Song is Senior Lecturer in Christian Ethics in the Department of Theology and Religion, Durham University. He is the author of *Christianity and Liberal Society* (1997) and *Human Genetics: Fabricating the Future* (2002) as well as many articles across the fields of Christian ethics and social and political theology. His research interests centre on the theology and ethics of medicine and the life sciences, particularly in relation to reproductive and genetic technologies and technological interventions in the human body. He is an adviser to the Church of England House of Bishops Working Group on Human Sexuality, and is currently working on a book on posthumanism and Christian ethics.

Xenia Zeiler studied South Asian Classical and Ancient Studies at Humboldt-University Berlin and Jawaharlal Nehru University, New Delhi. She concluded her Ph.D. in Cultural and Religious History of South Asia (Classical Indology) at the South Asia Institute, University of Heidelberg, in 2009. In her dissertation, she applied an ethno-indological approach, analysing the Sanskrit textual Tantric background of the goddess Dhūmāvatī and her contextual recent transformation processes, including her rise to an urban district deity in Benares. She published a monograph on Dhūmāvatī and several articles and book chapters, mainly on South Asian goddesses and their transformations.

Her research interests include Ethno-Indology, transformations in recent urban Hinduism, and Hinduism and Modern Mass Media. Since 2008, Xenia Zeiler is a Lecturer for South Asian Religions at the University of Bremen, Germany.

Introduction

Celia Deane-Drummond and David Clough

While non-human animals have frequently been the objects of various religious practices, and in the context of religion subjected to human interests and power in myriad ways, they have rarely been the subjects of religious thinking or scholarship. This is particularly obvious given that the question of the place and significance of animals has been one of the most pressing cultural and academic concerns to surface in the last decade.[1] Animal studies have proliferated through many disciplines, as have critical questions about the role of non-human animals in shaping human societies. Examples where other animals are the subject of attention – such as the Jewish philosopher and theologian Philo of Alexandria's treatise *De animalibus* (On Animals) composed *c.* 50 CE[2] – merely make conspicuous the comparative rarity in the context of religious thought of giving sustained attention to animals, and suggest that scholars of religion need to address the question of where animals belong in schemes of religious thought and practice. This collection aims to be at once an initial response to the need

---

[1] It is important here to add a note about our use of 'animal' in this conversation across disciplines. Those engaged in critical animal studies have struggled to find a way of expressing discourse about animals that does not repeat the critique implicit in this discussion by using the language of 'animal' and 'human' as opposite categories. One way round this difficulty is to refer to animals as 'non-human animals', or to suggest 'other animals', as a reminder that humans are animals as well. We have discussed the particular problems of terminology in an earlier volume, C. Deane-Drummond, and D. Clough, 'Introduction', *Creaturely Theology: On God, Humans and Other Animals* (C. Deane-Drummond, and D. Clough (eds); London: SCM Press, 2009), pp. 1–18. The specific theological issues associated with the way other animals have been classified are raised in David Clough's chapter in this volume. In this introduction, we use the term 'animal' in recognition of its systematic ambiguity as to whether or not humans are included in the term. Other authors in this volume take up this issue from a variety of angles.

[2] Philo of Alexandria, *Philonis Alexandrini de Animalibus* (A. Terian (ed. and trans.); Studies in Hellenistic Judaism; Chico, CA: Scholars Press, 1981).

for new work at the interface of religious studies, theology, and animals, and a stimulus for further enquiry.[3]

When the significance of the subject of animals is explored in relation to specific religious traditions, some fascinating cross-cultural conversations on other animals are opened up in a way that informs and enriches both the field of animal studies and the study of religious traditions. How have human beings thought about animals historically in religious terms? What are the reciprocal implications for religious understandings of the human condition? In what way and for what reasons do particular religious beliefs specifically shape human attitudes to other animals? How might theological approaches to other animals from Christian perspectives shift in response to a greater cultural awareness of the importance of other animals? Can we begin to point to ways in which religious traditions might respond to specific ethical issues and the contribution they might make in navigating ethical quandaries about the status and use of other animals? The collection of essays in this volume represents the outcome of an academic conversation on these and other questions. It shows multidisciplinarity at its very best, namely, a rigorous approach within one discipline in conversation with others around a common theme. The disciplines most relevant to this conversation are represented here, namely, philosophy, anthropology, religious studies, theology, history of religions, archaeology, and cultural studies. This work was energized by the third biennial conference of the European Forum for the Study of Religion and Environment, also called *Animals as Religious Subjects*, at Gladstone's Library, Hawarden, and a second conference entitled *Animals as Medical Subjects* held in May 2011 and hosted by the Centre for Religion and the Biosciences of the University of Chester. Many authors take into account scientific studies of other animals and weave this into their discussion, in some cases inspired by the public address given at the beginning of the first conference by ethologist Professor Marc Bekoff.

---

[3] In our Introduction to *Creaturely Theology*, we noted a number of thinkers who had contributed to the project of theological thinking about animals, most notably Stephen R. L. Clark and Andrew Linzey. In the broader context of this volume, we should note the following examples of works that have offered reflections relevant to the interface between animal studies and religious studies: T. Ingold (ed.), *What Is an Animal?* (London: Routledge, 1988); G. Kowalski, *The Souls of Animals* (Walpole, NH: Stillpoint Publishing, 1991); C. Adams, and J. Donovan (eds), *Animals and Women: Feminist Theological Explorations* (Durham, NC: Duke University Press, 1995); P. Waldau, *The Specter of Speciesism: Buddhist and Christian Views of Animals* (Oxford: Oxford University Press, 2002); C. Patterson, *Eternal Treblinka: Our Treatment of Animals and the Holocaust* (New York: Lantern Books, 2002); P. Waldau, and K. Patton (eds), *A Communion of Subjects: Animals in Religion, Science, and Ethics* (New York: Columbia University Press, 2006); I. S. Gilhus, *Animals, Gods, and Humans: Changing Attitudes to Animals in Greek, Roman, and Early Christian Ideas* (London and New York: Routledge, 2006).

The work is divided into four sections. The first section, 'Animals as Subjects of Religious Thought', explores philosophical, anthropological, and religious perspectives, raising general questions about the human perception of animals and its crucial cultural significance. The second section, 'Animals as Subjects of Religious Symbolism', explores the intriguing topic of the way animals have been used historically as religious symbols and in religious rituals, in some cases having negative connotations for traditional Christian religious belief through association with paganism, but also becoming incorporated into that tradition. The third section, 'Animals as Subjects of Theological Enquiry', re-examines some Christian theological and biblical approaches to animals in the light of current concerns. The final fourth section, 'Animals as Subjects of Religious Ethics', extends the implications of traditional views about other animals to more specific ethical theories and practices.

The first section, 'Animals as Subjects of Religious Thought', opens with a provocative piece by philosopher Stephen Clark, 'Ask Now the Beasts and They Shall Teach Thee'. In this chapter, he argues that it has been axiomatic in Western culture to suppose, with Plutarch, that 'nature has given to the brutes an imperfect affection for their kind, one neither marked by justice nor going beyond commodity: whereas to man, a logical and social animal, she has taught justice and law, and honour to the gods, and building of cities, and philanthropy'.[4] So also Emile Durkheim: 'Animals know only one world, the one which they perceive by experience, internal as well as external. Men alone have the faculty of conceiving the ideal, of adding something to the real.'[5] Animals, in other words, can be neither truly moral nor yet 'religious'. Clark argues, on the contrary, that this unexamined axiom can be disputed on the basis of both a better understanding of 'animal' life and a clearer vision of what 'piety' or 'religion' means. He suggests that animals engage in rituals that channel and evoke emotions that seem of a piece with our experience of 'religion', and can even – it seems – experience the sudden shift of attention that we associate with conversion or repentance. It is even possible to understand 'religion' exactly as a way of silencing the fat, relentless ego, and its distracting monologue – in other words, if 'animals' are dumb, this may be just what we need ourselves. He brings up specific religious insights that reinforces this position, so that, according to Buddhist legend, in the Jatakas, non-human animals can display, through their self-sacrifice, the very spirit of enlightenment: more literally, the Buddha

---

[4]   Cited in Clark, this volume.
[5]   Ibid.

was born many times in non-human form, teaching lessons of humility and generosity through his actions. He also points out that Christian preachers, as well as pagan philosophers, have often drawn out lessons from the behaviour of ants, mice, and sparrows. He concludes with the thought that maybe it is time to recognize that our non-human cousins have a lot to teach us.

In the second chapter in this section, anthropologist Tim Ingold invites us to go 'Walking with Dragons: An Anthropological Excursion on the Wild Side'. Here he points out that contemporary scientists often compare the natural world to a book whose contents can be read by those with the requisite expertise. There is indeed a parallel in the modern constitution between the book of nature and the nature of the book. For mainstream science the division between what there is and what we know seems self-evident; the problem lies in reaching an accommodation between them. Ingold argues, however, that the opposite is true. The hard thing is to force a rupture between the existence of a world and the possibility of our knowing it. Moving through the world, rather than roaming its surface, our knowledge is not built up on the outside of our earthly being but unfolds from the inside. We grow into the world, as the world grows in us. Perhaps this grounding of knowing in being is key to the kind of sensibility we call 'religious'. It is because of the way it subverts the effort to divide knowing from being that religious sensibility seems to collide with objective science. For science turns the relation between knowing and being inside out. This inversion has silenced both nature and the book. Drawing on studies of medieval monasticism and of indigenous peoples, with particular reference to encounters with other-than-human beings, Ingold suggests an alternative way of reading which allows us to take counsel from the voices of the pages and of the world around us, and to heal the rupture between the world and our imagination of it.

In the last chapter of this first section, Aaron Gross takes up in a provocative way the topic 'The Study of Religion After the Animal'. Gross argues that from Emile Durkheim to Mircea Eliade to J. Z. Smith, the discipline of religious studies took the human/animal boundary as one of its founding questions. His paper reviews the history of the exclusion of 'the animal' from the study of religion and considers emerging challenges to that stance within religious studies. Drawing on Tim Ingold's work on hunter-gatherer ontologies and Jacques Derrida's theorizations of 'the question of the animal', Gross makes the case that the kinds of subjectivity that might qualify as religious should not be limited to the human. Religious phenomena are not best conceived as a dimension of human culture but, to quote Ingold's characterization of hunter-gatherer ontologies, a dimension of 'the total field of relations embracing all living things'.[6] Gross suggests that by limiting the religious subject to a human subject the study of religion has become implicated in what Derrida calls a 'disavowal' (dénégation) of regard for animals and a 'war' (guerra) against them.[7] Gross argues that both Derrida's and Ingold's critical insights converge in unsettling a simple exclusion of animals from the sphere of the religious. He concludes that there needs to be a revision of our understanding of the religious subject, making both nonhuman and human animals eligible for participation in the phenomenon we call religion.

The second section, 'Animals as Subjects of Religious Symbolism', begins with Sabine Obermaier's investigation of 'Hedgehog Skin and Golden Calf: Animals as Symbols for Paganism in Medieval German Literature'. In this chapter, she seeks to demonstrate how medieval German authors use animals to symbolize pagans and paganism. Obermaier focuses on the Middle High German crusade epics, including Konrad's *Rolandslied* (c. 1170) and Wolfram's of Eschenbach *Willehalm* (about 1210 to 1220). In addition, she explores Wolfram's *Parzival* (about 1200 to 1210), where – as in other grail romances – the oriental world is of specific interest. The first part of this chapter deals with the oriental fauna that is also part of the pagans' equipment; the second examines specific pagan animal-related customs, for instance the deification of animals. But Obermaier's main interest is directed towards the description of pagans by 'animal means'. The third section of the chapter moves the discussion to consider, first, animal comparisons and animals as metaphors for pagans and, second, pagans with animal-like body-parts. In the course of this exploration, she finds that examining the relationship between Christians and pagans through the lens of animals and humans opens up new and interesting comparisons between different authors. While in the older *Rolandslied* 'animal means' are used to stress the pagan's strangeness, dangerousness, sinfulness, monstrosity, and inferiority to Christians, which supports the author's negative view of the pagans, Wolfram of Eschenbach alters the animal features according to the author's higher developed view not only of mankind, but also of animals.

The fifth chapter by Adam Dodd pursues a novel exploration of 'The Daemonic Insect: *Mantis religiosa*'. The praying mantis (*Mantis religiosa*, Linnaeus, 1758), as its name implies, has been associated with theological and occult powers in European folklore for centuries, largely owing to its striking and easily anthropomorphized 'praying' aspect. With the almost total

---

[6]   Cited in Gross, this volume.
[7]   Ibid.

secularization of entomology in the early twentieth century, the mantis surfaced in Surrealist art and literature as a signifier of the unconscious, and specifically, as a living embodiment of the monstrous, castrating female, owing to its tendency to devour the male during copulation. More recently still, the figure of the mantis recurs in testimonies of so-called 'alien abduction' and in clinical trials of the powerful hallucinogen, Dimethyltryptamine, or DMT. Dodd reviews the twentieth-century figuration of the praying mantis and examines its persistent ability to evoke notions of religious horror and awe in the human observer, asking what this might suggest about human-insect relations in general. He considers the Mantis as an entheogenic insect, that is, as a 'revealer of the divine within', and as a mediator between 'worlds' – the so-called 'insect world' and the everyday world of the human subject. Dodd then broadens this inquiry with a discussion of the extent to which the insect world and the microscopic world can be seen to have functioned as spatial metaphors for the unconscious mind, concluding that the Mantis persists as a potent yet poorly understood symbol of 'intercosmic', interspecies relations unaccounted for by the strictures of biological determinism.

The sixth chapter, by religious studies scholar Xenia Zeiler, invites us to consider 'Benevolent Bulls and Baleful Buffalos: Male Bovines versus the "Holy Cow" in Hinduism'. In Hindu religious traditions, animals play a very significant role as religious subjects for several reasons. First, one important aspect of the veneration given to animals, and accordingly one reason for their incorporation in ritual and worship, is the representation of 'deified' animals as escorts and companions of deities throughout Hindu mythology. This practice can be traced back to the very beginning of textual tradition in South Asia. From Vedic mythology onwards animals are depicted as a crucial part of the pantheon. This is the case especially in the later Hindu concept of vāhana ('vehicle, draught-animal, carriage-animal'), though animals are understood to be much more than just mounts. Rather, they are incorporated in the pantheon as close attendants to deities and act as their assistants in the everlasting battle against evil. In general, every Hindu deity is connected to a certain vāhana, a deified animal companion. The close bond between the specific animal and the respective deity shows clearly not only in mythology, but also in ritual and iconography, where deity and an accompanying animal are very often positioned side by side. Hindu mythology, developed from the epic period onwards, repeatedly places animals in very prominent roles and on a par with anthropomorphic deities. This goes as far as to present animals as religious and ritual subjects in their own right, without accentuating the link to their affiliated deity in certain mythological contexts. Following preliminary remarks on the general position and function of animals as part of the Hindu pantheon, this chapter discusses details from representations of the admired and much-loved bull, lion and tiger, on the one hand, and the unpopular and often feared crow, on the other hand. Important questions that are raised in this chapter include, why did certain animals gain special significance in Hinduism, and why are some more popular than others? Can we trace a pattern of how and why certain animals are affiliated with Hindu deities?

In the final chapter of this second section, Ingvild Sælid Gilhus considers another aspect of the relationship between religion and animals, treating their cultural and religious trajectory in 'From Sacrifices to Symbols: Animals in Late Antiquity and Early Christianity'. The societies and economies of the Mediterranean were completely dependent on animals. First, animals served basic human physiological needs for nourishment and clothing; second, animal ingredients were important in magic and medicine; third, animals were used for transport; fourth, they met needs for safety; fifth, they were part of the entertainment industry; sixth, animals fulfilled needs for friendship and intimacy; seventh, they functioned as status symbols; eighth, they were the subject of natural histories and philosophical debates; and finally, animals were used for religious purposes in sacrifice, divination, and magic. The theme of this chapter is the religious evaluation and treatment of animals in the Roman Empire and the changes that occurred during the first centuries CE. Sacrifice, divination, and magic were based on interactions between humans and culturally postulated superhuman beings. The religious language of the empire was a sacrificial language. During the sacrificial process, animals were conceived of as intermediaries between humans and gods, but at the same time, the sacrifice functioned as a justification for killing them. The chapter explores a number of questions concerning the ways that perspectives developed in a religious context, such as the status of animals, the critique of animal sacrifice, and the religious process of individualization. In the final section of the chapter, Gilhus discusses what she considers to be the most significant elements in the ancient Christian views of animals: a) a postulated fundamental division between humans and animals (based on a combination of Christian canonical texts and Stoic ideas); b) the end of sacrifice and the secularization of slaughtering; and c) a metaphorical use of animals that made it possible to speak about humans in a sort of code.

The third section, 'Animals as Subjects of Theological Enquiry', begins with theologian Forrest Clingerman's philosophical and theological analysis of experiential aspects of a particular creature in 'Butterflies Dwell Betwixt and Between:

Non-Human Animals, Theology, and Dwelling in Place'. He begins this chapter by setting out its intent as a theological reflection on the redemptive opportunity that butterflies offer humans – and the spiritual and religious relationship between humans and non-humans more generally. Clingerman begins with a brief characterization of two challenges that theology has previously faced in taking animals on their own terms. On one hand, animals have been objects of religious reflection, not subjects: animals have served as mere symbols, or have been treated only in terms of their relationship to humans. On the other hand, in cases where non-human animals are seen as having individual value, theology sometimes replicates the split in environmental ethics between discussions of animal rights and environmental ethics. In order to overcome these challenges, he suggests that one way of integrating the concern for individual animals on their own terms with concern for environments more generally is through reflecting on who and what 'dwells in place'. The advantage of this focus on dwelling becomes clearer as Clingerman develops this chapter. First, an emphasis on dwelling treats individuals as subjects, while also acknowledging how they might serve to convey meaning for others. Second, it diminishes the separation between individual and collective, and this has implications for the relationship between discourses about animal rights and environmental ethics. In the final section of this chapter, he explicitly ties the concern for dwelling into theological discourse. He achieves this by suggesting how dwelling in place emerges as a spiritual practice – one that includes human and non-human animals, and other beings that dwell in a particular place. The trajectory for truly and fully dwelling aims at the flourishing of individuals in place, which means that both the individual inhabitants and the environment itself are of concern. There is, therefore, a redemptive element to this flourishing, so that not only can we follow other theologians in saying that non-human animals might be redeemed, but more importantly non-humans participate in the inter-subjective work of redemption in active ways.

The ninth chapter, by Eric Daryl Meier, invites us to 'Marvel at the Intelligence of Unthinking Creatures!: Contemplative Animals in Gregory of Nazianzus and Evagrius of Pontus'. To refute the claim that bees and ants display rationality in arranging their societies for the benefit of each and all, Gregory and Nemesius and Evagrius of Pontus explain away the appearance of reason by externalizing the source of this animal behaviour. Each argues that the creative Logos of God implants instincts for rational behaviour within 'irrational animals'. Yet it is God's wisdom on display, not the faculties of these creatures. Gregory and Evagrius thus inscribe the gap between human beings and other animals as the difference of discursive rationality and freedom: the human is free and reflective while other animals act on instinct. The instinctual behaviour of animals appears rational because they are acting out the implanted rationality of God, not because they possess reason. Intriguingly, though they use differing terms to do so, each of these theologians has a common strategy, each describes the proper goal of human life by approaching God through disciplined contemplation, and each describes a relation to the divine Logos that fosters a mode of subjectivity indistinguishable from that of animals, even though these are the very beasts that have been explicitly denied the conditions of the possibility of religious subjectivity. This chapter examines the interplay of subjectivity and instinct in order to argue that, for Gregory of Nazianzus and Evagrius of Pontus, the perfected mode of religious subjectivity is structurally identical to the instinctual 'subjectivity' of animals (a subjectivity nevertheless disavowed), such that any subject – human or otherwise – approaching God becomes more like an 'animal' rather than less.

The final chapter in this section is by theological ethicist David Clough, who draws attention to the significance of how humans group and name animals in 'Putting Animals in their Place: On the Theological Classification of Creatures'. Clough takes as a starting point the frontispiece to one of the editions of Linnaeus's *Systema naturae*, in which Linnaeus pictures himself as a second Adam in Eden, naming the creatures God brings before him, continuing in the tradition of Francis Bacon in which the classification of organisms was seen as a way of re-establishing a dominion over them lost in the Fall. The chapter surveys a wide range of perspectives on how to make sense of creaturely differences, from Plato's *Timaeus*, through Origen, Basil of Caesarea, Augustine, Aquinas, and on to ideas of the Great Chain of Being in the eighteenth century and beyond. Particular attention is devoted to the theological rendering of the human/non-human difference in the doctrine of humanity made in the image of God and the doctrine of the incarnation. Clough argues that there are good theological reasons to reject the possibility of any unilinear scale of creaturely difference: instead, theologians should accept a plurality of categorizations of creatures in biblical texts and beyond. He notes that the philosopher of biology, John Dupré, makes an independent argument for such plurality in organizing organisms. The recognition that theology does not provide a justification for a univocal ordering of creatures has an important consequence of destabilizing conventional accounts of the relative importance of different creatures before God, which points to the need for further theological work in this area.

The final and fourth section, 'Animals as Subjects of Religious Ethics', begins with Raymond Person's critical review in the eleventh chapter of biblical practices through a consideration of '"Your Wives, Your Children, and Your Livestock": Domesticated Beings as Religious Objects in the Book of Deuteronomy'. As is widely acknowledged, biblical law is written from not only an anthropocentric position, but also an androcentric one. In the book of Deuteronomy, various dualities exist in its symbolic religious world, as that, for example between 'land' and 'wilderness'. Person shows that in a variety of places a duality is created between men and other beings in the patriarchal household expressed in the triad of 'wives', 'children', and 'livestock' (for example, Deut. 3.19), all of whom live in the 'land'. By contrast, the 'beasts' or wild animals live in the uninhabited/uninhabitable 'wilderness'. He demonstrates that in some places the text subtly hints that these dualities can be somewhat flexible – for example, the lists of clean and unclean animals (Deut. 14.3–21) include domesticated livestock as well as wild animals that were hunted for their meat in the ancient world. However, this duality of men and women-children-livestock nevertheless influenced some of the legal material in the book of Deuteronomy, thereby promoting patriarchal and anthropocentric values, for example, the law concerning the spoils of war in Deuteronomy 20. After describing the anthropocentric and androcentric character of Deuteronomy, the chapter concludes with a critique of this position, beginning with a discussion of the book of Jonah, a work that is widely understood as satirizing the Deuteronomic understanding of prophecy. Here Person believes that the book of Jonah satirically criticizes the duality of men and women-children-livestock in the Deuteronomic worldview and, in fact, places all of creation, including, the fish, the worm, and the Ninevite livestock, on a par with humans as active subjects who can obey God's commands. He ends his critique with some reflections on how modern people of faith might adopt a critical reading of Deuteronomy's understanding of household as an appropriate aid to developing a more holistic approach to the environmental crisis.

The twelfth chapter, Robert Song's 'Transgenic Animals and Ethics: Recognizing an Appropriate Dignity', is explicit about the implications of thinking about animals for contemporary ethical issues. Developments in medical research are leading to the creation of animals that contain human genetic material and are becoming the subject of increasing ethical interest. After a brief account of the kinds of experimental developments involved – genetically modified sheep which produce human insulin, growing human livers in pigs for subsequent transplantation to human beings, for example – this chapter explores the theological and moral issues raised by transgenic animals. It proceeds through a critique of a 2001 document on xenotransplantation produced by the Pontifical Academy for Life, and the subsequent discussion of this document by senior Roman Catholic moral theologians. While agreeing with their rejection of Lockean approaches to personhood, these approaches, Song suggests, mistakenly assume that the fundamental issue at stake in animal trans-genesis is *human* dignity. Instead, Song argues that the real ethical concern needs to be *animal* dignity, and, further, that recognizing animal dignity does not require a dilution of respect for human dignity, and that we need to develop an understanding of 'appropriate dignity' for human and non-human animals alike.

The final chapter, by theologian and ethicist Charles Camosy, offers a challenge to theological assumptions about other animals by considering 'Other Animals as Persons? — A Roman Catholic Inquiry'. Secular utilitarians like Peter Singer, often in defence of the ethical treatment of other animals, sometimes criticize a traditional Christian ethic as 'speciesist'. Thomas Aquinas, in particular, has been singled out as a particularly important part of the unjustified privileging of the species *Homo sapiens*. But in this essay, which focuses specifically on claims about moral status and personhood, Camosy shows that the narrative generally offered in support of this view is inadequate. Roman Catholic theology, and the work of Thomas Aquinas in particular, have taken personhood outside the species *Homo sapiens* seriously with regard to angels, and this leaves an important opening to talk about the moral status of non-human animals. Camosy argues that one can use a Thomistic approach to show that the image of God, and not only the likeness, should be seen as subsisting in various creatures along a spectrum related to their ability to know and to love. This not only avoids arbitrarily putting human beings at the top of a hierarchy of moral value, since angels far exceed humans, but also clears the conceptual space for exploring whether other animals have a moral status similar to that of human beings.

The diversity, depth, and fruitfulness of these investigations concerning religion and animals indicates that there is much to be gained by further work at the interface between religious studies, theology, and animals. In addition to providing new insights about how animals have been considered and treated in religious contexts, the essays in this volume make clear that reflection on the human/non-human animal boundary has the potential to change the way we understand both broader religious questions, such as what it means to be human, and still wider methodological questions, such as the impact of the human/non-human boundary on the structure of the discipline of religious studies. The essays gathered here make no claim to be comprehensive in their depiction of the interactions between animal studies, religious studies, and theology. In fact, they demonstrate quite the reverse: through uncovering and pursuing such a fascinating range of new questions for the various disciplines of their authors, they show how much more remains to be explored. We hope, therefore that in addition to informing readers about the topics addressed, these essays will whet appetites for further research that recognizes the interest and significance of taking animals as religious subjects.

Bibliography

Adams, C. J., and J. Donovan (eds), *Animals and Women: Feminist Theological Explorations* (Durham, NC: Duke University Press, 1995).

Deane-Drummond, C., and D. Clough, 'Introduction', *Creaturely Theology: On God, Humans and Other Animals* (C. Deane-Drummond, and D. Clough (eds); London: SCM Press, 2009), pp. 1–18.

Derrida, J., 'L'animal que donc je suis', *L'animal Autobiographique: Autour De Jacques Derrida* (M. L. Mallet (ed.); Paris: Galilee, 1999).

—*The Animal That Therefore I Am*, (David Wills (trans.) and Marie-Louise Mallet (ed.), Perspectives in Continental Philosophy (M.-L. Mallet (ed.); D. Wills (trans.); New York: Fordham University Press, 2008).

Durkheim, E., *The Elementary Forms of the Religious Life: A Study in Religious Sociology* (J. W. Swain (trans.); London: Allen & Unwin, 1915).

Gilhus, I. S., *Animals, Gods, and Humans: Changing Attitudes to Animals in Greek, Roman, and Early Christian Ideas* (London and New York: Routledge, 2006).

Ingold, T., 'Hunting and Gathering as Ways of Perceiving the Environment', *Animals and the Human Imagination* (A. Gross, and A. Vallely (eds); New York: Columbia University Press, 2012), pp. 31–54.

—(ed.), *What Is an Animal?* (London: Routledge, 1988).

Kowalski, G. A., *The Souls of Animals* (Walpole, NH: Stillpoint Publishing, 1991).

Patterson, C., *Eternal Treblinka: Our Treatment of Animals and the Holocaust* (New York: Lantern Books, 2002).

Philo of Alexandria, *Philonis Alexandrini de Animalibus* (A. Terian (ed. and trans.); Studies in Hellenistic Judaism; Chico, CA: Scholars Press, 1981).

Plutarch, 'On Love to One's Offspring', *Plutarch's Morals* (A. R. Shilleto (trans.); Charleston: Bibliolife, 2009).

Waldau, P., *The Specter of Speciesism: Buddhist and Christian Views of Animals* (Oxford: Oxford University Press, 2002).

Waldau, P., and K. C. Patton (eds), *A Communion of Subjects: Animals in Religion, Science, and Ethics* (New York: Columbia University Press, 2006).

Part One

Animals as Subjects of Religious Thought

1

'Ask now the beasts and they shall teach thee'[1]

Stephen R. L. Clark

I. Can Animals Be Religious?[2]

In speaking of 'animals as religious subjects' the organizers of the conference at which this paper was first presented probably intended us to consider what religious thought has to say about animals, or how religious practice involves them. This topic in turn is part of a larger enquiry: what practical and rhetorical use do people make of animals, and what is their significance in human life? Animals are good to eat and also good to think with, as Plutarch observed some centuries before Lévi-Strauss.[3] They – or their stereotypical images – may be used to represent all manner of human possibilities, for good or ill. Their actual selves are used for all manner of human purposes: to clothe, feed, and amuse us, to labour on our behalf, and to serve our medical and scientific ends. Historically, we have usually sanctified most of these uses by obedience to some ritual: the Christians of Paul's day could not be sure that the meat on offer had not been taken from animals sacrificed to idols, and might be well advised to refrain from eating it.[4]

The particular angle on the topic that I am choosing to address involves a slightly different reading of the title. Can animals be religious *subjects*, as

---

[1] Job 12.7. The passage has mostly been used to validate the allegorical use of animals, as in the medieval bestiary: see M. Curley, *Physiologus: A Medieval Book of Nature Lore* (Chicago: University of Chicago Press, 2009). All biblical references in this chapter are from the NIV.

[2] This paper was originally composed for a conference – *Animals as Religious Subjects* – at the Gladstone Library, Hawarden, UK, 21 May–24 May 2011.

[3] Plutarch, 'On Isis and Osiris', 380F–381F: *Moralia* (F. Babbitt (trans.); Loeb Classical Library, vol. 5; London: Heinemann, 1936), pp. 171–7; C. Lévi-Strauss, *Totemism* (R. Needham (trans.); Boston: Beacon Press, 1963), p. 89. See also G. Lloyd, *Science, Religion and Ideology* (Cambridge: Cambridge University Press, 1983), p. 12.

[4] I Corinthians 8.4–13; 10.18–33; cf. Acts 15.29, Revelation 2.20.

distinct from religious *objects*? This is to echo the question that I sought to answer many years ago, in a short volume entitled *The Nature of the Beast: Are Animals Moral?* Are non-human animals, that is, moral *agents* as well as moral *patients*? My eventual answer, years ago, was that non-human animals were 'ethical', in the sense that they were often motivated by considerations that also influence human beings for the better, but that they were not strictly 'moral', in that they had no interest in doing things simply because it was *right* that they should, and no way of assessing their own motives to see whether these were such as *should* be acted on here-now.[5] Later evidence suggests that they may be more 'moral', in that sense, than I had supposed: at any rate, it can be shown experimentally that some non-human primates have something like 'a sense of justice', and require fair play in their dealings with each other and with us. And more creatures seem to be 'self-aware' than we used to think. But I am not now concerned with the origins of 'morality', but of 'religion'. Are non-human animals 'religious'? And what would it mean for them, or for us, to be thus 'religious'?

Of course, this very enquiry will seem to some to be ridiculous. It has been axiomatic in the Western tradition (or at least in the mainstream traditions that Oswald Spengler called the 'Classical' and the 'Faustian'[6]) for three thousand years or more that non-human animals can have no sense of justice, let alone religion, and are moved only by 'natural' lusts and affections. Once upon a time this doctrine also implied that the things that animals desire are not really good, even when these are things that we too, as animals, desire (health, pleasure, friendly faces): 'there is no good except where there is a place for reason'.[7] Even when that stark message is forgotten we have usually continued to suppose that 'dumb animals' have no grasp of good or evil, and that nothing that happens to them is ever either very good or very bad. That this makes little sense is not my present concern. The relevant claim in this context is that reason and religion alike require us to open our eyes and minds to a larger world than the senses can reveal, and to construct symbolic and intellectual structures that have not previously existed in the world. Non-human animals (and also human children, slaves, and barbarians) live – it was thought – by sense alone, and its accompanying impulses. Even Plutarch of Chaeronea (46–122) who had a

[5] S. R. L. Clark, *The Nature of the Beast* (Oxford: Oxford University Press, 1982), p. 107.

[6] O. Spengler, *Decline of the West: Form and Actuality* (C. Atkinson (trans.); vol. 1; New York: Albert A. Knopf, 1926).

[7] Seneca, 'Letters', 124.13–14: *The Hellenistic Philosophers* (A. Long, and D. Sedley (eds); vol. 1; Cambridge: Cambridge University Press, 1987), p. 371 (60H).

more generous view of non-human life and thought than the Classical norm, argued that 'nature has given to the brutes an imperfect affection for their kind, one neither marked by justice nor going beyond commodity: whereas to man, a logical and social animal, she has taught justice and law, and honour to the gods, and building of cities, and philanthropy'.[8] Human feeling and action may be rooted in 'animal impulses', but are developed far beyond them. We can be moved by the sight of beauty, and not just by amorous or parental affection. We can be outraged by injustices, saddened by misfortunes that do not touch us directly. We can plant trees whose final growth we shall never see. We can imagine ourselves elsewhere, and think of things that are absent or even quite imaginary. We can acknowledge, and respect, the immortal gods: which is as much as to say that we can look past our own lives and circumstances and feel that some good things will endure. 'To plant a tree, to cultivate a field, to beget children: meritorious acts, according to the religion of Zoroaster'.[9]

Even when we do the very same things as our non-human kin, we do it – as we suppose – with a difference. Like them, we eat and drink, have sex, and care for our offspring. Like them we take shelter from storms, seek out our food, and try not to be food for others. But we also place all these acts in context, and surround them with evocative rituals, with personal and tribal memories, hopes, and personal commitments. So far from being *rational* animals, adapting ourselves and our actions to clearly defined ends, we are *ritualistic* and *symbolizing* animals, eager to see our circumstances and perform our acts in the light of a larger universe, in service to the gods. It is not entirely absurd to argue that 'the world', the encircling cosmos, is made to suit the purposes of gods and human beings – as Stoic philosophers and their disciples have supposed – because 'the world' does not exist for anyone but gods and human beings. 'Animals know only one world, the one which they perceive by experience, internal as well as external. Men alone have the faculty of conceiving the ideal, of adding something to the real'.[10] Or so we say.

Even modern anthropologists who are persuaded that 'religion' and 'the religious impulse' are natural, and for that reason unlikely to be swiftly eliminated from human history, usually suppose that they are specifically *human* adaptations, or at least confined to hominids.

---

[8] Plutarch, 'On Love to One's Offspring', *Plutarch's Morals* (A. Shilleto (trans.); Charleston: Bibliolife, 2009), p. 37.
[9] D. Hume, *Enquiry Concerning the Principles of Morals* (J. Schneewind (eds), first published 1751; Indianapolis: Hackett, 1983), p. 18.
[10] E. Durkheim, *The Elementary Forms of the Religious Life: A Study in Religious Sociology* (J. Swain (trans.); London: Allen & Unwin, 1915), p. 421.

Unlike other social animals [so Pascal Boyer claims], humans are very good at establishing and maintaining relations with agents beyond their physical presence; social hierarchies and coalitions, for instance, include temporarily absent members. This goes even further. From childhood, humans form enduring, stable and important social relationships with fictional characters, imaginary friends, deceased relatives, unseen heroes and fantasized mates. Indeed, the extraordinary social skills of humans, compared with other primates, may be honed by constant practice with imagined or absent partners. … Religious concepts and activities hijack our cognitive resources, as do music, visual art, cuisine, politics, economic institutions and fashion. This hijacking occurs simply because religion provides some form of what psychologists would call super stimuli. Just as visual art is more symmetrical and its colours more saturated than what is generally found in nature, religious agents are highly simplified versions of absent human agents, and religious rituals are highly stylized versions of precautionary procedures.[11]

Is it really obvious that other creatures are so different? Are not they also aware of *absences,* perhaps especially when their worlds are permeated by scent markers? Do they not engage in seemingly impractical rituals or vastly elaborated displays? Maybe the difference is that they are *more* religious, not less!

II. What Is Religion?

Pascal Boyer's account deliberately ignores the *metaphysical* claims that particular 'religious believers' make. What is of interest is what they do, especially when they are not consciously matching their behaviour to the doctrines they profess. And what they do, by his account, is gossip about imagined, powerful entities as much like themselves as they can manage to conceive, and engage in ritualistic activities not wholly unlike the symptoms of obsessive compulsive disorder (OCD). His characterization of 'religion', of course, seems limited even by anthropological standards. Not every religious person, or religious culture, seeks to get the rituals 'just right'. And most are well aware that God or the gods are very different from us. Emile Durkheim's discussion, for all its faults, offers a more plausible account of the role of cult, and social solidarity, in religion.[12]

---

[11] P. Boyer, 'Being Human: Religion: Bound to Believe?', *Nature* 455 (23 October 2008), pp. 1038–9; see also P. Boyer, *Religion Explained: The Human Instincts That Fashion Gods, Spirits and Ancestors* (London: Heinemann, 2001).

[12] Durkheim, *The Elementary Forms of the Religious Life*, pp. 415–47. See also E. Evans-Pritchard, *Theories of Primitive Religion* (Oxford: Clarendon Press, 1965).

'God', or the order sanctioned by God or by the gods, is the ideal, originative, inspiring form of the community (as even believers can in part agree).[13] 'Religious believers' of a rather different sort would prefer to say that the great traditions are a form of intellectual and emotional askesis, a deliberate effort to avoid idolatry – but they too will acknowledge the significance of the public cult.

> The ancient traditions of devotion and reflection, of worship and enquiry, have seen themselves as *schools*. Christianity and Vedantic Hinduism, Judaism and Buddhism and Islam are schools ... whose pedagogy has the twofold purpose – however differently conceived and executed in the different traditions – of weaning us from our idolatry and purifying our desire.[14]

Sometimes this purification is also a moral and political act.

> When you come to appear before me, who has asked this of you, this trampling of my courts? Stop bringing meaningless offerings! Your incense is detestable to me. New Moons, Sabbaths and convocations: I cannot bear your evil assemblies. Your New Moon festivals and your appointed feasts my soul hates. They have become a burden to me; I am weary of bearing them. When you spread out your hands in prayer, I will hide my eyes from you; even if you offer many prayers, I will not listen. Your hands are full of blood; wash and make yourselves clean. Take your evil deeds out of my sight! Stop doing wrong, learn to do right! Seek justice, encourage the oppressed. Defend the cause of the fatherless, plead the case of the widow.[15]

Sometimes, on the other hand, it is a deliberate withdrawal from the moral and political spheres, as irrevocably corrupt. 'This is the life of gods and of godlike and blessed men, deliverance from the things of this world, a life which takes no delight in the things of this world, escape in solitude to the solitary'.[16]

---

[13] According to Kant (but I have not been able to find his source), the Tibetan lamas told Francesco Orazio Olivieri della Penna (1680–1747; the head of the Capuchin mission in Lhasa from 1725 to 1733, and principal author of the first Tibetan-Italian dictionary) that 'God is the gathering of all the blessed [or holy] ones'. I. Kant, *Kant's Political Writings* (H. Reiss (ed.); Cambridge: Cambridge University Press, 1970), p. 107.

[14] N. Lash, *The Beginning and the End of 'Religion'* (Cambridge: Cambridge University Press, 1996), p. 21. See also M. Maimonides, *The Guide of the Perplexed*, (J. Guttmann (ed.); C. Rabin (trans.); original version 1190; Hackett: Indianapolis, 1995), Bk. 3, ch. 29, p. 178: 'the first purpose of the whole law is to remove idolatry and to wipe out its traces and all that belongs to it, even in memory'. The idea is also discussed by Jan Assman in *Moses the Egyptian* (Cambridge: Harvard University Press, 1997), p. 58.

[15] Isaiah 1.12–17.

[16] Plotinus, *Ennead*, VI. 9 [9].11, 48–51: *Enneads* (A. Armstrong (trans.); Loeb Classical Library, vol. 7; London: Heinemann, 1988), p. 345. This is not to say that Plotinus despised the world, nor that he disdained ordinary 'religion'. The route he preferred was, in a way, a solitary one – but it was also a reversal of the fall: and that fall was because 'as if [the souls] were tired of being together, they each go to their own' (*Ennead*, IV.8 [6].4, 11ff.). But that is another story.

And the route to that outcome, by Plotinus's account, is to 'try to bring back the god in you to the divine in the All',[17] without relying on public rituals or conversations with imagined (which is not necessarily to say 'imaginary') spirits. Even a forced exile may be salutary:

> What kind of life will a wise man have if he is abandoned by his friends and hurled into prison or isolated in some foreign country or detained on a long voyage or cast out onto a desert shore? It will be like the life of Zeus, at the time when the world is dissolved and the gods have been blended together into one, when nature comes to a stop for a while; he reposes in himself given over to his thoughts.[18]

A wiser man, perhaps, might recognize that Zeus is already present everywhere, and that everything, correspondingly, is already charged with the grandeur of God, 'like shining from shook foil'.[19] I shall return to that theme. But it is plausible enough, or at least agreeable, to think that metaphysics, mysticism, and morality require an intellectual range that is probably beyond non-human animals – or at any rate we are unlikely ever to find the evidence. Other elements associated with 'religion' are perhaps more easily – though still questionably – found among the non-human. Lionel Tiger, asked whether animals can be 'religious', replied as follows:

> Religion in the sense that there are periods during the day, normal day of a group of chimps when they seem to engage in what we would, could call a religious type service, that is after they have had breakfast, they've closed their nests and so on and they feel safe they'll usually sit in someplace which is like a clearing and they're protected by trees. You might well say that it's almost cathedral-like, depending on where they are and they exist with very reduced tension. The dominant males don't bother the youngsters as much. The females interact with each other and the youngsters and there is a lot of grooming that goes on. People ... not people, chimps grooming each other and that lasts for awhile and then they go back to their regular business and so you could see that there is in our repertoire a predisposition to some kind of let's take time off behavior and just be friendly to each other'.[20]

---

[17] Plotinus on his death bed, according to Porphyry's account, in *Life of Plotinus*, ch. 2: *The Enneads* (A. Armstrong (trans.); Loeb Classical Library, vol. 1; London: Heinemann, 1966), p. 7.

[18] Seneca, Letters, 9.16: *The Hellenistic Philosophers*, p. 277 (46O).

[19] G. M. Hopkins, 'God's Grandeur', *Poems* (W. Gardner, and N. Mackenzie (eds); Oxford: Oxford University Press, 1967), p. 66.

[20] L. Tiger, 'Can Animals be Religious?', *BigThink.com* (20 May 2010), http://bigthink.com/ideas/20164 (accessed 24 July 2012); see also L. Tiger and M. McGuire, *God's Brain* (New York: Prometheus Books, 2010).

Jane Goodall, interviewed on the same question, 'considers the implications of the behaviour of chimpanzees she has observed in the wilderness staring transfixed at a rushing waterfall. She characterizes this transfixed state as 'awe', suggesting that primate expressions of awe at a waterfall site 'may resemble the emotions that led early humans to religion'. In other words, her decades of familiarity with the chimpanzees leads her to place their response on the spectrum of religious consciousness rather than utterly apart from it.[21]

So both peaceful togetherness, 'time off' or 'time out', and expressions of awe (whether at the size, the volume, or even the beauty of a waterfall) may be identified at least among other primates, and associated by at least some commentators with 'religion', or with the bundle of responses that are often wrapped up in 'religion'. It is also common to suspect that domestic dogs are bound to their human masters in something like the way that human beings may be focused on their gods – whether those gods are visible or not. Piety, of a sort, is shown in submission (though I suspect that we elevate our own importance to dogs by this comparison, and perhaps forget that even dogs, especially dogs, may sometimes be quite 'cynical' about their imagined deities).[22] What else can be identified as vaguely 'religious'? We are not the only animals that sometimes act 'out of character', though we are probably the only ones that notice what we have done, and give a name to the invading spirit, whether we reckon it a demon or a god. So Aphrodite, goddess of sexual attraction, herself desiring the mortal man Anchises, came down to Mount Ida disguised as a young girl:

> After her went fawning the grey wolves and fierce-eyed lions, bears and swift leopards insatiable for deer. Seeing them, she was glad at heart; in their breasts too she cast longing, and they all lay down in pairs in their shadowy haunts.[23]

Gods (and demons) are, at least, the binding spirits, the sudden convulsions and conversions that may come on individuals, on couples, and on groups, whether human or non-human. Human beings, perhaps, are unusual in giving them back-stories, as it were, that place them in context and give us an opportunity to *decide* between them or to invoke an opposing spirit. But it is evident that

---

[21]　K. Patton, ' "He Who Sits in the Heavens Laughs": Recovering Animal Theology in the Abrahamic Traditions', *The Harvard Theological Review* 93 (2000), pp. 401–34 (425), citing P. Miller, 'Jane Goodall', *National Geographic* 188.6 (1995), pp. 102–28.

[22]　J. Masson and S. McCarthy, *When Elephants Weep: The Emotional Lives of Animals* (London: Vintage, 2nd edn, 1996), pp. 203–4, citing E. Thomas, *The Hidden Life of Dogs* (Boston: Houghton Mifflin, 1993), pp. xvii–xviii.

[23]　M. West (ed. and trans.), 'Homeric Hymn to Aphrodite', *Homeric Hymns. Homeric Apocrypha. Lives of Homer* (Loeb Classical Library; London: Heinemann, 2003), lines 69–74, p. 165.

human beings are not the only mortals to be affected by them. If we are the only ones who tell these stories, we may also be the only ones who might possibly, with great difficulty, sometimes defy them (rather as Richard Dawkins hopes, without much evidence, to defy his 'selfish genes').

It should already be clear that there is a long tradition even in the West that sees more in animals than mainstream 'Faustian' or 'Classical' thinkers reckon, a tradition perhaps to be associated with what Spengler called the 'Magian', which speaks rather of constant transformations, and places us all, human or non-human, in the service of a transcendent, non-anthropomorphic God.[24]

> Pliny the Elder (23–79 CE) claimed that elephants, the animal 'closest to man,' not only recognized the language of their homeland, obeyed orders, and remembered what they learned, but also had been seen 'worshipping the sun and stars, and purifying [themselves] at the new moon, bathing in the river, and invoking the heavens'.[25]

This is a step beyond the 'awe' that Goodall detected in the attitude, the brief attentive silence of her chimpanzees. Religion includes a worship that is not merely obedience to a mortal master (as the dog's devotion might be), but also an impulse to 'purification' and – maybe – invocation. Whether Pliny was correct is difficult to assess: the most that other, more recent, commentators have acknowledged from their own experience is that elephants do seem to feel deeply about their offspring and companions, can learn and themselves devise quite complicated strategies, and perform what look like 'rituals' – not in the sense identified by Boyer, that they obsessively repeat some stereotyped movements without any obvious 'practical' effect, but that they behave *attentively* in ways having nothing clearly to do with sex or food or parenting or even simple togetherness. Of course – to state the obvious – it is not enough that non-human animals should position themselves or their limbs in ways that vaguely resemble human gestures: 'praying mantises' have other aims, at least, than prayer. But it does not follow that there may not be a serious convergence of style and attention which convinces careful observers that the animal is indeed doing something rather like whatever it is that prayerful humans do.

---

[24] O. Spengler, *The Decline of the West: Perspectives of World History* (C. Atkinson (trans.); vol. 2; New York: Alfred A. Knopf, 1928), pp. 233ff.

[25] P. Waldau, 'Religion and Other Animals', *Sightings* (29 May 2008), http://divinity.uchicago.edu/martycenter/publications/sightings/archive_2008/0529.shtml (accessed 24 July 2012), quoting Pliny, *Natural History*, 8.1. See also M. de Montaigne, *Apology for Raymond Sebond* (R. Ariew, and M. Grene (trans.); Indianapolis: Hackett, 2003), p. 30. This is one of those stories that seem to be passed on without much serious comment by philosophers: it may be correct, but I would be happier if there were more, and more contemporary, detail.

Oddly, indeed, it may be that the prayerful humans have always taken their cue from animals![26] Ritual, among humans, involves a lot of dressing up, usually in ways that enhance the participants' height or bulk or beauty. We put on fur or feathers, jewels, and shiny fabrics to get the spectators' attention (and of course the spectators may themselves dress up and join in the parades, the choirs, the dances, and the ceremonial sacrifices). Often indeed we try to impersonate *animals*, and so invoke the spirit associated, symbolically or even really, with the beast we choose to portray. Sometimes this may serve the very same functions as courtship dances among the non-human – but even those dances probably engage the dancers' attention in more than a merely utilitarian way: they (human or non-human) are not just thinking about getting laid, even when the effect of a particularly splendid performance is to encourage just that outcome! Whatever the origins of religious or theatrical performances (and the point is that there is in origin not much to choose between these descriptions) we now enjoy them for themselves and hope thereby to invoke some more enduring spirit. And what is to say that this is not also true for the non-human? Birds build bowers, lay out dancing floors, and sing complex melodies. Jane Goodall reports that the young male chimpanzee 'Mike' rose to alpha status through the innovative use of empty kerosene cans from the scientists' camp.[27] Our performances are, at least to our eyes, more complex ones – but perhaps we do not see the complexities or variations in the non-human sort, and far too quickly assume that they have just the one familiar goal – of getting laid. And even that goal, remember, is an invocation.

> Eternity is passion, girl or boy
> Cry at the onset of their sexual joy
> 'For ever and for ever'; then awake
> Ignorant what Dramatis Personae spake.[28]

Wedding ceremonies are attempts to bring down gods to help sustain us over a lifetime together. Military ceremonies invoke courage and loyalty to a sacred symbol, so that our soldiers do not run and hide. We mark out every serious event and institution – and our failure to take those ceremonies seriously hints that we do not much care about those events and institutions. Human 'religious'

---

[26] Self-transformation has often 'been associated with the imitation of other species'. F. Fernández-Armesto, *So You Think You're Human? A Brief History of Humankind* (Oxford: Oxford University Press, 2004), p. 42.

[27] J. Goodall, *In the Shadow of Man* (New York: Houghton Mifflin, 1971), pp. 113–14.

[28] W. B. Yeats, 'Supernatural Songs VIII', *Collected Poems* (London: Wordsworth Editions, 1994), p. 247.

rituals are not really much like those tedious duties that victims of OCD create to provide some order in their lives and to avoid anxiety. They have a positive and not just a preemptive role. And perhaps the same is true of stereotypy among zoo animals: the polar bear that is constantly pacing and figure-eight swimming is not necessarily deranged, though he may indeed be responding to an environment that is otherwise terminally boring. He is summoning a spirit, and the question whether this is to come from his own 'inner depths' or from 'the deeps' is not one that he has any need to raise, even if he had the cognitive skills to raise it. As Temple Grandin suggests, stereotypies are sometimes satisfactory ways of coping: in one group of (very poorly housed and managed) mink it was the mink who engaged in stereotypies who were calmer and less fearful.[29] This is not to say that such stereotypies are not also, often, a signal, precisely, that the animals are poorly housed and managed. And some of them are so far lost to the wider world as indeed to seem deranged.

Even when we *can* rationalize what non-human animals do, we cannot altogether dismiss the notion that they are feeling something like 'religion'. 'As the Quran says, "Seest thou not that it is Allah Whose praises all beings in the heavens and on earth do celebrate and the birds (of the air) with wings outspread? Each one knows its own mode of prayer and praise. And Allah knows well all that they do".[30] So also in the Franciscan tradition:

> One time when Francis was walking with another friar in the Venetian marshes, they came upon a huge flock of birds, singing among the reeds. When he saw them, the saint said to his companion, 'Our sisters the birds are praising their creator. We will go in among them and sing God's praise, chanting the divine office.' They went in among the birds, which remained where they were, so that the friars could not hear themselves singing the office, they were making so much noise. Eventually the saint turned to them and said, 'My sisters, stop singing until we have given God the praise to which He has a right.' The birds were silent immediately and remained that way until Francis gave them permission to sing again, after they had taken plenty of time to say the office and had finished their praises. Then the birds began again, as usual.[31]

Quite why Francis thought it right thus to interrupt the birds' worship I do not know!

But his conviction that the birds were indeed 'praising God' is widely shared – even by people who seem to feel no compunction about killing and eating their

---

[29]   T. Grandin and C. Johnson, *Animals Make Us Human* (Orlando: Houghton Mifflin, 2009), p. 19.
[30]   Patton, ' "He Who Sits in the Heavens Laughs" ', p. 417, citing *Koran* 24.41.
[31]   Ibid., pp. 420–21, citing Bonaventure, *Major Life of St. Francis*, 8.9.

fellow worshippers (a topic that I must put on one side)! The obvious, rationalist response is that the birds (it is supposed) do not have the mental apparatus to conceive of God, nor indeed of any invisible spirit who should elicit worship. Surely, the birds are only asserting their territorial rights, even if it is difficult not to concede that they are also *enjoying* it. But this is to bring in metaphysical considerations that – perhaps – are out of place. 'Praising God' is not, even for human believers, much like complimenting a visible, mortal superior, nor even wooing a lover: 'praising God' is the name we give to a bundle of feelings and behaviours, in which the worshipper's spirit is in some way 'exalted', 'carried outside itself', 'absorbed in the very act'. That spirit itself – we could summarize – is God (or at any rate, a god). The best life of all, so Aristotle says, is *theoria,* and that life, in which other animals – he supposes – have no share, is God.[32] Other theorists, as Aristotle acknowledges, may have other, rather more vulgar, ideas of where to find the divine. Having sex, enthusiastically, is Aphrodite. Berserk rage is Ares. Music and mathematics is Apollo. Confident, cunning enterprise is Athena, who stands ready to pull us round from error. In Homer's *Iliad* the error from which Athena saves Achilles is murder: Plotinus hoped that 'if someone is able to turn around, either by himself or having the good luck to have his hair pulled by Athena herself, he will see God and himself and the all. … He will stop marking himself off from all being and will come to all the All without going out anywhere'.[33] That is a larger hope than most humans, let alone non-humans, have, but it is not too far removed from the ordinary experience. Anecdotally I can remark that I have seen a cat suffer that sudden reversal: some years ago we had added a hamster to the domestic economy, who did occasionally wander freely around the house. One of our cats, spotting the hamster, momentarily poised to spring – and then suddenly stopped, as one remembering that this was indeed a *domestic* hamster, a member of the household, and looked away in some embarrassment.

You will notice, of course, that I am drawing my examples from 'pagan' practice, poetry and philosophy, and only gesturing toward the more familiar monotheistic forms, mostly Abrahamic. This is deliberate. Modern misreadings – as I suppose – of the Abrahamic traditions – make it difficult to consider that non-human animals could be 'theists', since 'theism' is popularly supposed to involve us in metaphysical hypotheses that hardly any *human* beings understand

---

[32] Aristotle, *Metaphysics*, 12.1072ᵇ28. On the claim that the other animals have no share in this worshipful activity, see *Nicomachean Ethics*, 10.1178ᵇ24–30.
[33] Plotinus, *Ennead*, VI.5 [23].7, 9ff.: *Enneads* (A. Armstrong (trans.); Loeb Classical Library, vol. 6; London: Heinemann, 1988), p. 341, after Homer's *Iliad* I.197ff.

or find persuasive. It is also popularly supposed that 'religion' creates divisions between 'soul' and 'body', 'earth' and 'heaven', 'sin' and 'righteousness', that modern liberals and materialists find objectionable. It is easier to work with pagan poetry and even some pagan philosophy, and so to see that talk of 'the divine' is not about a peculiar being or quasi-spatial region hidden away from ordinary eyes, and inaccessible to creatures who lack the necessary cognitive powers to escape from *sensibilia*. The life-world even of militant atheists is full of ghosts and memories, spirits, and subversive sensibilities: even if it is true that 'in reality there are only atoms and the void, and all else is by convention', as Democritus decreed,[34] it is still impossible in practice to escape those conventions! Even eliminative materialists do not manage, in practice, to efface their own awareness that they are surrounded by things that cannot be described by us merely as matter in motion. The rest of us cannot even make that attempt, and some of us see more clearly.

> How do you know but ev'ry Bird that cuts the airy way,
> Is an immense world of delight, close'd by your senses five?[35]

And again:

> 'What', it will be Question'd, 'When the Sun rises do you not see a round Disk of fire somewhat like a Guinea?' O no, no, I see an Innumerable company of the Heavenly host crying 'Holy, Holy, Holy is the Lord God Almighty'.[36]

There is a difference between the life-worlds of 'believers' and 'unbelievers': it is not simply that the former group believe in the existence of an extra entity (Super-yeti) in a world still characterized as the unbelievers do![37] Nor do we come to believe by any neutral experiment.

> Bacchanals did not say, 'Let us discover whether there is a god of wine'. They enjoyed wine so much that they cried out naturally to the god of it. Christians did not say, 'A few experiments will show us whether there is a god of goodness'. They loved good so much that they knew that it was a god. Moreover, all the great religions always loved passionately and poetically the symbols and machinery by which they worked – the temple, the coloured robes, the altar,

[34] Democritus, DK68B9: G. Kirk, J. Raven, and M. Schofield, *The Presocratic Philosophers: A Critical History with a Selection of Texts* (Cambridge: Cambridge University Press, 2nd edn, 1983), p. 410.
[35] W. Blake, 'The Marriage of Heaven and Hell', *Complete Writings* (G. Keynes (ed.); Oxford: Oxford University Press, 1966), p. 150.
[36] W. Blake, 'A Vision of the Last Judgement', *Complete Writings* (G. Keynes (ed.); Oxford: Oxford University Press, 1966), p. 617.
[37] See A. MacIntyre, *God, Philosophy, Universities: A History of the Catholic Philosophical Tradition* (London: Rowman & Littlefield, 2009), p. 8.

the symbolic flowers, or the sacrificial fire. It made these things beautiful: it laid itself open to the charge of idolatry.[38]

Everything in the believers' world is significant, and the significance is spelled out with stories, songs, and rituals. 'Religion', or the bundle of sayings, practices, and attitudes that we call 'religious', is a way, or rather a set of ways, of organizing our experience and the life-world that we, all of us, create together. That 'we', by the way, includes all living creatures here on Earth (at least): it is one of the oddest features of modern sensibility that the chattering classes constantly forget that the very air and soil on which they live is built and adorned by living creatures, and that such creatures as seek to build *their own* worlds without consideration for the wider world on which they depend and which is constantly being built and re-built around them, are bound to be eroding their own lives and projects. But that too is another story.

III. Metaphysics, Mysticism and Morals

And what about the metaphysical, mystical, or moral elements of 'religion'? Even if human beings incorporate in their 'religious' lives many elements that they share with other creatures (and it would be very surprising if they did not), must it not still be true that they, that we, have made much more of them than the non-human ever could? We dress up as animals, draw moral lessons from their actual or their imaginary behaviour, and are often awed by them.[39] '[Primitives] say that the wisest of all animals, the most powerful and divine of all beings, is the elephant, and then comes the python or the lion, and only then comes man'.[40] And there is something wonderful and beautiful in even the smallest, commonest, and apparently 'base' of living creatures, as Aristotle said.[41] Is it enough to say that non-human animals do not make these comparisons, and are not awed either by size or beauty? As Chesterton observed, only human beings really notice that they resemble other creatures, and so differ from them even in their similarity. 'The fish does not trace the fish-bone pattern in the

---

[38] G. K. Chesterton, 'Skepticism and Spiritualism', *Illustrated London News* (14 April 1906).
[39] We do not always respond well to feeling awe-struck: the very creatures before whom we are momentarily silenced must then be trapped and diminished, to prove to ourselves that we are, after all, their masters.
[40] C. G. Jung, *Zarathustra Seminar* (J. Jarrett (ed.); Princeton: Princeton University Press, 1988), p. 1393–4; M. Sabini (ed.), *The Earth has a Soul: The Nature Writings of C. G. Jung* (Berkeley, CA: North Atlantic Books, 2005), p. 84.
[41] Aristotle, *De Partibus Animalium*, 1.645a15ff.

fowls of the air; or the elephant and the emu compare skeletons'.[42] Probably that
is true – but of course this habit of mind is not in fact found among all human
beings, and neither is the impulse to systematize our morals or metaphysics.
Mystics in particular usually deny that there is any way of systematizing or even
describing what is revealed, perhaps, to them and take especial pains to make
such dogmas as they do proclaim as opaque as possible! By some accounts the
whole of human reasoning is a grand diversion from an original unity, and
'religion' is a way of numbing the mind into a primordial daze. Whether that is
a good thing or a bad thing may need some further thinking.

Suppose, however, for the moment, that this last description, for good or ill,
does catch something of the point of 'religious' practice. Getting ourselves –
and especially 'the fat, relentless ego'[43] – just to shut up for once is enormously
difficult: we need all the help we can get. But if the goal is to shut up, to halt the
constant rationalizing, self-dramatizing, and self-critical monologue that drives
us all (and sometimes drives us mad), may not we wonder whether the creatures
whom we routinely dismiss, precisely, as *not* rational, *not* self-conscious,
have the better part? The difference that rationalists especially in the Western
tradition have often identified between 'animals' and us is that they do not need
to *choose*, nor yet to *think*, but follow the law unconsciously and easily. Human
beings are able *not* to do what they should, and reckon that they are therefore
superior – except that they also fantasize about a heavenly realm in which they
can no longer, ever, 'sin'. 'In a way the animal is more pious than man, because
it fulfils the divine law more completely than man ever can. ... He can deviate,
he can be disobedient, because he has consciousness [or more exactly, *self*-
consciousness]'.[44] More precise investigations may reveal that other animals may
also be *self*-conscious, and also sometimes *choose*. The idea that they do all and
only what 'God and Nature' demands of them, and without any effort, may be
mistaken. It seems plausible that chimpanzees, for example, sometimes *choose*
to assist an injured companion, though nothing in their nature demands that
they do. The cat I mentioned earlier *chose* not to catch the hamster. Evolutionary
change may depend, more often than we easily suppose, on *choices*: some one
or some group changed their way of life, and so were subject to rather different

---

[42]   G. K. Chesterton, *The Everlasting Man* (London: Hodder & Stoughton, 1925), p. 307.
[43]   I. Murdoch, *The Sovereignty of Good* (London: Routledge & Kegan Paul, 1970), p. 51.
[44]   C. G. Jung, *Letters* (G. Adler (ed.); vol. 1; Princeton: Princeton University Press, 1975), pp. 483–6,
       cited by Sabini (ed.), *The Earth has a Soul*, p. 12. See also C. G. Jung *Visions: Notes of the Seminar
       Given in 1930–1934* (C. Douglas (ed.); Princeton: Princeton University Press, 1997), p. 144; Sabini
       (ed.), *The Earth has a Soul*, p. 170.

evolutionary pressures than otherwise they would have been.[45] And it is also not as clear to me as it has been to more traditional thinkers that 'the law' – the law, that is, of predation – has any strictly moral weight! I do not myself think that we can discover the laws of righteousness merely by understanding what the laws of nature say: that is, an accurate description of what happens here does not tell us what would be best to happen, nor yet what we should do.

> Lay up these things within your heart and listen now to right, ceasing altogether to think of violence. For the son of Cronos has ordained this law for men, that fishes and beasts and winged fowls should devour one another, for right is not in them; but to mankind he gave right which proves far the best.[46]

Hesiod, like many other theologians and philosophers, assumes that 'fish and beasts and winged fowl' have no share in justice, whereas we may. He may have been mistaken in this. But it is true enough that justice does not, at the moment, prevail. We are living in a 'fallen' world. According to that strange mystic and natural scientist Empedocles, we are embedded in a fallen world, by our canni-balistic error, very much as Hesiod's gods may be condemned to lie frozen by the Styx when they break their oath.[47] Zuntz's aphorism is almost correct: 'the banished god described by Hesiod is – Man'.[48] Almost correct, but not exactly: for Empedocles' point is that the banished god *is not* human, even if it is born among humans 'as prophets, bards, doctors and princes'[49] – and among beasts as lions, or laurels among trees. Our collective sin is cannibalism: 'will you not cease from the din of slaughter? Do you not see that you are devouring each other in the heedlessness of your minds?'[50] According to Buddhist legend, in the Jatakas, non-human animals can display, through their self-sacrifice, the very spirit of enlightenment: more literally, the Buddha was born many times in non-human form, teaching lessons of humility and generosity through his actions.[51]

Religion, even of the mystical variety, may pull in opposite directions. On the one hand, the proper state to achieve is to go with the flow, to stop judging

---

[45] See A. Hardy, *The Living Stream: A Restatement of Evolution Theory and Its Relation to the Spirit of Man* (London: Collins, 1965).

[46] Hesiod, *Works and Days*, 274–6: *Theogony and Works and Days* (M. West (trans.); Oxford: Oxford University Press, 2008).

[47] Hesiod, *Theogony*, 775–806: *Theogony and Works and Days* (M. West (trans.); Oxford: Oxford University Press, 2008).

[48] G. Zuntz, *Persephone: Three Essays on Religion and Thought in Magna Graecia* (Oxford: Clarendon Press, 1971), p. 267.

[49] Kirk, Raven, and Schofield, *The Presocratic Philosophers*, p. 317.

[50] Sextus Empiricus, 'Against the Mathematicians', 9.129: Kirk, Raven, and Schofield, *The Presocratic Philosophers*, p. 319.

[51] The generosity, perhaps, was sometimes excessive! See also E. Heathcote-James, *Psychic Pets: How Animal Intuition and Perception Has Changed Human Lives* (London: John Blake, 2007).

oneself and others, to rediscover the life of brutes. Cynic philosophers as well
as Christian preachers took lessons from sparrows and mice: especially, not to
be worried about tomorrow.[52] On the other hand, we need to repent of the sins
that brought us here, and that we ceaselessly repeat (that is our punishment,
to be forever repeating the sin). Religious traditions may emphasize either
goal, and are as liable to corruption and confusion as any other institution, as
any other mortal creature. So can we learn from our brothers and sisters, the
non-human, how to cope, how to endure? One answer is already implicit in
what I have said already: we have been learning from them, and copying them,
from the beginning. My point is not the one that theologians, I suspect, prefer:
I do not mean only that we have found useful *symbols* among animals, and can
then happily ignore the actual creatures. It is all too common for theists in the
Western tradition to sing happily of the Lamb of God but think that this gives
them no reason at all to wonder about the lives of real lambs, or to reckon that
the Four Living Creatures who stand around the throne of God, in *Revelation*,
have anything to do with any real living creatures. Our ancestors, from the
beginning, took advice from animals, without supposing that they were always
right, but knowing that they sometimes were. We may still attend to the animals
we now encounter, and learn a little about how to live together in peace. Or at
least to imagine that we should:

> The wolf will live with the lamb, the panther lie down with the kid, calf, lion
> and fat-stock beast together, with a little boy to lead them. The cow and the bear
> will graze, their young will lie down together. The lion will eat hay like the ox.
> The infant will play over the den of the adder; the baby will put his hand into
> the viper's lair. No hurt, no harm will be done on all my holy mountain, for the
> country will be full of the knowledge of Yahweh as the waters cover the sea. [53]

Things are not much like that now. Religion, as Marx declared, may be the opium
of the people, the dream of a better world than this.[54] The non-human animals
who live in this world with us may have their dreams as well[55]: what reason have
we to think that they are less deserving? According to Xenophanes of Colophon

---

[52] Diogenes Laertius, *Lives*, 6.2.3, 9.11.68; Matthew 6.25–34. See F. Downing, *Cynics and Christian Origins* (London: Routledge, 1992).

[53] Isaiah 11.6–9.

[54] The full claim is 'Religion is the sigh of the oppressed creature, the heart of a heartless world, and the soul of soulless conditions. It is the opium of the people'. Karl Marx, 'Introduction', *The Critique of Hegel's Philosophy of Right* (J. O'Malley (ed.); first published 1843–4; Cambridge: Cambridge University Press, 1970).

[55] R. Brooke, 'Heaven', *Collected Poems* (vol. 4; New York: John Lane, 1916): 'And in that Heaven of all their wish, there shall be no more land, say fish'.

(*c*.570–*c*.475 BC): 'if cattle and horses or lions had hands, or were able to draw with their hands and do the works that men do, horses would draw the forms of the gods like horses, and cattle like cattle'.[56] The usual philosophical moral has been that God or the gods must actually be quite otherwise, that anthropomorphic conceptions of the ultimate cause and final judge of all things are as foolish as would be a hippomorphic one. Our only hope, it has been supposed, is an intellectual detachment from merely earthly, merely animal, imaginings. But perhaps the proper moral is a different one, and Xenophanes' aphorism has more bite than we suppose: the God of intellectuals is very likely to be thus 'intellectual', but the reality is something else. It is 'through our inarticulate groans [that] the Spirit himself is pleading for us'![57] And once it is admitted that it is not by our careful reasonings and splendid speeches that we shall be saved, it is surely time to notice that there are other creatures in the world than us, and that they too are groaning. 'The created universe waits with eager expectation for God's children to be revealed'[58]: that too is religion, and what shape or style God's children will turn out to have is not as clear as we have usually supposed.

> And though the last lights off the black West went
> Oh, morning, at the brown brink eastward, springs—
> Because the Holy Ghost over the bent
> World broods with warm breast and with ah! bright wings.[59]

Bibliography

Abram, D., *The Spell of the Sensuous: Perception and Language in a More-than-Human World* (New York: Pantheon Books, 1996).

Aristotle, *Metaphysics*.

—*Nicomachean Ethics*.

—*De Partibus Animalium*.

Assman, J., *Moses the Egyptian* (Cambridge: Harvard University Press, 1997).

Blake, W., 'The Marriage of Heaven and Hell', *Complete Writings* (G. Keynes (ed.); Oxford: Oxford University Press, 1966).

—'A Vision of the Last Judgement', *Complete Writings* (G. Keynes (ed.); Oxford: Oxford University Press, 1966).

Bonaventure, St., *Major Life of St. Francis*.

---

[56] Kirk, Raven, and Schofield, *The Presocratic Philosophers*, p. 169.
[57] Romans 8.26.
[58] Romans 8.19.
[59] Hopkins, 'God's Grandeur', p. 66.

Boyer, P., 'Being Human: Religion: Bound to Believe?', *Nature* 455 (23 October 2008), pp. 1038–9.

—*Religion Explained: The Human Instincts That Fashion Gods, Spirits and Ancestors* (London: Heinemann, 2001).

Brooke, R., 'Heaven', *Collected Poems* (vol. 4; New York: John Lane, 1916).

Chesterton, G. K., *The Everlasting Man* (London: Hodder & Stoughton, 1925).

—'Skepticism and Spiritualism', *Illustrated London News* (14 April 1906).

Clark, S. R. L., *The Nature of the Beast* (Oxford: Oxford University Press, 1982).

Curley, M. J., *Physiologus: A Medieval Book of Nature Lore* (Chicago: University of Chicago Press, 2009).

Diogenes Laertius, *Lives of the Eminent Philosophers* (R. D. Hicks (trans.); Loeb Classical Library; London: Heinemann, 1925).

Downing, F. G., *Cynics and Christian Origins* (London: Routledge, 1992).

Durkheim, E., *The Elementary Forms of the Religious Life: A Study in Religious Sociology* (J. W. Swain (trans.); London: Allen & Unwin, 1915).

Epistles of the Brethren of Purity: The Case of the Animals versus Man Before the King of the Jinn: An Arabic Critical Edition and English translation of Epistle 22 (L. E. Goodman, and R. McGregor (eds); New York: Oxford University Press, 2010).

Evans-Pritchard, E. E., *Theories of Primitive Religion* (Oxford: Clarendon Press, 1965).

Fernández-Armesto, F., *So You Think You're Human? A Brief History of Humankind* (Oxford: Oxford University Press, 2004).

Goodall, J., *In the Shadow of Man* (New York: Houghton Mifflin, 1971).

Grandin T., and C. Johnson, *Animals Make Us Human* (Orlando: Houghton Mifflin, 2009).

Hardy, A. C., *The Living Stream: A Restatement of Evolution Theory and Its Relation to the Spirit of Man* (London: Collins, 1965).

Heathcote-James, E., *Psychic Pets: How Animal Intuition and Perception Has Changed Human Lives* (London: John Blake, 2007).

Hesiod, *Theogony and Works and Days* (M. L. West (trans.); Oxford: Oxford University Press, 2008).

Hopkins, G. M., 'God's Grandeur', *Poems* (W. H. Gardner, and N. H. Mackenzie (eds); Oxford: Oxford University Press, 1967).

Hume, D., *Enquiry Concerning the Principles of Morals* (J. B. Schneewind (eds); Indianapolis: Hackett, 1983).

Jung, C. G., *Letters* (G. Adler (ed.); vol. 1; Princeton: Princeton University Press, 1975).

—*Visions: Notes of the Seminar Given in 1930–1934* (C. Douglas (ed.); Princeton: Princeton University Press, 1997).

— *Zarathustra Seminar* (J. Jarrett (ed.); Princeton: Princeton University Press, 1988).

Kant, I., *Kant's Political Writings* (H. Reiss (ed.); Cambridge: Cambridge University Press, 1970).

Kirk, G. S., J. E. Raven, and M. Schofield, *The Presocratic Philosophers: A Critical*

History with a Selection of Texts (Cambridge: Cambridge University Press, 2nd edn, 1983).

Lash, N., *The Beginning and the End of 'Religion'* (Cambridge: Cambridge University Press, 1996).

Lévi-Strauss, C., *Totemism* (R. Needham (trans.); Boston: Beacon Press, 1963).

Lloyd, G. E. R., *Science, Religion and Ideology* (Cambridge: Cambridge University Press, 1983).

MacIntyre, A., *God, Philosophy, Universities: A History of the Catholic Philosophical Tradition* (London: Rowman & Littlefield, 2009).

Maimonides, M., *The Guide of the Perplexed* (J. Guttmann (ed.); C. Rabin (trans.); Indianapolis: Hackett,1995).

Marx, K., 'Introduction', *The Critique of Hegel's Philosophy of Right* (J. O'Malley (ed.); first published 1843–4; Cambridge: Cambridge University Press, 1970).

Masson, J., and S. McCarthy, *When Elephants Weep: The Emotional Lives of Animals* (London: Vintage, 2nd edn, 1996).

Miller, P., 'Jane Goodall', *National Geographic* 188.6 (1995), pp. 102–28.

Montaigne, M. de, *Apology for Raymond Sebond* (R. Ariew, and M. Grene (trans.); Indianapolis: Hackett, 2003).

Murdoch, I., *The Sovereignty of Good* (London: Routledge & Kegan Paul, 1970).

Patton, K., ' "He Who Sits in the Heavens Laughs": Recovering Animal Theology in the Abrahamic Traditions', *Harvard Theological Review* 93.4 (2000), pp. 401–34.

Pliny, *Natural History*.

Plotinus, *Ennead*, in *Enneads* (A. Armstrong (trans.); Loeb Classical Library, vol. 6 and 7; London: Heinemann, 1988).

Plutarch, 'On Isis and Osiris', *Moralia* (F. Babbitt (trans.); Loeb Classical Library, vol. 5; London: Heinemann, 1936).

—'On Love to One's Offspring', *Plutarch's Morals* (A. Shilleto (trans.); Charleston: Bibliolife, 2009).

Porphyry, *Life of Plotinus*, in *The Enneads* (A. Armstrong (trans.); Loeb Classical Library, vol. 1; London: Heinemann, 1966).

Sabini, M. (ed.), *The Earth Has a Soul: The Nature Writings of C. G. Jung* (Berkeley, CA: North Atlantic Books, 2005).

Seneca, *Letters*, in *The Hellenistic Philosophers* (A. Long, and D. Sedley (eds); vol. 1; Cambridge: Cambridge University Press, 1987).

Spengler, O., *Decline of the West: Form and Actuality* (C. Atkinson (trans.); vol. 1; New York: Albert A. Knopf, 1926).

—*The Decline of the West: Perspectives of World History* (C. Atkinson (trans.); vol. 2; New York: Alfred A. Knopf, 1928).

Thomas, E., *The Hidden Life of Dogs* (Boston: Houghton Mifflin, 1993).

Tiger, L., 'Can Animals be Religious?', *Big Think* (20 May 2010), http://bigthink.com/ideas/20164 (accessed 24 July 2012).

Tiger, L., and M. McGuire, *God's Brain* (New York: Prometheus Books, 2010).

Waldau, P., 'Religion and Other Animals', *Sightings* (29 May 2008), http://divinity. uchicago.edu/martycenter/publications/sightings/archive_2008/0529.sht ml (accessed 24 July 2012).

West, M. (ed. and trans.), 'Homeric Hymn to Aphrodite', *Homeric Hymns. Homeric pocrypha. Lives of Homer* (Loeb Classical Library; London: Heinemann, 2003).

Yeats, W. B., 'Supernatural Songs VIII', *Collected Poems* (London: Wordsworth Editions, 1994).

Zuntz, G., *Persephone. Three Essays on Religion and Thought in Magna Graecia* (Oxford: Clarendon Press, 1971).

2

Walking with Dragons: An Anthropological Excursion on the Wild Side

Tim Ingold

I. Facing the Facts

In the year 1620, the English philosopher-statesman Francis Bacon set out a plan for what was to be a massive work of science, entitled *The Great Instauration*. Dedicated to King James I, who had recently appointed Bacon as his Lord Chancellor, the work was never completed. In his prolegomenon, however, Bacon railed against traditional ways of knowing that continually mixed up the reality of the world with its configurations in the minds of men. If only the mind was as clear and even as a perfect mirror, then – said Bacon – it would 'reflect the genuine rays of things'. But it is not. Cracked and deformed by flaws both innate and acquired, by instinct and indoctrination, the mind distorts the images that are cast upon its surface, by way of the senses, and cannot – if left to its own devices – be relied upon to deliver a true account of things as they are. There is but one way out of this predicament, Bacon argued, and that is by appeal to the facts. 'Those', he wrote, 'who aspire not to guess and divine, but to discover and know, who propose not to devise mimic and fabulous worlds of their own, but to examine and dissect the nature of this very world itself, must go to the facts themselves for everything'.[1]

Bacon's words have an unmistakeable contemporary ring. Today's science continues to found its legitimacy upon its recourse to the data, which are repeatedly checked and rechecked in a never-ending search for truth through

---

[1] Citations from *The Great Instauration: The Plan of the Work* are drawn from the standard translation by J. Spedding, R. Ellis, and D. Heath, *Works of Francis Bacon, Baron of Verulam, Viscount St. Alban and Lord High Chancellor of England, Vol. IV* (London: Spottiswoode, 1858), pp. 22–33 (27–8), http://www.constitution.org/bacon/instauration.htm (accessed 9 August 2012).

the elimination of error.[2] And for the most part the sciences of mind and culture, psychology and anthropology, have ridden on the back of the same enterprise. That is to say, they have colluded in the division between what Bacon called the 'world itself', the reality of nature that can be discovered only through systematic scientific investigation, and the various imaginary worlds that people in different times and places have conjured up and which – in their ignorance of science and its methods – they have taken for reality. Where anthropologists busy themselves with the comparative analysis of these imaginary worlds, psychologists purport to study the mechanisms, presumed to be universal, that govern their construction. All agree that the realms of reality and the imagination should on no account be confused. For the very authority of science rests upon its claim to disclose, behind the home-made 'figments' that the imagination paints before our eyes, the facts of what is really there. One can of course study figment as well as fact so as to deliver what many anthropologists still call 'emic' rather than 'etic' accounts, but to mix the two is to allow our judgement to be clouded by error and illusion. 'For God forbid', as Bacon put it, 'that we should give out a dream of our imagination for a pattern of the world'.[3]

I want to argue in this chapter that Bacon's injunction, which modern science has taken to its heart, has had fateful consequences for human life and habitation, cutting the imagination adrift from its earthly moorings and leaving it to float like a mirage above the road we tread in our material life.[4] With our hopes and dreams suffused in the ether of illusion, life itself appears diminished. Reduced to biochemical function, it no longer gives cause for wonder or astonishment. Indeed, for those of us educated into the values of a society in which the authority of scientific knowledge reigns supreme, the division of real life and the imagination into the two mutually exclusive realms of fact and fable has become so engrained as to be self-evident. The problem, in our estimation, has been one of how to reach some kind of accommodation between the two. How can we make a space for art and literature, for religion, or for the beliefs

---

[2] At the time of writing, a team of scientists led by Professor Antonio Ereditato has just reported that the neutrinos they have been blasting through a tunnel under the Alps have reached speeds faster than that of light. The team's findings, based on some fifteen thousand separate observations, have caused consternation in the world of particle physics. Commenting on the furore, the lead writer in *The Guardian* opined that 'the first thing in science is to face the facts; making sense of them has to come second'. *Plus ça change...* 'Unthinkable? Faster than light', *The Guardian* (24 September 2011), http://www.guardian.co.uk/commentisfree/2011/sep/23/unthinkable-faster-than-light-editorial (accessed 9 August 2012).

[3] Bacon, *The Great Instauration*, pp. 32–3.

[4] Here, I am developing an argument initially sketched out in an essay entitled 'Life Beyond the Edge of Nature? Or, the Mirage of Society', *The Mark of the Social* (J. Greenwood (ed.); Lanham, MD: Rowman and Littlefield, 1997), pp. 231–52, see p. 238.

and practices of indigenous peoples, in an economy of knowledge in which the search for the true nature of things has become the exclusive prerogative of rational science? Do we suffer the imagination to persist in our midst, or tolerate its penchant for fantasy, out of a compensatory wish for enchantment in a world that has otherwise ceased to enthral? Do we keep it as a sign of creativity, as a badge of civilization, out of respect for cultural diversity, or merely for our own entertainment?[5] Such questions are endemic, yet the one thing we forget in posing them is how hard it is, in our experience, to split the reality of our life in the world, and of the world in which we live, from the meditative currents of our imagination. Indeed the problem is the very opposite of what we take it to be: not of how to reconcile the dreams of our imagination with patterns in the world, but of how to separate them in the first place.

Historically, this separation was but slowly and painfully achieved in the religious upheavals of the Reformation and the turbulent beginnings of early modern science, in which Bacon – along with his exact contemporary, Galileo – played a pivotal part. But the historical process is recapitulated today in the education of every schoolchild who is taught, on pain of failure in his or her examinations, to distrust the sensuous, to prize intellect over intuition, and to regard the imagination as an escape from real life rather than its impulse. Almost by definition, it seems, the imaginary is unreal: it is our word for what does *not* exist. As every modern parent knows, for example, there is no such thing as a dragon. We grown-ups are convinced that dragons are creatures of the imagination. Yet most of us would have no difficulty in describing one. Having seen pictures of dragons in the books we read when we were children, and that we in turn read to our own offspring, we are familiar with their general appearance: green scaly bodies, long forked tails, flared nostrils, sabre-like teeth, and flaming mouths. These monsters roam the virtual terrain of children's literature alongside a host of other creatures of similarly fictive provenance. Some of them, of course, have real zoological counterparts. While the ever-popular *Tyrannosaurus rex*, perhaps the nearest thing to a dragon that ever lived, is conveniently extinct, other animals – from cobras to crocodiles and from bears to lions – are still around and occasionally claim human lives.[6] Encountered in the flesh, we do well to fear them.

---

[5] This latter view is exemplified in the pronouncements of science policy makers who support public funding for scholarship in the arts and humanities on the grounds of its direct or indirect contribution to the 'creative industries'.

[6] To this list could be added the *komodo dragon*, the largest extant species of lizard in the world, which inhabits the islands of south-eastern Indonesia. Though rare, these animals are extremely dangerous, and attacks on humans have increased in recent years.

Their fictive cousins, however, give no cause for alarm, for the only people they can eat are as imaginary as themselves. Along with the stuff of nightmares, these creatures are sequestered in a zone of apparitions and illusions that is rigorously distinguished from the domain of real life. We calm the sleeper who wakes in terror, at the point of being consumed by a monster, with the reassuring words, 'don't worry, it was only a dream'. Thus, the boundary between fact and phantasm, which had seemed momentarily in doubt at the point of waking, is immediately restored. What, then, are we to make of the following story, which comes from the *Life of St. Benedict of Nursia*, composed by Gregory the Great in the year AD 594? The story tells of a monk who encountered a dragon. This monk was restless: his mind was given to wandering and he was itching to escape from the cloistered confines of monastic life. Eventually the venerable father Benedict, having had enough of the monk's whingeing, ordered him to leave. No sooner had he stepped outside the precincts of the monastery, however, than the monk was horrified to find his path blocked by a dragon with gaping jaws. Convinced that the dragon was about to eat him up, and trembling with fear, he shouted to his brothers for help. They came running. Not one of them, however, could see any dragon. They nevertheless led their renegade colleague – still shaking from his experience – back inside the monastery. And from that day on he never again went astray, or even thought of doing so. It was thanks to Benedict's prayers, the story concludes, that the monk 'had seen, standing in his path, the dragon that previously he had followed without seeing it'.[7]

II. The Shape of Fear

Perhaps the monk of this cautionary tale was merely suffering from nightmares. Medieval people, however, would not have been so readily reassured as their modern counterparts by the realization that, in their encounters with dragons and other monsters, what they had seen was but a dream. They were not, of course, so gullible as to suppose that dragons *exist*, in the specific sense of existence invoked by modern people when they assert, to the contrary, that dragons do *not* exist. It is not as though the monk, in our story, came face to face with some other creature that, with the benefit of scientifically informed

---

[7] From M. Carruthers, *The Craft of Thought: Meditation, Rhetoric and the Making of Images, 400–1200* (Cambridge: Cambridge University Press, 1998), p. 185, author's translation.

hindsight, we moderns can recognize, say, as a species of reptile. Remember that the brothers who came to his rescue saw no dragon. They saw nothing there at all. What they did see however, as Gregory's account repeatedly testifies, was that the monk was trembling. No doubt they saw the look of terror etched in his face. And yet, when the monk cried out to be saved from the jaws of the dragon, his brothers understood his predicament at once. They did not react to his outburst – as the modern psychiatrist might react to the ravings of a lunatic escaped from the asylum – as the idiosyncratic, possibly drug-induced halluci-nations of a fevered and unsettled mind that would be best recaptured and shut away, in solitary confinement, to avoid further contagion. Rather, they immedi-ately recognized, in the vision of the dragon, the form of the monk's otherwise inarticulable agitation, and imperilled themselves in responding, affectively and effectively, to his distress.[8] The monk was on the point of being consumed by fear and already felt the accompanying symptoms of personal disintegration. The dragon was not the objective cause of fear; it was the shape of fear itself.

For the brethren of monastic communities, this shape would have been entirely conventional and well-known to all, drummed in through rigorous discipline of mind and body. In this training, stories and pictures of dragons and of other, equally terrifying monsters were used not as we would today, to create a comfort zone of safety and security by consigning everything that might be frightening to the realms of make-believe, but to instil fear in novices, so that they might experience it, recognize its manifestations and – through a stern regime of mental and bodily exercise – overcome it. As the manifest form of a fundamental human feeling, the dragon was the palpable incarnation of what it meant to 'know' fear. Thus, in medieval ontology, the dragon existed as fear exists, not as an exterior threat but as an affliction instilled at the core of the sufferer's very being. As such, it was as real as his facial expression and the urgency in his voice. But unlike the latter, it neither could be seen nor heard save by the one who was himself afeared. That is why the monk's rescuers saw no dragon themselves. They were most likely motivated by a feeling of compassion, which may for them – in the idiom of the time – have called to mind the image of a saintly figure, radiating light. Both saints and dragons, in the monastic imagination, were concocted from fragments of text and pictures shown to novices in the course of their instruction. In that sense, to adopt the apt term of the historian Mary Carruthers, they were 'figmented'.[9] But these figments of

---

[8] I am grateful to Godelieve Orye for this insight.
[9] Carruthers, *The Craft of Thought*, p. 187.

the imagination, far from being cordoned off in a domain separate from that of 'real life', were for medieval thinkers the outward forms of embodied human experience, lived in the space of rupture between Heaven and Hell.

The monk of the story was of course torn between the two. Expelled from the monastery by the saintly Benedict, the devil – in the shape of the dragon – was waiting for him outside. Rescued in the nick of time, he was led back in. Thus, the story unfolds along a path of movement, from inside to outside and then back inside again. From the very beginning, we are told, the mind of the monk was prone to wandering. Indeed in a puzzling twist at the end of his tale, Gregory recounts that for all that time, the monk was following the dragon *without actually seeing it*. What happened when he stepped outside was a complete loss of bearings, the kind of bodily disorientation that occurs when one is thrust into a totally unknown environment. It was as though the ground had been pulled away from under his feet. He panicked and at that moment the dragon reared up before his eyes, blocking his path. He found he could no longer carry on. So in truth, the story concludes, Benedict did the monk a good turn by throwing him out, since it led him to see – and thus to know – the dragon that he had otherwise blindly followed. For writers in the monastic tradition, as the narrative brings out so clearly, knowing depended on seeing, and both proceeded along trajectories of movement. To understand what they meant, we have to think of cognition, as Carruthers explains, 'in terms of paths or "ways"'. The medieval thinker, in a nutshell, was a wayfarer, who would travel in his mind from place to place, composing his thoughts as he went along.[10]

III. Dreams and Reality

I shall return in due course to the question of wayfaring. In the meantime, let me introduce another example. Among the Ojibwa, indigenous hunters and trappers of the Canadian North, there is said to be a bird whose sound, as it swoops across the sky, is a peal of thunder. Few have seen it, and those who have are credited with exceptional powers of revelatory vision. One such person, according the ethnographer A. Irving Hallowell, was a boy of about twelve years of age. During a severe thunderstorm, Hallowell recounts, the boy ran out of his tent and saw a strange bird lying on the rocks. He ran back to call his parents, but by the time they arrived the bird had disappeared. The boy

---

[10] Ibid., p. 70. See also T. Ingold, *Lines: A Brief History* (London: Routledge, 2007), pp. 15–16, 95.

was sure it was *pinési*, the Thunder Bird, but his elders were unconvinced. The matter was clinched, and the boy's account accepted, only when a man who had *dreamed* of the Bird verified the boy's description.[11] Clearly, *pinési* is no ordinary bird, just as the dragon is no ordinary reptile. Like the sound of thunder itself, the Thunder Bird makes its presence felt not as an object of the natural world but, more fundamentally, as a phenomenon of experience.[12] It is the incarnate form of a sound that reverberates through the atmosphere and overwhelms the consciousness of all who hear it. Just as the monk's brethren, as they rushed outside, saw no dragon, so the boy's parents did not themselves witness *pinési*. But as the conventional shape of a powerful auditory sensation, it would have been entirely familiar to them. The Thunder Bird may be a figment of the imagination, but it is an imagination that has saturated the fullness of phenomenal experience.

Recall that the boy's observation, in this case, was confirmed by a dream. Bacon would have been mortified. For us moderns it is more usual, and certainly more acceptable, for dreams to be confirmed by observation. A well-known instance is the story of how the chemist Friedrich August Kekulé discovered the structure of the benzene molecule, comprised of a ring of six carbon atoms. According to Kekulé's own, admittedly retrospective and possibly embellished account – in a speech delivered during a celebration held in Berlin City Hall in 1890 to mark the 25th anniversary of his discovery – it happened one night in 1865, while he was staying in the Belgian city of Ghent. He had been up late in his study, at work on a textbook. Making little progress, he had turned his chair towards the fire and dozed off. In his reverie, atoms gambolled before his eyes, twining and twisting in snake-like motion.

> But look! What was that? One of the snakes had seized hold of its own tail, and the form whirled mockingly before my eyes. As if by a flash of lightning I awoke; …
> I spent the rest of the night in working out the consequences of the hypothesis.[13]

Whatever Kekulé might have felt at the moment of waking, we can be sure that once the flash that shook him from his slumber was extinguished, the

---

[11] The story is told in A. Hallowell, 'Ojibwa Ontology, Behavior and World View', *Culture in History: Essays in Honor of Paul Radin* (S. Diamond (ed.); New York: Columbia University Press, 1960), pp. 19–52(32).

[12] On this distinction, see T. Ingold, *The Perception of the Environment: Essays on Livelihood, Dwelling and Skill* (London: Routledge, 2000), pp. 278–9.

[13] An English translation of Kekulé's address by O. Theodore Benfey was published in 1958, see 'August Kekulé and the Birth of the Structural Theory of Organic Chemistry in 1858', *Journal of Chemical Education* 35.1 (1958), pp. 21–3 (22). See also R. Roberts, *Serendipity: Accidental Discoveries in Science* (New York: Wiley, 1989), pp. 75–81.

gyrating serpent of his dream was no longer an affectation of vision but an abstract figure of thought – a snake 'good to think with' – that was peculiarly apt for deciphering the structure of a given reality. Thus, the serpent and the benzene ring fall unequivocally on either side of an impermeable ontological division between imagination and reality. It is this that allows the one to stand metaphorically for the other. The congruity between serpent and ring reinforces the division rather than breaking it down.

The dream-induced conjecture, however, is but a chimera until subjected to empirical test. It was in precisely this vein that Kekulé went on to advise his audience: 'Let us learn to dream, gentlemen, then perhaps we shall find the truth … But let us beware of publishing our dreams till they have been tested by waking understanding.'[14] Indeed, subsequent experimental work in the laboratory proved Kekulé's hypothesis to be substantially correct, and it went on to become a cornerstone of the emerging field of organic chemistry. The dream itself, however, did not. In the harsh light of day, the dream vanished into oblivion. Thus, science concedes to the imagination the power of conjecture – or, as we say, to think 'outside the box' – but only by banishing imagination from the very reality to which it affords insight. For the Ojibwa, by contrast, it would have been quite the other way around. For them, the truth of things is not only found but also tested by personal oneiric experience, which is why the boy's sighting of *pinési* could be corroborated by his elder's dream. In this quest for knowledge through experience, the powerful more-than-human beings that inhabit the Ojibwa cosmos, including Thunder Birds, are not analogical resources but vital interlocutors. This cosmos is polyglot, a medley of voices by which different beings, in their several tongues, announce their presence, make themselves felt, and have effects. To carry on your life as an Ojibwa person you have to tune into these voices and listen and respond to what they are telling you.

Another Thunder Bird story from Hallowell – admittedly one told to him by an informant – perfectly illustrates the point. Hallowell's informant was sitting in a tent, one stormy afternoon, with an old man and his wife. The thunder rolled and clapped. At once, the old man turned to his wife. 'Did you hear what was said?' he asked. 'No,' came the reply, 'I didn't quite catch it.' Commenting on the exchange, Hallowell remarks that the old man 'was reacting to this sound in the same way as he would respond to a human being whose words he did not

---

[14] Benfey, 'August Kekulé and the Birth of the Structural Theory of Organic Chemistry in 1858', p. 22.

understand'.[15] This was not, however, a simple failure of translation. It was not as though the Thunder Bird had a message for the old man that he failed to grasp because of his imperfect command of Bird language. 'By and large', Hallowell observes, 'the Ojibwa do not attune themselves to receiving messages every time a thunderstorm occurs'. It transpires that this particular man had, in his youth, become acquainted with the Thunder Bird through the dreams of his puberty fast, and had gone on to develop a close relationship of tutelage with *pinési*.[16] In the context of this relationship, listening and responding to thunder was a matter not of translation but of empathy, of establishing a communion of feeling and affect or, in short, of opening oneself up to the being of another.[17] And it is above all in dreaming, where the boundaries that surround the self in waking life are dissolved, that this opening up occurs.

Such exposure, however, was not something that a sober scientist like Kekulé could even contemplate. For him, the path to true knowledge lay not in opening up a dialogue with beings of the more-than-human world, but in an exact and literal reading of the facts already deposited there. The investigator who would 'follow the paths of the Pathfinders', Kekulé advised, 'must note every footprint, every bent twig, every fallen leaf. Then, standing at the extreme point reached by his predecessors, it will be easy for him to perceive where the foot of a further pioneer may find solid ground.'[18] The object, as Bacon had put it, was to write a 'true vision of the footsteps of the Creator', inscribed in the works of His creation.[19] It was a matter of unlocking the secrets of nature. For that you need a key or rather several keys, to unlock door after door. Kekulé's serpent offered one such key, in the figure of a ring. In his book *The Assayer*, dating from 1623, Galileo found his keys in the characters of mathematics, in the 'triangles, circles and other geometric figures', which comprise its special language. 'Philosophy is written in this grand book, the universe', wrote Galileo, 'which stands continually open to our gaze. But the book cannot be understood

---

[15] Hallowell, 'Ojibwa Ontology, Behavior and World View', p. 34.

[16] This crucial qualification appears in one of Hallowell's last papers on the Ojibwa, first published in 1966. See A. Hallowell, 'The Role of Dreams in Ojibwa Culture', *Contributions to Anthropology: Selected Papers of A. Irving Hallowell* (R. Fogelson, F. Eggan, M. Spiro, G. Stocking, A. Wallace, and W. Washburn (eds): Chicago: University of Chicago Press), pp. 449–74 (459).

[17] I have discussed the distinction between translation and empathy, drawing on Hallowell's example, in *The Perception of the Environment*, p. 106. For an exploration of the significance of empathy within relations of tutelage, see T. Gieser, 'Embodiment, Emotion and Empathy: A Phenomenological Approach to Apprenticeship Learning', *Anthropological Theory* 8.3 (2008), pp. 299–318.

[18] Benfey, 'August Kekulé and the Birth of the Structural Theory of Organic Chemistry in 1858', p. 23.

[19] Bacon, *The Great Instauration*, p. 33.

unless one first learns to comprehend the language and read the letters in which it is composed'.[20]

IV. Of Words and Works

The idea of the book of the universe, or of nature, is of considerable antiquity, and was as current among medieval scholars as it was subsequently to become in the rise of modern science. It rested, at root, on a homology between the *word* of God (*verbum Dei*), in the composition of the scriptures, and the *works* of God, in the creation of the world and its creatures. The question was: 'how could humans read those twin books?'[21] With this, we can return to the monks of the medieval era, for whom – as I have already observed – the meditative practice of reading liturgical texts was a process of wayfaring. Over and over again, they would compare their texts to a terrain through which they would make their way like hunters on the trail, drawing on, or 'pulling in', the things they encountered, or the events to which they bore witness, along the paths they travelled. The word in Latin for this drawing or pulling in was *tractare*, from which is derived the English 'treatise' in the sense of a written composition. As they proceeded, the various personages whom they would meet on the way, and whose stories were inscribed on the pages, would speak to them, with words of wisdom and guidance, to which they would listen and from which they would learn. These were known as the *voces paginarum*, 'voices of the pages'.[22] Indeed, reading was itself a vocal practice: typically, monastic libraries were abuzz with the sounds of reading as the monks, murmuring the voices of the pages, would engage with them as though they were present and audible. To read, in its original medieval sense, was to be advised by these voices, or to take counsel, much as the old Ojibwa man would have been advised by the voice of his mentor the Thunder Bird – if only he had heard what it said![23]

Surrounded by the voices of the pages as the hunter is surrounded by the voices of the land, the medieval reader was a follower of tradition. In his

---

[20] Galileo Galilei, *Discoveries and Opinions of Galileo* (S. Drake (trans.); Garden City, NY: Doubleday Anchor, 1957), p. 237.

[21] J. Bono, *The Word of God and the Languages of Man: Interpreting Nature in Early Modern Science and Medicine* (Madison, WI: University of Wisconsin Press, 1995), p. 11.

[22] See Dom J. Leclercq, *The Love of Learning and the Desire for God* (C. Misrahi (trans.); New York: Fordham University Press, 1961), p. 19; D. Olson, *The World on Paper: The Conceptual and Cognitive Implications of Writing and Reading* (Cambridge: Cambridge University Press, 1994), pp. 184–5; see Ingold, *Lines*, pp. 14–15.

[23] On the early medieval sense of reading, see N. Howe, 'The Cultural Construction of Reading in Anglo-Saxon England', *The Ethnography of Reading* (J. Boyarin (ed.); Berkeley, CA: University of California Press, 1992).

encyclopaedic survey of animals in myth, legend, and literature, Boria Sax points out that the word 'tradition' comes from 'trade', which originally meant 'track'. 'To study a tradition', Sax writes, 'is to track a creature, as though one were a hunter, back through time'.[24] Each creature *is* its story, its tradition, and to follow it is at once to perform an act of remembrance and to move on, in continuity with the values of the past. Often, the name of the creature is itself a condensed story, so that in its very utterance, the story is carried on. But it is carried on, too, in the calls or vocalizations of the creatures themselves – if they have a voice – as well as in their manifest, visible presence and activity.[25] As a node or knot in a skein of interwoven depictions, stories, calls, sightings, and observations, none of which is ontologically prior to, or in any sense more 'real' than, any other, every creature – we could say – is not so much a living thing as the instantiation of a certain way of being alive, each of which, to the medieval mind, would open up a pathway to the experience of God. And so it was, too, with the letters and figures of the manuscript which, according to Isidore of Seville, writing in the seventh century, enable readers to hear again and retain in memory the voices of those not actually present.[26] Thus was the book of nature mirrored in the nature of the book: a second nature comprised not of works but of words.[27]

For Isidore, reading should be done quietly, but it could not be altogether silent since it depended on gestures of the throat and mouth.[28] This was because, at that time, there were no spaces between the words of a manuscript. The only way to read, then, was to read *out*, following the line of letters much as one would follow a line of musical notation, allowing the words to emerge or 'fall out' from the performance itself. In the twelfth and early thirteenth centuries, however, there gradually came about a shift towards reading with the eyes alone, unaccompanied by voice or gesture. What made this possible was the division of the line of text into word-length segments, each of which could be taken in at a glance, with spaces in between. The medievalist and palaeographer Paul Saenger

---

[24] B. Sax, *The Mythical Zoo: An Encyclopaedia of Animals in World Myth, Legend and Literature* (Santa Barbara, CA: ABC-CLIO, 2001), p. x. I am grateful to Maan Barua for bringing this work to my attention.

[25] I have discussed the ways in which the naming and vocalizations of animals enact their own stories in my essay 'Naming as Storytelling: Speaking of Animals Among the Koyukon of Akaska', *Being Alive: Essays on Movement, Knowledge and Description* (London: Routledge, 2011), pp. 165–75.

[26] M. Carruthers, *The Book of Memory: A Study of Memory in Medieval Culture* (Cambridge: Cambridge University Press, 1990), p. 106.

[27] F. Clingerman, 'Reading the Book of Nature: A Hermeneutical Account of Nature for Philosophical Theology', *Worldviews: Global Religions, Culture, Ecology* 13.1 (2009), pp. 72–91.

[28] P. Saenger, 'Silent Reading: Its Impact on Late Medieval Script and Society', *Viator* 13 (1982), pp. 367–414 (384).

has shown how, with such visual reading, the voices of the pages were effectively silenced.[29] As long as everyone in a monastic library was reading aloud, the sound of one's own voice would have sufficed to screen out the voices of others. But as every modern student knows, when one is trying to read silently, the slightest sound can be a source of distraction. So it was that silence came to reign within the cloistered confines of the monastery. In the world outside the monastery, however, in lay society, oral reading continued to predominate well into the fourteenth and fifteenth centuries. As the historian of cognition David Olson has pointed out, it was the Reformation that heralded the key transition in ways of reading, from reading *between* the lines to reading what was *on* them, or from the search for revelations or 'epiphanies' to the discovery of the one literal meaning lodged in the text, and available to anyone with the necessary key to extract it.[30]

V. Reading the New Book of Nature

In the early sixteenth century, Martin Luther urged readers to abandon the dreams and fantasies that their predecessors had found in their attunements to voices that they felt were speaking to them through the pages of the manuscript, and to draw a line in the sand between the given meanings of words and their subsequent interpretations.[31] And from there it was but a short step to extend the same reasoning from words to works, that is, to the reading of the book of nature. Thus did Bacon, a century later, insist on an absolute distinction between dreams of the imagination and patterns of the world. I would like to draw attention, in particular, to three corollaries of this transition in ways of reading the natural world. The first has to do with the imagination of what is yet to come. Reading the voices of nature, of the more-than-human world, medieval people were advised by them and would follow this advice, in parallel with their own experience, in laying a path into the future. With a sensibility attuned by an intimate perceptual engagement with their surroundings, they could *tell*, not only of what has been, but also of what will come to pass. But such foretelling, as Olson shows, has to be clearly distinguished from the kind of prediction to which a scientific reading of the book of nature aspires.[32] For to predict is not

---

[29] Ibid., pp. 378, 397.
[30] Olson, *The World on Paper*, pp. 143–4.
[31] Ibid., pp. 153–4.
[32] Ibid., pp. 174–5.

to open up a path through the world but to fix an end-point in advance. Where foretelling is guided by a dialogue with nature, prediction extrapolates from observable facts. Drawing on these facts, it is to speculate *about* the future rather than to see *into* it.

The second corollary concerns performance. I have shown how for medieval readers, meaning was generated in the vocal-gestural activity of reading *out*. Doing and knowing, here, were as clearly coupled as chewing and digestion – an analogy explicitly drawn in the ancient characterization of thinking as a process of rumination. To ruminate, we still say, is to chew things over – as cattle chew the cud – and to digest their meanings.[33] Moreover medieval people, as we have seen, would have read the book of nature in the same manner, through their practices of wayfaring. Thus, knowledge of nature was forged in movement, in the course of going about in it. This knowledge was performative in the strict sense that it was *formed through* the comings and goings of inhabitants. Reading as performance, in short, was both word-forming and world-forming. As the case of the Ojibwa and the Thunder Bird clearly demonstrates, in a way of knowing that is performative – that *goes along* – any boundaries between self and other or between mind and world, far from being set in stone, are provisional and fundamentally insecure. In a science constructed in the spirit of Bacon, however, to know is no longer to join *with* the world in performance but to be informed *by* what is already set down there. Rather than seeking to follow the trails of a familiar terrain that is continually unfolding, the scientist sets out to map a *terra incognita* that is ready made – that is, to discover, through some process of decoding or deciphering, what exists in fact. The book of nature having been *in*-scribed by the Creator in the language of things, the task of the scientist – for Bacon, as indeed for Galileo – was to *de-in*-scribe, or in a word, to 'describe' what was written there.[34] This is to obtain knowledge not by reading *out* but by reading *off.* And from the moment when reading out gave way to reading off, the world ceased to offer counsel or advice and became instead a repository of data that, in themselves, afforded no guidance on what should be done with them. The facts are one thing, values quite another, and the latter had their source not in nature but in human society. Thenceforth, wisdom took second place to information.

The third corollary takes us back to the idea that animals, and other beings of the more-than-human world, were known in medieval times by their traditions,

---

[33] Carruthers, *The Book of Memory*, pp. 164–5; see Ingold, *Lines*, p. 17.
[34] On Bacon and the 'new *de-in-scriptive* hermeneutics of nature', see Bono, *The Word of God and the Languages of Man*, p. 244.

as skeins of stories, depictions, and observations. To track an animal in the book of nature was like following a line of text. But just as the introduction of word-spacing broke the line into segments, so also – in the book of nature – creatures began to appear as discrete, bounded entities rather than as ever-extending lines of becoming. Nature, thus, became amenable to the project not of trail-following but of classification. The lines were broken, but the resulting objects could be sorted and arranged, on the basis of perceived likeness or difference, into the compartments of a taxonomy. One could speak, for the first time, of the building blocks of nature, rather than its weave, and of its architectonics. Nature, in short, was perceived to be built up from elements rather than woven from lines. And the creatures of this natural world were no longer known as traditions but as species. Those creatures, however, that were known *only* by their traditions, and for which no corroborating evidence could be found in the facts of nature, fell through the cracks. There are no dragons or Thunder Birds in scientific taxonomies. It is not just that they *do not* exist in the new book of nature; they *cannot*, since their story-bound constitution is fundamentally at odds with the project of classification. Dragons, along with other beings that rear up or make their presence felt along the ways of the world, can be told but they cannot be categorized. Nor, of course, can they be precisely located, as on a cartographic map. Just as they fell through the cracks of taxonomy, so also they were 'pushed into the wings', as Michel de Certeau put it, of a scientific cartography that had no place for the movements and itineraries of life.[35] The same, of course, is true of experiences of fear, and of the sounds of thunder. They, too, can be neither classified nor mapped. But this does not make them any less real for a person who is frightened or caught in the eye of a storm.

VI. Science and Silence

It seems, then, that as the pages lost their voice with the onset of the modern era, so the book of nature was also silenced. No longer does it speak to us, or tell us things. And yet, this allegedly silent nature can be, and often is, a deafeningly noisy place. As philosopher Stephen Vogel observes,[36] the world of nature abounds in movement and gesture, and much of this movement is manifested as sound: think of the clap of thunder and the howling of the wind, the cracking

[35] M. de Certeau, *The Practice of Everyday Life* (S. Rendall (trans.); Berkeley, CA: University of California Press, 1984), pp. 120–1.
[36] S. Vogel, 'The Silence of Nature', *Environmental Values* 15.2 (2006), pp. 145–71.

of ice and the roar of the waterfall, the rustling of trees and the calls of birds. We may also admit that at one level, human talk may also be understood as vocal gesture, and that the voice manifests human presence in the world just as the call manifests the presence of the bird and the clap the presence of thunder. On this level, voice, call, and thunder are ontologically equivalent: as the voice *is* human being in its sonic manifestation, so the call *is* the bird, and the clap *is* thunder. Yet none of this, Vogel maintains, warrants the conclusion that natural entities actually *converse* with human beings, let alone with one another. This is for two principal reasons. Firstly, conversation requires participants to attend and respond, in turn, to one another. Humans do indeed attend and respond to the sounds of nature: they listen out for bird calls and are moved, even terrified, by thunder. But does nature, Vogel asks, respond to us? 'Do the self-speaking entities we attend and respond to in nature ever give us their full attention…, engage us, respond to our claims?'[37] The answer, he is convinced, is 'no'. The sounds of nature, he suggests, are more like the commands of a monarch who is deaf to his subjects but compels their obedience. Secondly, a conversation is necessarily *about* something.[38] It enables participants to compare each other's perceptions of the world in the common task of figuring out how it actually *is*. Human interlocutors do this, but birds, trees, rivers, thunder, and the winds do not. It is not that they are irresponsible interlocutors; rather, they are not interlocutors at all.[39]

For Vogel, then, the silence of nature means that however much noise it makes, it takes no part in the conversations we hold about it. It might sound to us *as if* nature is speaking, but that is a delusion. 'I have listened carefully', writes Vogel, 'and I hear nothing'.[40] Recall the old Ojibwa man and the Thunder Bird. He thought the thunder was speaking to him, but could not comprehend what it said. Was this a failure of translation, as Hallowell seems to suggest? I have argued that it was rather a failure of empathy. For Vogel, however, had the old man comprehended thunder's speech, he would have succeeded neither in translating it nor in empathizing with it. He would rather have performed an act of ventriloquism. For whereas the translator speaks for another but in his own tongue, the ventriloquist projects his own words onto a mute object while creating the illusion that it is the object speaking for itself.[41] This charge

---

[37] Ibid., p. 148.
[38] Ibid., pp. 151–2.
[39] Ibid., p. 157.
[40] Ibid., p. 167.
[41] Ibid., p. 162.

of ventriloquism is of course the foundation for the scientific abhorrence of anthropomorphism, where those who claim empathy with non-human creatures, or to know what they are feeling, stand accused of merely projecting their own thoughts and sentiments onto their unwitting subjects. It is an accusation, however, that has not gone unchallenged. In an important debate conducted in the pages of the journal *Environmental Values*, Nicole Klenk has entered on the other side. She replies that non-humans *can and do* respond to human voice, gesture, and presence in ways that are meaningful both to them and to us.[42]

It is true that non-humans may not compare their perceptions of the environment with humans in a collaborative effort to establish the truth of what is actually 'out there'. But to insist that conversations can only take this form, Klenk argues, is to take such a narrow view of conversation that it would exclude most of what we commonly call conversation in the human world. For most people, most of the time, conversation is a matter of understanding what others are telling us – of 'getting the story right', not of verifying the rightness of the story.[43] Thus, human beings who take it upon themselves to render in words what nature is saying are indeed translators and not ventriloquists. For Klenk, this is precisely what happens in scientific work. Were this not the case, she concludes, scientific interpretations would be mere fictions created through dialogue among humans, rather than the results of careful interaction with – and observation of – components of the natural world. But in this, I believe Klenk is mistaken. Or more to the point, she is mistaken so long as we remain bound by the methodological protocols of normal science. For the claim of science is that as a specialized knowledge practice, it *does* seek to verify the rightness of the story, rather than merely getting the story right. Ever since Bacon, science has insisted on discovering the literal truth of what is there, and, thus, on the strict separation of fact and interpretation. Reading what is *on* the lines of the book of nature, rather than between them, the one thing that scientists insist they do *not* do is what Klenk takes to be their number one priority: 'to listen to the voices of those beings they interact with'.[44] Arguably, indeed, scientists do all

---

[42] N. Klenk, 'Listening to the Birds: A Pragmatic Proposal for Forestry', *Environmental Values* 17.3 (2008), pp. 331–51.

[43] Ibid., p. 333.

[44] Ibid., p. 334. The exception to this are advocates of Goethean science for whom to engage in scientific study is to 'enter into a conversation with nature [and] listen to what nature has to say'. C. Holdrege, 'Doing Goethean Science', *Janus Head* 8.1 (2005), pp. 27–52. The contempt in which the Goethean approach is held by mainstream science reveals it, however, to be an exception that proves the rule.

they can to *avoid* listening, for fear that it would interfere with or compromise the objectivity of their results.

VII. Knowing in Being

So there is, I contend, a real parallel in the modern constitution between the book of nature and the nature of the book, as a completed work whose contents can be read by those with the keys to decipher it. The parallel lies in the idea that both are to be read in silence: not in the course of an on-going conversation whose manifold participants open up to one another and whose stories intertwine, but as a record of results that – rendered inert and impassive, in objective and objectified forms – have turned their back on us, presenting to our inspection only what Mae-Wan Ho has called an 'opaque, flat, frozen surface of literalness'.[45] To science, the facts are given; they comprise what are called the 'data'. But the world does not ostensibly give of itself to science as part of any offering or commitment. What is 'given', in science, is precisely that which has fallen out of circulation and has settled as a kind of residue, cast off from the give and take of life. It is this residue – dredged, sampled, and purified – that is then subjected to a process of analysis, the end results of which appear on the written page in the forms of words, figures, and diagrams. Thus, the knowledge so constituted is created as an overlay or wrap-around on the outside of being. Having silenced the world, we find knowledge in the silence of the book. Indeed, the very concept of the human, in its modern incarnation, expresses the dilemma of a creature that can know the world of which it is existentially a part only by leaving it. Yet in our experience as inhabitants, moving through the world rather than roaming its outer surface, our knowledge is not built up as an external accretion but rather grows and unfolds from the very inside of our earthly being. We grow into the world, as the world grows in us. Perhaps this grounding of knowing in being lies at the heart of the kind of sensibility we are apt to call 'religious'.

But was it not in the name of religion that leaders of the Reformation insisted on turning the relation between knowing and being inside out? In its stress on the literal truth of words and works, the religion of the reformists was trumped by the very science it unloosed. For in any contest over the facts, science is

---

[45] M.-W. Ho, 'The Role of Action in Evolution: Evolution by Process and the Ecological Approach to Perception', *Cultural Dynamics* 4.3 (1991), pp. 336–54 (348).

bound to win, and religion to lose, leaving the puzzle of why people – including, it must be said, many scientists – tenaciously adhere to representations of reality that are demonstrably false.[46] Yet questions about which can better *represent* the world, religion or science, are wrongly posed, for the real contest lies elsewhere. It turns on the question of whether or not our ways of knowing and imagining are enshrined within an existential commitment to the world in which we find ourselves. To compare religion and science in terms of their respective purchase on a reality from which we ourselves are fully disengaged is to assume that they are not – in other words, that in our conscious deliberations, whether scientific or spiritual, the world owes nothing to us, nor we to the world. But if, on the other hand, we owe our very existence to the world, and if the world, at least in some measure, owes its existence to us, then we need to ask instead: what is the nature of these owings, these commitments? How can knowing and imagining let us, and the creatures around us, *be*? For it is surely in their discharge into being – that is, in the recognition, as anthropologist Stuart McLean puts it, of an essential continuity between 'human acts of imagining' and 'the processes shaping and transforming the material universe' – that the common ground between religion and science is to be found.[47]

This is where Klenk might be right after all. All science depends on observation, and observation depends in turn on a close and immediate coupling, in perception and action, between the observer and those aspects of the world that are the focus of attention.[48] Perhaps the most striking characteristic of modern science lies in the lengths to which it has gone to deny or cover up the practical, observational commitments on which it depends. To highlight these commitments – to attend to the practices of science rather than its formal prescriptions – means recovering those very experiential and performative engagements which, unwritten and unsung, have fallen through the cracks or been pushed into the wings of scientific conceptualizations. Let us not forget the advice of Kekulé, that to 'follow the paths of the Pathfinders [one] must note every footprint, every bent twig, every fallen leaf'. Scientists in practice are as much

---

[46] There is an ever-growing literature devoted to this puzzle, which frames the problem in exactly these terms: why is the human imagination primed to come up with representations of entities, such as spirits, which – if they existed in fact – would violate obvious principles of physical or biological causation? See, for example, P. Boyer, 'Functional Origins of Religious Concepts: Ontological and Strategic Selection in Evolved Minds', *Journal of the Royal Anthropological Institute* 6.2 (2000), pp. 195–214. From the perspective advanced here, this literature, which treats religion as a domain of cognitive illusion, completely misses the point.

[47] S. McLean, 'Stories and Cosmogonies: Imagining Creativity Beyond "Nature" and "Culture"', *Cultural Anthropology* 24.2 (2009), pp. 213–45.

[48] Ingold, *Being Alive*, p. 75.

wayfarers as are people of faith, and must perforce tread where others have gone before, ever attentive and responsive to the rustlings and whisperings of their surroundings. Joining with things in the processes of their formation, rather than merely being informed by what has already precipitated out, practising scientists do not just *collect* but *accept* what the world has to offer them. They may, in deference to official protocols, feign not to listen to the voices of beings around them, but listen they must, if they are to advance beyond the bare pick-up of information towards real understanding. Like it or not, they too are beholden to the world. And it is in this more humble profession, rather than in arrogating to itself the exclusive authority to represent a given reality, that scientific inquiry converges with religious sensibility as a way of knowing-in-being. This is the way of imagination.

VII. The Bible and the Land

Let me conclude with one further example from the ethnography of the circumpolar North. It comes from a recent study by Peter Loovers, carried out among Teetł'it Gwich'in people living in and around Fort McPherson, in the Northwest Territories of Canada.[49] The study is exceptional in combining a sensitive account of the ways in which people relate to their environment as they hunt, trap, and move around on land and water, with a detailed history of Gwich'in engagements with the written word – above all in the translation and reception of the Christian Bible. The immense work of translation was undertaken by Archdeacon Robert McDonald. Born in 1829 of a Scottish father – an employee of the Hudson's Bay Company – and an Ojibwa mother, McDonald was educated at the Anglican mission school at the Red River settlement and spent a decade serving with the Ojibwa people before embarking, in 1862, on a mission to bring the Anglican faith to the people of the Mackenzie River district. Over the ensuing decades, McDonald worked tirelessly to introduce Christian teachings to native Gwich'in communities and many of the men and women whom he encountered on his travels became key advisers in helping him to transcribe liturgical texts into their own language, known at the time as

---

[49] J. Loovers, ' "You Have to Live It": Pedagogy and Literacy with Tweetł'it Gwich'in (PhD thesis, University of Aberdeen, 2010). It was my privilege to supervise Peter's work, alongside my colleague David Anderson, and it was my experience of helping him pull together the sections of his thesis on literacy and living on the land that first planted the idea for this chapter in my mind.

Tadukh. For McDonald, the translation of the entire Bible into Tadukh was a lifelong endeavour, and the work was not completed until 1898.

Though the Tadukh Bible was warmly received by the Gwich'in, this reception was not quite as McDonald intended. Unlike his rivals from the Catholic mission, who took a rather more relaxed attitude, McDonald was steeped in the traditions of the reformed church and believed that the text of the Bible was to be read literally, as the unalterable record of a singular truth that is not open to negotiation. Much to his discomfort, however, many Gwich'in people, including several of McDonald's own pupils, began to experience dreams and visions in which, it seemed, the pages of the Bible were talking to them, issuing instructions, and revealing prophecies. These pages spoke with the voices of their elders, the people with whom McDonald had been working in transcribing the text (and whose particular dialectal idiosyncrasies had become incorporated into it), and even with the voice of McDonald himself. Thus, for the Gwich'in, to read the Bible was to open up a conversation with these elders, to listen to their voices, to be taught by them, and to learn. For his part, McDonald was mightily displeased and felt compelled to denounce the 'false prophecies' that were being mouthed by the people.[50] The mismatch between these ways of reading was not, however, confined to the Bible. It has continued to surface in other contexts, most notably in the interpretation of treaties and land claims agreements drawn up with officials of the Canadian government. In these cases the dismay was on the side of the Gwich'in, who were surprised to discover that documents which they had thought to open up to on-going dialogue with those whose voices were incorporated therein, were treated by officialdom as set in stone, silent, and unyielding.[51]

Exactly the same mismatch, as Loovers elegantly shows, can be found in ways of reading the land. For colonizers, explorers, scientists, and others who have come to the land from outside, whether on a mission to civilize it, to develop it, to research it, or to appreciate its natural beauty, there is no disputing that what is there is already fixed, awaiting discovery, explanation, and possibly transformation by the hands and minds of men. For the Gwich'in, however, it is quite different. To read the land, for them, is to attend to the multiple clues that reveal the activities and intentions of its manifold human and more-than-human inhabitants. These clues, Loovers tells us, 'include animal movements, trails, old and new camps and cabins, marks on the land, wood, snow and ice

---

[50] Ibid., p. 117.
[51] Ibid., p. 138.

conditions in winter, river-banks in summer, and places where events have unfolded'.[52] Wherever they go, Gwich'in are listening, remembering, learning, *taking counsel* from the land. It is their teacher, not just a repository from which can be extracted materials for the construction of propositional knowledge. Thus, the land speaks to people with many voices, just as the Bible does. Should we then go along with Archdeacon McDonald and conclude that such a way of reading the land is equally false, or that it rests on the kinds of delusions to which in western colonial eyes, allegedly primitive, native peoples have always been supposed to be prone? Even McDonald, with his Ojibwa upbringing, would have known that there is more to indigenous understandings than this. And so, in light of what I have argued in this chapter, do we.

VIII. Epilogue

There's No Such Thing as a Dragon. That's the title of one of the great classics of children's literature, authored by Jack Kent.[53] It tells the story of a little boy, Billy Bixbee, who wakes one morning to find a dragon in his bedroom. It is pretty small and wags its tail in a friendly way. Billy takes the dragon down to breakfast, and introduces it to his mother. 'There's no such thing as a dragon', she declares firmly, and carries on preparing pancakes for breakfast. Billy sits at the breakfast table; the dragon sits *on* it. Sitting on the table is not normally permitted in the Bixbee household, but there was nothing to be done, since if a dragon does not exist, you cannot tell it to get down from the table. The dragon is hungry and eats most of the pancakes, though Billy does not mind. As his mother continues to ignore the new arrival, the dragon begins to swell. It swells and swells. Soon it occupies most of the hallway, and Billy's mother has difficulties cleaning the house as she can only get from one room to another by way of the windows. All the doors are blocked. The dragon swells and swells – now it is as big as the whole house. Then the house is lifted off its foundations and careers off down the street on the dragon's back. Billy's father, home from work, is surprised to find that his house has vanished. But a helpful neighbour points in the direction it went. Eventually the family is reunited, and by this time Billy's mother has reluctantly acknowledged that perhaps the dragon does exist after all. Immediately, the dragon begins to shrink, until it is once again

---

[52] Ibid., p. 300.
[53] J. Kent, *There's No Such Thing as a Dragon* (New York: Random House Children's Books, 2009).

of a manageable size. 'I don't mind dragons when they're this size', Mrs Bixbee admits, as she sits comfortably in an armchair giving the dragon a good stroke.

The moral of this story, of course, is that initially small problems – if we are afraid to recognize them or to speak their name, for fear of infringing the norms of rational conduct – can grow and grow to the point at which ordinary social life can no longer be sustained. I think, in the present day, that there is a dragon in our midst, and that it is growing to the point at which it is becoming increasingly difficult to lead sustainable lives. This dragon inhabits the rupture we have created between the world and our imagination of it. We know from experience that the rupture is unsustainable, and yet we are reluctant to acknowledge its existence since to do so would fly in the face of accepted scientific rationality. I believe such acknowledgement is long overdue. In this chapter I have suggested how studies of medieval monasticism and of so-called indigenous ontologies could suggest alternative ways of reading, and of writing, which might allow us once again to take counsel from both the voices of the pages and the world around us, to listen and be advised by what they are telling us, and to heal the rupture between being and knowing. This healing must be a first step towards establishing a more open-ended and sustainable way to live. Perhaps, then, the dragon will subside.

Bibliography

Bacon, F., *The Great Instauration: The Plan of the Work: Works of Francis Bacon, Baron of Verulam, Viscount St. Alban and Lord High Chancellor of England, Vol. IV* (J. Spedding, R. L. Ellis, and D. D. Heath (eds); London: Spottiswoode, 1858), pp. 22–33.

Benfey, O. T., 'August Kekulé and the Birth of the Structural Theory of Organic Chemistry in 1858', *Journal of Chemical Education* 35.1 (1958), pp. 21–3.

Bono, J. J., *The Word of God and the Languages of Man: Interpreting Nature in Early Modern Science and Medicine* (Madison, WI: University of Wisconsin Press, 1995).

Boyer, P., 'Functional Origins of Religious Concepts: Ontological and Strategic Selection in Evolved Minds', *Journal of the Royal Anthropological Institute* 6.2 (2000), pp. 195–214.

Carruthers, M., *The Book of Memory: A Study of Memory in Medieval Culture* (Cambridge: Cambridge University Press, 1990).

—*The Craft of Thought: Meditation, Rhetoric and the Making of Images, 400–1200* (Cambridge: Cambridge University Press, 1998).

Certeau, M. de, *The Practice of Everyday Life* (S. Rendall (trans.); Berkeley, CA: University of California Press, 1984).

Clingerman, F., 'Reading the Book of Nature: A Hermeneutical Account of Nature for Philosophical Theology', *Worldviews: Global Religions, Culture, Ecology* 13.1 (2009), pp. 72–91.

Galilei, G., *Discoveries and Opinions of Galileo* (S. Drake (trans.); Garden City, NY: Doubleday Anchor, 1957).

Gieser, T., 'Embodiment, Emotion and Empathy: A Phenomenological Approach to Apprenticeship Learning', *Anthropological Theory* 8.3 (2008), pp. 299–318.

Hallowell, A. I., 'Ojibwa Ontology, Behavior and World View', *Culture in History: Essays in Honor of Paul Radin* (S. Diamond (ed.); New York: Columbia University Press, 1960), pp. 19–52.

—'The Role of Dreams in Ojibwa Culture', *Contributions to Anthropology: Selected Papers of A. Irving Hallowell* (R. D. Fogelson, F. Eggan, M. E. Spiro, G. W. Stocking, A. F. C. Wallace, and W. E. Washburn (eds); Chicago: University of Chicago Press), pp. 449–74.

Ho, M.-W., 'The Role of Action in Evolution: Evolution by Process and the Ecological Approach to Perception', *Cultural Dynamics* 4.3 (1991), pp. 336–54.

Holdrege, C., 'Doing Goethean Science', *Janus Head* 8.1 (2005), pp. 27–52.

Howe, N., 'The Cultural Construction of Reading in Anglo-Saxon England', *The Ethnography of Reading* (J. Boyarin (ed.); Berkeley, CA: University of California Press, 1992).

Ingold, T., *Being Alive: Essays on Movement, Knowledge and Description* (London: Routledge, 2011).

—'Life Beyond the Edge of Nature? Or, the Mirage of Society', *The Mark of the Social* (J. B. Greenwood (ed.); Lanham, MD: Rowman and Littlefield, 1997), pp. 231–52.

—*Lines: A Brief History* (London: Routledge, 2007).

—*The Perception of the Environment: Essays on Livelihood, Dwelling and Skill* (London: Routledge, 2000).

Kent, J., *There's No Such Thing as a Dragon* (New York: Random House Children's Books, 2009).

Klenk, N., 'Listening to the Birds: A Pragmatic Proposal for Forestry', *Environmental Values* 17.3 (2008), pp. 331–51.

Leclercq, J., *The Love of Learning and the Desire for God* (C. Misrahi (trans.); New York: Fordham University Press, 1961).

Loovers, J. P. L., *"You Have to Live It": Pedagogy and Literacy with Tweetl'it Gwich'in* (unpublished Ph.D. thesis, University of Aberdeen, 2010).

McLean, S., 'Stories and Cosmogonies: Imagining Creativity Beyond "Nature" and "Culture"', *Cultural Anthropology* 24.2 (2009), pp. 213–45.

Olson, D. R., *The World on Paper: The Conceptual and Cognitive Implications of Writing and Reading* (Cambridge: Cambridge University Press, 1994).

Roberts, R. M., *Serendipity: Accidental Discoveries in Science* (New York: Wiley, 1989).

Saenger, P., 'Silent Reading: Its Impact on Late Medieval Script and Society', *Viator* 13 (1982), pp. 367–414.

Sax, B., *The Mythical Zoo: An Encyclopaedia of Animals in World Myth, Legend and Literature* (Santa Barbara, CA: ABC-CLIO, 2001).

'Unthinkable? Faster than light', *The Guardian* (24 September 2011), http://www.guardian.co.uk/commentisfree/2011/sep/23/unthinkable-faster-than-light-editorial (accessed 9 August 2012).

Vogel, S., 'The Silence of Nature', *Environmental Values* 15.2 (2006), pp. 145–71.

3

The Study of Religion after the Animal

Aaron Gross

The inquiry now taking place into 'animals and religion', to which this edited collection contributes, is noteworthy for taking into account the ethical challenges regarding our treatment of animals that have been raised with special force since the 1970s,[1] while simultaneously pursuing theoretical, historical, and theological issues related to animals and religion. This broad and rich exploration of 'animals and religion' has generally been considered something new under the academic sun, or, at most, three or four decades old. Something new certainly is happening as religious practitioners and scholars increasingly accept the idea of animals as religious subjects of one kind or another; however, serious questions about animals and religion are not, despite appearances, 'cutting edge', nor did they first emerge alongside the political struggles for animal protection that arose in the academy in the 1970s. Questions about what animals are, and whether animals can participate in the phenomena of religion, are also *founding* questions in religious studies.

Certain ways of imagining and engaging animals and the human/animal border have helped define the academic study of religion since its inception and continue to do so. More specifically, the founding theorists of religious studies who, significantly, were following the intellectual trajectory of Jewish and Christian theologians, have uncritically deployed discourses about animals and the human/animal border in order to imagine humanity, religion, the categories used to study religion, and the very space of the humanities and social sciences.

---

[1] For example, the work of scholars like Peter Singer, who tends to ignore religion or see it as part of the problem (though that may be changing); Andrew Linzey, who emphasizes Christianity's liberatory potential in regard to our treatment of animals; and Mary Midgley, who sees in religion neither the root of the problem nor the primary solution in our troubled relationship with other animals.

Scholars and religious practitioners interested in animals and religion cannot simply study the topic as if it were any one of a number of new inquiries. Rather, we need to remember what could be called the 'absent presence' animals have always had in our discipline and confront it. In the first part of this essay, I focus on following the intertwinement of the question of the animal as it founds the academic study of religion and questions about animals that later arise in this discipline. In the second part, I suggest the value of the scholarship of the philosopher Jacques Derrida and the anthropologist Tim Ingold for scholars of religion as we confront the theoretical challenges posed by the study of animals' religious subjectivities.

I. Scholarship on Animals and Religion

To begin, I offer some general observations about the present state of scholarship on animals and religion. In order to briefly sketch a pair of well-articulated approaches that can orient us to the field, I mention only two scholars of religious studies: Paul Waldau and Kimberley Patton, who are also the editors of the first edited, scholarly volume devoted specifically to the nexus of animals and religion, *A Communion of Subjects*. In Waldau's attempts to imagine the field of animals and religion, for example, in his 2006 essay 'Seeing the Terrain We Walk: Features of the Contemporary Landscape of "Religion and Animals"', he envisions the subfield in expansive terms as virtually any inquiry in the academy that bears on religious phenomena and what he calls, in a poignant phrase, '*the nearby biological individuals outside human communities*'.[2] That is, his emphasis is – quite rightly – on the fundamental and surprisingly complicated task of ensuring that actual animals are discussed. Kimberley Patton's work, as she herself notes, is ambiguously suspended between constructive theology and comparative religion. Patton argues – both theologically out of a multiplicity of traditions and as a historian of religions – that animals, or rather human-animal relationships, are something *holy*. In her ground-breaking essay published in 2000, '"He Who Sits in the Heavens and Laughs": Recovering Animal Theology in the Abrahamic Traditions', Patton highlights three themes by which the Abrahamic traditions have imagined the sacrality of animal subjectivities: 'first, divine compassion or special regard for animals; second,

---

[2] P. Waldau, 'Seeing the Terrain We Walk: Features of the Contemporary Landscape of "Religion and Animals"', *A Communion of Subjects: Animals in Religion, Science, and Ethics* (P. Waldau, and K. Patton (eds); New York: Columbia University Press, 2006), p. 40.

communication and mutual awareness between God and animals; and third, animal veneration of God'.[3] More recently, Patton has argued that the human-animal relationship is and always has been, 'something charged, something holy, something that social construction can only partially interpret, but to which the religious imagination, with its unflinching reach into the depths of the human heart, must instead respond'.[4] These two orientations – Waldau's concern with a robust consideration of actual animals and Patton's imagination of the human-animal relationship as sacred – remain crucial and are in need of development in their own right. I wish to argue, however, that today a third approach, which is already vibrant in some areas of philosophy and anthropology, should be *integrated* with these, namely, attending to how the question of the animal founds the very discourses that now, belatedly, have turned to inquire about animals. It is by addressing this knottiest of issues that we can create the space in the study of religion to fully confront animals.

II. The Absent Presence: Theorizing Animals and Religion in the History of Religious Studies

I now turn to a survey of three influential theorists of religious studies. I begin with the founding figure of Emile Durkheim, then proceed to the scholar who arguably has had the most influence on the theoretical foundations of religious studies departments, Mircea Eliade, and conclude with the highly regarded contemporary scholar of religion, Jonathan Z. Smith. Attending to their engagement with animals at crucial moments in their respective oeuvres will show the central role animals have played in the study of religion; significantly, I could have chosen numerous other theoretical giants and the results would have been no different.

a. Emile Durkheim

Emile Durkheim's foundational contribution to the study of religion in his 1912 classic *The Elementary Forms of Religious Life* was to imagine the study of

---

[3] K. Patton, '"He Who Sits in the Heavens Laughs": Recovering Animal Theology in the Abrahamic Traditions,' *Harvard Theological Review* 93.4 (2000), p. 409.

[4] K. Patton, '"Caught with Ourselves in the Net of Life and Time": Traditional Views of Animals in Religion,' *A Communion of Subjects: Animals in Religion, Science, and Ethics* (P. Waldau, and K. Patton (eds); New York: Columbia University Press, 2006), p. 37.

religion as a study of the sacred-profane binary as it arises in all aspects of life – in economy, in governance, in family structure, in ritual, and so on. Rather than a sociology of religion that would bring the tools of sociology to bear upon religion, Durkheim imagined a religious sociology that refused reductionist approaches.[5] Durkheim's inquiry into religion is simultaneously an inquiry into the origins of conceptual thought, the emergence of the human out of animality, and the foundations of society – all four of these inquiries are intimately bound together.

For Durkheim, the human being is distinct from all other animals because the human form is uniquely indeterminate. In his 1903 work with Marcel Mauss, *Primitive Classification*, Durkheim explains that 'humanity in the beginning lacks the most indispensable conditions for the classificatory function'.[6] 'It would be impossible to exaggerate, in fact, the state of indistinction from which the human mind developed.'[7] Refining this thinking, he later wrote that 'the categories of human thought are never fixed in a definite form; they are cease-lessly made, unmade, and remade; they vary according to time and place'.[8] This biological indeterminacy, he goes on to theorize, demands completion by human society. Only when the categories of thought – including the decisive categories of the sacred and profane – are socially completed does thought become 'truly and peculiarly human'.[9] Humans are not born but produced in the socially assisted completion of our biologically indeterminate classificatory function. The emergence of the human from animality and the emergence of properly conceptual thought is one and the same process.

Society, Durkheim argues, also originates in this process. Society is under-stood to be simultaneously constituting (society completes human biological indeterminacy) and constituted (society itself is made in the process of thus completing human indeterminacy). The sociologist Peter Berger, who is a perfect Durkheimian in this regard, explains in his classic *The Sacred Canopy*,

---

[5] J. Alexander, *Durkheimian Sociology: Cultural Studies* (Cambridge: Cambridge University Press, 1988), pp. 5–6.

[6] E. Durkheim, and M. Mauss, *Primitive Classification* (Chicago: University of Chicago Press, 1963), p. 7.

[7] Ibid., p. 5. Significantly, in *Primitive Classification*, Durkheim argues for the original state of indis-tinction primarily by showing that certain non-Western communities do not distinguish between humans and animals in the same manner with which we are accustomed. He appears to take for granted the naturalness and reasonableness of the familiar human-animal binary. A culture without this binary, he problematically concludes, is surely just in an early, primitive state 'of confusion' (p. 6).

[8] E. Durkheim, *The Elementary Forms of Religious Life* (K. Fields (trans.); New York: Free Press, 1995), p. 14.

[9] Ibid., p. 446.

'man cannot exist apart from society. The two statements, that society is the product of man and that man is the product of society, are not contradictory. They rather reflect the inherently dialectic character of the societal phenomenon'.[10]

Finally, we come to religion. Religion, for Durkheim, is *not* reducible to thought, to the human, or to society but is the very knot that laces these three realities together. When human communities gather for intense ritual practices in the obscure moment of what Durkheim calls 'collective effervescence',[11] the experience of the difference between the sacred (space, times, and actions) and profane founds 'the religious idea'.[12] The individual, in a state of exaltation and surrounded by particular sancta in particular times and places, becomes religious by acquiring an understanding of the sacred-profane binary.

Acquiring this binary, and other categories, Durkheim theorizes, is nothing other than the formation of conceptual thought itself; with this, the human emerges from animality and society is constituted (and, dialectically, constituting). Religion, understood as the division of the world into sacred and profane, is not only for Durkheim a universal characteristic of human culture (something necessitated by our uniquely neotenic biology), but the very production of the properly human from the fodder of the peculiar, indeterminate animality into which we are born.

Interestingly, while Durkheim ultimately is arguing for a radical break between the human and all other animals, he does not rest this difference in biology. Durkheim insists, 'From a physical point of view … and from the mental point of view … [man] differs from the animal only in degree'. Human distinction is *constructed*. 'And yet', Durkheim continues,

> society conceives him and requires that we conceive him as being endowed with a *sui generis* character that insulates and shields him from all reckless infringement—in other words, that imposes respect. This status, which puts him in a class by himself, seems to us to be one of his distinctive attributes, even though no basis for it can be found in the empirical nature.[13]

While human uniqueness is constructed, this does not, for Durkheim make it any less real. Human uniqueness – and the special moral and ethical status of

---

[10] P. Berger, *The Sacred Canopy: Elements of a Sociological Theory of Religion* (New York: Anchor Books, 1990), p. 4.
[11] Durkheim, *The Elementary Forms of Religious Life*, pp. 220, 228.
[12] Ibid., p. 220.
[13] Ibid., p. 229.

human life – is simply grounded in a different kind of reality than are 'brute' biological features like the opposable thumb.[14]

More work would be necessary to properly explicate Durkheim's tight binding together of religion, conceptual thought, the properly human, and society. For our purposes, though, the crucial detail is simply the more generic observation that, for Durkheim, both society and religion are imaginable only on the previous assumption of a radical break between the almost infinitely malleable human and 'animals', who, for Durkheim, have a fixed nature and thus are utterly cut off from any participation in the phenomena of religion, conceptual thought, or society. The question of the animal and the difficulties associated with it turn out to be at the very heart of Durkheim's foundational contribution to the future of the scholarly study of both religion and society.

b. Mircea Eliade

Both Eliade and Smith have followed Durkheim in intertwining the study of religion with a demarcation of the properly human from the animal. First, we can note that the scholarship of both Eliade and Smith relies in crucial ways on the Durkheimian sacred-profane binary, which, as we have seen, is intimately interwoven with the human/animal binary. Producing this distinction between sacred and profane is, for Eliade, what distinguishes the human from the animal. For Eliade, the sacred-profane binary is crucial to the definition of his most central scholarly category, 'myth'. Myth, he argues, always involves a break-through of the sacred into profane life. Smith develops and critiques Eliade's understanding of myth, constructing an ever larger body of scholarship on the basis of these foundational binaries. Though not immediately visible, the animal again undergirds the imagination of religion.

Just as for Durkheim the human arises or reproduces itself from a kind of animality by enacting the sacred-profane binary, for Eliade the human is produced in the act of myth-making, which is essentially an act of meaning-making. In both *The Quest* and the first volume of his monumental three volume *A History of Religious Ideas,* Elide writes, 'it is difficult to imagine how

---

[14] Durkheim here offers a secular parallel to a wide variety of theological arguments for the human distinction from animals that suggest human uniqueness is not found in the animal body, but rather in the unique human soul, in unique divine mandates, in unique abilities of humans to transcend animality, and in similar conceptions. In place of such uniquely human features, Durkheim places his interwoven conception of conceptual thought and society. What remains consistent in both cases is the articulation of the human through a dramatic division between the animal and human – a division, often used to authorize violence to animals, that Durkheim has clearly absorbed from ancient streams of both Jewish and Christian thought.

the human mind could function without the conviction that there is something irreducibly *real* in the world; and it is impossible to imagine how consciousness could appear without conferring a *meaning* on man's impulses and experiences'.[15] To be human is to be *homo religiosus* – an animal that transcends its animality by making myths and thus meaning.

For both Durkheim and Eliade, the phenomenon of religion can be found persistently through time and space because it is rooted in the uniquely religious character of the properly human. Religion, for both thinkers, begins where the animal ends. As Eliade has it, 'In other words, to be—or, rather, to become—*a man* signifies being "religious"'.[16]

Thus, in *A History of Religious Ideas,* first published in 1976, Eliade gives the distinction between humans and animals the pride of the opening line. Here Eliade addresses the centrality of the demarcation between human and animal to the study of religion, while, oddly, denying that he will discuss this demarcation. Eliade writes, 'Despite its importance for an understanding of the religious phenomenon, we shall not here discuss the problem of "hominization"' – that is, the process of the animal *homo sapiens* becoming a human being. 'It is sufficient to recall that the vertical posture already marks a transcending of the condition typical of the primates. … It is because of man's vertical posture that space is organized in a structure inaccessible to the prehominians.'[17] From these lines forward, Eliade, like Durkheim before him, proceeds in the manner of the great philosophers to articulate a careful demarcation between the human and primate that simultaneously presents his view of the human being as inherently religious.

Eliade enumerates three basic differences that separate 'primate and human' which create the conditions in which the properly human can emerge: verticality, tools (technology), and, most intriguingly, the decision to kill and eat animals. Verticality, the upright posture of the human, Eliade argues, provides the condition for the possibility of viewing some space as sacred space. Animals may have territory, mating grounds, and other intimate relations with land, but only the human creates sacred space. The use of tools, fire especially, Eliade continues, further distinguishes human and animal. Even though other animals do make tools, Eliade asserts that only the human 'use of tools is not confined to a particular situation or a specific moment, as is the case with monkeys'.[18]

---

[15] M. Eliade, *A History of Religious Ideas Volume 1: From the Stone Age to the Eleusinian Mysteries* (W. Trask (trans.); 3 vols.; Chicago: University of Chicago Press, 1981), p. xiii.
[16] Ibid.
[17] Ibid., p. 3.
[18] Ibid., p. 4.

The final demarcation holds special interest for anyone interested in the question of the animal and religion. '[M]an', Eliade argues, 'is the final product of a decision to kill in order to live. In short, the hominians succeeded in outstripping their ancestors by becoming flesh-eaters'.[19] This decision to kill, Eliade continues, ultimately leads to the production of gender differentiation and the structure of sacrifice. This sacrificial structure emerges, Eliade speculates, because 'the ceaseless pursuit and killing of game ended by creating a unique system of relationships between the hunter and the slain animals … [A] 'mystical solidarity' between the hunter and his victims is revealed by the mere act of killing: the shed blood is similar in every respect to human blood'.[20] A special kind of killing is therefore required and sacrifice emerges. Eliade's view, which I have summarized in a few sentences, is ultimately unfolded in over 1,000 pages of analysis in *A History of Religious Ideas* and I would urge readers not to view the above as an adequate summary. Far more time would be needed to make Eliade's view fully intelligible and thus put us in a position to understand it well enough to properly critique or endorse it, but this is not necessary for the present purposes. It is in any case clear that the foundational imagination of religion and the key categories used to understand it, such as myth and sacred space, are, for Eliade, bound up intimately with his views about animals.

These views have immediate practical consequences. For example, the study of animal behaviour, ethology, could never, on Eliade's or Durkheim's view, teach us anything essential about religion. Their picture excludes, or at least constrains, the potential importance of the controversial and problematic, but I think productive, proposals of scholars, such as Fritz Staal,[21] Walter Burkert,[22] and Robert Bellah,[23] who have attempted to place religion in an evolutionary frame and understand religious practice as sharing certain important continuities with particular animal behaviours. It also unnecessarily curtails the potential significance of related scholarly attempts to bring the humanities into closer dialog with the life sciences – for example, Anne Taves's suggestion that we theorize religion through an identification of more basic 'building blocks'

---

[19] Ibid.

[20] Ibid., p. 5.

[21] F. Staal, *Rules without Meaning: Ritual, Mantras, and the Human Sciences* (Toronto Studies in Religion; vol. 4; New York: P. Lang, 1990).

[22] W. Burkert, *Creation of the Sacred: Tracks of Biology in Early Religions* (Cambridge: Harvard University Press, 1996).

[23] R. Bellah, *Religion in Human Evolution: From the Paleolithic to the Axial Age* (Cambridge, MA: Belknap Press of Harvard University Press, 2011).

that 'reflect basic affective and cognitive processes common to humans and perhaps to other animals as well'.[24]

It is possible, of course, to take on a perspective that makes room for serious consideration of continuities between religious activity and animal behaviour in the manner of Bellah, Burkert, Stall, or Taves while still restricting the domain of the 'truly' religious to the human (and this is largely what these four scholars do). In this sense, Durkheim's and Eliade's theories of religion do not absolutely rule out the *relevance* of animals to religion; their views could be stretched to consider animal behaviour as helpful for understanding the ground from which religion springs. That said, as Durkheim's and Eliade's lack of interest in even 'proto-religious' behaviour among animals suggests, the actual functioning of their theorization of religion as exclusively human, which plays into a larger and deeply entrenched narrative about the gulf separating human from animal that is only now being fully deconstructed, has led and continues to lead to a more thoroughgoing exclusion of animals. Even among scholars that have overcome a total exclusion of animals from the theorization of religion, it is arguable that a largely unquestioned dogma asserting that religion is exclusively human prevails at decisive moments. For example, Bellah, in the context of his argument that the evolution of empathy plays an important role in religion, explains, 'The capacities that develop from the emergence of parental care are absolutely basic to the entire story I want to tell from here on, basic to the development of empathy and ethics, even among many species of animals, and ultimately religion among humans'.[25] The adverb 'ultimately' is symptomatic. Without wishing to challenge the coherence of the particular demarcations Bellah puts forth, after critically considering his masterful study one nonetheless is left with the impression that the narrative of religion as uniquely human (and as a pinnacle achievement of evolution – as something 'ultimate') is determined in advance of any investigation, and that definitions are crafted and data assembled so that this *ultimately-religion-among-humans-alone* sentiment is inevitable. Our imagination of the human and religion is constrained less because of evidence than because of a hidden theologically and culturally specific assumption. Examples could be multiplied.

---

[24] A. Taves, *Religious Experience Reconsidered: A Building Block Approach to the Study of Religion and Other Special Things* (Princeton, NJ: Princeton University Press, 2009), p. 163. See also A. Taves, 'No Field Is an Island: Fostering Collaboration between the Academic Study of Religion and the Sciences', *Method and Theory in the Study of Religion* 22 (2010), pp. 170–88.

[25] Bellah, *Religion in Human Evolution*, p. 70.

c. Jonathan Z. Smith

Smith, who is both a great champion and critic of Eliade's sometimes insufficient attention to historical and political contexts, can be viewed as radicalizing the humanistic legacy of Durkheim and Eliade. Smith is keen to remind scholars that the study of religion is, at bottom, the study of the human. Consider his well-known quip from the preface to his 1982 classic *Imagining Religion*: 'while there is a staggering amount of data…that might be characterized in one culture or another, by one criterion or another, as religious—*there is no data for religion. Religion is solely the creation of the scholar's study*'.[26] So if religion itself does not present data to us, where does the scholar look for the potential examples of religious phenomena that Smith argues are central to his or her endeavour? Quite simply, we are to look at *human* activities. For Smith, there is no natural or necessary line to be drawn between the study of religion and the study of the human; different scholars draw different lines and can do so legitimately. While not strictly necessitated by this position, the unspoken correlate to Smith's thesis is that there is a line to be drawn between the study of religion and the study of the animal.

As expansive as Smith's view is and despite its potential to be modified to leave open the question of animals as religious subjects, its tacit horizon is the animal. As the rest of Smith's text makes clear his bold quip that '*there is no data for religion*' is meant to remind scholars that the entire idea of a study of religion located in the *human* sciences was once so radical as to appear a contradiction in terms.[27] Smith explains that titles such as 'religion and the human sciences' are so *familiar* that we no longer appreciate 'their daring' and their 'highly polemical' nature.[28] The nontheological study of religion became possible only when it became intelligible to pull 'religion' from the divine side of the human/ divine binary over to the human side (at least partially), thus making it plausible to use the tools of the human sciences where once only the methods of the 'divine sciences' – theology – appeared appropriate. As Smith emphasizes, the inclusion of religion in the human sciences was once so disruptive because the human sciences were defined precisely in opposition to the divine sciences. The deeply-rooted human/divine binary had to be reconsidered for religious studies to emerge in its contemporary form. In much the same way, this essay

---

[26] J. Z. Smith, *Imagining Religion: From Babylon to Jonestown* (Chicago Studies in the History of Judaism; Chicago: University of Chicago Press, 1988), p. xi.
[27] Ibid., p. 102.
[28] Ibid.

will propose in its conclusion a reconsideration of the human/animal binary – a step Smith does not take, though he might have and perhaps will.

In any case Smith does bring critical meta-reflection to the human/animal border, which is absent in his predecessors. While Smith, like Durkheim and Eliade before him, ends up resting an important theoretical foundation of his scholarship on this ultimately obscure distinction, he begins to highlight the problematic nature of it. Smith does not so much problematize the human/animal binary itself but shows how this division of the world into human and nonhuman frequently threatens to become a distinction between people-like-us and people-not-like-us.

With great perceptiveness Smith argues in his 1978 collection of essays *Map is Not Territory* that one of the ironies of our intellectual history is that in an attempt to understand 'those activities of man which are unique', we have split the world into 'human beings (who are generally like-us) and non-human beings (who are generally not-like-us), into the "we" and the "them" '.[29] Despite mitigating this legacy in the contemporary era, Smith argues that the study of religion has not escaped it: 'the twentieth century interpretation suggests, at best, that the primitive is another kind of human… On the conceptual level it robs them of their humanity, of those perceptions of discrepancy and discord which give rise to the symbolic project that we identify as the very essence of being human'.[30]

Again, Smith's views require more explication, but we have already learned enough for the purposes of the present argument. We have yet another theorist for whom the demarcation between the human and the animal creates the horizon of what may be considered religion, however expansive and constructed that understanding of religion may be. A crucial difference with Smith is that he brings frontal, critical reflection on some aspects of the violence inherent in this demarcation and thus anticipates to a certain degree the present inquires into animals as religious subjects.

Taken together these three thinkers – Durkheim, Eliade, and Smith – represent a century-long intellectual arc in the study of religion, particularly the history of religions that at bottom *imagines religion as that aspect of the human that is not shared with the animal*. Religion, for these and many other theorists is imagined and even produced in the very distinction between human and animal. Crucially, these examples could be greatly multiplied. I do not mean

[29] J. Z. Smith, *Map Is Not Territory: Studies in the History of Religions* (Chicago: University of Chicago Press, 1993), p. 294.
[30] Ibid., p. 297.

to 'pick on' Durkheim, Eliade, and Smith; the stunning fact is that my own research gives me the impression that the overwhelming majority of theorists of religion – perhaps all of them – at some point in their corpus find themselves falling back upon the human/animal binary for support. The 'problem of the animal,' so to speak, is more profound and pervasive than any survey could hope to capture.

In his book, *The Open,* Giorgio Agamben has helpfully called this structure, whereby the human/animal binary generates the human subject and other crucial categories of thought, an 'anthropological machine' that executes the fundamental operation of 'anthropogenesis'. Rather than defining the human positively, the anthropological machine holds the human 'suspended between a celestial and a terrestrial nature, between animal and human—and thus, his being always less and more than himself'.[31]

Just as I have shown the persistent and foundational work of this 'machine' in the history of the study of religion, Agamben shows its operation in a much broader arc of Western theological, philosophical, and literary thought. More particularly he argues for the dependence of Western understandings of life – and the basic divisions of life (vegetal and relational, organic and animal, etc.) – on a more primary and intimate division within the human species between the animal and the human, 'a mobile border within living man' without which 'the very decision of what is human and what is not would probably not be possible'.[32] It is this fraught border that Agamben rightly asks us to attend to with new vigour. 'We must learn', Agamben insists, to read the Western tradition as creating the human 'from the incongruity of these two elements [humanity and animality], and investigate not the metaphysical mystery of conjunction, but rather the practical political mystery of separation'.[33] Agamben insists that 'it is more urgent to work on these divisions ... than it is to take positions on the great issues of so called human rights and values'.[34] Intensifying a direction Smith gestures towards in warning of the dangers of making distinctions between 'human beings ... and non-human beings',[35] Agamben links the problematics of the human/animal binary with the most extreme forms of violence: 'Perhaps concentration and extermination camps are ... an extreme

---

[31] G. Agamben, *The Open: Man and Animal* (K. Attell (trans.); Stanford, CA: Stanford University Press, 2004), p. 29.
[32] Ibid., p. 15.
[33] Ibid., p. 16.
[34] Ibid.
[35] Smith, *Map is Not Territory*, p. 294.

and monstrous attempt to decide between the human and the inhuman, which has ended up dragging the very possibility of the distinction to its ruin.'[36]

Still, Agamben – and I would follow him here – does not suggest it is any simple matter to avoid this fundamental distinction. The closing and haunting question of *The Open* is whether there is, in fact, a way to stop the anthropological machine. This is a pertinent question for scholars of religion. Do even those scholars most keen to move 'beyond' the human/animal binary really have the conceptual resources to think beyond the human/animal binary? Can the study of religion think of a subject that is neither human nor animal?

Agamben also emphasizes another point that I should like to highlight in concluding this first section of my essay. 'Perhaps', Agamben wonders, 'the aporias [the gaps and irresolvable conflicts] of the philosophy of our time coincide with the aporias of this body that is irreducibly drawn and divided between animality and humanity.'[37] The question of the animal is not parallel to other knotty points in the imagination of the human or religion.

> It is as if determining the border between human and animal were not just one question among many discussed by philosophers, theologians, scientists and politicians, but rather a fundamental metaphysico-political operation in which alone something like 'man' can be decided upon and produced.[38]

We therefore must, per Waldau, 'see the terrain we walk' (and have always walked) while also seeking new ground – a 'clearing of the space for the *event* of what we call animals.'[39]

The study of religion cannot *simply* talk about 'animals and religion' because it then would already be under the sway of the operations of the anthropological machine. Thus, in tandem with the effort to 'make present' actual animals, which I have emphasized above particularly in connection with the scholarship of Waldau, and a serious consideration of animals as a site of the sacred, which I emphasized in relation to the scholarship of Patton, the study of religion today would do well to attend to how 'animals' found our field, the humanities, and ultimately the very space of our humanity.

In sum, I am arguing that though the category 'animal' has not generally been imagined as a 'great word' in the study of religion, it should be. It always has been a great word, but we scholars somehow forget or disavow this. Scholarship,

[36] Agamben, *The Open*, p. 22.
[37] Ibid., p. 12.
[38] Ibid., p. 6.
[39] M. Calarco, *Zoographies: The Question of the Animal from Heidegger to Derrida* (New York: Columbia University Press, 2008), p. 4.

like Perseus in battle with the Gorgon, needs to look simultaneously at its own reflection to properly approach the question of the animal. The study of religion needs to follow the question of the animal into this hermeneutical circle – to follow this circular movement as it produces a *knot* in which the human sciences, religion, the human, the animal, and much we cannot touch upon here are laced together.

III. Clearing a Space for Animals: Theorizing Animals and Religion Moving Forward

The scholarship of both Tim Ingold and Jacques Derrida, and the broader modes of scholarship they represent, provide some particularly powerful resources that might contribute to this 'rethinking'. Ingold represents an anthropological ethos that, following Claude Lévi-Strauss, has paid careful attention to both the human/animal binary and the closely associated culture/nature binary. This anthropological ethos is rooted in a sensitivity to the paradox inherent in the anthropological effort to interpret other 'cultures' when those cultures lack the nature/culture binary. Jacques Derrida, who is also responding to Lévi-Strauss, has argued throughout his career, but especially in his last years, for the centrality of 'the question of the animal' to virtually every issue of pragmatic or philosophical concern. More precisely, Derrida (who has generally resisted the idea 'centrality') finds animals inside the 'most economical torsion'[40] of the knot of concepts that constitute our subjectivity.

To anticipate my conclusion, the motivation behind my preference for these two thinkers is the hypothesis that the subjects and kinds of subjectivity that count as religious, or count as participants in the phenomenon of religion, should not be limited, without specific qualification, to the human. The religious dimension that the academic study of religion analyses and works over is not so much a dimension of human culture as a dimension of a unified field of relations that (can be but) need not be divided into human and animal. As Ingold has described it, 'Relations that human beings have with one another form just one part of the total field of relations embracing all living things'.[41]

Despite the challenges critical reflection on animals pose to the theoretical foundations of the lineage I have traced from Durkheim to Smith, the present

---

[40] J. Derrida, *Of Spirit: Heidegger and the Question* (G. Bennington, and R. Bowlby (trans.); Chicago and London: University of Chicago Press, 1989), p. 9.
[41] T. Ingold, 'Hunting and Gathering as Ways of Perceiving the Environment', *Animals and the Human Imagination* (A. Gross, and A. Vallely (eds); New York: Columbia University Press, 2012), p. 49.

study still proceeds in many important ways within this lineage. I am not arguing that this lineage be supplanted with an absolutely different kind of study. Rather, I am suggesting that the most fundamental phenomena with which the Durkheim to Smith lineage are concerned – the diverse phenomena that scholars variously identify as 'religious' – never were, despite initial scholarly intuitions, exclusively human. The grand idea of a 'science' of religion that stands independently of any particular traditional religious heritage never required the exclusion of animals and, in fact, has suffered from their exile.

a. Tim Ingold

Certain features that arise commonly among hunter-gatherers, which Ingold highlights, can help the study of religion attend to the peculiarity of our way of imagining religion through what Derrida would call a 'disavowal' or obfuscation of animals' subjectivities. Ingold draws upon ethnographic literature concerning a range of hunger-gatherers: (1) tropical hunter-gatherer peoples (Batek Negritos of Malaysia, Mbuti Pygmies of the Ituri Forest, and Nayaka forest-dwelling hunter-gatherers of Tamil Nadu), (2) northern hunters, especially the Cree (northeast Canada), (3) aboriginal Australian peoples (especially the Pintupi of the Gibson Desert of Western Australia), and (4) peoples of subarctic Alaska (especially the Koyukon). The most important characteristic of these hunter-gatherer communities for our purposes is not something they have but something they lack: the human/animal, culture/nature binary.[42] Attending to this lack of the animal, much like attending to animals, can make visible, and help us to gain purchase on, our own uncritical use of the human/animal binary. Ultimately, the lack of the human/animal, subject/object binary among hunter-gatherers gives us grounds to imagine a religious subject that is no longer a classical (human) subject.

Ingold can be helpfully understood as engaging the same problematic that troubles Agamben but from a different direction: how can we imagine a world, like that of hunter-gatherers, without already splitting it into human and animal, nature and culture, subjects and objects? How can we stop what Agamben calls the anthropological machine – an especially pointed challenge for an anthropologist? Agamben turns to Walter Benjamin for assistance in deconstructing the

---

[42] A long tradition describes hunter-gatherers through the image of a 'lack' *in a pejorative sense* and it is precisely this tradition (and its implication that hunter-gatherers are, for better or worse, less culturally evolved) that I aim to critique be redeploying the image of a lack here as a mark of sophistication.

anthropological machine. Agamben argues, 'Several of Benjamin's texts propose an entirely different image of the relationship between man and nature and between nature and history: an image in which the anthropological machine seems to be completely out of play'.[43] While space does not allow us to consider how Agamben reads Benjamin, when I turn in a moment to Derrida I will be drawing on related Western 'counter' intellectual traditions that have challenged dominant conceptions of animality. Both Benjamin and Derrida are, for example, heirs to a common intellectual heritage on the question of the animal: heirs to Adorno, Kafka, Freud, Horkheimer, Marx, Nietzsche, and to certain aspects of the rabbinic tradition, all of which challenged dominant conceptions of the animal and/or animality.[44] Ingold, circling similar terrain, finds in hunter-gatherers no anthropological machine to begin with and seeks to make available to his readers the capacity of hunter-gatherers to be immersed in an 'active, practical and perceptual engagement with constituents of the dwelt-in world'[45] – their own 'enskillment' rather than enculturation.[46] '[W]hat *we* distinguish as humanity and nature merge, for [the Koyukon hunters of Alaska], into a single field of relationships ... we find nothing corresponding to the Western concept of nature in hunter-gatherers' representations, for they see no essential difference between the ways one relates to humans and to nonhuman constituents of the environment.'[47] I have focused on Ingold because his almost poetic prose, which I cannot do justice to here, is especially skilful in taking the reader beyond the *ideas* discussed here and allowing an imaginative leap of sorts into what he calls 'hunter-gatherer ontology'. Ingold, however, hardly stands alone in advocating these insights, as any perusal of the current literature on hunter-gatherers will show.

b. Jacques Derrida

If Ingold, and the broader insights of ethnographic work with hunter-gatherers that he makes accessible, gives us a glimpse of a world without the human/

---

[43] Agamben, *The Open*, p. 81.

[44] For further consideration of this powerful but minority stream in the Jewish context, see my essay 'Jewish Animal Ethics', *Oxford Handbook of Jewish Ethics and Morality* (E. Dorff, and J. Crane (eds); Oxford: Oxford University Press, 2012), pp. 422–9.

[45] Ingold, 'Hunting and Gathering', p. 34.

[46] T. Ingold, *Perception of the Environment: Essays on Livelihood, Dwelling & Skill* (London and New York: Routledge, 2008), pp. 36–7, 55, 357, 416.

[47] T. Ingold, 'From Trust to Domination: An Alternative History of Human-Animals Relations', *The Perception of the Environment: Essays in Livelihood, Dwelling and Skill* (T. Ingold (ed.); London: Routledge, 2008), p. 75.

animal binary, Derrida's specialty is alerting us to just how deeply this binary is rooted in a dominant Western understanding of self and world. Derrida not only helps us attend to animals differently but also to the *knot* in which the animal is bound to other core concepts. Rather than leading us from animals to subjects of 'greater importance' to which animals are connected (for example, looking at animals for the sake of understanding humanity), Derrida shows how we need to reconsider our own subjectivity to responsibly consider animals, and how we must confront our own being-confronted by animals to reconsider our own subjectivity.

Derrida argues that the dominant Western relationship with animals in modernity has taken the form of a 'disavowal' (*dénégation*), a 'war' (*guerra*), and a 'sacrifice'. Each of these words signal a particular interpretive strategy for Derrida and following these words provides entry into Derrida's reflections on animals at the points in which his writings are most productive for re-imagining the religious subject. To anticipate what I elaborate elsewhere and can only gesture at here,[48] we could say that *disavowal* brings to bear an existential and loosely psychoanalytic hermeneutic. For Derrida, whether one is seen by an animal ultimately comes down to whether one *avows* being seen. We are all seen by animals. For Derrida, this is a basic datum, a naked fact: we animals, human and nonhuman, look at each other. We cannot avoid this, but only deny or forget it in disavowal.

War brings a pragmatic-political hermeneutic. Like the conventional use of the term 'war', it signals an immense mobilization of resources, social planning, an intensified use of technologies, destruction of environments, and mass killing. And just as war has become intensified in modernity, so has the war against animals. Derrida marks this intensification as an 'event' [événement].[49] At one level, Derrida wants to mark something new in human/animal relations, an intensification of violence that amounts to war; at another level, however, the language of war is used to emphasize a continuity with what is most ancient. More specifically, Derrida is arguing that the developments that have culminated in today's war with animals begin with the very formation of the 'world' we live in, including our fundamental understanding of what counts as knowledge (the privileging of reason, the denial of reason to animals),

---

[48] See the fifth chapter of my forthcoming book, *The Question of the Animal and Religion* (New York: Columbia University Press, forthcoming 2013).

[49] J. Derrida, 'L'animal que donc je suis', *L'animal Autobiographique: Autour De Jacques Derrida* (M. Mallet (ed.); Paris: Galilee, 1999), p. 276; J. Derrida, *The Animal That Therefore I Am* (M. Mallet (ed.); D. Wills (trans.); Perspectives in Continental Philosophy; New York: Fordham University Press, 2008), p. 25.

history (animals have only biological evolution, no history; natural history is not history; prehistory is not history), and technology (man as the toolmaker; technology makes the human uniquely open to new possibilities in comparison to animals). The 'modern' war against animals has been occurring, according to Derrida, ' "for about two centuries," as though such a point of reference were rigorously possible in speaking of a process that is no doubt as old as man, as old as what he calls his world, his knowledge, his history and his technology'.[50]

Sacrifice, recasting structuralist themes, locates the human-animal relationship in the context of the Abrahamic traditions. Derrida argues that thinking itself (questioning, speaking, and responding – at least as traditionally understood) repeats an older structure, or gesture, of violence to animals and to other others: a sacrifice of them for the sake of what must remain unscathed, namely, the human (often idealized as the virile male). The disavowed sacrifice of animals 'could not be the figure of just one disavowal among others. It institutes what is proper to man, the relation to itself of a humanity that is above all anxious about, and jealous of, what is proper to it'. Further, Derrida is arguing ahistorically for persistent associations and alliances in which the human/animal binary is knotted up with others – with discourses that privilege the phallus and logos, for example.[51] These associations and alliances do not so much occur within historical time as at the 'genesis of time'[52] – at the very moment of the institution of 'what is proper to man',[53] at the moment the subject becomes subject.

Extending and particularizing Derrida's critique, I would argue that, by limiting the religious subject to a human subject, the study of religion has become implicated in both the 'disavowal' of regard for animals and the 'war' against them of which Derrida speaks. Rather than study the 'sacrifice' of animals, religious studies has participated in it. Both Derrida's and Ingold's critical insights converge in unsettling a simple exclusion of animals from the sphere of the social, the cultural, or – our present focus – the religious. Ingold, by imploring us to take seriously the hunter-gatherer ontologies he explicates, and Derrida, through his deconstructive analysis of 'the animal', both suggest

[50] Derrida, *The Animal*, p. 24. In the French, ' "à peu près deux siècles », comme si un tel repérage était possible, en toute rigueur, dans un processus qui est aussi vieux, sans doute, que l'homme, ce qu'il appelle son monde, son savoir, son histoire et sa technique?' (Derrida, 'L'animal', p. 275.)

[51] J. Derrida, ' "Eating Well," or the Calculation of the Subject', *Points … Interviews, 1974–1994* (E. Weber (ed.); Stanford, CA: Stanford University Press, 1995), pp. 255–87.

[52] Derrida, *The Animal*, p. 17; Derrida, 'L'animal', p. 268.

[53] Derrida, *The Animal*, p. 14; Derrida, 'L'animal', p. 265.

that the study of religion would do well to revise its impoverishing self-under-standing as the study of certain dimensions of human life.

I see no need to ignore all the productive intellectual work that the human/animal binary has accomplished, but I also see no need to continue to imagine religion as exclusively human. If Derrida and Agamben are correct, then the human/animal binary of the Western intellectual heritage is, at least, too steeped in a history of violence to continue to use it in the simplistic way theorists of religion have typically done. Scholarship will probably not be able to do without the human/animal binary entirely anytime soon, but we may be able to do with less of it in the study of religion. This begins with a simple avowal, the clearing of a space where animals too may be participants in the phenomena of religion. What religion will be after the animal, after we face animals, cannot be known in advance.

The argument of this paper is expanded in Gross, *The Question of the Animal*, chapters 3–5.

Bibliography

Agamben, G., *The Open: Man and Animal* (K. Attell (trans.); Stanford, CA: Stanford University Press, 2004).

Alexander, J. C., *Durkheimian Sociology: Cultural Studies* (Cambridge: Cambridge University Press, 1988).

Bellah, R. N., *Religion in Human Evolution: From the Paleolithic to the Axial Age* (Cambridge, MA: Belknap Press of Harvard University Press, 2011).

Berger, P. L., *The Sacred Canopy: Elements of a Sociological Theory of Religion* (New York: Anchor Books, 1990).

Burkert, W., *Creation of the Sacred: Tracks of Biology in Early Religions* (Cambridge: Harvard University Press, 1996).

Calarco, M., *Zoographies: The Question of the Animal from Heidegger to Derrida* (New York: Columbia University Press, 2008).

Derrida, J., *The Animal That Therefore I Am* (M.-L. Mallet (ed.); D. Wills (trans.); Perspectives in Continental Philosophy; New York: Fordham University Press, 2008).

—' "Eating Well," or the Calculation of the Subject', *Points … Interviews, 1974–1994* (E. Weber (ed.); Stanford, CA: Stanford University Press, 1995), pp. 255–87.

—'L'animal Que Donc Je Suis', *L'animal Autobiographique: Autour De Jacques Derrida* (M. L. Mallet (ed.); Paris: Galilee, 1999).

—*Of Spirit: Heidegger and the Question* (G. Bennington, and R. Bowlby (trans.); Chicago and London: University of Chicago Press, 1989).

Durkheim, E., *The Elementary Forms of Religious Life* (K. E. Fields (trans.); New York: Free Press, 1995, 1912).

Durkheim, E., and M. Mauss, *Primitive Classification* (Chicago: University of Chicago Press, 1963).

Eliade, M., *A History of Religious Ideas, Volume 1: From the Stone Age to the Eleusinian Mysteries* (W. R. Trask (trans.); 3 vols; Chicago: University of Chicago Press, 1981, 1978, 1976 in French).

Gross, A., 'Jewish Animal Ethics', *Oxford Handbook of Jewish Ethics and Morality* (E. Dorff, and J. Crane (eds); Oxford: Oxford University Press, 2012), pp. 422–9.

—*The Question of the Animal and Religion* (New York: Columbia University Press, forthcoming 2013).

Ingold, T., 'From Trust to Domination: An Alternative History of Human-Animals Relations', *The Perception of the Environment: Essays in Livelihood, Dwelling and Skill* (T. Ingold (ed.); London: Routledge, 2008), pp. 61–76.

—'Hunting and Gathering as Ways of Perceiving the Environment', *Animals and the Human Imagination* (A. Gross, and A. Vallely (eds); New York: Columbia University Press, 2012), pp. 31–54.

—*Perception of the Environment: Essays on Livelihood, Dwelling & Skill* (London and New York: Routledge, 2008, 2000).

Patton, K., ' "Caught with Ourselves in the Net of Life and Time": Traditional Views of Animals in Religion', *A Communion of Subjects: Animals in Religion, Science, and Ethics* (P. Waldau, and K. Patton (eds); New York: Columbia University Press, 2006).

—' "He Who Sits in the Heavens Laughs": Recovering Animal Theology in the Abrahamic Traditions', *Harvard Theological Review* 93.4 (2000), pp. 401–34.

Smith, J. Z., *Imagining Religion: From Babylon to Jonestown* (Chicago Studies in the History of Judaism; Chicago: University of Chicago Press, 1988).

—*Map Is Not Territory: Studies in the History of Religions* (Chicago: University of Chicago Press, 1993).

Staal, F., *Rules without Meaning: Ritual, Mantras, and the Human Sciences* (Toronto Studies in Religion; vol. 4; New York: P. Lang, 1990).

Taves, A., 'No Field Is an Island: Fostering Collaboration between the Academic Study of Religion and the Sciences', *Method and Theory in the Study of Religion* 22 (2010), pp. 170–88.

—*Religious Experience Reconsidered: A Building Block Approach to the Study of Religion and Other Special Things* (Princeton, NJ: Princeton University Press, 2009).

Waldau, P., 'Seeing the Terrain We Walk: Features of the Contemporary Landscape of "Religion and Animals" ', *A Communion of Subjects: Animals in Religion, Science, and Ethics* (P. Waldau, and K. Patton (eds); New York: Columbia University Press, 2006).

Part Two

Animals as Subjects of Religious Symbolism

4

Hedgehog Skin and Golden Calf: Animals as Symbols for Paganism in Medieval German Literature

Sabine Obermaier

From the *Physiologus* and the bestiary tradition to the clerical bias of the great nature encyclopaedias, animals of medieval literature are usually tied to Christian culture. Against this background, this paper is dedicated to examining animals as symbols for pagans and paganism in medieval German literature.

The antagonism between pagans and Christians is the central subject of medieval crusade literature. Therefore, I will focus on the two most important Middle High German crusade epics: Konrad's *Rolandslied* (1170)[1] and Wolfram of Eschenbach's *Willehalm* (1210–20).[2] To better understand Wolfram, I will include an exploration of Wolfram's *Parzival* (1200–10)[3] in which, more than in the other grail romances, the oriental world is of specific interest. While these three texts do not cover the whole spectrum of orient-related texts in medieval German literature, they will suffice in pointing out what I wish to argue, though, when necessary, I shall refer to other texts as well.

The *Rolandslied* is about the battle of Roncevalles in which the Emperor Charlemagne looses his rear-guard, led by the famous Christian knight Roland. The Christian defeat is made possible by the betrayal of Roland's adversary Genelun who collaborates with the pagans. In the last battle, however, the Christians are victorious and Genelun receives his just punishment in a trial by combat. In *Willehalm* the confrontation between Christians and pagans is motivated by a love-story: the Christian margrave Willehalm abducts and marries princess Arabel, the daughter of the pagan emperor Terramer and former wife of the pagan ruler Tybalt. Arabel converts to the Christian faith, now calling herself Gyburc. This story is told in retrospective and the epic itself

---

[1] Das *Rolandslied* des Pfaffen Konrad (C. Wesle, and P. Wapneswki (eds); Tübingen: Niemeyer, 1985).
[2] Wolfram of Eschenbach, *Willehalm* (A. Leitzmann (ed.); Tübingen: Niemeyer, 1963).
[3] Wolfram of Eschenbach, *Parzival* (K. Lachmann, and B. Schirok (eds); Berlin: de Gruyter, 1998).

follows the two battles at Alischanz fought between Christians and pagans. Because *Willehalm* is a fragment, the end of the story is missing. The grail romance *Parzival* tells the story of Parzival's struggle to become grail king. Although he becomes the foremost knight at King Arthur's court, he fails to ask the saving question during his first visit to the grail castle; however, after a long period of searching and struggling he is finally able to fulfil his destiny.

The first part of this chapter will focus on oriental fauna as one part of the pagan equipment, which also included other transported goods such as armaments and clothing. The second part will be dedicated to specific pagan animal-related customs, for instance, the deification of animals. But our main interest is directed towards how pagans are described by 'animal means': on the one hand, animals are used as comparisons and metaphors for pagans, on the other hand, pagans are described as having animal-like body parts.

I. Oriental Fauna

The natural habitat of pagans in medieval German literature was the East, particularly Asia, or what we call the Orient, where the earthly paradise and the legendary Christian kingdom of Prester John was located. It was the Greeks, namely Herodotus, Ktesias of Knidos, and Megasthenes, who were responsible for the Western conception of the remote East, especially of India.[4] Through the writings of Pliny and Solinus, Macrobius, and Martianus Capella, the medieval writers became familiar with the classical stories of the 'marvels of the East',[5] to which belong exotic animals and the famous monstrous races.

In the Alexander romances (one of the main sources for medieval knowledge about the Orient besides the fictitious letter of Prester John), Alexander's knights are confronted not only with wild and exotic beasts and un-real fantastic creatures,[6] but also with foreign or well-known animals turned into monstrous beings.[7]

None of these features is part of the two German crusade epics *Rolandslied* and *Willehalm*, perhaps because these stories are not set in the oriental world. In these

---

[4] R. Wittkower, 'Marvels of the East. A Study in the History of Monsters', *Journal of the Warburg and Courtauld Institutes* 5 (1942), pp. 159–97 (159).
[5] Ibid., p. 169.
[6] J. Brummack, *Die Darstellung des Orients in den deutschen Alexandergeschichten des Mittelalters* (Berlin: Erich Schmidt, 1966), pp. 118–21.
[7] See S. Obermaier, 'Antike Irrtümer und ihre mittelalterlichen Folgen: Das Flusspferd', *Antike Naturwissenschaft und ihre Rezeption* 21 (2011), pp. 135–79.

epics, the oriental fauna is, as a matter of course, part of the pagan equipment. Pagans use camels, dromedaries, and elephants (the most important representatives of the domestic oriental fauna) as *draught and pack animals* for food and luxury goods:[8]

> *die heiden vluhen vor durch nôt:*
> *olbenden und dromendarîs*
> *dâ beliben, geladen in manegen wîs*
> *mit wîne und mit spîse.*[9]

Exotic animals, however, are also offered as *presents* (often meant as temptations) from pagan kings to Christian kings. During the pagan's council in Konrad's *Rolandslied*, Blanscandiz recommends that the pagan king Marsilie offers treasures and exotic animals, such as lions and bears, horses and young falcons, mules and camels, to the Christian emperor Charlemagne.[10] Charlemagne, however, is not tempted by these rich gifts. He says:

> *ir mûle un[de] ir olbenden,*
> *enrûche ich nicht mere*
> *wider der armen sele.*[11]

In Wolfram's *Willehalm*, Arofel, the Persian king and Terramer's brother, offers in vain *drîzec helfande* (thirty elephants) laden with gold as a ransom.[12]

In contrast to the Alexander romances, the crusade epics do not mention elephants as part of the usual pagan *military equipment*. Exotic animals, however, are used for *clothing and armour*; for example, in Wolfram's *Willehalm*, Rennewart, the son of Emperor Terramer, chooses a *surkôt von kemmelîn* (a tunic made of camel hair).[13] Tybalt, Gyburc's first husband, is the owner of a buckler, a tunic, and a horse blanket made of salamander skin.[14] And Purrel, the king of Nubiant, wears a coat of mail and a helmet, both made from the skin of *neitûn* and *muntunzel*,[15] two very strange *wurme* (usually the word for reptiles),

---

[8] See Albrecht von Scharfenberg, *Der Jüngere Titurel* (W. Wolf, and K. Nyholm (eds); 4 vols; Berlin: Akademie-Verlag, 1955–95), 852.1–4 and 4460.1–4.

[9] 'The pagans have to flee: They leave camels and dromedaries, variously laden with wine and food'. *Willehalm*, 90.30–91.3.

[10] *Rolandslied*, 459–79; see also 744–52.

[11] 'I do not need their mules and camels – for I am interested in the salvation of the poor soul'. *Rolandslied*, 1078–80.

[12] *Willehalm*, 79.16; see also 203.20–5.

[13] *Willehalm*, 196.2.

[14] *Willehalm*, 366.4–13.

[15] J. Vorderstemann, 'NEITUN und MUNTUNZEL. Zu "Willehalm" 425,25–426,30', *Kritische Bewahrung. Beiträge zur deutschen Philologie. Festschrift für Werner Schröder zum 60 Geburtstag* (E.-J. Schmidt (ed.); Berlin: Erich Schmidt, 1974), pp. 328–34. See also *Willehalm*, 425.30 and 426.11.

which we are unable to identify. We can only safely assume that this armour is made of a very exotic, strange, and impenetrable material.

Apart from camels, dromedaries, and elephants, fabulous *merrinder* (literally translated sea cattle, sea cows, or sea oxen) are used for transport, for example, to carry pagan idols.[16] Here, the prefix *mer-* is not related to the sea, it simply means 'strange'. *Merrinder* are also mentioned by Irmenschart, the mother of the Christian protagonist Willehalm: *ich teile in durch dich, liebez kint, / swaz ahtzehen merrint / bisande mugen geziehen.*[17] Here, the *merrinder* have the literary function of giving an impression of the pagan-like abundance of Irmenschart's gift.

In contrast, there are only minor differences between Christians and pagans concerning their individual *armorial bearings* (Table 1).

Table 1: Animals as armorial bearings

Christians	**Pagans**
Rolandslied	*Rolandslied*
Roland: lion (3,986); dragon (3,285)	Falsaron: golden eagle (4,220)
	Paligan: dragon (8,125)
Willehalm	*Willehalm*
No animals as armorial bearings	Tedalun, Poidjus: ecidemôn (379.25; 44.8)
	Josweiz: white swan with black beak and feet (386.12)
	Terramer: Kahun on griffin (356.28)

On both sides, if we find animals at all, they are heraldic animals of high value. But it seems that Wolfram stresses the exotic character of the pagans' armorial bearings a little bit more, particularly in summary descriptions.[18] No difference, however, is made concerning their *mounts*: Christian knights ride on horseback and, usually, in the German crusade epics, oriental pagan knights ride on horseback, too.[19] In fact, being a knight implies horse riding.[20] In the Alexander romances and in Albrecht's grail epic *Der Jüngere Titurel*,

---

[16] *Willehalm*, 352.1–9.

[17] 'I give you from my treasures, dear child, as much gold coins as eighteen *merrinder* are able to carry', *Willehalm*, 161.1–3.

[18] *Willehalm*, 400.26 to 401.1.

[19] Terramer's horse, Brahâne, has a name and is decorated like Christian horses (*Willehalm*, 360.13).

[20] See U. Friedrich, 'Der Ritter und sein Pferd. Semantisierungsstrategien einer Mensch-Tier-Verbindung im Mittelalter', *Text und Kultur. Mittelalterliche Literatur 1150–1450* (U. Peters (ed.); Stuttgart, Weimar: Metzler, 2001), pp. 245–67; and D. Peschel-Rentsch, 'Pferdemänner. Kleine Studie zum Selbstbewußtsein eines Ritters', *Pferdemänner. Sieben Essays über Sozialisation und ihre Wirkungen in mittelalterlicher Literatur* (Erlangen, Jena: Palm & Enke, 1998), pp. 12–47.

pagan knights sometimes have special mounts, such as *merrinder*, camels, or elephants.[21] In Wolfram's *Parzival*, the monstrous creatures Cundrie and her brother Malcreatiure are riding on mules or other inferior horses,[22] but they are no crusaders.

To summarize, exotic animals in the two medieval crusade epics have different kinds of narrative functions:

- Mentioning elephants, camels, and other exotic animals as part of everyday knightly life is the easiest and most economic way to *identify* pagans as pagans, or at least as being of oriental origin.
- Mentioning exotic animals as part of everyday knightly life enables the medieval author to stress the difference between Christian and pagan knights; thus, exotic animals are used as a device to *indicate strangeness* which sometimes also implies *dangerousness*.
- By mentioning well-known precious and exclusive animals of representative quality in great quantities, exotic fauna become a *sign of pagan luxury*. For Wolfram, luxury is part of both Christian and pagan courtly life, but Konrad uses this device to stress the contrast between Christian modesty and pagan luxury.

In both texts it is only in regard to knighthood that there is little difference between pagans and Christians. Obviously, it is important to medieval authors that Christian knights have adversaries of equal chivalric qualities.

II. Pagan Animal-Related Customs

Some animal-related customs also indicate paganism. In the *Rolandslied*, some of the pagan tribes *eat horses*: *si ezzent diu ros*.[23] For Christian readers, eating horses is related to pre-Christian times and only allowed during times of famine.[24] Moreover, the Middle High German word *ros* indicates that pagans do not flinch from eating the knightly warhorse, the *destrier*. For Christians, such behaviour would have caused horror and revulsion

---

[21] Ulrich of Etzenbach, *Alexander* (W. Toischer (ed.); Reprint Stuttgart/Tübingen: Bibliothek des Litterarischen Vereins, 1888; Hildesheim: Olms, 1974), 12110–12 and 12861ff.; Albrecht, *Jüngerer Titurel*, 3262.2f.

[22] *Parzival*, 312.7 and 520.7.

[23] *Rolandslied*, 2690.

[24] Cf. the commentary by D. Kartschoke, *Das Rolandslied des Pfaffen Konrad* (D. Kartschoke (ed., trans., com.); Stuttgart: Reclam, 1993), p. 688.

and the pagans would have appeared as monsters – a point to which I will return.

In medieval crusade narratives, the belief that pagans worship animals is rather underrepresented, although the biblical narration of the Golden Calf suggests that pagans usually tend to *worship animals*. However, in the crusade epics, animals only carry their idols.[25] The illustration accompanying the *Rolandslied* in manuscript P[26] shows an idol in calf form, which the text itself does not mention.[27] I am certain, though, that this pictorial representation is due to the influential iconographical tradition of the Golden Calf.

In Wolfram's *Parzival*, the narrator tells us that Flegetanis, who was the first to tell about the grail, worshipped a calf:

> *Er was ein heiden vaterhalp,*
> *Flegetânîs, der an ein kalp*
> *bette als ob ez wær sîn got.*
> *wie mac der tievel selhen spot*
> *gefüegen an sô wîser diet,*
> *daz si niht scheidet ode schiet*
> *dâ von der treit die hôhsten hant*
> *unt dem elliu wunder sint bekant?*[28]

The consternation uttered by Wofram's narrator shows that worshipping an animal (or an idol in form of an animal)[29] is interpreted as an aberration, as a going astray. Nevertheless, Wolfram's narrator is able to admit that Flegetanis is a wise man in spite of his faith.

What is also interesting is that in the *Rolandslied*, the pagans *throw their idols among dogs and pigs* after their defeat:

> *di gote hiezen si weruen*
> *under di hunde,*
> *etliche in des wages grunde.*[30]

---

[25] *Willehalm*, 441.4f.; cf. 441.14f.; and 442.9.

[26] This illustrated manuscript is held at the library of the University of Heidelberg (cod. pal. germ. 112, folio 32ᵛ).

[27] *Rolandslied*, 2372f.: Genelun and the pagans *swuren uf Appollen* [!] *uf Rolandes tot* [they swear by Apollo to kill Roland].

[28] Instead of translating line by line, I only want to paraphrase this passage: 'Flegetanis had a pagan father and worshipped a calf, as if it were his god. Why does the devil deride such wise people, so that God cannot part them from such ridiculousness?' *Parzival*, 454.1–8.

[29] The phrase *der an ein kalp / bette* suggests that by the calf what is meant is the real animal and not an artificial idol. But, for medieval Christians, perhaps this makes no great difference.

[30] 'They gave the instruction to throw their gods [i.e. their idols] among the dogs, some of them into the sea.' *Rolandslied*, 7137–9.

[Marsilie] sprach: ,waz machten mir die gote frum sin?
ich hiz sie werfen unter die swin […].'[31]

These incidents illustrate a complete inversion of God's word in Matthew 7.6: *Nolite dare sanctum canibus, neque mittatis margaritas vestras ante porcos, ne forte conculcent eas pedibus suis.*[32] The defeated pagans act in antagonism to the Holy Bible and to the Christian God. Here, pagans are not only non-Christians; they are seen as anti-Christian.

In summary, the two German authors are very cautious in their descriptions of pagan animal-related customs. The idols worshipped by pagans seldom have animal form and no animal deities are mentioned. Instead, the German authors describe the pagans worshiping three (!) different Gods (one of them is Mohammed, the Islamic prophet; the others are often taken from antiquity). This conception, which totally opposes the rigorous monotheism of the Islamic religion, reflects a deeper problem earnestly discussed by medieval scholars: given the Christian concept of the Trinity, Islam seems to be the 'more' monotheistic religion. I believe this is the reason why the authors favour a polytheistic conception instead of an animist one.

III. The Description of Pagans by 'Animal Means'

a. Animal Comparisons and Animals as Metaphors for Pagans

Based on Psalms 21.17/21 and Psalm 58.7 (according to the Vulgata), the *Rolandslied* usually compares pagans with dogs.[33]

diu ir scar also dicke
gelagen an dem gewicke
sam die hunte unraine[.][34]

di haiden we sungen,
si grinen sam die hunde[.][35]

---

[31] '[Marsilie] said: "For what purpose could these gods be useful to me? I gave the instruction to throw them among pigs."' *Rolandslied*, 7277f.

[32] 'Do not give what is holy to dogs, and do not throw pearls before swine, lest they trample them under their feet, and turn and tear you to pieces'. See also Kartschoke, 'Commentary', p. 730. For all biblical references I use the text of the *Biblia sacra iuxta Vulgatam versionem* (R. Weber et al., (ed.); Stuttgart: Deutsche Bibelgesellschaft, 1983).

[33] Cf. Kartschoke, 'Commentary', p. 708. See also *Rolandslied*, 5156–8; 5422f; 8309f.

[34] 'Their numerous legions were situated near the fork like mangy dogs'. *Rolandslied*, 4527–9.

[35] 'The pagans lamented, they cried like dogs'. *Rolandslied*, 4837.

Even Charlemagne equates the pagans with dogs in his prayer: *erlose uns von den hunden.*[36] In the light of the Biblical references, comparing pagans to dogs indicates that these people are seen as detestable enemies of God. The comparisons with impure dogs also suggest that the pagans have less honour than the Christians. However, such plain demagogy is found only in the (earlier) *Rolandslied*, which was written in the rigid spirit of Bernard of Clairvaux. Wolfram of Eschenbach does not compare pagans with dogs.[37]

At one point in Wolfram's *Willehalm*, Willehalm complains angrily about the superior numbers of the pagan army:

> *ir gunêrten Sarrazin,*
> *ob beidiu hunt unde swîn*
> *iuch trüegen und dâ zuo diu wîp,*
> *sus manegen werlîchen lîp,*
> *vür wâr möhte ich wol sprechen doch,*
> *daz iuwer ze vil wære dannoch.*[38]

Willehalm tries to give himself some kind of rational explanation for the great number of pagans confronting him. Wolfram lets his protagonist use the old, and usually negative, dog and swine comparison in a totally new way: dogs and pigs are cited because of their aptitude for proliferation[39] and not because they represent the detestable enemies of God. Neither Willehalm nor Wolfram really believes that pagans descend from dogs or pigs.

Dogs and pigs, however, are used not only to depreciate the pagans: even in *Rolandslied*, the dog could also carry positive connotations, but then only in regard to Christians.

> *si [= the pagans] fluhen ze den stunden*
> *sam der hirz uor den hunden.*[40]

The stag-hunting image has two aspects: first, here the dogs signify successful hunting by the Christians; second, the stag represents the noble quarry that is

---

[36] 'Save us from the dogs'. *Rolandslied*, 8420.

[37] In this, Wolfram differs also from his French model *Aliscans*, see N. Harris, 'Animal, Vegetable, Mineral. Some Observations on the Presentation and Function of Natural Phenomena in Willehalm and in the Old French Aliscans', *Wolfram's 'Willehalm'. Fifteen Essays* (M. Jones, and T. McFarland (eds); Columbia, SC: Camden House, 2002), pp. 211–29 (213).

[38] 'Damned Saracens, whether you many were born by dogs and pigs and also by human women, anyhow I should say, that you are too many'. *Willehalm*, 58.15–19.

[39] For the concupiscence of dogs and pigs, see R. Schenda, 'Hund', *Enzyklopädie des Märchens* 6 (1990), col. 1317–40 (1319f.); and H.-J. Uther, 'Schwein', *Enzyklopädie des Märchens* 12 (2007), col. 393–8 (394).

[40] 'The pagans flew immediately like the stag flees the hunting dogs'. *Rolandslied*, 6314f.

worth hunting. Sometimes the warriors from both sides are likened to boars.[41] As an animal related with courtly hunting, the boar comparison serves to underline the high value and bravery of any warrior.[42]

Animal metaphors sometimes are used in a negative way with regard to Christians: when Genelun, the Christian traitor, is asked by Charlemagne to carry a message to the pagans' camp, he looks around like a wolf (*er tete die wûluine blicke*).[43] Likening Genelun's behaviour to a wolf's has clearly negative connotations: according to Horst Richter, here the wolf symbolizes rapacity or even the devil himself.[44] Using an animal metaphor with negative connotations, normally reserved for pagans, within the context of the description of the Christian Genelun is quite logical, for Genelun is betraying the Christians to the pagans and is, therefore, no longer a Christian knight in the full sense; he has mutated, as it were, into someone pagan-like.

With regard to the angry Willehalm, Wolfram chooses the ironic comparison of a wolf looking 'innocently' into a sheep pen.[45] By stressing *ira*, anger, Willehalm is depicted as an ambiguous heroic character.[46]

Christian-like pagans also can be depicted through the use of positive animal images. In introducing Rennewart, Terramer's son who helps the Christians against the pagans, Wolfram uses the image of the eaglet that is able to successfully pass its father's examination.[47] In this image taken from the *Physiologus* and the bestiary tradition, Wolfram accentuates Rennewart's *verdacte tugent*, his 'hidden virtue', meaning his Christian-like qualities.[48]

In Konrad's *Rolandslied*, animals are also used as *dream symbols*. Two series of dreams are attributed to Charlemagne. In the first dream series, we find three different visions, in which the first – the vision of the broken lance – is without animals.[49] In the second dream vision, Charlemagne in his imperial domicile at

---

[41] On the Christian side: *Willehalm*, 327.3–5. On the pagan side: *Willehalm*, 418.16f.

[42] Cf. Harris, 'Animal, Vegetable, Mineral', p. 214.

[43] *Rolandslied*, 1418.

[44] H. Richter, *Kommentar zum Rolandslied des Pfaffen Konrad* (Teil I; Bern, Frankfurt: Herbert Lang & Cie, 1972) p. 241. See also A. Pluskowski, *Wolves and the Wilderness in the Middle Ages* (Woodbridge, Suffolk: Boydell Press, 2006) p. 133. The wolf is here also mentioned as a 'metaphor for fallen nobility'.

[45] *Willehalm*, 129.14–17.

[46] Cf. W. Haug, 'Parzivals *zwîvel* und Willehalms *zorn*. Zu Wolframs Wende vom höfischen Roman zur chanson de geste', *Strukturen als Schlüssel zur Welt. Kleine Schriften zur Erzähliteratur des Mittelalters* (Tübingen: Niemeyer, 1989), pp. 529–40 (533–7, 539); see also *Angers Past. The Social Uses of an Emotion in the Middle Ages* (B. Rosenwein (ed.); Ithaca and London: Cornell University Press, 1998).

[47] *Willehalm*, 189.2–24.

[48] C. Gerhardt, 'Wolframs Adlerbild ("Willehalm", 189, 2–24)', *Zeitschrift für deutsches Altertum* 99 (1970), pp. 213–22 (217).

[49] *Rolandslied*, 3068–81.

Aachen is attacked by a chained bear (or boar). The third vision is missing in the manuscript, but it is available in Stricker's *Karl*: Charlemagne sees himself in Paris being attacked by a leopard who comes from Spain.[50] Then, a male dog comes out of the palace, fights the leopard and defeats it. Regrettably, there is no explanation of these three dreams in the text, but we can safely assume that they foreshadow the loss of Roland, Charlemagne's right arm, by Genelun's betrayal.[51] Genelun breaks his allegiance and loyalty both to Charlemagne and to the Christian God much like the bear/boar breaks his chains.[52] The leopard coming from Spain may stand for Binabel, Genelun's nephew, who fights in place of Genelun at the trial and is defeated by the loyal Tirrich (represented by a male dog).[53]

In Charlemagne's second dream series,[54] which is characterized as a vision sent by God,[55] animals play an important role, too. The wild animals heavily afflicting the people are symbols for the pagans. Although it is impossible to attribute single animals to actual persons in the text, we clearly can see one point, which is highly important for the subject of this chapter: the kind of animal chosen is always well-considered. The wild and dangerous animals represent the pagans or Christian traitors. By contrast, the Christian side is represented (if at all) by comparison to a domestic animal, particularly to a courtly hunting animal, the dog. The distinction between 'domestic' and 'wild' animals or the distinction between animal and non-animal, animal and human,[56] is used to illustrate the predominance of the Christians over the pagans. The *Rolandslied* unmistakably sides with the Christians.

b. Animal Parts as Parts of the Pagan Body

Pagans can also appear as composite beings (half-human, half-animal) and so are likened to the classical monstrous races, handed down by Pliny and,

---

[50] The Stricker, *Karl der Große* (K. Bartsch (ed.); Berlin: de Gruyter, 1965), 3675–703.

[51] S. Fischer, *The Dream in the Middle High German Epic. Introduction to the Study of the Dream as a Literary Device to the Younger Contemporaries of Gottfried and Wolfram* (Bern, Frankfurt am Main Lang, and Las Vegas: Lang, 1978), p. 50; K.-E. Geith, 'Die Träume im Rolandslied des Pfaffen Konrad und in Strickers Karl', *Träume im Mittelalter. Ikonologische Studien* (A. Bagliani, and G. Stabile (eds); Stuttgart and Zürich: Belser, 1989), pp. 227–40 (232f.) (with references to older academic literature).

[52] Fischer, *The Dream in the Middle High German Epic*, p. 50.

[53] Geith, 'Träume im Rolandslied', p. 232.

[54] *Rolandslied*, 7084–127.

[55] *Rolandslied*, 7078–83. This is also shown in the illustration of manuscript P (University library of Heidelberg, cod. pal. germ. 112, folio 41ᵛ). See Geith, 'Träume im Rolandslied', pp. 234–6.

[56] Human body parts, for instance Charlemagne's arm, are only metaphors for Roland.

therefore, also called the 'Plinian races'.[57] In the *Rolandslied*, we encounter
Cynocephali, the Dog-Heads, among the twenty-two pagan kings who support
Marsilie and Paligan (*ir houbit scain sam der hunde*).[58] The members of another
pagan tribe have *pig bristles* on their back (*an dem rucke tragent si börsten sam
swin*).[59] In Wolfram's *Willehalm*, the narrator mentions people with *green horny
skin and animal voices* who follow King Gorhant whose kingdom is lies near the
River Ganges in India:

> *des volc was vorn und hinden horn,*
> *âne menschlich stimme erkorn:*
> *der dôn von ir munde*
> *gal sam die leithunde*
> *oder als ein kelber muoter lüet.*[60]

> [...] *niht ander wâpen si mohten hân:*
> *ir vel was horn in grüenem schîn,*
> *die truogen kolben stehelîn.*[61]

According to Claude Lecouteux, Wolfram here connects two different traditions:
first, the Germanic legend of Siegfried who becomes invincible after bathing in
dragon's blood, which renders his skin horny and impenetrable; second, the
myth of Indian people having green skin, which was probably handed down
by Solinus.[62] What is important is that Wolfram describes the green horny
skin as a kind of armour, which seems to be depicted in the illustration of the
Wolfenbüttel codex. (Although some scholars miss the illustration of King
Gorhant's knights, I am convinced that, according to Wolfram's description, the
knights in green tunics shown on folio 83r of the Wolfenbüttel codex should be
the knights of King Gorhant.)[63] By this, Wolfram obviously wants to lessen the

[57] J. Friedman, *The Monstrous Races in Medieval Art and Thought* (Cambridge, MA and London: Harvard University Press, 1981), ch. 1.
[58] *Rolandslied*, 2656. Some scholars think that here the pagans are just compared to dogs and do not consider the ancient tradition of monstrous races (Kartschoke, 'Commentary', p. 687, 2656), but the accentuation of the head makes the relation to the *Cynocephali* conception very probable.
[59] *Rolandslied*, 8046. Cf. Kartschoke, 'Commentary', p. 739: 'Abgesehen von der fabelhaften Physis dieses Heidenvolkes ist zu bedenken, daß der Vergleich mit dem Wildschwein nichts Ehrenrühriges hat, sondern zum traditionellen Repertoire heimischer Heldendarstellung gehört'.
[60] 'His followers have horned bodies for and aft and they lack a human voice: They bark like dogs or moo like cows'. *Willehalm*, 35.13–17.
[61] 'They fight – very unknightly – with iron clubs. And they have no other armour than their green horny skin.' *Willehalm*, 395.22–24.
[62] C. Lecouteux, *Les monstres dans la literature allemande du moyen âge* (3 vols; Göppingen: Kümmerle, 1982), vol. 2, p. 98, cf. p. 92. They are not to be confused with the *Cornuti* or *Gegetones*. Ibid., p. 90f., cf. J. B. Friedman, p. 16f.
[63] Herzog August Library at Wolfenbüttel, Cod. Guelf. 30.12 Aug. fol., fol. 83r.

monstrosity of the pagans by rationalizing their strangeness – a point to which I will return.

In his grail romance *Parzival*, Wolfram depicts two individual pagans who are humans with animal attributes: Cundrie and her brother Malcreatiure. Both are presents from the pagan queen Secundille to the Grail king Amfortas. Let us first look at Cundrie. When she arrives at King Arthur's court to condemn the protagonist Parzival, the narrator takes care to tell us that Cundrie is erudite: she speaks Latin, Arabian, and French[64] and is well versed in the sciences, such as dialectic, geometry, and astronomy[65] – this is reflected in her surname *surziere*,[66] the sorceress, the enchantress. In contrast to her high education and her courtly and precious dress,[67] her appearance is all the more shocking: her braided hair is black and strong (*linde als eins swînes rückehâr*),[68] she has a dog-like nose, and from her mouth two boar's teeth protrude (*si was genaset als ein hunt: / zwên ebers zene ir für den munt / giengen wol spannen lanc*).[69] Her eyebrows are bound in braids, towering to her hair-band.[70] She has bear-like ears (*Cundrî truoc ôren als ein ber*),[71] her face is hairy (*Rûch was ir antlütze erkant*),[72] and her hands are like ape's skin with fingernails like lion's claws (*gevar als eines affen hût / truoc hende diz gœbe trût. / die nagele wâren niht ze lieht; / wan mir diu âventiure gieht, si stüenden als eins lewen klân*).[73]

Her brother Malcreatiure who accompanies Orgeluse, the future wife of Gawain, is characterized in a similar way:

> *Malcrêatiure*
> *hiez der knappe fiere:*
> *Cundrîe la surziere*
> *was sîn swester wol getân:*
> *er muose ir antlütze hân*
> *gar, wan daz er was ein man.*
> *im stuont ouch ietweder zan*

---

[64] *Parzival*, 312.19–21.
[65] *Parzival*, 312.22–5.
[66] *Parzival*, 312.27.
[67] *Parzival*, 313.1–13.
[68] 'Smooth like a pig's bristles.' *Parzival*, 313.20.
[69] *Parzival*, 313.21–3.
[70] *Parzival*, 313.24–5.
[71] *Parzival*, 313.29.
[72] *Parzival*, 314.1.
[73] *Parzival*, 314.5f. When Cundrie arrives at Arthur's court a second time to pronounce the message that Parzival is destined to be the next grail king, the description of her half-human half-animal appearance is completed by information concerning the colour of her eyes and mouth: *ir ougen stuonden dennoch sus,/gel als ein thopazîus,/ir zene lanc: ir munt gap schîn/als ein viol weitîn* ('her eyes are yellow like a topaz, her mouth blue like a violet'). *Parzival*, 780.19–22.

als einem eber wilde,

ungelîch menschen bilde.

im was dez hâr ouch niht sô lanc

als ez Cundrien ûf den mûl dort swanc:

kurz, scharf als igels hût ez was.[74]

Within the context of Malcreatiure's description, Wolfram gives us some information on the origin of these kinds of creatures: they come from *Trîbalibôt* (which means India), near the river Ganges.[75] For Wolfram, Cundrie and Malcreatiure do not represent individual types of deformation, but they do belong to the monstrous races, which are placed at the margins of the known world where they are also placed on medieval world maps.[76] By retelling the legend of Adam's disobedient daughters,[77] Wolfram also gives an explanation for their strange appearance: Adam, who had been taught by God the name and the nature of all things on earth and above, forbade his daughters to eat of certain herbs when they were pregnant because this would turn their offspring into monsters, but the daughters did not obey and because of this their humanity was inverted (*sus wart verkêrt diu mennischeit*).[78]

In the Middle Ages, different tales were told to explain the origin of the so-called monstrous races. One of them was the apocryphal tale of the disobedience of Adam's children, particularly his daughters (sometimes they are also the daughters of Cain).[79] Another approach declares the monstrous races to be Cain's descendants:[80] some scholars even argue that Cain was not the son of Adam, but of the Serpent, the devil. After the murder of his brother Abel, Cain was punished with horns or lumps on his body and he had to live in exile and died like a savage animal.[81] Other medieval scholars consider Noah's son Ham as the after-flood father of the monstrous races.[82] Like Cain, Ham was cursed by

---

[74] 'The proud knave was called Malcreatiure. Cundrie the enchantress was his lovely sister. He looked like her, although he was a man. Wild boar's teeth stuck from his mouth – he didn't look like a human. His hair was not as long as Cundrie's, [it was] short, sharp like hedgehog skin.' *Parzival*, 780.19–22 to 517.16–27.

[75] *Parzival*, 780.19–22 to 517.28–30.

[76] Cf. R. Wisbey, 'Wunder des Ostens in der "Wiener Genesis" und in Wolframs "Parzival", *Studien zur frühmittelhochdeutschen Literatur. Cambridger Colloquium 1971* (L. Johnson, H.-H. Steinhoff, and R. Wisbey (eds); Berlin: Erich Schmidt, 1974), pp. 180–214 (202).

[77] *Parzival*, 518.1–519.1.

[78] *Parzival*, 518.29.

[79] Friedman, *The Monstrous Races*, p. 93.

[80] Ibid., pp. 95–9.

[81] Ibid., p. 96: 'The story of Cain's punishment, exile, and death influenced later views of his progeny, punished by deformity for their ancestor's crime, and, like him, exiled from mankind.'

[82] Ham can be seen as 'the spiritual if not physical heir of Cain' (Ibid., p. 99). In medieval orthography their names were often confused (Ibid. p. 100), and medieval illustrations suggest a 'typological identity of Cain and Ham' (Ibid.).

his father, who asked God to decree that Ham's descendants be black and to be the servants of his brother Shem's children.[83]

According to Roy Wisbey, Wolfram hesitates to identify Cundrie and Malcreatiure clearly with one of the monstrous races[84] and to relate them to the 'children of Cain'.[85] Although, as Paul Michel pointed out, a certain correspondence can be seen between Parzival who, by the murder of his relative Ither, repeated the sin of Cain, and Cundrie who, herself a 'daughter of Cain', first cursed and later rehabilitated Parzival.[86]

But what is the function of depicting pagans as half-human, half-animal monsters? In the tradition described above, the origin of the monstrous races is linked to disobedience, crime, and sin.[87] Therefore, linking the pagans with representatives of the monstrous races casts a damning light on the pagans. But it is striking that in both Konrad's *Rolandslied* and Wolfram's *Willehalm* the authors abstain from enumerating the whole catalogue of monstrous races. They concentrate on a small, but meaningful selection: on monsters with deformed heads (e.g., the Dog-Heads) or, more often, with monstrous-looking skin (e.g., people with pig-bristles on their back, with green horny skin, and also with numerous 'blackamoors'). Along with heads and skin, our attention is directed to body parts, which are the most important for descriptions of outward appearance and, especially, of beauty. By this, the medieval authors perhaps want to suggest that, in contrast to Adam, pagans are not created after the (beautiful) image of God.[88]

In my opinion, this is certainly true for the *Rolandslied*. For Wolfram's *Willehalm*, I believe other conditions apply. Here, the female protagonist Gyburc, who converted to Christianity out of love for the male protagonist Willehalm, delivers a speech to the council of the Christian knights in which she begs that the pagans, her relatives, be spared: *hoert eines tummen wîbes rât,/ schônet der gotes hantgetât* (Listen to the advice of a simple woman, spare – or be kind to – God's creation or to the children of God).[89] I do not want to enter

[83] Ibid., p. 101.
[84] Wisbey, 'Wunder des Ostens', p. 212.
[85] Ibid., p. 206.
[86] P. Michel, *Formosa deformitas. Bewältigungsformen des Häßlichen in mittelalterlicher Literatur* (Bonn: Bouvier, 1976), p. 67.
[87] As Friedman, *The Monstrous Races*, p. 88, showed, this tradition replaced the older view represented by Saint Augustine for whom the monstrous races were just part of God's creation.
[88] Cf. I. Kasten, 'Häßliche Frauenfiguren in der Literatur des Mittelalters', *Auf der Suche nach der Frau im Mittelalter* (B. Lundt (ed.); München: Wilhelm Fink, 1991), pp. 255–76 (260).
[89] *Willehalm*, 306.27. She then gives a lot of arguments why pagans should not be automatically condemned and why there is hope for salvation for the pagans, too: the first man, Adam, was also a pagan (*Willehalm*, 306.29). In the Old Testament, there are examples of redeemed pagans like Elias,

deeper into the complex theological discussion concerning what Wolfram really means by *gotes hantgetât* (God's handiwork), which may mean 'created by God' or even 'child of God'.[90] When Wolfram describes the green horny skin of the people following King Gorhant as a kind of armour, he not only reduces the monstrous character of these people, but also allows us to consider pagans as descendants of Adam, as Gyburc likely does.

By describing pagans as part of the monstrous races, Western medieval authors seem to deny, to some degree, the full human status of pagans. Indeed, medieval scholars earnestly discuss the problem whether a *monstrum* – be it a portentous individual birth or an unusual race[91] – is a human being or not, whether monstrosities are part of the creation or *contra naturam*, or whether a monster has reason and a soul.[92] Incidentally, similar questions are discussed in relation to animals: do animals have reason, do animals have a soul?[93]

Many of the medieval writers of the great nature encyclopaedias grant to the monstrous races only an inferior place in the Chain of Being, they are located somewhere between animals and humans, sometimes nearer to animals, sometimes nearer to humans (Table 2).[94] As Friedman pointed out, this way of thinking is oriented toward a European image of man.[95]

In comparing pagans to animals, in relating pagans to the monstrous races, the Christian authors seem to want to emphasize the 'subhumanity' of the pagans[96] and their vicinity to animality. The suggested inferiority of pagans to Christians is mirrored by the inferiority of animals to humans. When they refer to the animal world, medieval authors are more than simply using a handy metaphor. Here, animality has significance in itself. Being like an animal, even

---

Henoch, Noah, and Hiob (*Willehalm*, 307.1–6). Also the three Magi and even Maria were pagans (*Willehalm*, 307.7–14). Every child who is born is at first pagan before it is baptized (*Willehalm*, 307.17–25).

[90] The discussion was started by F. Knapp, 'Die Heiden und ihr Vater in den Versen 307, 27f. des 'Willehalm', *Zeitschrift für deutsches Altertum* 122 (1993), pp. 202–7; response by J. Heinzle, 'Die Heiden als Kinder Gottes. Notiz zum "Willehalm", *Zeitschrift für deutsches Altertum* 123 (1994), pp. 301–8; J. Heinzle, 'Noch einmal: Die Heiden als Kinder Gottes in Wolframs "Willehalm", *Zeitschrift für deutsche Philologie* 117 (1998), pp. 75–80; response by F. Knapp, 'Und noch einmal: Die Heiden als Kinder Gottes', *Zeitschrift für deutsches Altertum* 129 (2000), pp. 296–302.

[91] The Latin word *monstrum* has different meanings; see Friedman, *The Monstrous Races*, p. 3.

[92] Ibid., ch. 9.

[93] See P. Sobol, 'The Shadow of Reason', *The Medieval World of Nature: A Book of Essays* (J. Salisbury (ed.); New York and London: Garland Publishing, 1993), pp. 109–28; P. De Leemans and M. Klemm, 'Animals and Anthropology in Medieval Philosophy', *A Cultural History of Animals in the Medieval Age* (B. Resl (ed.); Oxford and New York: Berg, 2007), pp. 153–77.

[94] Friedman, *The Monstrous Races*, pp. 183–96.

[95] Ibid., p. 196: 'As long as the definition of "man" was based upon a Western model, the monstrous races could only be assigned a subordinate place in the Chain of Being'.

[96] Harris, 'Animal, Vegetable, Mineral', p. 213, speaks of the 'function of implicitly dehumanizing' the heathens.

Table 2: The Status of the Monstrous Races in the Chain of Being

Humans	
	▪ **Alexander of Hales** and **Ratramnus of Corbie**: as "inferior human", "better be considered men than beasts"
	▪ **Albert the Great**: "above apes but a step below man" (related to pygmies)
	▪ **Thomas of Cantimpré** and **Vincent of Beauvais**: slightly higher than animals
Animals	▪ **Lambert of Saint Omer**: created by God among the ordinary animals

a wild and impure animal, or being half-human, half-animal – all these literary animal images point to the meaning of being not fully human.

Yet, we have to keep in mind that Wolfram's *Willehalm* does not put forward the rigid views of pagans that the *Rolandslied* offers. Wolfram's monstrous Cundrie is to some extent better than Parzival whom she curses. In the person of Cundrie, Wolfram discusses the divergence between external ugliness and internal beauty. While Cundrie is civilized and learned, but horrible to look at, Parzival, at their first meeting, is beautiful to look at but inwardly ugly because he is a sinner.[97]

Conclusions

Let us come back to our main question: how do medieval authors use animals to symbolize pagans and paganism? They do this in different ways according to their different purposes. First, they use

- *Animals as real animals*. If animals appear as part of the pagan's everyday world, then the author refers to real animals. In such cases, the author may, for instance, refer to camels and elephants as draught animals or presents, or mention animals being worshipped or eaten by the pagans.

---

[97] A. Groos, 'Cundrie's Announcement ("Parzival" 781–2)', *Beiträge zur Geschichte der deutschen Sprache und Literatur* 113 (1991), pp. 384–414 (403); cf. Michel, *Formosa deformitas*, p. 66. For D. Böhland, 'Integrative Funktion durch exotische Distanz. Zur Cundrie-Figur in Wolframs *Parzival*', *Böse Frauen – gute Frauen. Darstellungskonventionen in Texten und Bildern des Mittelalters und der Frühen Neuzeit* (U. Gaebel, and E. Kartschoke (eds); Trier: Wissenschaftlicher Verlag, 2001), pp. 45–58 (58), Cundrie belongs to the rare description pattern, 'worin das Häßliche als das Nicht-Böse integrationsfähig ist'.

- *Animals as literary images.* Animals can also appear as comparisons and metaphors within descriptions of pagans or as dream images symbolizing individual pagans or pagans generally. In this case, the animal does not count as an animal itself but rather as a literary image transporting relatively fixed meanings.
- *Animals as representatives of animality.* Animal parts can appear as parts of the pagan's body. In this case, the animal represents animality rather than humanity.

Second, we have to distinguish between the kinds of animals the medieval authors select:

- *Exotic and fabulous animals*, such as camels, dromedaries, and elephants as well as *merrinder*, are used to describe the everyday environment of the pagans.
- *Wild and impure animals*, such as pigs and dogs as well as leopards, bears, and lions are often used as comparisons and metaphors for pagans; they may also figure as dream images.
- *Common animals,* particularly *animals with positive connotations* in the medieval world, such as hunting dogs, boars, and bears as well as lions, are also used in describing pagans. These animals represent animality itself and the single animal does not transport a specific meaning.

Incidentally, these last three categories correspond with the first ones. In addition, we can add a third group of observations, this time concerning the authors' purposes of using animal attributes to symbolize pagans and paganism.

- Real animals, particularly exotic animals, are used simply to *indicate* pagans as pagans, as part of the oriental world. Besides this, these animals also serve to *characterize* pagans as strangers, and, furthermore, at least in the *Rolandslied*, to *value* the pagans as lovers of luxury (meaning sinners).
- Wild and impure animals, in contrast to the domestic and highly esteemed animals representing Christians, are used by Konrad the priest not only to *characterize* the pagans as dangerous adversaries of the Christians, but also to *value* pagans as less worthy than Christians. In dreams they also serve to *indicate* individual pagans or paganism as a whole.
- Common animals are used to *indicate* monstrosity and thereby to *characterize* the pagans as descendants of Adam's disobedient daughters, of Cain, or of Ham. This implies that the animals used in this way also serve to *(de)value* the pagans as inferior to Christians and ultimately as not fully human.

It is necessary to emphasize once again that Konrad the Priest and Wolfram of Eschenbach each makes use of the 'animal means' in different ways. In the older *Rolandslied*, 'exotic' animals stand for condemnable luxury (as opposed to Christian modesty and humility), pagans are compared to wild and impure animals by the narrator or in Charlemagne's dreams, and their affiliation to the monstrous races is a sign of their sinfulness and of the absence of Christian belief. In the more modern *Willehalm*, 'exotic' luxury is part of the courtly culture, which the pagan knights share with their Christian opponents, and pagans are no longer compared to wild and impure animals. Nonetheless, some of them belong to the monstrous races, but, as I have pointed out, their strange appearance is here depicted as a kind of armour, not as a result of sin and disobedience. Already in his *Parzival*, Wolfram designed in Cundrie and Malcreatiure two oriental creatures that do not fit the usual binary value system: good or bad, familiar or strange, Christian or pagan.

When, in *Willehalm*, Wolfram has Gyburc express the revolutionary view that pagans, too, are part of God's creation (or even God's children) and has her think about the possibility of the pagans' salvation, this leads necessarily to a modification in the way pagans can be described. The common tradition of animal imagery is taken up but altered according to the author's higher-developed view of mankind. Thereby, Wolfram also increases the value of the image of animality.[98] In the *Rolandslied*, being an animal means being non-human and thus being inferior to humans; in Wolfram's texts, being an animal means also being a natural creature created by God, which sometimes includes the possibility of being superior, or at least equal, to humans. Thus, having analysed animal images used for the description of pagans, we have gained deeper insight into the medieval discussion not only on paganism and its relation to Christianity, but also on humanity and animality.

Bibliography

Albrecht of Scharfenberg, *Der Jüngere Titurel* (W. Wolf, and K. Nyholm (ed.); 4 vols; Berlin: Akademie-Verlag, 1955–95).

Biblia Sacra iuxta Vulgatam versionem (R. Weber et al., (ed.); Stuttgart: Deutsche Bibelgesellschaft, 1983).

---

[98] This corresponds with results and observations made by Harris, 'Animal, Vegetable, Mineral', p. 215, that Wolfram uses 'a notably wide range of animals' and 'was patently familiar […] with animal lore' (here referring to Gerhardt, 'Wolframs Adlerbild').

Böhland, D., 'Integrative Funktion durch exotische Distanz. Zur Cundrie-Figur in Wolframs *Parzival*', *Böse Frauen – gute Frauen. Darstellungskonventionen in Texten und Bildern des Mittelalters und der Frühen Neuzeit* (U. Gaebel, and E. Kartschoke (eds); Trier: Wissenschaftlicher Verlag, 2001), pp. 45–58.

Brummack, J., *Die Darstellung des Orients in den deutschen Alexandergeschichten des Mittelalters* (Berlin: Erich Schmidt, 1966).

Fasbender, C., ' "Willehalm" als Programmschrift gegen die "Kreuzzugsideologie" und "Dokument der Menschlichkeit" ', *Zeitschrift für deutsche Philologie* 116 (1997), pp. 16–31.

Fischer, S. R., *The Dream in the Middle High German Epic. Introduction to the Study of the Dream as a Literary Device to the Younger Contemporaries of Gottfried and Wolfram* (Bern, Frankfurt am Main, and Las Vegas: Lang, 1978).

Friedman, J. B., *The Monstrous Races in Medieval Art and Thought* (Cambridge, MA and London: Harvard University Press, 1981).

Friedrich, U., *Menschentier und Tiermensch. Diskurse der Grenzziehung und Grenzüberschreitung im Mittelalter* (Göttingen: Vandenhoeck & Ruprecht, 2009).

—'Der Ritter und sein Pferd. Semantisierungsstrategien einer Mensch-Tier-Verbindung im Mittelalter', *Text und Kultur. Mittelalterliche Literatur 1150–1450* (U. Peters (ed.); Stuttgart and Weimar: Metzler, 2001), pp. 245–67.

Geith, K.-E., 'Die Träume im *Rolandslied* des Pfaffen Konrad und in Strickers Karl', *Träume im Mittelalter. Ikonologische Studien* (A. P. Bagliani, and G. Stabile (eds); Stuttgart, Zürich: Belser, 1989), pp. 227–40.

Gerhardt, C., 'Wolframs Adlerbild ("Willehalm", 189, 2–24)', *Zeitschrift für deutsches Altertum* 99 (1970), pp. 213–22.

Groos, A., 'Cundrie's Announcement ("Parzival" 781–82)', *Beiträge zur Geschichte der deutschen Sprache und Literatur* 113 (1991), pp. 384–414.

Harris, N., 'Animal, Vegetable, Mineral. Some Observations on the Presentation and Function of Natural Phenomena in Willehalm and in the Old French Aliscans', *Wolfram's 'Willehalm'. Fifteen Essays* (M. H. Jones, and T. McFarland (eds); Columbia, SC: Camden House, 2002), pp. 211–29.

Haug, W., 'Parzivals *zwîvel* und Willehalms *zorn*. Zu Wolframs Wende vom höfischen Roman zur chanson de geste', *Strukturen als Schlüssel zur Welt. Kleine Schriften zur Erzählliteratur des Mittelalters* (Tübingen: Niemeyer, 1989), pp. 529–40.

Heinzle, J., 'Die Heiden als Kinder Gottes. Notiz zum "Willehalm" ', *Zeitschrift für deutsches Altertum* 123 (1994), pp. 301–8.

—'Noch einmal: Die Heiden als Kinder Gottes in Wolframs "Willehalm" ', *Zeitschrift für deutsche Philologie* 117 (1998), pp. 75–80.

Kartschoke, D., 'Commentary', *Das Rolandslied des Pfaffen Konrad* (D. Kartschoke (ed., trans., comm.); Stuttgart: Reclam, 1993), pp. 627–750.

Kasten, I., 'Häßliche Frauenfiguren in der Literatur des Mittelalters', *Auf der Suche nach der Frau im Mittelalter* (B. Lundt (ed.); München: Wilhelm Fink, 1991), pp. 255–76.

Knapp, F. P., 'Die Heiden und ihr Vater in den Versen 307,27f. des "Willehalm"', *Zeitschrift für deutsches Altertum* 122 (1993), pp. 202–7.

—'Und noch einmal: Die Heiden als Kinder Gottes', *Zeitschrift für deutsches Altertum* 129 (2000), pp. 296–302.

Konrad, *Rolandslied* (C. Wesle, and P. Wapneswki (eds); Tübingen: Niemeyer, 1985).

Lecouteux, C., *Les monstres dans la literature allemande du moyen âge* (3 vols; Göppingen: Kümmerle, 1982).

Leemans, P. de, and M. Klemm, 'Animals and Anthropology in Medieval Philosophy', *A Cultural History of Animals in the Medieval Age* (B. Resl (ed.); Oxford: Berg, 2007), pp. 153–77.

Michel, P., *Formosa deformitas. Bewältigungsformen des Häßlichen in mittelalterlicher Literatur* (Bonn: Bouvier, 1976).

Miquel, D. P., *Dictionnaire symbolique des animaux. Zoologie mystique* (Paris: Le Léopard d'Or, 1992).

Obermaier, S., 'Antike Irrtümer und ihre mittelalterlichen Folgen: Das Flusspferd', *Antike Naturwissenschaft und ihre Rezeption* 21 (2011), pp. 135–79.

Peschel-Rentsch, D., 'Pferdemänner. Kleine Studie zum Selbstbewußtsein eines Ritters', *Pferdemänner. Sieben Essays über Sozialisation und ihre Wirkungen in mittelalterlicher Literatur* (D. Peschel-Rentsch (ed.); Erlangen and Jena: Palm & Enke, 1998), pp. 12–47.

Pluskowski, A., *Wolves and the Wilderness in the Middle Ages* (Woodbridge, Suffolk: Boydell Press, 2006).

Richter, H., *Kommentar zum Rolandslied des Pfaffen Konrad* (Teil I; Bern and Frankfurt: Herbert Lang & Cie, 1972).

Schenda, R., 'Hund', *Enzyklopädie des Märchens* 6 (1990), col. 1317–40.

Sobol, P. G., 'The Shadow of Reason', *The Medieval World of Nature. A Book of Essays* (J. E. Salisbury (ed.); New York and London: Garland Publishing, 1993), pp. 109–28.

Speckenbach, K., 'Der Eber in der deutschen Literatur des Mittelalters', *Verbum et signum. Friedrich Ohly zum 60. Geburtstag überreicht* (H. Fromm (ed.); 2 vols; München: Fink, 1975), vol. 1, pp. 425–76.

The Stricker, *Karl der Große* (K. Bartsch (ed.); Berlin: de Gruyter, 1965).

Ulrich of Etzenbach, *Alexander* (W. Toischer (ed.); Reprint Stuttgart/Tübingen: Bibliothek des Litterarischen Vereins, 1888; Hildesheim: Olms, 1974).

Uther, H.-J., 'Schwein', *Enzyklopädie des Märchens* 12 (2007), col. 393–8.

Vorderstemann, J., 'NEITUN und MUNTUNZEL. Zu "Willehalm" 425,25–426,30', *Kritische Bewahrung. Beiträge zur deutschen Philologie. Festschrift für Werner Schröder zum 60. Geburtstag* (E.-J. Schmidt (ed.); Berlin: Erich Schmidt, 1974), pp. 328–34.

Wisbey, R. A., 'Wunder des Ostens in der "Wiener Genesis" und in Wolframs "Parzival", *Studien zur frühmittelhochdeutschen Literatur. Cambridger Colloquium 1971* (L. P. Johnson, H.-H. Steinhoff, and R. A. Wisbey (eds); Berlin: Erich Schmidt, 1974), pp. 180–214.

Wittkower, R., 'Marvels of the East. A Study in the History of Monsters', *Journal of the Warburg and Courtauld Institutes* 5 (1942), pp. 159–97.

Wolfram of Eschenbach, *Parzival* (K. Lachmann, and B. Schirok (eds); Berlin: de Gruyter, 1998).

—*Willehalm* (A. Leitzmann (ed.); Tübingen: Niemeyer, 1963).

5

The Daemonic Insect: *Mantis religiosa*

Adam Dodd

It occurred to me that by virtue of its name, form, and habits, the praying
mantis displayed [an] objective capacity to act directly on the emotions to
an exceptional degree; this is very useful in helping us to understand how
imaginative synthesis can be transmitted in a lyrical way.[1]

I. Introduction

The European mantis, or praying mantis (*Mantis religiosa*),[2] as its name suggests, has been regarded as an abnormally sentient insect in Europe for centuries, largely owing to its conspicuous and easily anthropomorphized morphology. In particular, its well-known 'praying' aspect has led to associations with theological and occult powers, while 'mantis' is derived from the Greek *mantikos* meaning either prophetic or oracular, as well as 'of divination' or 'prophecy'.[3] The serene benevolence of the mantid's apparently reverent posturing, however, is sharply contrasted by the animal's violent predation and occasional cannibalization of conspecifics, sometimes during copulation. Mantids are known to attack and consume creatures much larger than themselves, including reptiles, rodents, and birds. In cases of female-on-male sexual cannibalism among mantids, the male may continue copulation even after his head, and much of his body, has been consumed by the female. These qualities, suffice it to say, have rarely sat easily with European natural historians; consequently, mantids have been subject to a number of myths and misunderstandings, even within the modern field of entomology. The praying mantis is something of a paradox: given what

---

[1] R. Caillois, 'The Praying Mantis: From Biology to Psychoanalysis', *The Edge of Surrealism: A Roger Caillois Reader* (C. Frank (ed.); Durham and London: Duke University Press, 2003), pp. 69–81.

[2] C. Linnaeus, *Systema naturae per regna tria naturae: secundum classes, ordines, genera, species, cum characteribus, differentiis, synonymis, locis* (10th edn, 1758).

[3] A. Nicholls, *Goethe's Concept of the Daemonic: After the Ancients* (Rochester, NY: Camden House, 2006), p. 30.

is known about its habits, as many observers have wryly noted, the animal could perhaps be more appropriately called the 'preying mantis'.

The natural history of the mantis is inherently fascinating, but in this chapter I focus on this animal's presence in the numinous dimensions of the Western imagination. This will involve tracing the mantis through some strange and perhaps unfamiliar territory – beginning with early modern accounts of praying mantids in European natural history and folklore, through the insectoid fairylands of the nineteenth century, into the otherworldly realms of twentieth-century alien abduction, and the powerful hallucinations and visions enabled by N,N-Dimethyltryptamine (DMT). In order to orient this passage, I am employing, as a kind of theoretical compass, the concept of 'daemonic dread' as articulated by Rudolph Otto:

> This crudely naive and primordial emotional disturbance, and the fantastic images to which it gives rise, are later overborne and ousted by more highly-developed forms of the numinous emotion, with all its mysteriously impelling power. But even when this has long attained its higher and purer mode of expression it is possible for the primitive types of excitation that were formerly a part of it to break out in the soul in all their original naiveté and so to be experienced afresh.[4]

As I hope to show, the praying mantis, the figures it inspires, and the 'fresh experience' of such figures can be understood within this framework: the mantis does indeed constitute a kind of 'daemonic insect'. The mantis cannot be located neatly within any clearly defined religious category; it exhibits something of the numen but is not the numen itself. While we may regard the mantis with a mixture of horror and fascination, it does not constitute what Otto describes as the 'daemonic-divine object', which

> may appear to the mind an object of horror and dread, but at the same time it is no less something that allures with a potent charm, and the creature, who trembles before it, utterly cowed and cast down, has always at the same time the impulse to turn to it, nay even to make it somehow his own.[5]

However, in the case of 'aliens' and other mantid-like beings described by those reporting alien abduction and DMT experiences, it would seem that the mantis has come to inspire such 'daemonic-divine' objects.

---

[4] R. Otto, *The Idea of the Holy: An Inquiry into the Non-Rational Factor in the Idea of the Divine and its Relation to the Rational* (J. Harley (trans.); Oxford: Oxford University Press, 1936), p. 16.
[5] Ibid., p. 31.

While its influence extends beyond itself, into the domains of imagination, hallucination, and myth, the actual mantis has often been regarded as a kind of living monster, capable of inspiring religious horror and dread, and unsettling a number of fundamental ontological and aesthetic concepts. As Noël Carroll explains:

> Otto's numen is wholly other. It defies the application of predicates and even the manifold of predicability itself. But this is not the case with the monsters of horror. For even if they cannot be named outright in terms of the standing concepts of the culture, they can be situated in terms of those concepts as combinations, magnifications, etc. of what already is. That is, monsters are not wholly other, but derive their repulsive aspect from being, so to speak, contortions performed upon the known. They do not defy predication, but mix properties in nonstandard ways. They are not wholly unknown, and this is probably what accounts for their characteristic effect – disgust. Nor does one feel worthless before (or dependant upon) the monsters of horror as one might before a deity.[6]

A number of the figures inspired by the mantis, particularly the anthropomorphized aliens of abduction accounts, can be understood in this context, constituting what Carroll describes as fusion figures: '[composites that unite] attributes held to be categorically distinct and/or at odds in the cultural scheme of things in *unambiguously* one, spatio-temporally discrete entity'.[7] Examining the extent to which the praying mantis (and perhaps insects more generally) have inspired such figures, which have become central to a modern 'myth in the making', to paraphrase Jung, can clarify our understanding of the complex correspondences between nature, imagination, and culture. There is a religious – we might say, a 'spiritual' – aspect to these correspondences. However, as Stephanie Kelley-Romano has observed, 'unlike religions and other codified systems of belief, the alien abduction myth ... is still developing'[8] and so we should, from the outset, perhaps accept the inability to arrive at some final explanation of this process. Like the natural world from which they draw inspiration, the peopled realms of fairylore, alien abduction narratives, and DMT accounts exist in a state of perpetual flux; however, this should not deter us from acknowledging, documenting, and attempting to comprehend them. In order to

---

[6] N. Carroll, *The Philosophy of Horror; or, Paradoxes of the Heart* (New York: Routledge, 1990), p. 166.
[7] Ibid., p. 43.
[8] S. Kelley-Romano, 'Mythmaking in Alien Abduction Narratives', *Communication Quarterly* 54.3 (2006), p. 384.

do this, I suggest, we should turn our attention to the cultural history of insects in general, and praying mantids in particular.

II. The Dreaded Mantis and the Entomological Gaze

The praying mantis is exemplary among the insects in its ability to contain opposites and contradictions. Life and death, beauty and violence, the familiar and the strange – these and other fundamental dualisms begin to dissolve when we look closely at mantids. The mantid's ability to provoke this kind of dissolution can be seen as a factor contributing to its inspiration of mythic, imaginative, and religious forms. Although my focus is broadly on the Western context, it is worth noting that, historically, Eastern attitudes towards praying mantids have been significantly different – indeed, one is tempted to say, significantly more measured. Although in Europe, mantids (as with insects in general) first became the subjects of close, systematic investigation in the second half of the sixteenth century, in China mantids have been studied, included in art and literature, and used as objects of entertainment for at least 1,000 years. As Frederick Prete and M. Melissa Wolfe have observed:

> Perhaps due to their long-developed observational skills, the mantid's seemingly pious demeanor did not deceive observers in the Far East as it did those in western Asia, Africa, and Europe. In China (and later, Japan) the mantid became a symbol of strength, courage, and boldness, extending sometimes to foolhardiness. The conceptualization, based on the mantis's willingness to attack creatures as large as or larger than itself, was popularized in the Chinese proverb that states that the mantis is not strong enough to stop a bullock cart, although, the accompanying folktale goes, one actually thought it could do so.[9]

Eastern attitudes towards the mantis reflect a deeper accommodation of insect life in general, one that has developed over a considerable amount of time. As James Tsai notes, sericulture and silk technology in China dates back to 4,500–7,000 years ago[10] and the relationship between predator and prey was first studied in AD 52 with sphecid wasps.[11] By comparison, Europeans have come to know the insect only recently and within a significantly different cultural and

[9] F. Prete and M. Wolfe, 'Religious Supplicant, Seductive Cannibal, or Reflex Machine? In Search of the Praying Mantis', *Journal of the History of Biology* 21.1 (1992), p. 95.

[10] J. Tsai, 'Entomology in the People's Republic of China', *Journal of the New York Entomological Society* 90.3 (1982), p. 187.

[11] Ibid., p. 191.

philosophical milieu. In particular, anthropomorphic and theological interpretations of insect life, which are closely aligned both with teleological and
juvenile attitudes towards animals,[12] only began to widely subside in Western
scientific accounts at the turn of the twentieth century, and even since then, the
mantis has proved to be a stubbornly anthropomorphic animal.

The earliest documented recordings of mantids in Europe, such as those
found in Ulisse Aldrovandi's *De animalibus insectis* (1602), and Thomas
Muffet's[13] *Insectorum sive minimorum Animalium Theatrum* (1634), classify
the mantid as a rare kind of locust or grasshopper. Muffet's work, completed
as a manuscript in 1589, provides one of the earliest European accounts of the
mantid's environment, morphology, and folkloric significance. In the English
publication, *The Theater of Insects* (1658), Muffet described how

> they are called *Mantes, foretellers*, either because by their coming (for they first
> of all appear) they do shew the Spring to be at hand, so *Anacreon* the Poet sang;
> or else they foretell dearth and famine, as Caelius the Scholiast of Theocritus
> have observed. Or lastly, because it alwaies holds up its forefeet like hands
> praying as it were, after the manner of their Diviners ... So divine a creature
> is this esteemed, that if a childe ask the way to such a place, she will stretch
> out one of her feet, and shew him the right way, and seldome or never miss ...
> and as she resembleth those Diviners in the elevation of her hands, so also in
> likeness of motion; for they do not sport themselves as others do, nor leap, nor
> play; but walking softly, she retains her modesty, and shews forth a kinds of
> mature gravity.[14]

Muffet's description is somewhat typical of sixteenth-century European natural
history texts, being a mixture of directly observed facts, references to classical
sources, and unverified repetitions of more recent accounts. It also represents
part of a wider Renaissance conception of the world as a kind of theatre, in
which 'the scholar and the reader are seen as spectators who contemplate a
show, a "theater of the world" ... [In the Renaissance period] the term *theater*
begins to be employed in the titles of works that are summary expositions of
vast subjects'.[15] Employing the metaphor of the theatre as a model for scientific discourse had consequences for the ways in which the subjects of science

---

[12] See D. Shepardson, 'Bugs, Butterflies, and Spiders: Children's Understandings about Insects',
International Journal of Science Education 24 (2002), pp. 627–43.

[13] Elsewhere, 'Mouffet' and 'Moffet'.

[14] T. Muffet, *The Theater of Insects*: E. Topsell, *The History of Four-footed Beasts and Serpents* (London,
1658), pp. 982–3.

[15] C. Avramescu, *An Intellectual History of Cannibalism* (A. Blyth (trans.); Princeton and Oxford:
Princeton University Press, 2009), p. 7.

were understood. As Catalin Avramescu points out, when Hume wrote in *The Natural History of Religion* (1757) that: 'We are placed in this world, as in a great theatre, where the true springs and causes of every event are entirely concealed from us',[16] he was advocating the metaphor of the theatre as way to promote the new mechanical philosophy. But if the world was a kind of machine, it remained a machine based on ultimately elusive, invisible principles. Insects, as subjects and objects of knowledge within this episteme, thus became not only players in the spectacular theatre of nature, but indicators of the occult forces that underpin 'the show'.

To the contemporary entomologist, Muffet's work is of little scientific value. Of particular interest to the historian of insect-human relations, however, is Muffet's subjective impression of the mantid's 'mature gravity'. Elevated beyond what are perceived as childish habits (play), the mantis exhibits a deliberate purpose-fulness that, one may assume, is indicative of a certain sentience. This kind of perception would feed into late nineteenth and early twentieth-century portrayals of the mantis by Jean-Henri Fabre, the Surrealists, and later still in testimonials from so-called 'alien abductees', who almost universally describe their captors as purposeful, unemotional, and emitting an often paralyzing gravitas.

Prete and Wolfe situate the earliest unfavourable account of the mantis in the work of the German naturalist and painter, August Johann Rösel von Rosenhoff (1705–95). Rösel, inspired to raise and illustrate insects after encountering the highly refined work of Maria Sibylla Merian (1647–1717), placed several mantids in a glass jar for observation. He reported that they tended to fight violently with each other and that the winner always devoured the loser. As Prete and Wolfe note, however, 'more important than the fact that his young mantids devoured one another was Rösel's claim that they did not cease to attack, kill, and eat each other even when their hunger had been satisfied by an abundant supply of other, nourishing food'.[17] This claim, repeated many times after Rösel, paved the way for the mantid's reputation as the insect world's most sadistic, cannibalistic killer. Crucially, the violence of the mantis was usually juxtaposed with its enchanting or charming qualities. Prete and Wolfe cite numerous examples of this approach, which has since become a largely unques-tioned convention in the portrayal of praying mantids.

While cannibalism is a shared taboo across many cultures and historical periods, we can connect the Western reception of the mantid's cannibalistic

[16] Ibid.
[17] Prete and Wolfe, 'In Search of the Praying Mantis', p. 103.

behaviour, from Rösel onwards, to cannibalism as figured by pre-Enlightenment dialectics. Avramescu observes:

> Up until the eighteenth century … the wider world is viewed through the lens of a system of fundamental oppositions between city and nature … Thus beyond the boundaries of the premodern city extends an inverted world, the opposite of civilization, peopled by grotesque figures, inverted images of civic man … The state of nature invoked by philosophers, prior to being a thought experiment of modern science or a historical hypothesis, is part of this fundamental inversion, a grotesque theater of lawless figures … This is the natural anarchy against whose background the central figure of our narrative takes shape: the anthropophagus.[18]

Avramescu's focus is the figure of the human cannibal, the anthropophagus, yet his analysis sheds some light on the mantid's negative reception by European naturalists from the eighteenth century onward. For example, in their widely read *Introduction to Entomology* (1815–26), William Kirby and William Spence portray 'the insect world' in precisely these dialectical terms. By the time the *Introduction* was published, 'the insect world' trope had begun to facilitate a shared conception of the diverse habitats of insects as a kind of unified, orderly, self-regulating, harmonious realm – a natural analogue, that is, of the efficient, modern city. Kirby and Spence were aware that some insects preyed on members of other insect species, but this was seen as an inherent part of the insect world's self-maintenance, as instigated by the Creator: 'I cannot doubt that you will recognize the goodness of the Great Parent in providing such an army of counterchecks to the natural tendency of almost all insects to incalculable increase'.[19] Insects of the same species feeding on each other, however, were quite a different matter: 'But before I quit this subject I may call your attention to what may be denominated *cannibal insects*, since in spite of those disclaimers who would persuade us that man is the only animal that preys on his own species, a large number of insects are guilty of the same offence'.[20] The mantid, among a number of arthropods cited as culpable of this transgression, was thus portrayed in a way that emphasized not only its behavioural proximity to man, but the very worst in man: conscious, sadistic cannibalism. Wherever cannibalism was observed in the insect world, it was met with an appropriate degree of revulsion and the insect was itself deemed to be of barbaric character. In some spider species, too,

---

[18] Avramescu, *An Intellectual History of Cannibalism*, pp. 8–9.
[19] W. Kirby, and W. Spence, *An Introduction to Entomology: or Elements of the Natural History of Insects* (vol. 1, 3rd edn, London: Longman, Hurst, Rees, Orme and Brown, 1818), p. 278.
[20] Ibid.

the females do not yield to the Mantes in their unnatural cruelty to their mates. Woe be to the male spider that after an union does not with all speed make his escape from the fangs of his partner! Nay, [Charles] De Geer saw one that, in the midst of his preparatory caresses, was seized by the object of his attentions, enveloped by her in a web, and then devoured – a sight which, he observes, filled him with horror and indignation.[21]

The 'horror and indignation' felt by (usually male) European observers of arthropod cannibalism in general, and female-on-male sexual cannibalism between mantids in particular, should be seen not as an instinctive, acultural response, but rather as one deeply informed by the episteme within which such observations took place. Because of the mantid's easily anthropomorphized form, instances of mantid cannibalism were immediately suggestive of the even more outrageous notion of human cannibalism; in cases of female-on-male cannibalism (which became the most widely repeated instances at the exclusion of asexual cannibalism) the 'theatre of nature' seemed to be playing out what was perhaps the ultimate nightmare scenario for Renaissance patriarchs – a woman devouring a man during sexual intercourse, simply because she wanted to. Evocative of the anthropophagus, and hence of the brutal, chaotic world of nature left behind for the civilized world of the modern city (a world reflected in the admirable societies of bees and ants), these and other instances of routine violence observed in the daily lives of insects were intolerable and largely irreconcilable. As the elaboration of the insect world trope continued into the nineteenth century, an exceedingly romantic view of insect life began to take shape, compensating, perhaps, for sexualized violence and suffering with nostalgia, exaggerated beauty, poetry, and wistful imaginings of 'other worlds'. It was during the nineteenth century, too, that insect fusion figures noticeably entered popular culture and, by extension, the popular imagination.

III. The Surreal Mantis

The most notable illustrators to have popularized anthropomorphic images of insects in nineteenth-century Europe are Martin Disteli (1802–44) and caricaturist Jean Ignace Isidore Gérard (1803–47), better known as Grandville. As Charles Hogue[22] shows, these artists established representational conventions

---

[21] Ibid., p. 280.
[22] C. Hogue, 'The Bugfolk', *Terra* 17.4 (1979), pp. 36–8.

for the illustration of popular fables and for presenting anthropomorphized animals as satires of human life and society, as 'bugfolk'. Corresponding with the popularity of these images was an emergent fascination with fairies – fashioned as miniature, insect-winged inhabitants of obscure, natural realms of dubious benevolence. Of particular influence upon the nineteenth-century fairy and fairylore, as Nicola Bown has observed, was the ascendency of popular natural history and amateur entomology. Referring to a number of nineteenth-century examples, including L. M. Budgen's highly anthropomorphic *Episodes of Insect Life* (1849–51), Bown shows how:

> The study of insects becomes a way of enchanting the natural world, of covering over 'the bare, the barren, and the death-like' and turning it into fairyland… The 'multitude of happy creatures' who inhabit this enchanted natural world bear very little resemblance to insects, and perhaps this is the point. Insects as insects must always remind us of the alien strangeness of the processes of nature; what this apostrophe invokes is a kind of insect that is rather like a human, though much smaller and supernaturally magical: an insect, in fact, that is rather like a fairy.[23]

It was also during the nineteenth century, Bown demonstrates, that fairies became widely represented as miniature folk with insect wings. Previous winged figures, such as angels and *putti*, were regarded as intermediaries between *spiritual* realms, signified most visibly by their feathered wings. The nineteenth-century fairy, however, was very much a figure of the new miniature dimensions of the natural world opened up by the microscope; their insect wings thus signify their ability to move between *spatial* realms. This was a shift that reflected the tension and irreconcilability of the microscopic subject as spatially both imminent and distant: the new sense of proximity to insects, brought about by the explosion in natural history books and amateur microscopy, was tempered by the trope of 'the insect world' in such a way that insects, no matter how closely we may have known them, were always already 'otherworldly'.

Despite (or perhaps because of) its overtly anthropomorphic appearance, the mantis seems to have taken a backseat during the insectoid fairy craze of the nineteenth century. Most fairies, even those who abduct and manipulate human beings for their own purposes, are evocative of the insects traditionally considered most endearing to Europeans, such as butterflies, fireflies, and dragonflies. Yet the association of insects in general with a vaguely defined,

---

[23] N. Bown, *Fairies in Nineteenth-Century Art and Literature* (Cambridge: Cambridge University Press, 2001), pp. 127–8.

mythical 'otherworld' laid the groundwork for subsequent variations of 'the insect world' that could accommodate, not only emerging knowledge about 'outer space' and its attendant questions about the possibility of extra-terrestrial life, but contemporary developments in psychology and psychiatry. At the turn of the twentieth century, the insect could stand not simply for the literal, miniature recesses of nature that ordinarily escape our view, but the deeper, 'hidden' recesses of the human mind that ordinarily evade our conscious thought. This made the insect in general, and the mantis in particular, a suitable figure for the project of the Surrealists. Before I briefly turn to the Surrealists' fascination with the mantis, however, I want to discuss how this fascination was buoyed by the writings of the French amateur entomologist, Jean-Henri Fabre (1823–1915).

As William Pressly has observed: 'Although other insects perform identical sexual rites, the particular interest in the mantis [for the Surrealists] was largely due to its exceptionally anthropomorphic form and to the imaginative observations of J. H. Fabre, who documented this insect's habits with as much poetry as science'.[24] Arguably the late nineteenth century's greatest popularizer of insect life, Fabre published a ten-volume work of observations he had gathered (mostly from his garden) entitled *Souvenirs entomologiques* (1879–1907). These were translated into various English volumes in the early decades of the twentieth century. Fabre's connection of the miniature to the 'souvenir' implied that a reduction in the dimensions of what was studied did not produce a corresponding reduction in significance, but rather, to paraphrase Susan Stewart, represented the insect as a container of aphoristic and didactic thought.[25] Moreover, if nature had been for Renaissance natural historians a kind of 'theatre', by the end of the nineteenth century it was becoming, if not a kind of cinema, at least something that could be understood cinematically. Fabre's descriptive style illustrates this: his primary discursive tactic was seemingly to account for every movement and action occurring within a 'scene' and then to structure these as following methodically from one into another to ultimately comprise the whole 'event'. This technique results in vivid, narrative prose that seems to describe moving, magnified images. As Eileen Crist observes: 'Fabre offers [his] description as of something real, in the way that images on film are of something real'.[26]

---

[24] W. Pressly, 'The Praying Mantis in Surrealist Art', *The Art Bulletin* 55.4 (1973), p. 600.

[25] S. Stewart, *On Longing: Narratives of the Miniature, the Gigantic, the Souvenir, the Collection* (Durham, NC: Duke University Press, 1993), p. 43.

[26] E. Crist, *Images of Animals: Anthropomorphism and Animal Mind* (Philadelphia: Temple University Press, 1999), p. 77.

The filmic qualities of Fabre's writings were also appreciated by his contemporaries. In *Fabre, Poet of Science* (1913), G. V. Legros wrote that

> although in his portraits and descriptions Fabre is simple and exact, and so full of natural geniality; although he can so handle his words as to render them 'adequate' to reproduce the *moving pictures* of the tiny creatures he observes, his style touches on a higher level, flashes with colour, and grows rich with imagery when he seeks to interpret the feelings which animate them... [Italics mine].[27]

One of Fabre's most famous and influential passages is his description of the praying mantis, which he relates in his characteristically dramatic, precise, and microscopic detail. In *Social Life in the Insect World* (1912), Fabre initially seems to make a case for the common, benevolent, anthropomorphic interpretation of the praying mantis, only to undermine this with a portrayal that emphasizes its abhorrent, 'murderous' behaviour. He begins his chapter entitled 'The Mantis – The Chase' with a review of the symbolic heritage of the insect, in which 'for once the language of science and the vocabulary of the peasant agree. Both represent the Mantis as a priestess delivering oracles or as an ascetic in a mystic ecstasy'.[28] Fabre then replaces one anthropomorphic view for another, exclaiming:

> Good people, how very far astray your childlike simplicity has led you! These attitudes of prayer conceal the most atrocious habits; the supplicating arms are lethal weapons; these fingers tell no rosaries, but help to exterminate the unfortunate passer-by... It is the tiger of the peaceful insect peoples; the ogre in ambush which demands a tribute of living flesh. If it only had sufficient strength its bloodthirsty appetites, and its horrible perfection of concealment would make it the terror of the countryside. The *Prègo-Diéu* [creature which prays to God] would become a Satanic vampire.[29]

There is something daemonically dreadful about the horror evoked by Fabre's description, which, in the context of the entomology book, takes on the qualities of a lesson, and possibly a warning, about the natural world. Fabre also mused on the idea that the mantid was capable of hypnotizing or paralyzing its prey through the incitement of terror. The particular instance he described, between a mantis and a cricket, was orchestrated within one of his terrariums, the chance of interruption being completely removed so that every detail of the process could be observed and documented.

---

[27] G. V. Legros, *Fabre, Poet of Science* (B. Miall (trans.); London: T. Fisher Unwin, 1913), p. 254.
[28] J. Fabre, *Social Life in the Insect World* (B. Miall (trans.); London: T. Fisher Unwin, 1912), p. 68.
[29] Ibid., p. 69.

Once the mantis, the scene, and the tension of an imminent attack have been well-established, Fabre describes not the inevitable action but rather the quiescence of the mantis, as if to suspend the tension of the scene further still.

> Motionless in its weird position, the Mantis surveys the acridian, its gaze fixed upon it, its head turning gently as on a pivot as the other changes place. The object of this mimicry seems evident; the Mantis wishes to terrorize its powerful prey, to paralyze it with fright; for if not demoralized by fear the quarry might prove too dangerous.[30]

Such descriptions would resurface decades later in accounts of the 'staring procedures' endured by those reporting alien abduction, which I discuss below.

In contrast to his representation of the cricket as possessing an automatic or hypnotized consciousness, Fabre's portrayal of the mantis describes a sentient being that chooses its actions carefully and deliberately. This is reiterated by his observation that 'sometimes the great hinder thigh is seized by the knuckle, carried to the mouth, tasted, and crunched with a little air of satisfaction. The swollen thigh of the cricket might well be a choice 'cut' for the Mantis, as a leg of lamb is for us!'[31] To some degree Fabre's open enthusiasm for the mantis suggests a deliberate incitement of affinity between the human observer and their monstrous subject. The reader is so absorbed in the intense particularity of the scene described that the surrounding context is all but forgotten – excluded in much the same manner, that is, as a microscopic lens omitting detail not appearing with its frame, or upon the stage of the microscope itself.

After Fabre, Roger Caillois writes in his essay 'The Praying Mantis: From Biology to Psychoanalysis' that 'naturalists find in the praying mantis the most extreme form of the close bond that often seems to exist between the sensual pleasures of sexuality and those of nutrition'.[32] In addition, he notes that, like Fabre, both André Breton and Paul Eluard kept mantids in their homes and that Eluard 'viewed their habits as the ideal mode of sexual relationship'.[33] Caillois' writings about praying mantids both reflected and impacted the Surrealists' concerns, appealing to their shared sensitivity to the omnipresence of the unconscious. The mantis, once appropriated in a very decisive way, provided an effective motif with which to express many of their interests in the deeper, darker, or repressed dimensions of human sexuality and imagination. Most contemporary examinations of

---

[30] Ibid., p. 75.
[31] Ibid., p. 78.
[32] Caillois, 'The Praying Mantis', p. 77.
[33] Ibid., p. 76.

the appropriation of the mantis by the Surrealists observe the misogyny at play here; indeed, the 'femme fatale' was a central obsession of the movement. In 'Dream' (1935) Escher substituted the mantis for the traditional succubus, in a distinctly religious context (see Figure 2). While drawing freely (yet inconsistently) from the fields of biology and psychology, the Surrealists often contributed to widespread misconceptions of the mantis, specifically, overstating the frequency of female-on-male sexual cannibalism, in order to elevate it to the status of the symbolic and the transcendental. As Ruth Markus shows, 'the Surrealists, unaware of the scientific evidence [that refuted the idea that females always devour males during sex], reinforced the myth to such an extent that the Praying Mantis is universally associated with the preying female'.[34] The Surrealists certainly were not immune from grand, universalizing claims about the mantis and its impact upon the human emotions. Indeed, as noted in the introduction to this chapter, Caillois held that the mantis has 'an objective capacity to act directly upon emotions', and in 'The Praying Mantis' essay, he refers to numerous examples, from antiquity to his own time and across disparate cultures, to make his case. Tellingly, the obvious counterexample to his argument – China – is mentioned only in a footnote, in a somewhat condescending and superficial manner: 'Even the Chinese have been emotionally affected by the mantis. Indeed, they keep mantises in bamboo cages and watch their fights with passionate interest'.[35]

Space does not permit an extended discussion of the mantis motif in Surrealist art; the topic has been handled thoroughly by other authors, most notably Pressly (1973) and Markus (2000). But before I discuss the mantis as it appears in the surreal narratives of alien abduction and DMT accounts, it is worth pointing out two particularly vivid correspondences. Among the many instances of the mantid's appearance in Surrealist work, one is especially striking, particularly in light of the kind of subsequent imagery I will address below: *L'Aventure permanente* (1944) by Felix Labisse.[36] As an insectoid, feminine, fusion-figure, it pre-empts representations of the aliens allegedly responsible for a considerable number of abductions and quasi-medical procedures on unsuspecting victims from the early 1960s onwards, while advancing pre-existing myths about the horror and beauty of female mantids themselves. Presented as a portrait, a convention usually reserved for human subjects, the image achieves a bizarre familiarity despite

---

[34] R. Markus, 'Surrealism's Praying Mantis and Castrating Woman', *Woman's Art Journal* 21.1 (2000), p. 33.
[35] Caillois, 'The Praying Mantis', p. 73.
[36] A reproduction of the image can be found online at: http://imgur.com/9VDMQ (accessed 25 July 2012).

its visibly nonhuman subject. A similar technique would appear decades later in Ted Seth Jacob's famous cover art for Whitley Strieber's widely read autobiographical account of his abduction experiences, *Communion* (1987), showing an alien species commonly referred to as 'the greys' (see Figure 1).

The second significant correspondence between the work of the Surrealists and later appearances of the mantids appears in Caillois' essay, 'Mimicry and Legendary Psychasthenia', first published in *Minotaure* in 1935. Here Caillois' concern is with mimicry in nature, which he sees not as a defence mechanism but as a morphological expression of the death drive: the organism's propensity to become indissoluble with its surrounding environment. This is a process that extends to human beings; the various expressions of schizophrenics 'shed light on a single process: depersonalization by assimilation to space, i.e., what mimicry achieves morphologically in certain animal species ... This assimilation to space is necessarily accompanied by a decline in the feeling of personality and life'.[37] I will return to Caillois' description below when I address reports of bodily dissolution in alien abduction and DMT experiences.

IV: The Alien Mantis

Copious literature, of varying quality and reliability, exists on the topics of insects, fairies, and aliens, but very little of this work attempts to show how these three capricious groups correspond with each other. In a previous section, I briefly discussed the ways in which the insect informed figurations of the fairy in the nineteenth century. In the twentieth century and beyond, as Carol G. Silver observes, 'science fiction has transmuted fairies to the small green men from outer space ... [and] contemporary UFOlogists argue that the fairies really *are* the little green men – alien creatures from outer space who have come to join us'.[38] Silver reproduces the cover image from Whitley Strieber's *Communion* (1987) with the caption 'A New Age fairy', and points out that 'the connections between fairies and aliens are made explicit in ... *Communion* ... their queen is a sort of fairy *femme fatale*, though contact with her is more of a rape than a seduction'.[39] Strieber, noting the parallels between his own recalled experiences and the content of traditional fairylore, speculated: 'Maybe the fairy was a real

---

[37] R. Caillois, 'Mimicry and Legendary Psychasthenia', *October* 31 (1984) [J. Shepley (trans.)], p. 30.
[38] C. Silver, *Strange and Secret Peoples: Fairies and Victorian Consciousness* (Oxford: Oxford University Press, 1999), p. 210.
[39] Ibid., pp. 210–11.

Figure 1: Communion

species, for example. Perhaps they now floated around in unidentified flying objects and wielded insight-producing wands because they have enjoyed their own technological revolution'.[40] He further added:

> What is most interesting to me about this story is that it continues imagery that is present in my early horror novels. The visitors could be seen as the Wolfen, as Miriam Blaylock in *The Hunger*, and as the fairy queen Leannan and her soldiers in *Catmagic*. The theme is always the same: Mankind must face a harsh but enigmatically beautiful force that, as Miriam Blaylock describes herself, is

[40] W. Strieber, *Communion: A True Story* (New York: Avon, 1987), p. 105.

part of the justice of the world. This force is always hidden between the folds of experience.[41]

Strieber's description here approaches, but does not finally arrive at, the insect. Insects, of course, are also 'a harsh but enigmatically beautiful force' which 'Mankind must face' and which is 'always hidden between the folds of experience'. Unlike the Wolfen, the vampire, or the fairy queen, however, insects exist in the here and now. Although Strieber never considers the possibility that his descriptions of the aliens could be shaped, or at least informed, by what is widely known about insects, there are numerous allusions to praying mantids throughout *Communion*. While under hypnotic regression, Strieber recalls a childhood encounter with one of the beings – popularly known as 'the greys' – who are conducting the abductions. Many (by no means all) abduction testimonies are provided during hypnosis. Since the memories of such experiences are allegedly so traumatic (John Mack coined the term 'ontological shock' to describe the effect),[42] abductees typically 'bury' these memories in their unconscious, masking them with 'screen memories'. This typically results in testimonies that routinely blur the distinctions between dream, fantasy, hallucination, imagination, and waking consciousness. While hypnotized, Strieber recalled a memory of an incident that took place at his grandmother's house in 1967.

> I thought at first it was like a skeleton on a motorcycle or something. It was flying – no, it wasn't flying. I could just see it, and I see it almost does, really does, look like a praying mantis, only bigger. It's got great big eyes that just scare the hell out of you. Scare you real bad. Big, big eyes.[43]

Despite the relatively homogenous representation of the alien abductors that emerged throughout the 1980s and into the 1990s, variants do exist. Many of these, however, are distinguished from the most conventional portrayals simply through their exaggeration of existing aesthetic codes, and primarily, the codes of anthropomorphism. Some hark back to the Aryan 'space brothers' typical of the 'contactee' reports of the 1950s, or else seem consistent with the evil, anthropomorphized reptilian aliens most famously portrayed in the television mini-series, *V* (1983). In Joe Lewels's *The God Hypothesis: Extraterrestrial Life and its Implications for Science and Religion* (1997), for example, a number of distinct types of variant aliens are described, including the 'Tall Blondes' and the

---

[41] Ibid., pp. 24–5.
[42] J. Mack, *Abduction: Human Encounters with Aliens* (London: Simon and Schuster, 1995), p. 44.
[43] Strieber, *Communion*, p. 156.

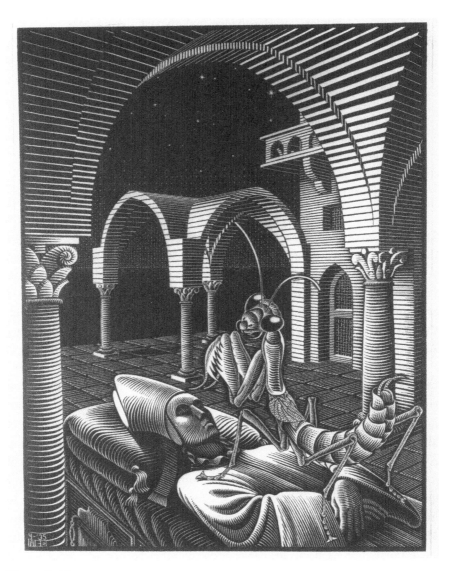

Figure 2: Dream

'Reptilians'. Within the abduction narratives, these beings seem to play a more subtle and mysterious role than the explicit pseudomedical activities carried out by 'the greys'. Of particular interest is a third variant, described by Lewels as the 'Praying Mantises', which seem to fulfil the Greek etymology of 'mantis' as diviner or prophet. The appearance of the mantis beings and the manner in which they, with the greys, effect a kind of ego death for the abductees, recalls both Caillois' 'legendary psychasthenia' and the paralyzing gaze of Fabre's mantis. Here, it is the alien gaze that functions to transform the human subject, now cast as a 'specimen':

> The Mantis type is also reported to participate in the "staring" procedure which has been described by various researchers, particularly Dr. David Jacobs of Temple University in his book *Secret Life*. This procedure involves a being placing its face "nose to nose" with the abductee and engaging in prolonged staring directly into the human's eyes. The effect, as described by those who have experienced it, is totally shattering to the human ego. Abductees often comment that it is as if "my mind and my soul were completely swallowed up by those eyes."[44]

There is, then, a kind of esoteric triangle involving insects, fairies, and aliens that we can observe in an historical context. During the nineteenth century, accounts of insects begin to resemble accounts of fairies, and fairies begin to resemble insects. In the twentieth century, accounts of aliens begin to resemble accounts of fairies, which in turn already resemble those of insects; the insect, the fairy, and alien reciprocate with one another in visible, if subtle ways. Among all of this, one insect tends to figure consistently: the praying mantis.

The figure of the mantis visibly surfaces in what can be seen as a 'modern myth in the making' that routinely hybridizes content from a range of sources: entomology, science fiction, and horror, Surrealist imagery, psychoanalysis, and non-ordinary states of consciousness. This hybridity takes shape in the figure of 'the grey' – an enigmatic creature who, incidentally, has been reported as participating in human-alien hybrid programs aboard UFOs.[45] In their aesthetic debt to images of insect life (where mimicry is commonplace), the greys are never quite what they seem, retaining what Caillois calls the 'primitive' tendency to imitate, combined with 'a belief in the efficacy of this imitation'.[46] As the late John Mack wrote in *Abduction*, based on the testimonies of numerous patients, 'the aliens themselves seem able to change or disguise their form, and ... may appear initially to the abductees as various kinds of animals, or even as ordinary human beings'.[47] As with insects, mimicry seems inherent to the aliens' raison d'être.

There is at least one more dimension to this strange arrangement, and this is the insect's – in particular, the mantid's – contemporary appearance

---

[44] Ibid., pp. 173–4.
[45] See, for example, D. Jacobs, *Secret Life: Firsthand Documented Accounts of UFO Abductions* (New York: Fireside/Simon and Schuster, 1992).
[46] Caillois, 'Mimicry and Legendary Psychasthenia', p. 27.
[47] Mack, *Abduction*, p. 396.

in testimonies of hallucinations and visions experienced under the influence of N,N-dimethyltryptamine, the most powerful hallucinogen (or entheogen) currently known.[48] The most recent clinical trials of DMT were performed by Rick Strassman in New Mexico and reported in his book, *DMT: The Spirit Molecule*. Strassman was interested in testing the hypothesis that there was a chemical basis for religious or 'visionary' experiences, and speculated that DMT might be produced spontaneously in the human pineal gland, thus accounting for so-called 'near death' or 'out of body' experiences. A fundamental challenge faced by Strassman was collating the diversity of DMT experiences; however, there were some consistencies across the many accounts. Strassman reports: 'We regularly heard comments such as "My body dissolved; I was pure awareness" and "I no longer had a body"'.[49] Between 1990 and 1995, Strassman had intravenously administered four hundred doses of DMT in various strengths to more than sixty volunteers in seven studies.[50] A number of his test subjects reported intense and highly vivid interaction with humanoid beings who exhibited insect-like features. One participant, 'Rex', stated:

When I was first going under there were these insect creatures all around me. They were clearly trying to break through. I was fighting letting go of who I am or was. The more I fought, the more demonic they became, probing into my psyche and being. I finally started letting go of parts of myself, as I could no longer keep so much of me together … As I accepted my death and dissolution into God's love, the insectoids began to feed on my heart, devouring the feelings of love and surrender. They were interested in emotion. As I was holding on to my last thought, that God equals love, they said, "Even here? Even here?" I said, "Yes, of course." They were still there but I was making love to them at the same time. They feasted as they made love to me. I don't know if they were male or female or something else, but it was extremely alien, though not necessarily unpleasant. The thought came to me with certainty that they were manipulating my DNA, changing its structure.[51]

---

[48] Strassman summarizes DMT as follows: 'DMT is a psychedelic substance found with great consistency within many living creatures, from psychoactive plants to the human body. Though we can describe its chemistry and pharmacology using the traditional tools and language of science, the subjective experiences of DMT are more difficult to place into a conceptual framework. Furthermore, its endogenicity and special but unknown role in normal brain function suggest that DMT exerts an impact on both extraordinary states of awareness during our lives and our fundamental perception of these lives'. R. Strassman, S. Wojtowicz, L. Eduardo, and E. Frecska, *Inner Paths to Outer Space: Journeys to Alien Worlds through Psychedelics and Other Spiritual Technologies* (Rochester, VT: Park Street Press, 2008), p. 80.

[49] R. Strassman, *DMT: The Spirit Molecule* (Rochester, VT: Park Street Press, 2001), p. 53.

[50] Ibid., p. 48.

[51] Ibid., pp. 68–9.

Another account is found in Daniel Pinchbeck's *Breaking Open the Head: A Psychedelic Journey into the Heart of Contemporary Shamanism*:

> Ten minutes later, John smoked the glass pipe, fell back, and went out. He came back screaming "We are! We are!" over and over again, until the lights in the other hotel rooms flicked on. A being had shown him its whirring praying mantis legs, he said. He saw a female entity sitting at something that looked like a computer. He told us how he had set free a praying mantis when he was five. The praying mantis had turned to look back at him before it hopped away, and at that moment he knew, with complete and utter certainty. He knew that the mantis knew him.[52]

These testimonials, which are subject to even less scholarly analysis than alien abduction accounts and are in the process of emerging, should always be taken in context as the earnest accounts of highly abnormal experiences which inherently expose the descriptive limits of vocabulary. Mantids appear in many, but not all, reports of DMT experiences. Still, the data gathered by Strassman was consistent enough for him to observe: 'These "beyond the veil" experiences share much with alien-abduction literature as it has been summarized by the late Harvard psychiatrist John Mack in his book *Abduction*'.[53]

V. Conclusion

What I have attempted in this chapter is an overview of the cultural history of the praying mantis that outlines some of the most salient ways the praying mantis has figured in the 'numinous imagination' as kind of daemonic insect. Unlike Caillois, I maintain that perceptions of, and emotional responses to, the mantis have their basis in cultural conditions. Praying mantids are real animals that exist in the manifold spaces of the natural world, whether we believe in them or not. But *what* we believe about them, as their cultural history shows, can vary significantly over time and, moreover, is constantly changing. We have yet much to learn about the praying mantis – and perhaps the praying mantis, in ways of which we are only now becoming conscious – has much to teach us.

---

[52] D. Pinchbeck, *Breaking Open the Head: A Psychedelic Journey into the Heart of Contemporary Shamanism* (New York: Broadway Books, 2003), p. 244.
[53] Strassman, Wojtowicz, Luna, and Frecska, *Inner Paths*, p. 73.

Bibliography

Avramescu, C., *An Intellectual History of Cannibalism* (A. I. Blyth (trans.); Princeton and Oxford: Princeton University Press, 2009).

Bown, N., *Fairies in Nineteenth-Century Art and Literature* (Cambridge: Cambridge University Press, 2001).

Caillois, R., 'Mimicry and Legendary Psychasthenia', *October* 31 (1984) (J. Shepley (trans.)), pp. 16–32.

—'The Praying Mantis: From Biology to Psychoanalysis', *The Edge of Surrealism: A Roger Caillois Reader* (C. Frank (ed.); Durham and London: Duke University Press, 2003), pp. 69–81.

Carroll, N., *The Philosophy of Horror; or, Paradoxes of the Heart* (New York: Routledge, 1990).

Crist, E., *Images of Animals: Anthropomorphism and Animal Mind* (Philadelphia: Temple University Press, 1999).

Fabre, J. H., *Social Life in the Insect World* (B. Miall (trans.); London: T. Fisher Unwin, 1912).

Hogue, C. L., 'The Bugfolk', *Terra* 17.4 (1979), pp. 36–8.

Jacobs, D.M., *Secret Life: Firsthand Documented Accounts of UFO Abductions* (New York: Fireside/Simon and Schuster, 1992).

Kelley-Romano, S., 'Mythmaking in Alien Abduction Narratives', *Communication Quarterly* 54.3 (2006), pp. 383–406.

Kirby, W., and W. Spence, *An Introduction to Entomology: or Elements of the Natural History of Insects* (vol. 1, 3rd edn; London: Longman, Hurst, Rees, Orme and Brown, 1818).

Legros, G. V., *Fabre, Poet of Science* (B. Miall (trans.); London: T. Fisher Unwin, 1913).

Lewels, J., *The God Hypothesis: Extraterrestrial Life and its Implications for Science and Religion* (Mill Spring, NC: Wildflower Press, 1997).

Linnaeus, C., *Systema naturae per regna tria naturae: secundum classes, ordines, genera, species, cum characteribus, differentiis, synonymis, locis* (10th edn, 1758).

Mack, J. E., *Abduction: Human Encounters with Aliens* (London: Simon and Schuster, 1995).

Markus, R., 'Surrealism's Praying Mantis and Castrating Woman', *Woman's Art Journal* 21.1 (2000), pp. 33–9.

Muffet, T., *The Theater of Insects*: E. Topsell, *The History of Four-footed Beasts and Serpents* (London, 1658).

Nicholls, A., *Goethe's Concept of the Daemonic: After the Ancients* (Rochester, NY: Camden House, 2006).

Otto, R., *The Idea of the Holy: An Inquiry into the Non-Rational Factor in the Idea of the Divine and its Relation to the Rational* (J. W. Harvey (trans.); Oxford: Oxford University Press, 1936).

Pinchbeck, D., *Breaking Open the Head: A Psychedelic Journey into the Heart of Contemporary Shamanism* (New York: Broadway Books, 2003).

Pressly, W. L., 'The Praying Mantis in Surrealist Art', *The Art Bulletin* 55.4 (1973), pp. 600–15.

Prete, F. R., and M. M. Wolfe., 'Religious Supplicant, Seductive Cannibal, or Reflex Machine? In Search of the Praying Mantis', *Journal of the History of Biology* 21.1 (1992), pp. 91–136.

Shepardson, D. P., 'Bugs, Butterflies, and Spiders: Children's Understandings about Insects', *International Journal of Science Education* 24 (2002), pp. 627–43.

Silver, C. G., *Strange and Secret Peoples: Fairies and Victorian Consciousness* (Oxford: Oxford University Press, 1999).

Stewart, S., *On Longing: Narratives of the Miniature, the Gigantic, the Souvenir, the Collection* (Durham, NC: Duke University Press, 1993).

Strassman, R., *DMT: The Spirit Molecule* (Rochester, VT: Park Street Press, 2001).

Strassman, R., S. Wojtowicz, L. Eduardo, and E. Frecska, *Inner Paths to Outer Space: Journeys to Alien Worlds through Psychedelics and Other Spiritual Technologies* (Rochester, VT: Park Street Press, 2008).

Strieber, W., *Communion: A True Story* (New York: Avon, 1987).

Tsai, J. H., 'Entomology in the People's Republic of China', *Journal of the New York Entomological Society* 90.3 (1982), pp. 186–212.

6

Benevolent Bulls and Baleful Buffalos: Male Bovines versus the 'Holy Cow' in Hinduism

Xenia Zeiler

In Hindu religious traditions, animals play a very significant role for several reasons. One important aspect of the veneration given to animals, and, accordingly, one reason for their incorporation in ritual and worship, is the representation of 'deified' animals as escorts and companions of deities throughout Hindu mythology. This practice can be traced back to the very beginning of textual traditions in South Asia when Vedic mythology already included animals in the pantheon. Especially in the later Hindu concept of *vāhana* ('vehicle, draught-animal, carriage-animal') animals are understood to be much more than just mounts; they are incorporated in the pantheon as close attendants to deities and act as their assistants in the everlasting battle against evil. In general, every Hindu deity is connected to a certain *vāhana*, a deified animal companion. The close bond between the specific animal and the respective deity is shown clearly not only in mythology, but also in iconography and ritual, where a deity and its accompanying animal are very often positioned side by side. Hindu religious traditions from the Epic period onward (from around the third to the second century BC) repeatedly place animals in prominent positions on par with anthropomorphic deities.

Following preliminary remarks on the general position, status, and function of animals as part of the Hindu pantheon, iconography, and ritual practice and on their religious authorization in these fields, this article analyzes details from representations of male Bovinae. By accentuating the male bull and buffalo over the much-discussed 'holy cow' in Hinduism,[1] the chapter aims at discussing

---

[1] Much has been written and (controversially) discussed on the 'holy cow' in Hinduism. Important and debated works include L. Alsdorf, *The History of Vegetarianism and Cow-Veneration in India* (W. Bollée (ed.); B. Patil (trans.); revised by N. Hayton; London and New York: Routledge, 2010); S. Batra, 'The Sacredness of the Cow in India', *Social Compass* 33.2–3 (1986), pp. 163–75; and

a broader perspective of sacred bovine animals in Hindu religious traditions, be they deified or demonized. Central questions discussed here are: why did certain bovine animals gain special significance in Hinduism and why are some more popular than others? Can we trace a pattern of how and why certain bovines are affiliated with certain Hindu deities? How, exactly, are male bovines represented in Hinduism and can we distinguish 'gender patterns' in representations of male bovine and the female 'holy cow'? This chapter focuses on bulls and male buffalos in Hindu mythology, iconography, and ritual and highlights their affiliation to two major Hindu deities. The god Śiva and the goddess Durgā are constantly connected to the bull and the buffalo, respectively.

I. Animals in Hindu Mythology, Iconography, and Ritual

Animals have been part of religious traditions in South Asia for a very long period. Already the oldest high culture in the region, the Indus Valley civilization flourishing *c.* 2500–1750 BC, depicted a large number of animals in apparently religious contexts. As the Indus script has yet to be deciphered, we have to rely on archaeological findings for information on social, cultural, and religious structures of this civilization. Among the major archaeological findings that give evidence of the religious belief system are square steatite seals. Up to the present, numerous such seals have been found showing animals on their own, arranged with objects (sometimes interpreted as ritual objects), with other animals, or with anthropomorphic figures. Animals depicted on seals or as statuettes in possibly religious contexts include both wild animals, such as the elephant, the tiger, or the rhinoceros, and domesticated animals, such as the bull or cow. Though there are indications of a widespread veneration of these animals at the time, we cannot verify if they were considered deified or sacred.

In the period following the Indus civilization, a new dominant cultural system developed in early South Asia: the Vedic civilization flourishing *c.*1750–500 BC. Indo-Iranian nomadic tribes invaded the northern parts of the subcontinent in several migration waves from Central Asia or the Caucasus

D. Jha, *The Myth of the Holy Cow* (London: Verso, 2002). For a detailed summary and discussion of the 'sacred cow debate' in social and cultural sciences and for a bibliography on cows in Hindu religious traditions, see F. Korom, 'Holy Cow! The Apotheosis of Zebu, or Why the Cow Is Sacred in Hinduism', *Asian Folklore Studies* 59.2 (2000), pp. 181–203. For important examples from this debate, see A. Heston, 'An Approach to the Sacred Cow of India', *Current Anthropology* 12.2 (1971), pp. 191–209; and F. Simoons et al., 'Questions in the Sacred-Cow Controversy [and Comments and Reply]', *Current Anthropology* 20.3 (1979), pp. 467–93.

and brought with them a complex mythology, a rich pantheon, and rituals based on Indo-European religious beliefs. They produced texts still held in high regard in present Hinduism, most notably the Vedas. Vedic literature gives a clearer, though ambivalent, picture of the position and function of animals in the religious belief system. Mythology includes animals in the pantheon and speaks, for instance, of deities' chariots drawn by horses, of desired bull qualities in gods, of doves as messengers of a goddess, etc. But, even though mythology repeatedly refers to animals as (positively) close to deities, there are few indications of actual animal worship in the Vedic period.

In addition, Vedic ritual practice points to a rather pragmatic approach towards animals. Vedic ritual essentially is one of fire sacrifice. This practice centres on food offerings, both vegetarian and non-vegetarian, which are placed in the ritual fire. The meat of several animals, including cattle and sheep, was ritually offered along with vegetarian products, such as butter, honey, and beverages, including milk and the intoxicant drink soma. *Ahiṃsā* ('non-harming' or 'nonviolence'), a concept with much influence in later Hindu and Buddhist religious traditions, was certainly not yet prevalent in early Vedic society.[2] It first appeared in later Vedic literature, for instance in the Upaniṣads, as part of a process which reformed Vedic religious thought and practice, especially ritual, and which finally lead to classical and modern Hinduism.

The development of *ahiṃsā* as one of the major foundations for most Hindu traditions was not the only significant change in the position, status, and function of animals in South Asia: the Hindu concept of *vāhana* was very influential as well. This important concept first appeared in Purāṇic literature from about the sixth century onward. From this time on, Hinduism regularly pairs deities with one or several animal companions or attendants. In mythology, iconography, and ritual alike, those animals regarded as *vāhanas* are attributed a deified status similar to that of anthropomorphic deities. At times this goes as far as to present certain animals as religious subjects in their own right, without accentuating the link to their affiliated deity in certain mythological, iconographical, or ritual contexts. This is true for many important *vāhanas*, as for the bull discussed here. The most significant and well-known example for this kind of religious 'animal autonomy' surely is the cow.

Nevertheless, a hierarchical order placing *vāhanas* in a subordinate or serving position to their deity masters is common. In the *vāhana* concept, deities

---

[2] For more information on the early development of *ahiṃsā* and for the institutionalization of the concept, see K. Jacobsen, 'The Institutionalization of the Ethics of 'Non-Injury towards All Beings in Ancient India', *Environmental Ethics* 16.3 (1994), pp. 287–302.

basically authorize the sacredness and deification of their animal companions. But the connection is reciprocal and also works the other way round: animal attendants are major symbols and emblems in the pantheon. They are consistently depicted in a key position supporting and even distinguishing a deity, and they are highly revered in Hinduism. Mythology gives much space to *vāhanas*: for instance, numerous mythological stories explain why a certain animal was associated with a certain deity. In iconography, *vāhanas* are mostly depicted alongside their deity masters or mistresses. At times, they are the only reliable mark helping to identify the deity in question. In ritual and popular worship, the *vāhana* and deity are often worshipped side by side.

Animals are of religious importance in Hindu traditions also in ways beyond the *vāhana* concept. This applies to both deified and living animals:

> A sacred animal in Hinduism is a divine being in animal form or with animal features, or a living animal that is worshipped and religiously valued. ... However, the divine beings in animal form do not become completely separated from the living species they represent. The sacredness of the divinity in animal form spills over to the living animals.[3]

Important sacred animals in Hindu traditions, besides the ones discussed in this article in detail, include the cow, the elephant, the monkey, the snake, and birds, such as the peacock, the swan, or the owl.[4] Besides these, animal deities may have zoocephalic forms in Hinduism. Such hybrid human-animal deities show a human body and an animal head as, for instance, the very popular gods Gaṇeśa and Hanumān.[5]

The deep reverence given to animals in Hindu religious traditions, in general, and the fact that this respect for animals is not limited to deified or sacred animals but is largely applied to living animals as well, was often interpreted as remarkable tolerance. The ethical dimension of animal reverence and worship in Hinduism is strongly interconnected with plant reverence and worship. The most important foundations for both are the underlying Hindu ideas that humans, animals, and plants share a common living (and religious) sphere and

---

[3] K. Jacobsen, 'Sacred Animals', *Brill's Encyclopedia of Hinduism, Vol. 1: Regions, Pilgrimage, Deities* (K. Jacobsen (ed.); Leiden: Brill, 2009), pp. 711–18 (711).

[4] For an overview on these individual animals in Hinduism, see for instance, K. Jacobsen, 'Sacred Animals', or N. Krishna, *Sacred Animals of India* (Delhi and London: Penguin Books, 2010).

[5] For a further discussion of the iconography and its symbolic and historical dimensions of Gaṇeśa, see A. Narain, 'Gaṇeśa: A Protohistory of the Idea and the Icon', *Ganesh. Studies of an Asian God* (R. Brown (ed.); Albany: State University of New York, 1991), pp. 19–48; for Hanumān, see I. Keul, *Hanuman, der Gott in Affengestalt. Entwicklung und Erscheinungsformen seiner Verehrung* (Berlin and New York: De Gruyter, 2002) and P. Lutgendorf, *Hanuman's Tale: The Messages of a Divine Monkey* (New York and Oxford: Oxford University Press, 2006).

that all are an expression of divinity.[6] Thus, ethical and ecological issues go hand in hand in most Hindu traditions.

II. The Bull in Ancient South Asian Iconography, Mythology, and Ritual

Bulls have been evidentially present in South Asian religious traditions for about five thousand years.[7] The oldest depictions of bulls in religious contexts on the subcontinent date from the Indus Valley period, from *c.* 2500–1750 BC. The Indus Valley civilization passed down numerous depictions of bulls, mainly on the steatite square seals typical for the culture.[8] Two motives stand out among these: first, bulls are shown alone with objects interpreted as ritual utensils; second, bulls are depicted along with other animals, often as part of a group of four – tiger, elephant, rhinoceros, and bull.[9] On most of these seals, the animals surround a figure seated in a position interpreted as a yoga posture. In addition, the (probably male) figure shows one more reference to bulls: he wears a headdress with spacious and broad horns, probably bull horns.[10] Several seals with such depictions have been found. A debate arose over the possible interpretation of this figure as a pre-form of the later prominent Hindu deity Śiva constantly connected to the bull (a 'Proto-Śiva').[11] Though the bull is only one

---

[6] See Jacobsen, 'Sacred Animals', p. 717. For a discussion of nature in traditional Hinduism, see A. Michaels, 'Notions of Nature in Traditional Hinduism', *Environment Across Cultures* (E. Ehlers, and C. Gethmann (eds); Berlin-Heidelberg: Springer, 2003), pp. 111–22. For Hinduism and ecology and for the sacred cow's position in it, see C. Robinson, and D. Cush, 'The Sacred Cow: Hinduism and Ecology', *Journal of Beliefs & Values* 18.1 (1997), pp. 25–37.

[7] For an overview on the bull in religious traditions worldwide, see B. Sax, *The Mythical Zoo: An Encyclopedia of Animals in World Myth, Legend, and Literature* (Santa Barbara: ABC-Clio, 2001), pp. 44–52; and H. Werness, *The Continuum Encyclopedia of Animal Symbolism in Art* (New York and London: Continuum, 2006), pp. 56–61.

[8] For other prominent archaeological findings, namely for bulls' ears, horns, hooves, and tails depicted on copper or clay platelets, or for clay masks with modelled bulls' ears and horns, see E. During Caspers, 'Rituals and Belief Systems in the Indus Valley Civilisation', *Ritual, State and History in South Asia: Essays in Honour of J. C. Heesterman* (A. Van den Hoeck, D. Kolff, and M. Oort (eds); Leiden: Brill, 1992), pp. 102–27 (107–8).

[9] For an interpretation of the bull as buffalo in such scenarios, see A. Hiltebeitel, 'The Indus Valley "Proto-Śiva", Reexamined through Reflections on the Goddess, the Buffalo, and the Symbolism of Vāhana', *Anthropos* 73.5–6 (1978), pp. 767–97. Also During Caspers prefers this reading, see 'Rituals and Belief Systems', p. 110.

[10] For an alternative reading of the headdress as buffalo horns, see Hiltebeitel, 'The Indus Valley "Proto-Śiva"', pp. 771–3.

[11] For a discussion and summary of this debate, see D. Srinivasan, 'The So-called Proto-Śiva Seal from Mohenjo-Daro: An Iconological Assessment', *Archives of Indian Art* 29 (1975–6), pp. 47–58; and D. Srinivasan, 'Unhinging Śiva from the Indus Civilization', *Journal of the Royal Asiatic Society of Great Britain and Ireland* (1984), pp. 77–89.

of several indicators, which seem to link the Indus figure on the seal with the Hindu god, it remains highly speculative to directly connect both. Irrespective of this, the bull was obviously revered already in the Indus Valley culture and most probably played an important role in its religious traditions.

This can be verified with reference to Vedic religious tradition and mythology. In general, Vedic texts refer to the bull as a representation of fertility and physical strength.[12] The most prominent gods of Vedic times, predominantly Indra, are described as having well regarded and desired bull qualities.[13] However, Vedic literature does not speak of bulls as deified or sacred, and they are not depicted as such in either mythology or ritual. On the contrary, a number of Vedic texts refer to bull slaughter and eating in non-ritual and, more seldom, ritual contexts. The oldest Vedic text, the Ṛgveda, dated 1750–1200 BC, for instance, depicts the major deities Indra and Agni as eaters of bulls[14] and speaks of slaughtering bulls for food.[15] Later Vedic texts give several examples of bull sacrifices and killings and of feastings on beef, which are recommended on special occasions, such as weddings, ancestor rituals, or regalement for distinguished guests.[16] It is thus debated whether the high rank of the bull already present in the ancient periods of South Asia in both Indus and Vedic civilizations formed the basis for the animals' prominent position in Hindu religious traditions. Though there are also indications of early bull reverence and esteem in religious contexts, there is no clear archaeological or textual evidence of a deification or even sacredness of the animal in this historical period in South Asia.

III. Nandī, the Sacred Bull

From around the third to the second century BC, a new historical period in South Asia commenced, including a new canon of literature and religious thought that later led to the development of Hindu religious traditions. Of course, these changes did not appear out of the blue. Classical Epic Hindu traditions drew on their antecedents on the subcontinent, just as today Hinduism still is based on

---

[12] For an introduction on bulls in Vedic literature and for a discussion of possible associations between bulls and mares in ancient Indo-European mythology, see W. O'Flaherty, *Women, Androgynes, and Other Mythical Beasts* (Chicago and London: Chicago University Press, 1980), pp. 241–4.

[13] See, for instance, Ṛgveda, VIII.19.

[14] Ṛgveda, X.86.13–14, respectively Ṛgveda, VIII.43.11.

[15] Ṛgveda, X.89.14.

[16] For a summary of citations on this matter and for the exact textual references from Brāhmaṇa, Sūtra and Smṛti literature, see M. Chakravarti, *The Concept of Rudra-Śiva through the Ages* (Delhi: Motilal Banarsidass, 1994), pp. 92–4.

older traditions and religious ideas passed down through history. Epic literature, unsurprisingly, shows a blend of innovative and even ground-breaking ideas, as well as building on previous religious ideas. Nevertheless, the two big epics of ancient India, Rāmāyaṇa and Mahābhārata, established a new religious age in South Asia, and they essentially shaped the developments leading to modern Hinduism. In general, this is true for almost all mythological, iconographical, and ritual aspects and more so for the perception of sacred animals.

From Epic times onward, from around the third to the second century BC, the bull is constantly incorporated in mythology, iconography, and ritual as sacred. In classical as well as in recent and contemporary Hinduism, the bull undoubtedly is one of the most popular sacred animals. It is important to specify here that Hindu religious traditions distinguish between different species of cattle. Though most of them are revered, it is especially the Zebu bull, Bos Indicus, which is considered sacred. This is most evident in one specific mythological bull figure, Nandī ('the happy one'), who is considered the *vāhana* of one of the most important Hindu deities, Śiva. Both inseparably belong together: the bull is only very seldom shown as the *vāhana* of another deity than Śiva, and he is by far the most important animal connected to this god.

Śiva is an integral god in Hinduism. He is part of the often so-called 'triad' or 'trinity' in the Hindu pantheon, *trimūrti* ('three-form'), including the male deities Brahma, Viṣṇu and Śiva. In this concept he is ascribed one major responsibility in the circle of life and death: he is believed to destroy life at the end of each cosmic circle, thus producing room for new creation. Of course, this is only one of the manifold agencies ascribed to Śiva in Hindu religious traditions. In mythology and ritual, the god is depicted in a variety of ways ranging from a meditating ascetic to a caring and loving husband and father. As an ascetic, he is depicted in mythology and iconography as Mahāyogin ('great practitioner of *yoga*') and is considered the ideal archetype of a sage leading a life of renunciation. In the context of his family, Śiva is shown as a husband encouraging the autonomy of his wife, as her very potent lover, and as a supporting father to his two sons. In either case, the god's *vāhana* Nandī is placed at his side (and often at the side of the family).

Hindu mythology gives a number of different origin stories for Nandī. Epic and several important Purāṇic texts speak of Nandī's birth and of the circumstances of him being connected to Śiva. The epics Mahābhārata[17] relates a story of how an important mythological figure, Dakṣa Prajāpati, offered a bull to Śiva

---

[17] Mahābhārata, Anuśāsanaparvan.

in order to appease him. Śiva accepted the gift and after some time made the bull his permanent *vāhana*. Later, in Purāṇic literature from around the fifth century onward, Nandī is taken up frequently as a mythological figure. Influential origin myths are included in the Śivapurāṇa and the Skandapurāṇa. The Śivapurāṇa[18] narrates how the sage Sālankāyana conducted hard ascetic practices in order to obtain a son. The god Viṣṇu pleased by the austerities granted the wish by creating the desired son out of himself. While appearing before the sage, Nandī (here called Nandīkeśvara) sprang from the right side of Viṣṇu as an anthropomorphic figure of a human with a bull's head. Nandī is immediately connected to Śiva in this narration, as the text expatiates on the strong resemblance of Nandī with Śiva. According to the Skandapurāṇa,[19] Dharma ('duty, justice, law, virtue'), the personified god of law and duty responsible for upholding the righteous order of the world, declared that he would assume the form of a bull and become the *vāhana* of Śiva. As he is believed to have done so, Nandī is also understood to be a defender and upholder of the *dharma* principle in modern Hinduism.

Nandī also repeatedly figures in Hindu texts, especially in Purāṇic literature, beyond the frame of origin myths. Mythology clearly denotes Nandī as chief of Śiva's *gaṇa* ('flock, troop, attendants'). As such and as defender of *dharma*, he carries a staff representing both the importance and specific character of his official position. The Śivapurāṇa, for instance, describes Nandī as he enters a mythological scene on his aerial chariot:

> He sat under a royal umbrella with a gemset handle, resembling the pure moon. He had three eyes. Even by his gestures he reminded one of the lord. He appeared like the untransgressable behest of the creator. He was one who blessed all. He stood directly in front of Śiva. He held an excellent trident. As the commander of the gaṇas he looked like another Viśveśvara *(another name of Śiva, the author)*. He could curb and bless the rulers of the universe. … He appeared like active efficiency. It seemed that the very salvation or the omniscient lord had come there.[20]

What is striking here is not only the way in which Nandī is elevated as a splendid, preeminent divine figure; it is also the very close connection to Śiva which gives him further sanction and authority. In this mythological passage, the bond between both almost goes so far as to identify Nandī with Śiva.

---

[18] Śivapurāṇa, Uttarāśatarudriyasaṃhitā, 3.
[19] Skandapurāṇa, Avantikhaṇḍa, 2.20.
[20] Śivapurāṇa, Vāyavīyasaṃhitā, 2, 41.28–32 in the translation of Shastri's edition 1995.

The interconnection and familiarity between Śiva and his chosen attendant also shows in another recurrent mythological motif. Nandī is frequently depicted as doorkeeper of Śiva's abode; in particular, he is assigned to guard the site (a bedroom, garden, or other location) of the god's lovemaking to his wife.[21] There are also several references to Nandī cursing or punishing Śiva's enemies or opponents[22] or actively battling them.[23] The Skandapurāṇa, for instance, depicts Nandī as a mighty warrior in a battle scene:

> The powerful Nandin caused great agitation among the Daityas and like a Śarabha (fabulous animal with eight feet) that seizes an elephant, he carried away Kāvya (Śukra) who was being protected by all the Daityas with nooses, swords, trees, boulders and rocks in their hands. The Asuras shouting with leonine roar followed him as though they would secure his release, even as he was caught by that powerful (Nandin) with the hairs dishevelled, ornaments dropped down and clothes slipping off. … the lord of the Gaṇas burned through the fire from his mouth, the hundreds of missiles. When the battle between the Asuras and the Devas became excessively fierce, he tormented the army of the enemies…[24]

Nevertheless, it is important to note, that even though Nandī may be depicted in mythology as acting without Śiva's direct orders, he never does so beyond a strictly defined boundary. Even in narratives where Nandī operates singly, he always stays restricted to a *vāhana* frame. Hindu mythology does not go beyond showing Nandī as an assistant or devotee of Śiva. This rather passive status is maintained in ritual and iconography as well. Though Nandī, of course, is included in the god's ritual as his *vāhana*, there is no indication of a single ritual procedure for the bull in classical Hindu texts. Nandī's worship and that of the sacred bull, in general, is inseparably intertwined with the worship of Śiva. This is clearly evident in iconography, as well. Statues or other iconographical depictions of Nandī alone are very rare. On the other hand, a statue of Nandī is found in nearly every temple of Śiva. Usually, the image is located in front of the sanctuary directly facing the main deity of the temple (see Figure 1). The bull may have a sanctuary of his own but is often placed in the open in a temple compound. At times, he is also depicted in *śaiva* goddess' temples next to Śiva (see Figure 2). Though authorized by the deity he accompanies, Nandī thus remains an ancillary associate or companion to the god in mythology, ritual, and iconography.

---

[21] For instance in Rāmāyaṇa, 7.16.1–10, Skandapurāṇa, 5.2.20.1–25 and 6.70–71 and Padmapurāṇa, 6.282.20–36. Quoted from O'Flaherty, *Women, Androgynes, and Other Mythical Beasts*, p. 253.

[22] For instance, in Śivapurāṇa, Rudrasamhitā, 26.19–54.

[23] For instance, in Skandapurāṇa, Kāśīkhaṇḍa, Pūrvārdha, 16.33–81.

[24] Skandapurāṇa, Kāśīkhaṇḍa, Pūrvārdha, 16.36–39, in the translation of Tagare's edition 2007.

Figure 1: Bronze Nandī facing the *liṅga* and included in its ritual in the temple of Ātmavīreśvar, Benares. Photograph by the author, September 2001.

Nandī's depiction in iconography is often rather naturalistic and unpretentious. Nandī is carved, drawn, sketched, etc. as a milk-white Zebu bull, Bos Indicus, with the characteristic hump on the back. There are only comparatively few examples of anthropomorphic depictions in iconography or mythology, representing Nandī as a human figure with a bull's head. Most frequently, he is shown as a bull, standing or lying down. In a lying position his left leg is usually bent, and at times this iconographic detail is included in popular ritual practice.[25] At several huge Nandī statues in India women wishing to have a child crawl through the hole of the bull's bent leg, which most likely points to notions of fertility attributed to the bull Nandī in popular belief. Commonly, he is adorned with some jewellery, often with necklaces and a bell or bells attached to his neck. At times, Nandī may be shown with a simply decorated coverlet or blanket, as well. As most *vāhanas*, he is far more than just a mount or vehicle. In iconography Nandī and Śiva are often placed side by side and the deity then rests his right arm on the back or hump of the bull.

[25] For an introduction to regional popular practices of worship and for festivals honouring Nandī, see Krishna, *Sacred Animals of India*, pp. 67–70.

Figure 2: Two white marble Nandīs incorporated in a compound with worshipped statues and *liṅgas* in the temple of the goddess Śītalā in Chetla, Kolkata. Photograph by the author, October 2011.

The strong bond between Nandī and Śiva has been interpreted primarily in two ways in academic research. First, the bull at Śiva's side was understood to be a reference to ancient ideas on fertility and potency related to the god.[26] This was often linked to Śiva's potential pre-forms, such as the 'Proto-Śiva' from the Indus civilization or the Vedic deity Rudra. Such links cannot be proven in detail. The second interpretation draws on ideas prevalent in Hindu religious traditions themselves. As Śiva is considered the Mahāyogin and ascetic par excellence, the bull's submission to him as his *vāhana* is also read as a metaphor for the god's conquest of his own animalistic passions or for (ascetically) controlled sexuality.[27] This belief may also illuminate why Nandī so constantly

[26] As one example of this interpretation, see Chakravarti, *The Concept of Rudra-Śiva through the Ages*, p. 101. He also names other supporters of this idea.

[27] As one example of this interpretation, see O'Flaherty, *Women, Androgynes, and Other Mythical Beasts*, p. 253. She also names other supporters of this idea.

is represented as the god's rather passive and submissive assistant and devotee throughout Hindu mythology, iconography, and ritual. Whatever the exact origins of pairing the god and the bull may be, we cannot verify them today. What is certain, nevertheless, is that from an early stage in Hinduism, from the very forming of the important deity Śiva onward, the sacred bull was placed at his side. And still today, Nandī is considered one of the most important animal companions in Hindu mythology, iconography, and ritual. This explicit divine authorization further contributed to the concept of the sacred bull that is most probably already inherent in ancient religious traditions of South Asia.

IV. Ambivalent Buffalos: Heroism, Danger, and Ritual Sacrifice

The high reverence given to the bull in Hindu traditions, especially in the deified form as Nandī, is not equally given to the buffalo. Though the buffalo, as much as the bull, had an ambivalent status including positive features in older South Asian religious traditions,[28] it is only seldom depicted in such a way in recent Hindu mythology, iconography, and ritual. In the Vedic textual tradition, buffalos do not figure as prominently as bulls or cows. For instance, while major deities, such as Indra, are often linked to bulls and bull qualities, they are only rarely associated with buffalos. The only Vedic god directly connected to a buffalo is Yama, who is described as the chief of the dead from the earliest Vedic texts onward, and who is perceived as the god of death in later Hinduism. This connection was established by the late Vedic period; it prevailed and the buffalo was attributed to Yama as his *vāhana* in the Hindu epics.[29] Buffalos, like bulls, were sacrificial animals in Vedic times.

There are indications, however, that the buffalo was worshipped by a number of pastoral tribes in South Asia from a very early period. Today, for instance, the pastoral Toda tribe in South India's Tamil Nadu still holds the buffalo to be sacred.[30] The buffalo is considered a totemic symbol by a small number of Central and South Indian tribes.[31] In Central and South India in particular,

---

[28] For an overview of the buffalo in religious traditions worldwide, especially North American Indian communities, see Werness, *The Continuum Encyclopedia of Animal Symbolism in Art*, pp. 55–6.

[29] For a discussion of Yama and his connection to the bull, see L. van den Bosch, 'Yama, the God on the Black Buffalo', *Visible Religion: Annual for Religious Iconography, Vol. 1: Commemorative Figures* (H. G. Kippenberg (ed.); Leiden: Brill, 1982), pp. 21–64.

[30] See, for instance, C. Berkson, *The Divine and Demoniac: Mahisa's Heroic Struggle with Durga* (Delhi: Oxford University Press, 1997), pp. 43–45; and Krishna, *Sacred Animals of India*, pp. 61–2.

[31] For the Kurubas, see Berkson, *The Divine and Demoniac*, p. 44. For the Gonds, see Krishna, *Sacred Animals of India*, pp. 62–3.

deified buffalos are included in local pantheons. Most of these figures have a highly ambivalent role: they are generally believed to be very heroic, but often a dangerous side is part of their representation as well.[32] In Hinduism, more so at the village or tribal level, such an ambiguity of deities in the intersection between benevolent and dangerous is not uncommon. Consequentially, many of these figures, including some buffalo deities, have very complex representations and multiple functions. One important example for such a multifaceted god is Mhasobā, who *inter alia* was a buffalo deity and is mainly worshipped by peasants in Western and Central India.[33]

Mhasobā (also called Mhaskobā) was a cattle deity of herding tribes in Central India, before he was transformed along with the living conditions of the people worshipping him. Along with the permanent settlement of the former cattle-raising worshippers and the alteration of their social and religious structures, including altered accentuations in the pantheon, processes of Sankritization contributed to the god's reconstruction and redefining.[34] Thus, Mhasobā is one major example of the changes in a deified buffalo's representation and function. In addition, he is one out of many examples of the (radical) transformation of 'folk' or popular non-urban deities in recent Hinduism resulting from sanskritized and brahmanical influence in general.[35] In the first stage, Mhasobā was identified with the well-known buffalo Mahiṣa of sanskritized brahmanical mythology.[36] In the second stage, Mhasobā was even merged with the major panhindu deity Śiva.[37] Thus, Mhasobā's buffalo background was successively concealed over a longer period of time. As a result of the process, the former minor, local deity was successfully incorporated into sanskritized and brahmanical Hinduism. This transformation was adjusted to

---

[32] For a short summary on present-day buffalo deities in South Asia and their highly ambivalent character, see, for instance, Berkson, *The Divine and Demoniac*, pp. 82–93; and Krishna, *Sacred Animals of India*, pp. 61–3.

[33] See G.-D. Sontheimer, *Pastoral Deities in Western India* (A. Feldhaus (trans.); New York and Oxford: Oxford University Press, 1989). For a shorter introduction to Mhasobā and the fluid transpositions between god, ghost, and demon in his representation based on Sontheimer's discussion, see Berkson, *The Divine and Demoniac*, pp. 85–93.

[34] See Sontheimer, *Pastoral Deities in Western India*, pp. 180–4.

[35] Such transformations of deities from formerly non-sanskritized and non-brahmanical traditions are widely accounted for – for tribal and village deities as much as for deities from alternative religious traditions and from the Tantric tradition. For one detailed example of the transformations of the Tantric goddess Dhūmāvatī, see X. Zeiler, 'Transformations in the Textual Tradition of Dhūmāvatī. Changes of the Tantric Mahāvidyā Goddess in Concept, Ritual, Function and Iconography', *Transformations and Transfer of Tantra in Asia and Beyond* (I. Keul (ed.); Berlin and New York: De Gruyter, 2012), pp. 165–94.

[36] See Berkson, *The Divine and Demoniac*, pp. 87–8, who also gives examples for this identification in certain locations.

[37] This process is traceable in both textual and lived tradition. See, for instance, Berkson *The Divine and Demoniac*, pp. 88–91.

social and religious changes, moving Mhasobā from an individual buffalo deity over a 'demonized' buffalo figure to a panhindu god without links to buffalos.

Interestingly, there are no indications that attempts were ever made to declare Mhasobā a buffalo *vāhana* of any deity, despite the fact that the buffalo is known as a *vāhana* in Hindu mythology. The buffalo is attributed to two deities: to Yama and, along with other animals, to the goddess Varāhī. It thus might seem consistent, at first glance, to redefine Mhasobā as a buffalo *vāhana* of, most probably, Śiva, since this god is already stably connected to a male bovine in Hindu mythology, iconography, and ritual. There are a number of possible points of contact between Nandī and Mhasobā. For instance, Śiva's established *vāhana* could have served quite easily as an identification figure for Mhasobā, or at least Mhasobā could have been declared a manifestation of Nandī. What probably prevented such a development is the firm embedding of the *vāhana* concept in sanskritized, brahmanical Hindu mythology. Obviously, it is one thing to identify a local deity with a popular panhindu deity who possesses enormous and increasing influence in tribal contexts; it is another thing to incorporate concepts from the Sanskrit high textual tradition into 'folk' religion, even if these concepts are well known.

The buffalo's ambivalent status in many 'folk' or non-sanskritized Hindu traditions is furthermore highlighted by the fact that he, unlike the bull, is still an important sacrificial animal today. In popular rituals including animal sacrifices, which are mainly given to a number of so-called *ugra* ('fierce, terrible, angry') goddesses in contemporary India, the male buffalo is a favourite (besides male goats). For instance, the Newars of Nepal still offer buffalos to Durgā or to goddesses identified as her manifestations in certain important festivals.[38] The killing of a buffalo is part of an appeasing ritual for the South Indian goddess Mara.[39] In South Indian villages, buffalos still today are considered the preferred sacrifice for goddesses.[40] They are ritually slain in festivals and on special occasions, for instance, to request healing from diseases.[41] Several tribal communities in Central and South India included and still include buffalo

---

[38] For blood sacrifices in Nepal, see A. Michaels, Blutopfer in Nepal', *Mythen des Blutes* (C. von Braun, and C. Wulf (eds); Frankfurt/Main: Campus, 2007), pp. 91–107.

[39] See Berkson, *The Divine and Demoniac*, p. 164.

[40] See E. Craddock, 'Reconstructing the Split Goddess as Śakti in a Tamil Village', *Seeking Mahādevī: Constructing Identities of the Hindu Great Goddess* (T. Pintchman (ed.); Albany: Albany University Press, 2001), pp. 145–98 (151–4); and Krishna, *Sacred Animals of India*, p. 61.

[41] For buffalo sacrifice in South India in order to appease goddesses connected to smallpox, see B. E. F. Beck, 'The Goddess and the Demon. A Local South Indian Festival and its Wider Context', *Autour de la Déesse Hindoue* (M. Biardeau (ed.); Paris: Éditions de l'École des Hautes Études en Sciences Sociales, 1981), pp. 83–136 (97); and A. Hiltebeitel, 'Rāma and Gilgamesh: The Sacrifices of the Water Buffalo and the Bull of Heaven', *History of Religions* 19.3 (1980), pp. 187–223 (188–200).

slaying in rituals at festivals or in times of epidemics.[42] Buffalo sacrifices in tribal contexts, especially, probably point to their pastoral background and at efforts to maintain human and agricultural fertility. In non-tribal Tamil village communities, the buffalo, more generally, is a symbol of power transferred to the goddess receiving the sacrifice.[43] But there is one more important reason why the buffalo of all animals is considered central to a number of Hindu goddesses' sacrificial rituals. It is revealed while analysing the most heroic and popular mythological deed of the goddess Durgā – the slaying of Mahiṣa.

V. The Buffalo and the Goddess: Mahiṣa and Durgā

What dominates the buffalo's representation in recent Hindu religious traditions is its identification with one important mythological figure. From about the fourth century onward, the buffalo-form of the *asura*[44] Mahiṣa ('great, powerful') has been continuously depicted in Hindu iconography. In mythology, the figure first appears (briefly) in the Mahābhārata.[45] The mythological motive of Mahiṣa is taken up in the Devīmāhātmya, the Devībhāgavatapurāṇa,[46] the Vāmanapurāṇa,[47] and the Vāmanapurāṇa.[48] First, the recurrent iconological motive of the (evil) *asura* Mahiṣa battling the (benign and superior) goddess Durgā is presented in detail in one of the most influential texts for the development of Hinduism, the

---

[42] Berkson, *The Divine and Demoniac*, pp. 164–8, 174–5, gives numerous examples. She also describes the usual ritual sequence involving a buffalo sacrifice. For a discussion and examples of a trend in the opposite direction, to substitute the buffalo with vegetarian offerings in tribal communities, see C. Mallebrein, 'When the Buffalo Becomes a Pumpkin: The Animal Sacrifice Contested', *Periphery and Centre: Studies in Orissan History, Religion and Anthropology* (G. Pfeffer (ed.); Delhi: Manohar, 2007), pp. 443–72.

[43] See Craddock, 'Reconstructing the Split Goddess as Śakti in a Tamil Village', p. 153.

[44] *Asuras* are a class of divine beings in Hindu mythology and are portrayed as opposed to the gods. Originally (as in some passages of older Vedic literature), *asuras* were believed to be another class of deities, besides the gods, without a strong negative connotation. This changed in later Vedic literature and since then *asuras* clearly have been perceived as evil spirits or demons. The everlasting battle between *devas* (deities) and *asuras*, that is, between good and evil, is the most important theme in Hindu mythology.

[45] Mahābhārata, 3.213–21. Here, Mahiṣa's killing is attributed to the male deity Skanda.

[46] Devībhāgavatapurāṇa, 5.2–20.

[47] Vāmanapurāṇa, 18–21.

[48] Vāmanapurāṇa, 89, 91–4. For a comparison of the four versions, see C. M. Brown, *The Triumph of the Goddess: The Canonical Models and Theological Visions of the Devī-Bhāgavata Purāṇa* (Delhi: Sri Satguru Publications, 1992), pp. 94–113.

Devīmāhātmya[49] section of the Mārkaṇḍeyapurāṇa.[50] The text stands out due to its complex and yet straightforward theology of an all-pervading female energy, personified as Durgā or Mahādevī ('great goddess'); the text, thus, constructs Hinduism's most important female deity up to the present.[51]

The mythological frame surrounding the final battle between the *asura* and the goddess begins with the empowering of Mahiṣa. As a result of intense ascetic practice, he gains supremacy over the three worlds and was granted a boon that he may be destroyed only by the hands of a female. Thus supposedly safe from all resistance, he established himself as ruler of all worlds including heaven. As the gods were deprived of their positions, they wandered about the world until a plan to annihilate Mahiṣa took shape. The male gods concentrated their powers, which emerged from them as rays of light, and bundled together, they created a female figure:

> Then from the face of Viṣṇu, filled with rage, came forth a great fiery splendor (*tejas*), (and also from the faces) of Brahmā and Śiva. And from the bodies of Indra and the other gods came forth a great fiery splendor ... That peerless splendor, born from the bodies of all the gods, unified, and pervading the triple world with her splendor, became a woman.[52]

The terrifying as well as overwhelmingly beautiful goddess was given a copy of each god's individual weapon and a lion as her *vāhana*. Thus supplied, she confronted Mahiṣa:

> The entire atmosphere was filled with her terrible noise, and with that measureless, overwhelming (noise) a great echo arose. All the worlds quaked, and the oceans shook. The earth trembled, and mountains tottered. ... Mahiṣāsura, having fumed in anger, "Ah, what is this?!," rushed toward the sound, surrounded by all the Asuras. Then he saw the Goddess, filling the triple world with her radiance, causing the earth to bow down at the tread of her feet, scratching the sky with her diadem."[53]

---

[49] For an excellent translation and analysis of the text, including its historical context, and for a discussion of the embedded theological structure, see T. Coburn, *Encountering the Goddess: A Translation of the Devī-Māhātmya and A Study of Its Interpretation* (Delhi: Sri Satguru Publications, 1992). For a shorter introduction of these same topics, see T. Coburn 'Devī. The Great Goddess', *Devī: Goddesses of India* (J. Hawley, J. Stratton, and D. Wulff (eds); Berkeley and Los Angeles: California University Press, 1996), pp. 31–48.

[50] Mārkaṇḍeyapurāṇa, 81–93.

[51] For just one example out of many of the contemporary relevance and living tradition of the text, see K. McLain, 'Holy Superheroine: A Comic Book Interpretation of the Hindu Devī Māhātmya Scripture', *Bulletin of SOAS* 71.2 (2008), pp. 297–322.

[52] Devīmāhātmya, 2.9–2.12, in the translation of Coburn, 'Devī. The Great Goddess'.

[53] Devīmāhātmya, 2.31–2.37, in the translation of Coburn, *Encountering the Goddess*.

Figure 3: Durgā attacking Mahiṣa, a human figure with a buffalo head. Relief from *c.* the seventh to the eighth century, Mahiṣamardinī cave, Mamallapuram. Photograph by the author, March 2010.

The battle began and after killing several of his generals, the goddess attacked Mahiṣa (see Figure 3). He continually changed his shape in the course of battle, trying to escape Durgā's weapons. Though Mahiṣa took many forms before he was slain in a buffalo form, none of his human or animal transformations became as influential as the last. It is the buffalo that is perceived as synonymous with Mahiṣāsura, one of Hindu mythology's best-known baleful, evil, and presumptuous figures. Consequentially, Mahiṣāsura is frequently called the 'buffalo-demon' throughout Hindu mythology and popular belief. And it is exactly in this mythological background that we find one important reason for buffalo sacrifice to the goddess. At festivals, especially at Navarātri ('nine nights'), the battle between the *asura* and the warrior goddess, perceived as a symbol for the general everlasting battle between evil and virtue, is annually ritually (re)staged. The festival, which is celebrated to mark the nine days and nights of battle,[54] may include buffalo sacrifices in order to enact Durgā's final victory. The Devīmāhātmya describes it such:

> When his own army was thus being destroyed, Mahiṣāsura in his own buffalo form caused [the Goddess's] troops to tremble. Some [he slew] with the blow of his snout, others with the stamping of his hooves; others [were] lashed with his tail, still others torn by his horns. ... Having seen the onrushing Asura, Caṇḍikā [*another name of Durgā*] got angry in order to slay him. Hurling a snare at him, she bound the great Asura. Thus bound in the great battle, he abandoned his buffalo form. Immediately thereupon he became a lion ... he appeared as a man ... Then he became a great elephant ... the great Asura resumed his buffalo form again. ... she mounted the great Asura. Having struck him with her foot, she beat him with her spear. Then he, struck with her foot, came forth out of his own mouth, completely hemmed in by the valor of the Goddess. That great Asura, who had come forth halfway fighting, was felled by the Goddess, who had cut off his head with a great sword.[55]

This exact position of Durgā and Mahiṣa in the battle's final moment is precisely the form that dominates iconographical depictions. The earliest reliefs and statues of Mahiṣāsuramardinī[56] ('slayer of Mahiṣāsura') date from around the fourth century.[57] We find them all over India, especially in the South. According to the textual specifications, Mahiṣāsuramardinī is usually portrayed with ten arms, but this number can go up to twenty. Her arms hold the weapons presented to her in her creation mythology by the individual gods. Mahiṣa mostly carries a sword and a shield. He may be depicted as a buffalo or as a human form with a buffalo's head (see Figure 4). Thus, the message is strikingly converted into iconography and it is made explicit in each of these depictions: the preeminent Hindu goddess, effortlessly, vanquishes personified evil, which has a buffalo form.

---

[54] For the detailed ritual of Durgā during the festival and for its interpretation, see H. Rodrigues, *Ritual Worship of the Great Goddess: The Liturgy of the Durga Puja with Interpretations* (Albany: Suny Press, 2003).

[55] Devīmāhātmya, 3.20–3.39, in the translation of Coburn, *Encountering the Goddess*.

[56] For a detailed analysis of the Mahiṣāsuramardinī motif in Hindu textual and iconographical traditions, see S. Nagar, *Mahishasuramardini in Indian Art* (New Delhi: Aditya Prakashan, 1988). For a shorter categorization of depictions according to a chronology, see Berkson, *The Divine and Demoniac*, pp. 220–9.

[57] There are references to depictions from an even earlier date, presumably dating back to the first century. However, the identification of these depictions as Mahiṣāsuramardinī is debated. See, for instance, T. Coburn, *Devī-Māhātmya: The Crystallisation of The Goddess Tradition* (Delhi: Motilal Banarsidass, 1988), pp. 227–9.

Figure 4: Durgā slaying Mahiṣa as he is turning from a human figure into a buffalo. Relief from *c.* the eighth century. Vaital temple Bhubaneśbar, Orissa. Photograph by the author, October 2011.

Conclusion

Bovines, both male and female, play a crucial role in Hindu religious traditions. As significant animals in South Asian culture and society, they were included in religious contexts at a very early stage and gradually became essential parts of Hindu mythology, iconography, and ritual. In recent Hindu society, they are revered both as mythological figures and as living animals. Some bovines, namely the bull and the cow, are highly respected and show nearly exclusively benevolent representations. Others, namely the male buffalo, have negative connotations as well. Male bovines in Hinduism, especially the bull and the buffalo, are considered sacred. But this sanctification includes both – deification as well as 'demonization'.

This alleged discrepancy might be explained by a number of factors. The most important of these lies in Hindu mythology. In the case of male bovines (as in many other cases) textually authorized mythological motives dictate their perception and along with it, their significance and popularity in recent lived tradition. The mythological background defines the respective animal's sphere of action, status, and position. Although the reciprocal influences of texts and lived religious practices on each other in the early stages of myth construction are certain, it is obvious that most contemporary Hindu traditions classify bulls and buffalos according to their respective passed down mythological settings. Still today, benevolence and victory clearly is assigned to Śiva's bull *vāhana* Nandī, as much as the buffalo-figure Mahiṣāsura is defined by his mythological evilness and impertinence. The affiliation of the bull and buffalo with the major Hindu deities Śiva and Durgā, respectively, is based on this mythological framework as well.

It is the battling, controlling, and vital 'qualities' of the bull and the male buffalo that are mainly stressed in mythology; while the emphasis in the cow's representation lies in idealized and standardized female 'qualities', such as nourishment. In this general sense, there are clearly defined gender patterns underlying the respective representations. But as with other male sacred animals in Hinduism, the bull especially is depicted with a gentle and benevolent character as well. Compared to the 'holy cow', none of the male bovines became as influential in Hinduism, but no other animal did either. Nevertheless, the bull and the male buffalo have been firmly incorporated in South Asian religious traditions presumably for five thousand years, which is as long as the cow has also been incorporated. The sacredness of bovine animals in Hinduism must thus be seen in a broader perspective than merely referring to cows, as reverence for Bovinae extends to the male species as well.

Bibliography

Alsdorf, L., *The History of Vegetarianism and Cow-Veneration in India* (W. Bollée (ed.); B. Patil (trans.); revised by N. Hayton; London and New York: Routledge, 2010).

Batra, S. M., 'The Sacredness of the Cow in India', *Social Compass* 33.2–3 (1986), pp. 163–75.

Beck, B. E. F., 'The Goddess and the Demon. A Local South Indian Festival and its Wider Context', *Autour de la Déesse Hindoue* (M. Biardeau (ed.); Paris: Éditions de l'École des Hautes Études en Sciences Sociales, 1981), pp. 83–136.

Berkson, C., *The Divine and Demoniac: Mahisa's Heroic Struggle with Durga* (Delhi: Oxford University Press, 1997).

Bosch, L. P. van den, 'Yama, the God on the Black Buffalo', *Visible Religion: Annual for Religious Iconography, Vol. 1, Commemorative Figures* (H. G. Kippenberg (ed.); Leiden: Brill, 1982), pp. 21–64.

Brown, C. M., *The Triumph of the Goddess: The Canonical Models and Theological Visions of the Devī-Bhāgavata Purāṇa* (Delhi: Sri Satguru Publications, 1992).

Chakravarti, M., *The Concept of Rudra-Śiva through the Ages* (Delhi: Motilal Banarsidass, 1994).

Coburn, T. B., 'Devī. The Great Goddess', *Devī. Goddesses of India* (J. S. Hawley, J. Stratton, and D. M. Wulff (eds); Berkeley and Los Angeles: California University Press, 1996), pp. 31–48.

—*Encountering the Goddess: A Translation of the Devī-Māhātmya and A Study of Its Interpretation* (Delhi: Sri Satguru Publications, 1992).

—*Devī-Māhātmya: The Crystallisation of The Goddess Tradition* (Delhi: Motilal Banarsidass, 1988).

Craddock, E., 'Reconstructing the Split Goddess as Śakti in a Tamil Village', *Seeking Mahādevī: Constructing Identities of the Hindu Great Goddess* (T. Pintchman (ed.); Albany: Albany University Press, 2001), pp. 145–98.

During Caspers, E. C. L., 'Rituals and Belief Systems in the Indus Valley Civilisation', *Ritual, State and History in South Asia: Essays in Honour of J. C. Heesterman* (A. W. Van den Hoeck, D. H. A. Kolff, and M. S. Oort (eds); Leiden: Brill, 1992), pp. 102–27.

Heston, A., 'An Approach to the Sacred Cow of India', *Current Anthropology* 12.2 (1971), pp. 191–209.

Hiltebeitel, A., 'Rāma and Gilgamesh: The Sacrifices of the Water Buffalo and the Bull of Heaven', *History of Religions* 19.3 (1980), pp. 187–223.

—'The Indus Valley "Proto-Śiva", Reexamined through Reflections on the Goddess, the Buffalo, and the Symbolism of Vāhana', *Anthropos* 73.5–6 (1978), pp. 767–97.

Jacobsen, K. A., 'Sacred Animals', *Brill's Encyclopedia of Hinduism, Vol. 1: Regions, Pilgrimage, Deities* (K. A. Jacobsen (ed.); Leiden: Brill, 2009), pp. 711–18.

—'The Institutionalization of the Ethics of 'Non-Injury towards All Beings in Ancient India', *Environmental Ethics* 16.3 (1994), pp. 287–302.

Jha, D. N., *The Myth of the Holy Cow* (London: Verso, 2002).

Keul, I., *Hanuman, der Gott in Affengestalt. Entwicklung und Erscheinungsformen seiner Verehrung* (Berlin and New York: De Gruyter, 2002).

Korom, F. J., 'Holy Cow! The Apotheosis of Zebu, or Why the Cow Is Sacred in Hinduism', *Asian Folklore Studies* 59.2 (2000), pp. 181–203.

Krishna, N., *Sacred Animals of India* (Delhi and London: Penguin Books, 2010).

Lutgendorf, P., *Hanuman's Tale: The Messages of a Divine Monkey* (New York and Oxford: Oxford University Press, 2006).

The Mahābhārata (J. A. van Biutenen (ed. and trans.); Chicago: University of Chicago Press, 1973–8.

Mallebrein, C., 'When the Buffalo Becomes a Pumpkin: The Animal Sacrifice Contested', *Periphery and Centre: Studies in Orissan History, Religion and Anthropology* (G. Pfeffer (ed.); Delhi: Manohar, 2007), pp. 443–72.

McLain, K., 'Holy Superheroine: A Comic Book Interpretation of the Hindu Devī Māhātmya Scripture', *Bulletin of SOAS* 71.2 (2008), pp. 297–322.

Michaels, A., 'Blutopfer in Nepal', *Mythen des Blutes* (C. von Braun, and C. Wulf (eds); Frankfurt/Main: Campus, 2007), pp. 91–107.

—'Notions of Nature in Traditional Hinduism', *Environment Across Cultures* (E. Ehlers, and C. F. Gethmann (eds); Berlin-Heidelberg: Springer, 2003), pp. 111–22.

Nagar, S. L., *Mahishasuramardini in Indian Art* (New Delhi: Aditya Prakashan, 1988).

Narain, A. K., 'Gaṇeśa: A Protohistory of the Idea and the Icon', *Ganesh: Studies of an Asian God* (R. L. Brown (ed.); Albany: State University of New York, 1991), pp. 19–48.

O'Flaherty, W. D., *Women, Androgynes, and Other Mythical Beasts* (Chicago and London: Chicago University Press, 1980).

Padmapurāṇa (N. A. Deshpande (ed. and trans.); Delhi: Motilal Banarsidass, 2009).

The Ramayan of Valmiki (R. T. H. Griffith (ed. and trans.); Benares: E. J. Lazarus, 1895).

Der Rig-Veda. Aus dem Sanskrit ins Deutsche übersetzt und mit einem laufenden Kommentar versehen von Karl Friedrich Geldner (Cambridge: Harvard University Press, 2003).

Robinson, C., and D. Cush, 'The Sacred Cow: Hinduism and Ecology', *Journal of Beliefs & Values* 18.1 (1997), pp. 25–37, http://dx.doi.org/10.1080/1361767970180104 (accessed 01 July 2012).

Rodrigues, H. P., *Ritual Worship of the Great Goddess: The Liturgy of the Durga Puja with Interpretations* (Albany: Suny Press, 2003).

Sax, B., *The Mythical Zoo: An Encyclopedia of Animals in World Myth, Legend, and Literature* (Santa Barbara: ABC-Clio, 2001).

Simoons, Frederick J., *et al.*, 'Questions in the Sacred-Cow Controversy [and Comments and Reply]', *Current Anthropology* 20.3 (1979), pp. 467–93.

Śivapurāṇa (J. L. Shastri (ed. and trans.); Delhi: Motilal Banarsidass, 1995).

Skandapurāṇa (G. V. Tagare (ed. and trans.); Delhi: Motilal Banarsidass, 2007).

Sontheimer, G.-D., *Pastoral Deities in Western India* (A. Feldhaus (trans.); New York and Oxford: Oxford University Press, 1989).

Srinivasan, D., 'The So-called Proto-Śiva Seal from Mohenjo-Daro: An Iconological Assessment', *Archives of Indian Art* 29 (1975–6), pp. 47–58.

—'Unhinging Śiva from the Indus Civilization', *Journal of the Royal Asiatic Society of Great Britain and Ireland* (1984), pp. 77–89.

Werness, H. B., *The Continuum Encyclopedia of Animal Symbolism in Art* (New York and London: Continuum, 2006).

Zeiler, X., 'Transformations in the Textual Tradition of Dhūmāvatī. Changes of the Tantric Mahāvidyā Goddess in Concept, Ritual, Function and Iconography', *Transformations and Transfer of Tantra in Asia and Beyond* (I. Keul (ed.); Berlin and New York: De Gruyter, 2012), pp. 165–94.

7

From Sacrifices to Symbols: Animals in Late Antiquity and Early Christianity

Ingvild Sælid Gilhus

I. Animals in the Roman Empire

The Mediterranean economy and societies were completely dependent on animals. Animals met all types of human needs.[1] They served basic physiological needs for nourishment and clothing. People were dependent on power based on animals' bodies. Oxen and horses pulled carts and chariots; donkeys worked the millstone and the wheels that were used to draw water from wells. Donkeys, horses, oxen, and camels trotted continually in all directions carrying people and goods, serving as mounts and beasts of burden. Animals and animal ingredients met needs for safety and were important in medicine, for example, in bloodletting and leech therapy. Animals were used for security reasons: cats and snakes hunted mice and rats; dogs protected people, houses, and farm animals; and horses served in the Roman armies. Animals were part of the entertainment industry, of its racing grounds, arenas, zoos, and temple parks. In their entertainment capacity, these institutions were probably also a safety measure, keeping people occupied and entertained; racing courses and arenas existed all over the empire. Animals fulfilled needs for friendship and intimacy: Odysseus' old dog Argus is a literary example of a companion animal, and dog burials are non-literary examples of the same. Children kept caged birds and mice as pets. Animals functioned as status symbols in various ways: social rank could, for instance, be defined by owning a horse. Status was given in relation to what sort of prey and how much a hunter killed – kings, for instance, hunted lions. Status was further connected to the number of animals a local ruler could

---

[1] See Abraham H. Maslow's pyramid of needs: basic physiological needs; safety in the form of personal security, financial security, health and wellbeing; love and belonging; esteem and respect; and self-realization.

afford to sacrifice, to the wild animals that were kept by Roman emperors, and to the peacocks that strutted around in the gardens of the elite. Animals were the subject of natural histories and philosophical debates. Last, but not least, they were used for religious purposes in sacrifice, divination, and magic.

The theme of this article is the religious interpretations and evaluation of animals in the Roman Empire and how their values changed during the first to the fourth century AD. Sacrifice, divination, and magic were based on interactions between humans on the one hand, and culturally postulated superhuman beings on the other, usually with an animal as the medium or connecting link. The religious language of the empire was a sacrificial language. During the sacrificial process, animals were conceived of as intermediaries between humans and gods, but at the same time the sacrifice was a justification for killing them.

What views of animals were reflected in the religious use of them? How was the relationship between humans and animals conceptualized and discussed in the religions of late antiquity? What were the cultural processes that contributed to changes in the conception of animals from the first to the fourth century AD? What did the transformation of a multi-religious empire into a Christian empire mean for the views and evaluation of animals?

The discussion of these questions will proceed in three steps. First, the chapter will present the religious uses of animals in the Roman Empire, especially the animal sacrifice, and ask what views of animals these uses reflect. Second, it will point out processes of religious change from the first to fourth century that influenced the status and meaning of animals. Finally, it will present the result of these processes, which was, mainly, the Christian conception of animals.

II. Religious Uses of Animals and Animals as Religious Subjects

The interactions between humans and animals were dependent on the context, social group, type of human institution, and the species of animal involved; they included a variety of different attitudes ranging from regarding and treating animals as objects/things to regarding and treating them as subjects. Animals could be seen as foes, food, and friends. In the last case, some animals were incorporated into the 'emotional family' of humans.[2]

---

[2] B. Børresen, 'Menneskets medfødte forutsetninger som vertskap for produksjonsdyr', *Dyreetikk* (A. Føllesdal (ed.); Oslo: Fagbokforlaget, 2000), pp. 16–39 (22).

When animals were companions and friends, they were given personal names and were usually not eaten. In many cases there was a mixture of attitudes towards an animal and sometimes a switch from one attitude to another. The standard example is farm animals, which could be treated as friends, but all the same were in the end slaughtered and made into meat and hide.

While some animals had names and were included in the emotional family of humans, humans were sometimes included in the same category as animals and seen as property and objects. *Lex Aquilia*, which was concerned with unlawfully inflicted damage, states: 'If anyone kills unlawfully a slave or a servant-girl belonging to someone else or a four-footed beast of the class of cattle, let him be condemned to pay the owner the highest value that the property had attained in the preceding year'.[3] The jurist Gaius makes a comment on this statute and stresses that it 'treats equally our slaves and our four-footed cattle which are kept in herds'.[4] Slaves and animals were sometimes treated together because their roles overlapped as they were often engaged in the same type of work.[5]

Animals were employed in important official institutions, such as sacrifice, divination, and the arenas. Sacrifice and divination were clearly religious institutions because they presupposed an interaction between humans and postulated superhuman beings by means of an animal as the mediator/medium. We can also note in passing that the third institution, the arenas, had religious dimensions. In the arenas the Romans staged their relationship with their surroundings and fought down enemies in the form of animals, fetched from all parts of the known world.[6] Mythological elements were often part of the spectacles. The Roman poet Martial describes a mythological tableaux[7] at the opening of the Flavian Amphitheatre (Colosseum) where people who fought in the arenas or were thrown to the beasts were identified with mythological heroes: the emperor Commodus attended the games dressed as Hercules and killed animals,[8] while

[3] *Lex Aquilia*, in *The Digest of Justinian* (T. Mommsen, and P. Krueger (eds); A. Watson (trans.); vol. 1–4; Philadelphia: University of Pennsylvania Press, 1985), 9.2.2; see also 9.2.5.22.
[4] Ibid., 9.2.2.2.
[5] Authors on agriculture associate slaves and animals with each other: Cato, *On Agriculture* (W. Hooper (trans.); Loeb Classical Library; London: Heinemann, 1967), 2.7; Columella, *On Agriculture* (H. Ash, E. Forester, and E. Heffner (trans.); Loeb Classical Library, 3 vols; London: Heinemann, 1955), 1.6.8; Varro, *On Agriculture* (W. Hooper (trans.); Loeb Classical Library; London: Heinemann, 1967), 1.17.1. Cato (*On Agriculture*, 2.3) advises to sell 'worn-out oxen, blemished cattle, blemished sheep, wool, hides, an old wagon, old tools, an old slave, a sickly slave, and whatever else is superfluous. The master should have the selling habit, not the buying habit'.
[6] See T. Wiedemann, *Emperors and Gladiators* (New York and London: Routledge, 1995).
[7] See K. Coleman, 'Fatal Charades: Roman Executions Staged as Mythological Enactments', *The Journal of Roman Studies* 80 (1990), pp. 44–73.
[8] M. Grant, *The Antonines: Roman Empire in Transition* (London and New York: Routledge, 1996), pp. 75–6.

the Christian martyrs Perpetua and her companions were presented to the audience in Carthage in the outfits of priests of Saturn and priestesses of Ceres.[9]

Different types of sacrifices were performed – animal, vegetal, and liquid – but the prototypical sacrifice was the butchering of a domestic animal.[10] Animals were sacrificed on the local farm as well as at official feasts involving the whole city. In the first case, the sacrifice could be a lamb or piglet; in the second case, several animals were killed. At the big events in Rome, for instance, when a new emperor was inaugurated, hundreds and hundreds of animals, including different species of animals, were sometimes sacrificed.

Most sacrifices included a gift exchange between gods and humans, expressed in the slogan *do ut des* ('I give so that you will give'), and the ritual usually culminated in a feasting on the meat of the slaughtered beast as the final part of the sacrifice. As Dio Chrysostom states: 'What sacrifice has proved pleasing to the gods unless men feast together?'[11] Stress was placed on the exchange between humans and gods on the one hand, and on cuisine, banquets, and commensality on the other.[12]

The idea of animals as subjects was sometimes present in a sacrifice in the form of a natural agreement between humans and animals and in a vague notion that the animal accepted its lot.[13] It was a good omen if animals were willing victims and a bad omen if they were resistant. The historian Ammianus Marcellinus, offering an example of resistant sacrificial animals and the disastrous consequence of the sacrifice, tells of Emperor Julian who dies immediately after this ill-omened attempt to make an offering to Mars the Avenger:

---

[9] *The Martyrdom of Saints Perpetua and Felicitas*, in *The Acts of the Christian Martyrs* (H. Musurillo (trans.); Oxford: Oxford University Press, 1972), 18, 4.

[10] Sacrifice is not a coherent category. This has recently been stressed by K. McClymond *Beyond Sacred Violence: A Comparative Study of Sacrifice* (Baltimore: The John Hopkins University Press, 2008); and J. Rives, 'The Theology of Animal Sacrifice in the Ancient Greek World: Origins and Developments', *Ancient Mediterranean Sacrifice* (J. Knust, and Z. Várhelyi (eds); Oxford: Oxford University Press, 2011), pp. 187–201.

[11] Dio Chrysostom, *Orations III*, in *Works* (J. Cohoon, and H. Lamar (trans.); Loeb Classical Library, 5 vols; London: Heinemann, 1932–51).

[12] See M. Detienne, 'Culinary Practices and the Spirit of Sacrifice', *The Cuisine of Sacrifice Among the Greeks* (M. Detienne, and J. Vernant (eds); Chicago and London: University of Chicago Press, 1989), pp. 1–20; and J. Vernant, *Mortals and Immortals: Collected Essays* (Princeton: Princeton University Press, 1991).

[13] It was discussed if there was a contract between animals and humans, but the existence of such a contract was usually denied, see J.-A. Shelton, 'Lucretius on the Use and Abuse of Animals', *Eranos* 94 (1996), pp. 48–64; and R. Sorabji, *Animal Minds and Human Morals: The Origins of the Western Debate* (London: Duckworth, 1993), pp. 121, 165. Cicero, for instance, said that 'animals have no rights in relation to humans [*homini nihil iuris esse cum bestiis*]', *De finibus bonorum et malorum* (H. Rackham (trans.); Loeb Classical Library; London: Heinemann, 1914), 3.67. Like the Stoics, the Epicureans denied justice to animals on the grounds that they were not rational. Accordingly, they could not make contracts, see Diogenes Laertius, *Epicurus* (R. Hicks (trans.); Loeb Classical Library, 2 vols; London: Heinemann, 1965), X, 150 (maxim 32).

... he prepared to offer many victims to Mars the Avenger; but of ten fine bulls that were brought for this purpose nine, even before they were brought to the altar, of their own accord sank in sadness to the ground; but the tenth broke his bonds and escaped, and after he had been with difficulty brought back and sacrificed, showed ominous signs. Upon seeing these, Julian in deep indignation cried out, and called Jove to witness, that he would make no more offerings to Mars; and he did not sacrifice again; since he was carried off by a speedy death.[14]

Ideally, the animal walked willingly to the altar: 'It has also been noted that calves are not usually acceptable if carried to the altars on a man's shoulders, and also that the gods are not propitiated if the victim is lame or is not of the appropriate sort, or if it drags itself away from the altar'.[15] Spelt and salt (*mola salsa*) or water was usually sprinkled on the head of an animal, and it could be given something to drink to make it bow its head and apparently make its assent to its own slaughter. In this way, there is a pretention, though vague, that animals were religious subjects. That reality sometimes differed from this is seen in the iron-rings bolted into the altars, signalling that reluctant animals could be tethered. In this case the voluntary consent of the sacrificial animal turns out to be 'no more than a formality'.[16]

Divination based on animals, for instance, on wild birds or chickens, was dependent on two closely related ideas. The first idea is that the gods made their will known by their influence on the behaviour of animals; the second idea is that they inscribed their message on the innards of the slaughtered animal, for instance, on the liver of an ox. In these cases the animals were more like media for the messages they were transmitting than messengers in their own right, and more like objects than subjects. The animals were not thought of as acting freely, but as being moved by external forces and as passive objects for these forces.[17]

In addition to the official religious institutions of sacrifice and divination, magic was an important technology that frequently involved animal ingredients and small animal sacrifices. In magic, animals were used in a systematic way that was built on the ideas of sympathies and antipathies, connecting and disconnecting the different things in the world. Richard Gordon has recently shown that the motif of presumed biological uniqueness loomed large in the

[14] Ammianus Marcellinus, *The History* (J. Rolfe (trans.); Loeb Classical Library, 3 vols; London: Heinemann, 1963–4), 24.6.17
[15] Pliny, *Natural History* (H. Rackham (trans.); Loeb Classical Library, 10 vols; London: Heinemann, 1962–7), 8.183.
[16] F. Van Straten, *Hiera Kala: Images of Animal Sacrifice in Archaic and Classical Greece* (Leiden: Brill, 1995), pp. 100–3.
[17] I. S. Gilhus, *Animals, Gods and Humans: Changing Attitudes to Animals in Greek, Roman and Early Christian Ideas* (London/New York: Routledge, 2006), pp. 120–1.

species that were used as 'privileged magical operators'.[18] If an animal did not conform to what one expected from an ordered and meaningful nature, as in the hyaena (sex-changing ability), the mole (blind), the cricket (walks backwards, bores into the earth, chirrups at night), the chameleon (neither eats nor drinks), and the tick (no anus, lives longer when not eating), it was seen as an especially potent magical remedy.[19] The magical use of animals reflects instrumental views of them as well as an interest in categorization.

In Greco-Roman religion, gods were usually not conceived of as animals, but specific animals were sometimes associated with them in an emblematic way – Zeus with an eagle, Athena with an owl. In myths, gods sometimes transformed themselves into animals, for instance, Zeus into a bull, a swan, and an eagle, while in the *Iliad*, Apollo and Athena took the shape of vultures and observed the preparations for battle from an oak tree.[20]

Egypt was seen as in some ways unique and the words of the historian Herodotus are frequently quoted: 'As the Egyptians have a climate peculiar to themselves, and their river is different in its nature from all other rivers, so have they made all their customs and laws of a kind contrary for the most part to those of all other men'.[21] One of the striking things in Egyptian religion, compared with its neighbours, was, according to Philostratus, that 'the mass of your shrines seem to have been erected in honour rather of irrational and ignoble animals than gods'.[22] When animals in Egypt were objects of cults, some of them were seen as sharing in the divine essence. Greek and Roman authors did their best to grasp the meaning of these animals, usually by giving them symbolic and allegorical explanations.[23] Animals were obviously vital elements in Egyptian religion in the Late Period and seem to have functioned as markers of cultural and religious boundaries: 'The choice of animal worship as a new national symbol at a time when the traditional gods no longer served

---

[18] R. Gordon, 'Magical Lessons in Natural History: Unique Animals in Graeco-Roman Natural Magic', *Myths, Martyrs, and Modernity. Studies in the History of Religions in Honour of Jan N. Bremmer* (J. Dijkstra, J. Kroesen, and Y. Kuiper (eds); Leiden and Boston: Brill, 2010), pp. 249–69 (268).

[19] Ibid.

[20] Homer, *The Iliad*, 7.58.

[21] Herodotus, *The Histories* (A. Godley (trans.); Loeb Classical Library, 4 vols; London: Heinemann, 1966), II, 35. David Frankfurter has recently argued that animal slaughter had a peripheral position in Egyptian religion, see 'Egyptian Religion and the Problem of the Category "Sacrifice"', *Ancient Mediterranean Sacrifice* (J. Knust, and Z. Várhelyi (eds); Oxford: Oxford University Press, 2011), pp. 75–93.

[22] Philostratus, *The Life of Apollonius of Tyana* (F. Conybeare (trans.); Loeb Classical Library, 2 vols; London: Heinemann, 1989–2000), 6.19.

[23] See Plutarch, (*On Isis and Osiris*) *De Iside et Osiride* (J. Griffiths (ed. and trans.); Cambridge: University of Wales Press, 1970), pp. 71–6.

as protectors of Egypt must correspond to the fact that animal worship struck foreigners as the most bizarre note of the entire Egyptian gamut'.[24]

III. Processes of Religious Change and the Conception of Animals

From the first to the fourth century, the Roman Empire went from being multi-religious and polytheistic to developing Christianity as its dominant religion and becoming moderately monotheistic, with a plethora of intermediate beings in the form of angels, demons, and saints. During these centuries, the religions and religious societies of the empire developed within the same cultural context, were part of the same processes of change, partook in a common religious language, and shared a pool of similar religious ideas and rituals.

During these centuries, there was a new focus on the animal sacrifice, which became a theme for discussion. James B. Rives has recently argued that 'philosophers of the imperial period took animal sacrifices much more seriously than did earlier philosophers and that only in this period did they develop a real theology of sacrifice – that is, a philosophical analysis that focused on the role of sacrifice as a cult act meant to establish connections between humans and the divine, and that located it within a large-scale and coherent understanding of the cosmos'.[25] He sees Neo-Pythagorean circles with the emblematic figure of Apollonius of Tyana as the source of a specific theology of sacrifice.[26] Daniel Ullucci has made a useful distinction between a sacrificial discourse and a sacrificial practice – that is, a difference between discursive and non-discursive action – and has pointed out that the sacrificial discourse became prominent during the empire.[27] The development of the emperor-cult and the strong connections that were made between the emperor and the sacrificial cult, as well as the increase in animal sacrifices at the big events in the Empire, probably contributed to discussions about sacrifice and to the development of explicit theologies of sacrifice.

---

[24] K. Smelik, and E. Hemelrijk, '"Who knows not what monsters demented Egypt worships?" Opinions on Egyptian Animal Worship in Antiquity as Part of the Ancient Conception of Egypt', *Aufstieg und Niedergang der Römischen Welt* 17.4 (Berlin and New York: Walter de Gruyter, 1984), pp. 1852–2357 (1863–4).

[25] Rives, 'The Theology of Animal Sacrifice', p. 187.

[26] Ibid., p. 197.

[27] D. Ullucci, 'Contesting the Meaning of Animal Sacrifice', *Ancient Mediterranean Sacrifice* (J. Knust, and Z. Várhelyi (eds); Oxford: Oxford University Press, 2011), pp. 57–74 (60); and also D. Ullucci, *The Christian Rejection of Animal Sacrifice* (Oxford: Oxford University Press, 2012).

Views of animals might change as a part of general cultural and religious changes. The change in India during the Axial Age implied that religion went from a Vedic sacrificial cult to a focus on bloodless rituals and from meat eating to vegetarianism, which was seen as a superior way of living.[28] A belief in non-violence (*ahimsa*) and in an encompassing reincarnation process, which included humans and animals in the cycle of continuous life and death, became the ideal.

This type of major change did not happen in the Mediterranean world in late antiquity, even if conceptions of sacrifice did change during these centuries, and even if animal sacrifices were eventually forbidden. The ban on animal sacrifice did not put an end to slaughtering; people continued to butcher animals and their meat was still eaten. What happened was that slaughtering went from being a prominent religious activity to becoming, on the whole, secularized and that sacrificial language was partly transferred from animals to humans.[29]

Aristotle had set animals on the agenda in a scientific approach to their nature and diversity. The Pythagorean revival from the first century BC focused on vegetarianism and reincarnation, and the expansion of encyclopaedic knowledge in the empire, seen for example in the *Natural History* of Pliny, helped kindle an interest in animals. The discussion of the status and value of animals that took place in these centuries is reflected in works, for instance, by Philo, Plutarch, Celsus, Origen, and Porphyry.[30] Important questions were raised and discussed. Chief among them was the question about reincarnation and whether humans and animals had the same type of soul, as well as the related question about the cognitive qualities of animals and whether animals had reason.

Some Platonists believed in reincarnation across species. It was never a majority view, but there were groups, such as the Pythagoreans, Orphics, and Cynics, who probably shared the idea of a transmigration of souls across the

[28] K. Jacobsen, 'The Institutionalization of the Ethics of "Non-Injury" Toward All "Beings" in Ancient India', *Environmental Ethics* 16 (1949), pp. 287–302.

[29] Gilhus, *Animals, Gods and Humans*; G. Heyman, *The Power of Sacrifice: Roman & Christian Discourses in Conflict* (Oxford: Oxford University Press, 2007); M.–Z. Petropoulou, *Animal Sacrifice in Ancient Greek Religion, Judaism, and Christianity, 100 BC to AD 200* (Oxford Classical Monographs; Oxford: Oxford University Press, 2008); J. Knust, and Z. Várhelyi (eds), *Ancient Mediterranean Sacrifice* (Oxford: Oxford University Press, 2011); Ullucci, *The Christian Rejection of Animal Sacrifice*.

[30] Origen, *Against Celsus* (H. Chadwick (trans.); Cambridge: Cambridge University Press, 1980); Philo, *Philonis Alexandrini De Animalibus* (A. Terian (trans.); Chico, CA: Scholars Press, 1981); Plutarch, *(Gryllus) Beasts are Rational* (H. Cherniss, and W. C. Helmbold (trans.); Loeb Classical Library; London: Heinemann, 1968); Porphyry, *On Abstinence from Killing Animals* (G. Clark (trans.); London: Duckworth, 2000).

human/animal divide.[31] These groups rejected animal sacrifice because, as Rives has recently stressed, they rejected food that included souls (*empsychos*) and preferred to eat food that was soulless (*apsychos*).[32]

In a similar way as the Pythagoreans, Orphics, and Cynics, the adherents of Mani believed in reincarnation across species and taught that all living beings had souls. The Manicheans included plants as well as animals in the cycle of births and rebirths and regarded plants, in some ways, to be on a higher level than animals because they contained spiritual elements in a purer form than animals did, which could be seen as a devaluation of the value of animals. In fact, the Manichean Elect thought they saved the spiritual light by eating specific species of fruits and vegetables.[33] Augustine, who had been a Manichean for nine years and who wrote several treatises and letters against them, presents an example of a fig and a raven in which the raven is about to eat the fig:

> In accord with your opinion, do you not suppose that the fig itself speaks and pleads with you in a pitiful fashion that you yourself should pick and bury it in your holy belly to be purified and resuscitated, rather that the raven should devour and mingle it with its dark body and from there send it on into other forms to be bound and tormented in them?[34]

This example illustrates that the Manicheans thought that the process of reincarnation included both plants and animals, and that at least some plants were considered to be on a higher level than animals.

In addition to the question whether humans and animals were united by soul, was the question if, and to what degree, they were divided by reason.[35] The Stoics made *logos* the categorical boundary marker between humans and animals: humans were rational while animals lacked reason; consequently, animals were frequently described as, *aloga*. The Stoic position became dominant and was adopted by Christianity.[36] Independent of whether one thought animals had reason or not, the question of empathy and emotions was sometimes raised. Plutarch wrote playful pieces in defence of animals and their abilities and in *On*

---

[31] Rives, 'The Theology of Animal Sacrifice', pp. 187–201, and Ullucci, *The Christian Rejection of Animal Sacrifice*.

[32] Ibid.; see also Ullucci, 'Contesting the Meaning of Animal Sacrifice', pp. 73–4.

[33] N. Pedersen, *Studies in The Sermon of the Great War: Investigations of a Manichean-Coptic Text from the Fourth Century* (Århus: Århus University Press, 1996), p. 295ff.; J. BeDuhn, *The Manichaean Body: In Discipline and Ritual* (Baltimore and London: The John Hopkins University Press, 2008).

[34] Augustine, *The Catholic Way of Life and the Manichean Way of Life*, in *The Manichean Debate* (Introduction and Notes by R. Teske; Works of Saint Augustine, I/19; Hyde Park: New City Press, 2006), Book II, 57.

[35] Gilhus, *Animals, Gods and* Humans, pp. 37–63.

[36] Sorabji, *Animal Minds and Human Morals*.

the Cleverness on Animals, argues that animals are rational and have sentient states: 'it is not those who make use of animals who do them wrong, but those who use them harmfully and heedlessly and in cruel ways'.[37]

A question that was sometimes raised was whether cruelty to animals should be condemned because of a concern and sympathy for animals, or because it had a brutalizing effect on humans, making men cruel towards each other. Eating meat was an object of similar considerations since vegetarianism was sometimes rooted in sympathy with the animals in question, but more often in a concern for pureness of diet as humans should not pollute themselves by eating animal food.[38] These two reasons for not eating meat – sympathy for the animal victim and fear of the impurity of meat – were sometimes mixed.

The criticism of animal sacrifice, voiced by non-Christian as well as by Christian authors, was only to a small degree concerned with animals and motivated by sympathy towards them. The critics mainly concentrated on the bad effects animal sacrifices had on humans and on the base/demonic qualities of gods who wanted such sacrifices. The bloody and messy business of slaughtering and the gods that craved such sacrifices, or could be bribed by means of them, were now looked down upon, at least by representatives of the elite, and were contrasted with less anthropomorphic and more spiritualized versions of divinity and ritual. Such views are found, for instance, in the satirical work of Lucian, *On Sacrifice*, as well as in *On Abstinence* by the Neoplatonist philosopher Porphyry.[39]

Views of animals were also dependent on other religious processes than those that were connected to the animal sacrifice. One such process, closely related to making religious practices into discourse and theology, is that of making religions out of a conglomeration of rituals, beliefs, myths, and values. Jörg Rüpke has presented two important phenomena that took place in the Hellenistic and Roman periods:

> The first is the transformation of religious practices and beliefs that led to the formation of boundary-conscious and knowledge-based religious groups that could be called "religions". At the same time, however, religious individuality

---

[37] Plutarch, *On the Cleverness of Animals* (H. Cherniss, and W. Helmbold (trans.); Loeb Classical Library; London: Heinemann, 1968), 965B; see also S. Newmyer, *Animals, Rights and Reason in Plutarch and Modern Ethics* (Oxford and New York: Oxford University Press, 2006).

[38] See J. Haussleiter, *Der Vegetarianismus in der Antike* (Berlin: Verlag von Alfred Töpelmann, 1935).

[39] Gilhus, *Animals, Gods and Humans*, pp. 138–60). According to Daniel Ullucci, 'Debate over the meaning of sacrifice must be understood as part of this ongoing competition between cultural producers, not as critiques of some essential or universal meaning or purpose of animal sacrifice.' Ullucci, 'Contesting the Meaning of Animal Sacrifice', p. 61.

is shown to be much more important than is usually admitted in dealing with ancient pre-Christian religion.[40]

Included in the focus on the individual is a preoccupation with the cosmos and with the place of humanity in it, as well as a belief in a human supra-biological life, which is a type of life that is conducted on a higher existential level than biological life and does not end with death.

There was an anthropocentric and individualistic trend in some religions and religious societies that interacted with the practice of sacrifice as well as with the discourse on sacrifice. The *taurobolium*, the Mithras cult, and the theurgical rites were examples of innovations in relation to Greco-Roman sacrificial religion, as was Christianity.[41] The taurobolium, in which an ox was killed, can be interpreted as a ritual and spiritual rebirth.[42] In the Mithras mysteries the mythological motif of killing the bull had symbolic meanings, and the mysteries seem to have been aimed at personal transformation and salvation.[43] According to a theurgical interpretation of sacrifice, a sacrifice works because it is part of a movement upwards in which matter is purified.[44] Sacrifices, real or symbolic, placed humans in a new cosmological context and promoted supra-biological life. They served the personal ambitions of those who sacrificed or took part in symbolic sacrifices, such as the Christian Eucharist. The goal was transformation and personal salvation.

IV. Christianities and Animals

Christianity was formed in the Roman Empire by a range of processes that moulded rituals, beliefs, myths, and values into a full-blown religion. Its views of animals were developed in the interplay between the interpretation of ancient texts and contemporary concerns. One of the roots of Christian conceptions of animals is the Hebrew Bible in which the main ideas were that humans, different

---

[40] See J. Rüpke, 'Hellenistic and Roman Empires and Euro-Mediterranean Religion', *Journal of Religion in Europe* 3 (2010), pp. 197–214, especially p. 197.

[41] See Gilhus, *Animals, Gods and* Humans, pp. 116–47.

[42] See G. Gasparro, *Soteriology and Mystic Aspects in the Cult of Cybele and Attis* (Leiden: Brill, 1985), p. 114f.

[43] See J. Alvar, *Romanising Oriental Gods: Myths, Salvation and Ethics in the Cults of Cybele, Isis and Mithras* (R. Gordon (ed.; trans.); Religion in the Graeco-Roman World; Leiden: Brill, 2008). pp. 126, 399–401.

[44] See G. Shaw, 'Theurgy: Rituals of Unification in the Neoplatonism of Iamblichus', *Traditio* 41 (1985), pp. 1–28; and G. Shaw, *Theurgy and the Soul: The Neoplatonism of Iamblichus* (University Park, PA: The Pennsylvania State University Press, 1995).

from animals, were made in the image and likeness of god, and that animals and the natural world were placed under human dominion (Gen 1.26–30). The Hebrew Bible focuses on animals, not least because the dietary laws made a sharp distinction between pure and impure animals.[45]

In the canonical gospels, animals appear in the contexts of fishing, pastoral farming, and the desert. There is, however, little focus on descriptions of 'real' animals. Animals are lifted out of the spheres of fishermen and shepherds and into the spheres of teachers and preachers, where they are used didactically. They have become subjects of parables and the stuff miracles and metaphors are made of: fish are, for instance, the ingredients of miracles and are used as metaphors for Christian souls; shepherds and sheep are used to describe Jesus and his adherents. In the desert scenario, animals represent antagonism, struggle, and forces that are opposed to humans (Mark 1.13).

In the Christian mythological universe, good and evil, God and Satan are cast as polar opposites. In accordance with the logic of this universe, when God becomes man, Satan is conceived of as a beast and evil forces tend to materialize in the form of animals. The Revelation of John excels in having animals and animal hybrids represent evil powers.

The tendency to use animals as actors in a mythological and polarized universe, found in Christian texts from the first century AD, and to use them as metaphors and symbols, was continued and developed in the next centuries.[46] Animals appear in key Christian scenarios, such as those of the martyrs and the ascetics.

The martyr scenario is closely related to the Roman arenas. The sentencing of humans to the beasts in the arenas – *damnatio ad bestias* – was a punishment for severe crimes and a shameful way to die. Christians sometimes became victims of this punishment, a theme that was treated in the Acts of the Martyrs and which became a new Christian genre. Characteristic of the genre of the Acts of the Martyrs is that it sides with the Christian victims and sees the struggle of the arenas as a struggle between God and Satan.[47] Sacrificial language permeates the

---

[45] See P. Garnsey, *Food and Society in Classical Antiquity* (Cambridge: Cambridge University Press, 1999); W. Houston, 'What was the Meaning of Classifying Animals as Clean or Unclean?', *Animals on the Agenda* (A. Linzey, and D. Yamamoto (eds); London: SCM Press, 1998), pp. 18–24.

[46] Even if a considerable part of Christian thinking about animals took place in an allegorical and symbolic mood, there were authors who were interested in real animals and used factual knowledge about them in their texts. Chief among them is Basil of Caesarea, who in his *Hexameron* reveals interest and knowledge about zoology.

[47] See J. Perkins, *The Suffering Self. Pain and Narrative Representations in the Early Christian Era* (London and New York: Routledge, 1995), pp. 24, 104–23; B. Shaw, 'Body/Power/Identity: Passions of the Martyrs', *Journal of Early Christian Studies* 4.3 (1996), pp. 269–312; K. Cooper, 'The Voice of the Victim. Martyrdom and the Subversion of Roman Power in late Antiquity', Lecture at the Theological Faculty, The University of Oslo, 25 April 2003.

Martyr Acts, and in these narratives the martyr takes on the role of the sacrificial animal. Polycarp, for instance, who was burned in Smyrna in the middle of the second century, is characterized as 'a noble ram chosen for an oblation from a great flock'[48] and as 'a rich and acceptable sacrifice'.[49] Perpetua, who was sentenced to the beasts in Carthage, argues that she and her companions should be led to the arenas 'in good condition [*pinguiores*]'.[50] The text uses a word that normally refers to sacrificial victims (*pinguis*).[51] The animals, which are mentioned in the Martyr Acts, are lions, leopards, bears, wild cows, oxen, wild boars, and dogs – occasionally strange animals appear as well, for instance the seals in the *Acts of Paul and Thecla*.[52] One of the peculiarities in these Acts is that the beasts seldom kill their human victims: the martyrs are in the end executed by humans.[53] This turn of events might be due to the fact that the sacrificial interpretation of martyrdom worked better if the martyrs were not killed or eaten by animals.

The carnivores in these texts are usually associated with cosmic/metaphysical evil and are seen as fighting for Satan. In some cases, however, animals act as friends and helpers of the Christian heroes. In *The Acts of Paul and Thecla*, Paul's lion, which he had baptized, refused to attack Paul, while Thecla's lioness fought on her behalf against a bear and tore it asunder before the brave animal was killed by a lion.[54] When these felines befriend humans they reflect anthropomorphic characteristics and Christian virtues.

The model text for the Christian ascetic life and an example of the ascetic scenario is *Vita Antonii*, written by Athanasius. It describes Antony's solitary life in the Egyptian desert. In this text, real animals run errands for demons; for example, hyaena and dogs – and fierce demons appear in the shape of animals and threaten Antony. The distinction between animals and demons in the form of animals is often blurred in this and similar texts. According to Origen, 'wild animals have something about them resembling evil, and although it is not evil, yet it is like it'.[55] Origen sees further some 'sort of kinship between the form of each species of demon and the form of each species of animal'.[56]

---

[48] *Martyrdom of Polycarp*, in *The Acts of the Christian Martyrs* (H. Musurillo (trans.); Oxford: Clarendon Press, 1972), 14.1.
[49] Ibid., 14.2.
[50] *The Martyrdom of Perpetua and Felicitas*, 16.3.
[51] P. Habermehl, *Perpetua und der Ägypter* (Berlin: Akademie Verlag, 1992), p. 193.
[52] *The Acts of Paul and Thecla*, in *Les Actes de Paul et ses lettres apocryphes* (Introduction, texts, traduction, and commentary by L. Vouaux; Paris: Libraire Letouzey et ané, 1913), 26–39.
[53] Gilhus, *Animals, Gods and Humans*, pp. 195–200.
[54] *The Acts of Paul and Thecla*, 26–39.
[55] Origen, *Against Celsus*, 4.92.21–2.
[56] Ibid., 4.93.14–15.

In the narratives of the desert fathers, as well as in the Apocryphal Acts of the Apostles, there are, in addition to the demonic and dangerous animals, also animals that are shown in a positive light. These animals have been tamed by the examples of the Christian heroes and have become human-like. In the *Acts of Paul*, Paul baptizes a lion;[57] in the *Acts of Philip*, a leopard argues on behalf of a kid and itself for their participation in a Eucharistic meal.[58]

When animals have been given roles in a mythological polarized universe, this type of mythological thinking sometimes rubs off on real animals, as when reptiles and predatory beasts are seen as incorporating metaphysical evil. Epiphanius is concerned to ensure that something similar does not happen with doves. Epiphanius makes a division between real doves and doves used as positive Christian metaphors when he says,

> in many ways doves are not admirable. They are incontinent and ceaselessly promiscuous, lecherous and devoted to the pleasures of the moment, and weak and small besides. But because of the harmlessness, patience and forbearance of doves – and even more, because the Holy Spirit has appeared in the form of a dove – the divine Word could have us imitate the will of the Holy Ghost and the harmlessness of the harmless dove, and be wise in good but innocent in evil.[59]

According to Epiphanius, the bird´s bad qualities ('incontinent and ceaselessly promiscuous, lecherous and devoted to the pleasures of the moment, and weak and small besides') far outweigh its good ones ('harmlessness, patience and forbearance'). When the bird is used, all the same, as a symbol for the Holy Spirit, it is not because it is a completely suitable vehicle for divinity, but because the dove is seen more like a metaphor. In this way, Epiphanius shows that the connection between 'real' doves and the Holy Spirit is slight and selective and that only some of the characteristics of the bird are suitable in relation to the Holy Spirit.

V. Conclusion

The end of animal sacrifice meant a secularization of slaughter. Power was no longer built on killing animals in a cultic setting and on feasting and distributing

---

[57] *Acts of Paul*, 7, Coptic papyrus in E. Hennecke and W. Schneemelcher, *New Testament Apocrypha, I-II* (London: SCM Press, 1973–5), pp. 387–90.

[58] *The Acts of Philip*, 12:2–5; 14:12–14, in *Acta Philippi, textus* (F. Bovon, B. Bouvier, and F. Amsler (eds); Turnhout: Brepols, 1999).

[59] Epiphanius, *The Panarion of Epiphanius of Salamis* (F. Williams (trans.); Nag Hammadi Studies, 35; Leiden: Brill, 1987–1994), Book I. 37.8–9.

their meat. The end of sacrifice accompanied a shift from real sacrifices of real animals to Christian metaphorical sacrifices connected to, for instance, Christ, the martyrs, ascetics, and the Eucharist. Christian views of animals were based on a combination of Christian canonical texts and Stoic ideas. These views implied that there was a fundamental division between humans and animals because animals, in opposition to humans, were seen as irrational, a view that was supported by Augustine.

In the Christian empire at the end of the fourth century, animals were still absolutely necessary for running society, and they still had a variety of different relationships to humans dependent on species and functions. However, their religious roles and status had changed: Christian attention was only rarely focused on the world of real animals; instead, the stress was on animals in a mythological polarized universe where they were demonized and/or humanized, and where they were seldom allowed to act as animals.

Bibliography

Acta Philippi, textus (F. Bovon, B. Bouvier, and F. Amsler (eds); Turnhout: Brepols, 1999).

Les Actes de Paul et ses lettres apocryphes (Introduction, texts, traduction, and commentary by Léon Vouaux; Paris: Librarie Letouzey et ané, 1913).

The Acts of the Christian Martyrs (Introduction, texts, and translation by H. Musurillo; Oxford: Clarendon Press, 1972).

Alvar, J., *Romanising Oriental Gods: Myths, Salvation and Ethics in the Cults of Cybele, Isis and Mithras* (R. Gordon (ed.; trans.); Religion in the Graeco-Roman World; Leiden: Brill, 2008).

Ammianus Marcellinus, *The History* (J. C. Rolfe (trans.); Loeb Classical Library, 3 vols; London: Heinemann, 1963–64).

Athanasius, St., *Vie d´Antoine* (Introduction, texte critique, traduction, notes et index par G. J. M. Bartelink; Sources Chrétiennes, 400; Paris: Cerf, 1994).

Augustine, St., *The Manichean Debate* (Introduction and Notes by Roland Teske; Works of Saint Augustine: A Translation for the 21st Century, I/19; Hyde Park: New City Press, 2006).

Basil, *The Hexaemeron* (P. Schaff, and H. Wace (ed.); B. Jackson (trans.); The Nicene and Post-Nicene Fathers, vol. 8; Edinburgh: T&T Clark, 1989).

BeDuhn, J. D., *The Manichaean Body: In Discipline and Ritual* (Baltimore and London: The John Hopkins University Press, 2008).

Børresen, B., 'Menneskets medfødte forutsetninger som vertskap for produksjonsdyr', *Dyreetikk* (A. Føllesdal (ed.); Oslo: Fagbokforlaget, 2000), pp. 16–39.

Cato, *On Agriculture* (W. D. Hooper (trans.); Loeb Classical Library; London: Heinemann, 1967).

Cicero, *De finibus bonorum et malorum* (About the Ends of Good and Evil) (H. Rackham (trans.); Loeb Classical Library; London: Heinemann, 1914).

Coleman, K. M., 'Fatal Charades: Roman Executions Staged as Mythological Enactments', *The Journal of Roman Studies* 80 (1990), pp. 44–73.

Columella, *On Agriculture* (H. B. Ash, E. S. Forester, and E. H. Heffner (trans.); Loeb Classical Library, 3 vols; London: Heinemann, 1955).

Cooper, K., 'The Voice of the Victim: Martyrdom and the Subversion of Roman Power in late Antiquity', Lecture at the Theological Faculty, The University of Oslo, 25 April 2003.

Detienne, M., 'Culinary Practices and the Spirit of Sacrifice', *The Cuisine of Sacrifice Among the Greeks* (M. Detienne, and J. P. Vernant (eds); Chicago and London: University of Chicago Press, 1989), pp. 1–20.

The Digest of Justinian (T. Mommsen, and P. Krueger (eds); A. Watson (trans.); vol. 1–4; Philadelphia: University of Pennsylvania Press, 1985).

Dio Chrysostom, *Works* (J. W. Cohoon, and H. Lamar (trans.); Loeb Classical Library, 5 vols; London: Heinemann, 1932–1951).

Diogenes Laertius, Epicurus (R. D. Hicks (trans.); Loeb Classical Library, 2 vols; London: Heinemann, 1965).

Epiphanius, *The Panarion of Epiphanius of Salamis* (F. Williams (trans.); Nag Hammadi Studies, 35; Leiden: Brill, 1987–94).

Frankfurter, D., 'Egyptian Religion and the Problem of the Category "Sacrifice"', *Ancient Mediterranean Sacrifice* (J. W. Knust, and Zsuzsanna Várhelyi (eds); Oxford: Oxford University Press, 2011), pp. 75–93.

Garnsey, P., *Food and Society in Classical Antiquity* (Cambridge: Cambridge University Press, 1999).

Gasparro, G. S., *Soteriology and Mystic Aspects in the Cult of Cybele and Attis* (Leiden: Brill, 1985).

Gilhus, I. S., *Animals, Gods and Humans: Changing Attitudes to Animals in Greek, Roman and Early Christian Ideas* (London and New York: Routledge, 2006).

Gordon, R., 'Magical Lessons in Natural History: Unique Animals in Graeco-Roman Natural Magic', *Myths, Martyrs, and Modernity. Studies in the History of Religions in Honour of Jan N. Bremmer* (J. Dijkstra, J. Kroesen, and Y. Kuiper (eds); Leiden and Boston: Brill, 2010), pp. 249–69.

Grant, M., *The Antonines: Roman Empire in Transition* (London and New York: Routledge, 1996).

Habermehl, P., *Perpetua und der Ägypter* (Berlin: Akademie Verlag, 1992).

Haussleiter, J., *Der Vegetarianismus in der Antike* (Berlin: Verlag von Alfred Töpelmann, 1935).

Hennecke, E., and W. Schneemelcher, *New Testament Apocrypha, I-II* (London: SCM Press, 1973–5).

Herodotus, *The Histories* (A. D. Godley (trans.); Loeb Classical Library, 4 vols; London: Heinemann, 1966).

Heyman, G., *The Power of Sacrifice: Roman & Christian Discourses in Conflict* (Oxford: Oxford University Press, 2007).

Houston, W., 'What was the Meaning of Classifying Animals as Clean or Unclean?', *Animals on the Agenda* (A. Linzey, and D. Yamamoto (eds); London: SCM Press, 1998), pp. 18–24.

Jacobsen, K. A., 'The Institutionalization of the Ethics of "Non-Injury" Toward All "Beings" in Ancient India', *Environmental Ethics* 16.3 (1994), pp. 287–302.

Knust. J. W., and Z. Várhelyi (eds), *Ancient Mediterranean Sacrifice* (Oxford: Oxford University Press, 2011).

Martial, *On the Spectacles, in Epigrams* (W. C. A. Ker (trans.); Loeb Classical Library, 2 vols; London: Heinemann, 1961).

The Martyrdom of Saints Perpetua and Felicitas, in *The Acts of the Christian Martyrs* (Introduction, texts and translation by H. Musurillo; Oxford: Oxford University Press, 1972), pp. 106–31.

McClymond, K., *Beyond Sacred Violence: A Comparative Study of Sacrifice* (Baltimore: The John Hopkins University Press, 2008).

Newmyer, S. T., *Animals, Rights and Reason in Plutarch and Modern Ethics* (Oxford and New York: Oxford University Press, 2006).

Origen, [*Against Celsus*] *Contra Celsum* (H. Chadwick (trans.); Cambridge: Cambridge University Press, 1980).

—*Contre Celse* (Introduction, texte critique, traduction et notes par M. Borret; Sources Chrétiennes, 132, 136, 147, 150, 227; Paris: Cerf, 1967–76).

Pedersen, N. A., *Studies in The Sermon of the Great War: Investigations of a Manichean-Coptic Text from the Fourth Century* (Århus: Århus University Press, 1996).

Perkins, J., *The Suffering Self: Pain and Narrative Representations in the Early Christian Era* (London and New York: Routledge, 1995).

Petropoulou, M.-Z., *Animal Sacrifice in Ancient Greek Religion, Judaism, and Christianity, 100 BC to AD 200* (Oxford Classical Monographs; Oxford: Oxford University Press, 2008).

Philo, *Philonis Alexandrini De Animalibus* (The Armenian Text with an introduction, translation, and commentary by A. Terian; California: Scholars Press, 1981).

Philostratus, *The Life of Apollonius of Tyana* (F. C. Conybeare (trans.); Loeb Classical Library, 2 vols; London: Heinemann, 1989–2000).

Pliny, *Natural History* (H. Rackham (trans.); Loeb Classical Library, 10 vols; London: Heinemann, 1962–7).

Plutarch, *(Gryllus) Beasts are Rational* (H. Cherniss, and W.C. Helmbold (trans.); Loeb Classical Library; London: Heinemann, 1968).

—(*On Isis and Osiris*) *De Iside et Osiride* (Edited with an introduction, translation, and commentary by J. G. Griffiths; Cambridge: University of Wales Press, 1970).

—*On the Cleverness of Animals* (H. Cherniss, and W. C. Helmbold (trans.); Loeb Classical Library; London: Heinemann, 1968).

—*On the Eating of Flesh* (H. Cherniss, and W. C. Helmbold (trans.); Loeb Classical Library; London: Heinemann, 1968).

Porphyry, *De l`abstinence* (J. Bouffartigue, M. Patillon, A. P. Segonds, and L. Brison (trans.); Budí series, 3 vols; Paris: Societe d´Edition "Les Belles Lettres", 1977–95).

—*On Abstinence from Killing Animals* (G. Clark (trans.); London: Duckworth, 2000).

Rives, J. B., 'The Theology of Animal Sacrifice in the Ancient Greek World: Origins and Developments', *Ancient Mediterranean Sacrifice* (J. W. Knust, and Z. Várhelyi (eds); Oxford: Oxford University Press, 2011), pp. 187–201.

Rüpke, J., 'Hellenistic and Roman Empires and Euro-Mediterranean Religion', *Journal of Religion in Europe* 3 (2010), pp. 197–214.

Shaw, B. D., 'Body/Power/Identity: Passions of the Martyrs', *Journal of Early Christian Studies* 4.3 (1996), pp. 269–312.

Shaw, G., 'Theurgy: Rituals of Unification in the Neoplatonism of Iamblichus', *Traditio* 41 (1985), pp. 1–28.

—*Theurgy and the Soul: The Neoplatonism of Iamblichus* (University Park, PA: The Pennsylvania State University Press, 1995).

Shelton, J.-A., 'Lucretius on the Use and Abuse of Animals', *Eranos* 94 (1996), pp. 48–64.

Smelik, K. A. D., and E. A. Hemelrijk, '"Who knows not what monsters demented Egypt worships?" Opinions on Egyptian Animal Worship in Antiquity as Part of the Ancient Conception of Egypt', *Aufstieg und Niedergang der Römischen Welt* 17.4 (Berlin and New York: Walter de Gruyter, 1984), pp. 1852–2357.

Sorabji, R., *Animal Minds and Human Morals: The Origins of the Western Debate* (London: Duckworth, 1993).

Straten, F. T. van, *Hiera Kala: Images of Animal Sacrifice in Archaic and Classical Greece* (Leiden: Brill, 1995).

Ullucci, D. C., *The Christian Rejection of Animal Sacrifice* (Oxford: Oxford University Press, 2012).

—'Contesting the Meaning of Animal Sacrifice', *Ancient Mediterranean Sacrifice* (J. W. Knust, and Z. Várhelyi (eds); Oxford: Oxford University Press, 2011), pp. 57–74.

Varro, *On Agriculture* (W. D. Hooper (trans.); Loeb Classical Library; London: Heinemann, 1967).

Vernant, J. P., *Mortals and Immortals: Collected Essays* (Princeton: Princeton University Press, 1991).

Wiedemann, T. E. J., *Emperors and Gladiators* (New York and London: Routledge, 1995).

Part Three

Animals as Subjects of Theological Inquiry

8

Butterflies Dwell Betwixt and Between: Non-Human Animals, Theology, and Dwelling in Place

Forrest Clingerman

I. Introduction

As spring progresses, new neighbours emerge. They first appear discretely – hidden away underneath flowers, or blending into leaves. But this seasonal influx of creatures is where the present chapter starts: a few summers ago, my daughter and I discovered a black swallowtail caterpillar casually browsing in our herb garden. Caterpillars, though small and easily missed, commonly share human space in warmer weather. With a slight touch of Sabina's finger, an orange, forked gland would reach out from the caterpillar's head. This gland would emit a rank odour meant to dissuade us from molesting the caterpillar further, but instead it focused our attention on the creature even more. Each day, we would visit the caterpillar and see him grow larger and larger. Then one day, he disappeared. Perhaps this sudden disappearance meant our caterpillar met an unhappy fate in a robin's beak. Or perhaps, we speculated, his continual repasts in our herb garden had made him drowsy and ready to be ensconced in a humble, camouflaged abode.

Monarchs and sulphurs, swallowtails and buckeyes live alongside us in the warm weather, flitting around our heads, always avoiding an excessive intrusion but nonetheless always present. Late in the summer, occasional days of cooler temperatures would result in dozens of butterflies adorning plants like flowers, wings open and beckoning but their scales sensitive to the slightest touch. Butterflies – whether crawling as caterpillars, absently hidden in cocoons, or brilliantly meandering in the air – surreptitiously become inhabitants that share our space. These small animals (are they really even that?) dwell among us, appearing before us, before ascending to the winds.

I begin with these encounters with butterflies, because at the heart of this chapter is the presumption that everyday encounters with non-human animals are in need of theological reflection. Clearly these creatures are quite different from humans – so how might we entertain the notion that these animals are religious subjects? To respond to this question, the theme of this chapter is how Christian theological reflection might approach non-human animals. Any response to this question must deal with a tension: human mythmaking and worldviews make valuable use of other animals for allegorical and metaphorical purposes, but there is also an ethical need to value animals as living beings that exist independently from human interpretations and uses. It is a tension between how we think of animals within our conceptual frameworks and what animals are in their own right. Theologically, this tension translates how we embody an orientation toward the integrity of all forms of life on the planet. To approach this theme, my thesis has two parts. First, I wish to suggest that our relationship with non-human animals is a relation of interpretation, focused on the concept of dwelling. The ways that we dwell in our environment, and simultaneously acknowledge the different ways other animals dwell, lead us to see particular non-human animals as inhabiting our interpretations of the world. Second, it is important to acknowledge that the diversity of human and non-human ways of dwelling nonetheless occur within a single place. This unity in the midst of diversity points to the limits of our interpretation of the world, and thereby leads us to seek the spiritual depth – the 'ground of our existence', as Paul Tillich would suggest – to our definitions of self, other, and place. Non-humans participate in redemption, especially those transformative beings that bestow their power upon us.

II. Butterflies as Theological Subjects

a. Animals as Religious Subjects

The first step of this discussion is to reflect on how Christians have religiously engaged other non-human animals *in general*. Indeed, whether we talk of butterflies or baboons, there has been much discussion on the religious place of non-human animals within Christianity. Recent Christian theologians (including pioneering works by theologians Andrew Linzey and Jay McDaniel[1])

---

[1] A. Linzey, *Animal Theology* (Urbana, IL: University of Illinois Press, 1995); J. McDaniel, *Of God and Pelicans: A Theology of Reverence for Life* (Louisville, KY: Westminster/John Knox Press, 1989).

have presented theological reflections that attempt to include all creatures in God's community of salvation; they seek to provide a theology *for* animals, not simply a theology *of* animals. This emphasis is a relatively recent occurrence within Christianity, however, because it is not especially easy for theology to determine the best ways to approach animals as a whole – both non-human creatures and the human as animal. The difficulty becomes rapidly clear: as Celia Deane-Drummond and David Clough explain, few beings outside the boundaries of humanity engage in theological reflection (as they say, we are not looking for a 'chimpanzee St. Augustine'), but, at the same time, there *is* a need to theologize from the perspective of creatureliness.[2] Thus, even when humans see a theological rationale for a theology for non-human creatures, such a theology is framed within the context of the unique capability (and fallibility) of humans.

Given the need for such a creaturely theology, how *should* the Christian theologian define the non-human animal in spiritual, intellectual, and ethical concerns? Christian theologians have reflected upon animals in every age of the tradition, but these discussions take a variety of forms. Somewhat reductively, we can classify these forms as resting between two poles. On one side, the non-human animal (as an individual or as a species) is an allegory, a metaphor, and not taken on its own terms. For example, animal imagery is common in Jesus' ministry (e.g., the lost sheep in Luke 15.1–7 and the story of Legion and the herd of swine in Mark 5.1–20). These animals are symbols, rather than actual beasts, and were chosen to bestow certain qualities on the meaning of the narrative.[3] We also might think of later discussions of animals as metaphors of more general truths: for instance, in the stories of the Desert Fathers combating beasts in the wilderness, these animals served as proxies for Satan.[4] In these stories, combatting reptiles in the wasteland of the desert was a form of spiritual warfare against the demonic.[5] Thus, some cases simply anthropomorphize animals to turn them into subjects of religious reflection. In other cases, however, animals

---

[2] C. Deane-Drummond, and D. Clough, 'Introduction', *Creaturely Theology: On God, Humans and Other Animals* (C. Deane-Drummond, and D. Clough (eds); London: SCM Press, 2009), p. 1.

[3] Commenting on a draft of this chapter, Celia Deane-Drummond suggested an important reflection on this point: interpreters must clarify the difference between the intended meaning of animal imagery and the various possible interpretations of the text. For example, allegorical readings are not always undertaken for thoughtful reasons, and sometimes theologians offer an allegorical interpretation for a text that was not intended as allegory. In some instances, animals serve as allegories merely out of convenience. Individuals and faith communities also might choose allegorical readings to confirm pre-existing theological or philosophical convictions.

[4] For example, in her footnote describing the combat of desert monks and serpents, Benedicta Ward notes that the term used for the serpent – a 'dragon' – was a term used to refer to the devil. B. Ward (ed.), *The Lives of the Desert Fathers* (Kalamazoo, MI: Cistercian Publications, 1981), p. 132.

[5] T. Ingold, this volume.

are taken on their own terms, as beings to be understood as unique and (at least somewhat) outside the domesticated sphere of the human world. For example, we can look to Aquinas' reflections on the qualities of animals in the *Summa Theologica*, while Francis preaches to the birds and delivers a stern rebuke to the wolf of Gubbio.[6] Likewise, blessing animals has occurred with some regularity in Christianity, usually associated with specific saints (Laura Hobgood-Oster has written about the recent popularity of such rituals in the US, explaining how such rituals conflate the image of animals with their actual presence in the sanctuary[7]). In these cases, the non-human animal is understood as unique, irreducible, and not limited to human use or meaning. It is even possible to go further, saying that animals are religious subjects insofar as religion befits and speaks to them on their own terms.

Elsewhere in this volume, philosopher Stephen R. L. Clark reflects on the difference between animals as subjects and moral agents, rather than merely as objects and moral patients.[8] While Clark's distinction is correct, I would like to suggest a slightly different terminology to distinguish between the two readings of animals as religious subjects in the last paragraph: in the first case (non-human animals as illustrations or allegories), animals are *grammatical* subjects, whereas in the second case (non-human animals as encountered on their own terms), they are *ontological* subjects. In the majority of cases, then, Christian theology has taken non-human animals as grammatical subjects – that is, as a mere marker in a sentence or phrase. In many cases the animal is not intended to be embodied in the theological text, but this is increasingly changing. Certainly in response to environmental ethics and the biological sciences, it seems appropriate that theologians have a responsibility to take animals as ontological subjects in their own right. Or, as Clark writes,

> I do not mean only that we have found useful symbols among animals, and can then happily ignore the actual creatures. It is all too common for theists in the Western tradition to sing happily of the Lamb of God but think that this gives them no reason at all to wonder about the lives of real lambs, or to reckon that

---

[6] Stories of Francis' relationship with the animals are common in texts such as St. Bonaventure's *Life of Saint Francis* and the anonymous *The Little Flowers of Saint Francis of Assisi*. See Bonaventure, *The Soul's Journey into God/The Tree of Life/The Life of Saint Francis* (E. Cousins (trans.); New York: Paulist Press, 1978), especially pp. 250–61; R. Huddleston (trans.), *The Little Flowers of Saint Francis of Assisi* (Springfield, IL: Templegate, 1988), pp. 56–9.

[7] L. Hobgood-Oster, *Holy Dogs & Asses: Animals in the Christian Tradition* (Urbana, IL: University of Illinois Press, 2008), pp. 107–28.

[8] S. R. L. Clark, 'Ask Now the Beasts and They Shall Teach Thee', this volume.

the Four Living Creatures who stand around the throne of God, in Revelation, have anything to do with any real living creatures.[9]

Although there is a need for a theology for animals, to see non-humans as ontological subjects, it faces a few challenges. Foremost, there is the difficulty of ascertaining the connection between humans and non-humans from the perspective of a Christian theology. Especially after the Reformation, there is a strong strand of Christian theology that deems religion as an exclusively individualistic and human affair. Should we conclude, for instance, that the *imago dei* quantitatively disconnects humans from other living things?[10] To upend this tradition means we must entertain the notion that animals can sit beside humans (metaphorically at least) in the pews. Or perhaps these fundamentally and fantastically different creatures participate in their own religion – something which Clark elegantly suggests and the work of Marc Bekoff on animal justice and morality can be seen to raise as a possibility[11] – apart from the human world? Second, as we have already pointed out, regardless of the connection between actual animals and humans, animals have served as symbols and examples in theological discussions. For example, because of its mundane existence as caterpillar, its seeming death in the cocoon, and its subsequent transformation in the chrysalis, the butterfly has a *symbolic* connection with the new life in Christ. But can this symbolic transformation ever evolve into an existential connection between a particular, individual butterfly and the resurrection? Finally, in cases where non-human animals are seen as having individual value, theology sometimes replicates the split between discussions of animal rights and environmental ethics. Within Anglo-American environmental ethics, especially, there has been a long-running debate regarding the worth of individual animals on the one hand, and the value of ecosystems or species on the other.[12] This has been a spirited

---

[9] Ibid.

[10] Elsewhere in this volume, Charles Camosy reflects on elements of the 'image and likeness of God' from a Thomistic, Roman Catholic theological position. He places the issue of the image of God within a careful balance between maintaining the possibility of hierarchically differentiating animals (including humans) from one another, while at the same time arguing for the moral conscience and personhood of creatures – indeed, even participation in the *imago dei* – beyond the human.

[11] See M. Bekoff, 'The Evolution of Animal Play, Emotions, And Social Morality: On Science, Theology, Spirituality, Personhood, and Love', *Zygon* 36 (2001), pp. 615–55; M. Bekoff, 'Minding Animals, Minding Earth: Old Brains, New Bottlenecks', *Zygon* 38 (2003), pp. 911–41; M. Bekoff, 'Considering Animals—Not "Higher" Primates', *Zygon* 38 (2003), 229–45; and J. McDaniel, 'All Animals Matter: Marc Bekoff's Contribution to Constructive Christian Theology', *Zygon* 41 (2006), pp. 29–58.

[12] A starting point for this conversation might be traced back to J. Callicott, 'Animal Liberation: A Triangular Affair', *Environmental Ethics* 2 (1980), pp. 311–38 and the many responses to this essay.

debate, asking: should we value an individual life at the cost of a greater whole, or should the ecosystem be valued over an individual life? These questions are raised precisely because we acknowledge the tension in the theological status of non-human animals.

b. Theology for Butterflies

If we seek to define animals as ontological subjects, a new dilemma presents itself: when we take non-human animals on their own terms, we immediately confront the *multiplicity* of species. The multitude of animals means that we cannot pattern a uniform theological response; a multiplicity of theological responses is necessary and appropriate in light of the diversity of species. That is to say, a theology for animals is in reality a variety of theologies. Our next step, then, is to discuss the different species of animal theologies (or more plainly, to show how to engage in theological reflections on different species).

I seek to illustrate this by looking at a single family, the butterfly, with a sense that even this can be narrowed to individual species (for we could ask the theological differences between Monarchs and Red Admirals, and so on). Butterflies are undeniably animals; the many species of butterflies '... share common descent with everything from protozoans to whales and humans'.[13] More specifically, they are insects. The first true butterflies dated from over fifty million years ago (moths over one hundred million years before them); though many of these early species can be attached to contemporary species families, these ancient butterflies were more muted whites, browns, and blacks.[14] What joins the various species together is the scaly wings each possesses: 'Butterflies and moths are members of the insect order Lepidoptera (from the Greek words *lepis*, meaning 'scale,' and *pteron*, meaning 'wing') because they share a single defining characteristic: scales cover their bodies and wings. The scales, which are really modified hairs, give the wings their colors and patterns, overlapping like roof tiles or shingles to, in most cases, cover the wings completely'.[15] While their colourful wings set them apart, their lifecycle is equally well-known. The butterfly is an insect that goes through a full metamorphosis: from egg, to cater-pillar, to chrysalis, and finally to adult (or imago). After reaching adulthood, most species will only live for weeks, save some unusual cases. Throughout this lifecycle, these insects feed on plants and nectar. There are 165,000 species in

[13] R. Pyle, *A Handbook for Butterfly Watchers* (New York: Scribner's, 1984), p. 12.
[14] Ibid., p. 6.
[15] P. Schappert, *A World For Butterflies* (Buffalo: Firefly Books, 2000), p. 20.

the order – second only to the beetles for the largest group of similar species.[16] Furthermore, they are found nearly everywhere on earth, excluding the poles. This geographic diversity is particularly amazing, considering the physical limits of the butterfly. 'The average butterfly is small… A small mass and large surface area allows them to gain heat quickly—and to lose heat quickly. Butterflies must, therefore, choose their flight plans carefully if they are to avoid being grounded by cold thoracic muscles in an inhospitable place.'[17] A temperate day can ground a butterfly, leaving it defenceless while it opens its wings and attempts to warm itself. Though separable from other species, butterflies share traits with insects and other animals that place them firmly in the kingdom of animals.

Butterflies appear to be unique and quite different from the furry and feathered animals that typically come to mind when using the term 'animal'. If we wish to speak of 'animals as religious subjects', what do butterflies – these un-creaturely creatures – contribute to the discussion? One contribution they make is this: butterflies are theologically interesting because they can be defined as *transformative*. Humans, of course, are transformative creatures in a number of ways: we manipulate the matter of the world through science and technology, we create art, and we conceptualize our surroundings in novel and ever-changing ways. Furthermore, humans are transformative in ways that are best described as theological: for example, one interpretation of the opening chapters of Genesis is that humanity has the role of guiding creation in order to fulfil the divine mandate to be stewards. Also, humans are offered a transformed 'new life' through grace and redemption. How are *butterflies* transformative and, through this transformation, do they have a place in theological thinking? Are they ontological subjects of religion in some way? The suggestion I wish to make is that butterflies are not only meaningful for theology, but also that the transformative butterfly transforms us.

The lives of butterflies – from start to finish – are defined by transformation. As a species, they inherently are always becoming something new. Furthermore, the human love of butterflies sensitizes our experience of any surroundings that contain these fragile and captivating creatures. As a species, butterflies have infiltrated our religious symbolism and cultural heritage: there is a pre-reflective, aesthetic, and emotional connection to these creatures that is manifested in art

---

[16] Ibid., p. 21.
[17] M. Douglas, *The Lives of Butterflies* (Ann Arbor: University of Michigan Press, 1986), p. 80. The famous monarch pilgrimage is the result of this. Monarch butterflies from North America have a unique life cycle that allows one generation to migrate to the hills of central Mexico during the cold winter. Once there, they weigh down trees when huddling close to each other, warming until a new generation can return north.

and myth alike. A rather provocative example of this is Damien Hirst's recent collages of butterfly wings.[18] Hirst's artworks illustrate the ways that religion and butterflies are connected in visual and, perhaps, emotional ways. In Hirst's work, actual butterfly wings are incorporated into the imagery of stained glass. The butterfly is transformed from colourful insect to the substance of artwork. In looking at these works, the recognizable shape of individual wings is still apparent, but together these remains provide a cumulative image of a church window. Simultaneously, then, our perception recognizes a mundane species and an element of religious architecture, creating a feeling of horror (at the death of such fragile, beautiful creatures) mixed with astonishment (at the beauty of the iridescent, consuming work). Further, we are confronted with the moral ambiguity of purposely killing beautiful creatures in order to create human works of beauty. This is a reaction, in other words, that occurs when we acknowledge the simple fact that these were once living, particular, and individual creatures. While Hirst pushes us toward the complexity of our aesthetic and emotional engagement in extreme ways, the pastime of collecting butterflies has a similar complexity. After all, the collector appreciates aesthetic depth of these creatures and seeks an ever-deeper knowledge of them while capturing the delicate flutter of the butterfly as a specimen. Though less extreme, other ways of encountering butterflies – for example, building a butterfly garden, visiting butterfly houses, or viewing other artistic portrayals – add depth to this complex relationship.

Hirst's mosaics of actual butterflies intimate some of the complexities of our relationship with butterflies. Most importantly, they force us to confront the fact that all sorts of animals participate in religion by becoming *embedded* in human places and artefacts. Here, the strange nature of the concrete case of butterflies (if we can really attribute the word 'concrete' to such delicate, otherworldly creatures) becomes sharper. For the term 'animals' frequently brings to mind the brutish, the earthly, the wild, the material, and the base. But butterflies – flitting for only a few weeks, ethereal and atmospheric, joyously beautiful, and at home in the bursting colour of flowers – are animals, too. But what if butterflies, by being far removed from the beastly and mundane, transform us in ways that our nearer kin do not?

---

[18] D. Hirst, *Superstition* (Beverly Hills: Gagosian Gallery, 2007).

III. Dwelling, Place, and Non-Human Animals

I suggest that a transformative power is located in the particularity of animals. Butterflies are not unique in this regard; certainly, we meet other creatures as individuals (pets are examples that quickly come to mind[19]). But butterflies seem to live beyond categories of 'wild' and 'domesticated', just as they appear aloof from the category of 'animal' itself. As seen in the example we started with, we approach the individual butterfly as an individual, most likely without even meaning to do so. We attend to their radical particularity by watching them animate flowers, or by watching their unpredictable flights around us. More significantly, we mentally and physically chase after them, not to destroy but to witness these little beings. Theologically, then, we cannot merely reduce such singular experiences to abstract categories.

A theology for animals, in other words, approaches not only non-human animals as a group, but also asks how we (as human animals) attend to individual non-human animals in our daily lives and theological musings. In fact, through Hirst's images we are left with the irreducible uniqueness of each individual creature. Our perception of Hirst's 'windows' is not limited to the visual force of the whole. Rather, we are drawn to see each unique wing that contributes to the overall image. The coloration and shape of a particular wing is not simply the result of the traits of each species – unique qualities are the marks of individuals. In like manner, taking animals as religious subjects means balancing individuals with species (and the animal kingdom on a whole), in a way that does not reduce either to a mere placeholder or resource. How might we understand animals on their own terms, while at the same time acknowledging the important functions that animals have symbolically in Christian theology? The current section addresses one way of integrating the concern for individual animals on their own terms with a concern for animals and environments more generally, by suggesting the need for reflection on who and what 'dwells in place'.

I define 'dwelling' from the context of a *hermeneutical* ecological theology, that is, a theology that approaches nature through a reflection on how we interpret the *meaning* of nature. The meaning of self and other – the 'depth dimension', to use Paul Tillich's metaphor for the sacred dimension of existence – is at the core of our theological understanding. To discuss human meaning

---

[19] A. Petersen, 'Recreate, Relate, Decenter: Environmental Ethics and Domestic Animals', *Placing Nature on the Borders of Religion, Philosophy and Ethics* (F. Clingerman, and M. Dixon (eds); Aldershot: Ashgate, 2011), pp. 165–82.

is to talk about something that rests *between* subject and object, *through* the interplay between particular and the general, *among* individuals, and *in the midst of* a context that transcends and embodies the individual. In other words, *meaning is negotiated betwixt and between* the whole of nature and individuals within nature.

Dwelling is a hermeneutical concept, I argue, because it functions as a conceptual framework for identifying the emergence of the *meaning* of particular individuals as constitutive elements of a place, when place is seen as the spatio-temporal whole that contextualizes and embeds the individual. Dwelling, in other words, allows us to define individuals as some*where*, while simultaneously thinking about how a place is defined by *who* is there. Environmental theology can approach nature by interpreting the particular individual as situated in a place made up of individuals, while also interpreting the whole place in light of each individual that makes up this place.

I am suggesting, then, that there is a need to investigate an 'environmental hermeneutical circle'. Typically the hermeneutical circle describes the process through which we interpret texts in a dialectical relationship between parts and whole. That is, we understand the whole of the narrative by understanding the different parts of the narrative, and simultaneously understand the parts through the narrative on a whole. By negotiating between parts and whole, the reader enters the world of the text. My suggestion is that there is an environmental hermeneutical circle that is not only intellectually, but also physically, inhabited. In fact, our physical and mental inhabitation occurs alongside other ways of being in place that together make the place being interpreted. Therefore, there is a specific hermeneutical play involved in environmental theology: it is a reflection on the meaning of place that involves *both* interpretation of the place on the whole, and *also* on the individual beings that make up that whole. In the case of nature, meaning does not emerge from the abstract whole (just as we do not interpret literature per se); we interpret meaning through *particular* places, landscapes, and environments. Thus, we can correlate the hermeneutical circle to place and inhabitants: we cannot understand the whole without the parts, nor can we understand the parts without the whole.

If environmental theology seeks to engage this environmental hermeneutical circle, it not only must look to interpret actual places (that is, the 'work' or the whole under interpretation), but it also must clarify what constitutes one of the 'parts' of these places. Some of these individual, non-human animals, approach place in ways similar to us: they live, attempt to belong to their environment, and interact with other inhabitants in diverse ways (some predictable, some not). They *dwell*. Admittedly, non-human animals most likely do not attain the complexity and reflexivity that characterize human interpretations of place. But even more simplified forms of dwelling suggest a form of individuality within place, within nature.

Dwelling names a framework of interpreting the meaning of the self in the world – of one being that is a part of the whole of place. In turn, this helps us understand our relationship with non-human animals, for it offers a concept through which to *understand* the different hermeneutical interactions we have, especially with other beings who dwell in place. Aaron Gross has helpfully argued that our interactions with non-human animals include pragmatic, ontological, and structural dimensions.[20] Reflection on the concept of dwelling complements and furthers Gross' discussion by allowing us to situate self and other in a spatio-temporal hermeneutical circle. That is to say, it provides the opportunity for yet another level: the reflexive. By dwelling on the meaning of place, we contextualize the individual within the whole, and the whole within the individual.

In the context of an environmental hermeneutical circle, how might we define 'dwelling'? Most basically, dwelling is *a work: the work of inhabiting a place, of encountering and embodying the meaning of a place, of when I become what I am through another, insofar as I participate in creating where others dwell.* Dwelling is a work of *participating in place*; it is becoming oneself by caring for others in and through the place in which we belong. Dwelling is fundamental to the narrative of place, and in turn the narrative of place grounds our self-identity as a narrative of self and other.

Elsewhere, I have discussed the Heideggerian notion of human dwelling, and this has bearing on the present discussion.[21] For Heidegger, dwelling is a poetic, meditative reflection on who and what we are as we are thrown into the world. Thus, dwelling is the 'basic character of Being'. That is to say, to dwell is to live in place, among other inhabitants, in such a way as to be secure and safe as what one is. Heidegger writes, 'To dwell, to be set at peace, means to remain at peace within the free, the preserve, the free sphere that safeguards each thing in its

---

[20] Gross writes, 'The pragmatic rigour, which deserves a certain priority, calls us to attend to the day-to-day, 'local' interactions with animals... The ontological rigour allows us to see that these biological animals are always both intertwined with symbolic ones and with an imagination of 'the animal' that delimits 'the human'. Finally, the structural rigour reminds us that an encounter with animals never takes place on one plane...' A. Gross, 'The Question of the Creature: Animals, Theology and Levinas' Dog', *Creaturely Theology* (C. Deane-Drummond, and D. Clough (eds); London: SCM Press, 2009), p. 121.
[21] F. Clingerman, 'The Intimate Distance of Herons: Theological Travels Through Nature, Place, and Migration', *Ethics, Place & Environment: A Journal of Philosophy and Geography* 11 (2008), pp. 313–25.

essence. *The fundamental character of dwelling is this sparing and preserving*.[22] Sparing, says Heidegger, means that we 'free' something to be what it is 'in its own nature'.[23] Such dwelling is neither autonomous nor self-centred; instead, it includes a sense of *caring for* others and allowing them to dwell. Thus, Michael Zimmerman explains, 'To dwell, then, means to be the silent openness that we always already are – a curious feat! In learning to be this open realm, we become attuned to Logos. We learn to be in the service of the Being of beings. That is, we learn to let beings bring themselves to appearance by giving voice to themselves through us'.[24]

What does this admittedly brief description of dwelling mean? Foremost, it connects the individual with the environment and, in so doing, allows for the possibility of connecting the individual with other individuals as well. To put this in the structure of the hermeneutical circle: individual inhabitants uniquely dwell in place, and place is where inhabitants become inhabitants through dwelling. Therefore, dwelling is a mode of *particular* existence, but a mode that is inevitably *intersubjective* and *situated*. For Heidegger, only humans can fulfil the task of dwelling. However, parting ways with Heidegger, I wish to suggest that there are different ways of inhabiting a place – herons migrate, bears hibernate, humans build. Each creature uniquely dwells in a location, providing one element that contributes to the instantiation of place. In each case, dwelling refocuses our attention toward more intersubjective descriptions: a theological discussion of dwelling seeks to interpret how animals (human and non-human alike) transform space and time in care of others.

Because of its emphasis on balancing relationality and uniqueness, a focus on dwelling, in fact, can be seen to share some affinities to David Cunningham's advocacy for the more theological term 'flesh'. For Cunningham, the difficulty with postulating a distinction between humans and non-humans in Christianity is that the distinction must be formulated from a specifically theological perspective. Although the most common theological starting point is the *imago dei*, Cunningham argues that the characterization of humans as the only creatures made in the image of God is mistaken; this is a claim that Charles Camosy also makes, elsewhere in this volume. Whether or not one agrees with Cunningham and Camosy on the uniqueness of the *imago dei*, both are seeking

[22] M. Heidegger, 'Building Dwelling Thinking', *Poetry, Language, Thought* (New York: Harper, 1971), p. 148.

[23] Ibid.

[24] M. Zimmerman, 'The Role of Spiritual Discipline in Learning to Dwell on Earth', *Dwelling, Place, and Environment: Toward a Phenomenology of Person and World* (D. Seamon, and R. Mugerauer (eds); New York: Columbia University Press, 1985), p. 253.

to ground our theological discussions of non-humans in a necessary humility; that is, both, correctly, wish to uncover the theological interconnection between human and non-human as equally creatures under God. Thus, for Cunningham, we should turn to the biblical characterization of 'flesh'. Cunningham argues that the *imago dei* connects humans and non-humans: 'The primary focus of God's relational life ad extra is not only with human beings; it extends to all flesh, all living creatures'.[25] At the same time, there are differences among creatures of flesh: flesh unites creatures but allows us to see what differentiates them as well. 'All living creatures share flesh, and they also share a relationship with God; but the category of flesh has certain distinguishing marks within it, such that (for example) cold-blooded and warm-blooded animals are both understood to have flesh, but different kinds of flesh'.[26] A focus on what it means to dwell shares a similar dynamic with the biblical notion of 'flesh' – we see how creatures are gathered together in such a way that allows for a sense of uniqueness and particularity.

Second, the task of dwelling is intimately tied to uncovering the narrative of a place – of seeing how individuals interact and create a place as place. Unlike a focus on flesh, dwelling embraces the temporal and spatial location of our embodiment. In other words, a theological reflection on dwelling concretizes our finitude, while maintaining the multiplicity and relatedness of particular embodiments. Dwelling takes up the symbolic and yet dwelling is a mediation of a non-metaphorical presence as well. But then this also means that dwelling *is an interpretive task in and through the particular individual in the midst of the general*. Dwelling is a work of mediation that occurs when the *individual* navigates *within* a locale, thereby discovering an intersubjective narrative that is the meaning of place, and thus the meaning of selfhood. At the same time, dwelling is a *social* work: individuals participate in the task of co-constituting a meaning of the shared narrative of what is other than the individual.

Finally, by focusing on dwelling, we are meant to treat individuals as subjects, while also acknowledging how they might serve to convey meaning for others. The presumption that an individual being is the sole locus of value (the one-sided viewpoint of animal rights) is mediated by the necessity of the whole as the framework for intersubjective meaning (the one-sided viewpoint of deep ecology, land ethics, and some forms of biodiversity protection). The obverse is similarly true: the whole is mediated by the uniqueness of the individual. This

---

[25] D. Cunningham, 'The Way of All Flesh: Rethinking the Imago Dei', *Creaturely Theology* (C. Deane-Drummond, and D. Clough (eds); London: SCM Press, 2009), p. 114.

[26] Ibid., p. 115.

diminishes the separation between individual and collective, or between animal rights and environmental ethics. Instead, part of authentic dwelling is to allow others to dwell: we revel in the individuals that together gather in place, while also acknowledging the value of the work and gathering that the place itself embodies.

Of course, butterflies are quite dissimilar to humans. Among other things, they cannot reflectively or reflexively think as humans do. But from egg to pupa to chrysalis to imago, they encounter the world in different ways, and so are continually involved in self-transformation. Thus, they challenge and add complexity to our limited approach to place and nature – in their transformation, they transform us. Indeed, we can point to the work of scholars such as Marc Bekoff to see how other animals teach us new and different ways of encountering the world. And so, if we assume other creatures also have forms of dwelling, can we ask: how do butterflies dwell?[27] This, I think, is the proper question of a theology that takes butterflies seriously. How might the short life span change their localization? How does the reliance on sunlight to warm their wings influence movement and space itself, or the dormancy or migration that marks the winter of many species? What meaning do they see in the world, and what meaning do they bring to our lives? How do butterflies dwell, not only in our concepts and visions of the world, but in the places and narratives that we together create? How might butterflies tarry and create a locale in ways that care for humans? And, in turn, how might humans dwell to care for butterflies? This can only be understood when we begin to reflect on the multiplicity of use, aesthetics, ecologies, and communities that defines the ways that others dwell, accepting that dwelling appears in us only insofar as others dwell alongside us.

IV. Dwelling, Spirituality, and Redemption

The final portion of this chapter suggests that dwelling in place has theological implications, insofar as dwelling is ultimately a spiritual practice – one that

---

[27] While the present chapter brings up the question of butterflies, it is important to note that we can ask similar questions of other species. For example, Freya Mathews has brought out some of the philosophical and ethical dimensions of the collapse of honeybee colonies with a recognition of the unique individuality of bees as members of the hive. Her analysis, I would argue, could easily be placed into dialogue with questions concerning a sense of how honeybees dwell. See F. Mathews, 'Planetary Collapse Disorder: The Honeybee as Portent of the Limits of the Ethical', *Environmental Ethics* 32 (2010), pp. 353–67.

includes human and non-human animals and other beings that dwell in a particular place.

Dwelling, as it has been discussed, is not simply a descriptive task, nor is it concerned exclusively with physical needs. Rather, it is a normative task – we seek to *fully* and *properly* dwell – and as such it extends to an almost Tillichian 'spiritual depth' of place. In other words, dwelling is oriented toward what David Klemm and William Schweiker have called 'the integrity of life before God'. The integrity of life, for Klemm and Schweiker, means that we have a fruitful and balanced life that consists of freedom and access to the basic, reflective, social, and spiritual goods of life. While Schweiker and Klemm are defining this view of integrity in the context of a renewed theological humanism, their conception of humanism is not oriented exclusively toward the value and needs of humanity. I would argue, then, that such integrity becomes an essential quality for assessing the dwelling of all creatures, not simply humans. Put plainly, all creatures should hope for an existence defined by integrity appropriate to a life before God.

Therefore, integrity cannot happen individually; it can only occur in relationship, in light of, to use the words of Todorov, 'the autonomy of the I, the finality of the you, and the universality of the they'.[28] This phrase characterizes what occurs when we properly dwell. To truly and fully dwell aims at the flourishing of individuals in place, not simply living, but living with integrity. In the integrity of life, the self meets the other and the individual inhabitants gather together within the locality of the environment itself. What I am suggesting aligns with Peter Scott's discussion of how humanity images God through sociality, temporality, and spatiality. Certainly we can see the social and temporal dimensions of the integrity of life. What is most intriguing, however, is that Scott's anthropological reading of spatiality offers a theological rationale through which we can show why human dwelling and human integrity are intimately tied together:

> Spatiality refers us to the reality of nature (including humanity) and its givenness by God: the character of humanity's place in its environment. The natural conditions of human life are part of the givenness of the blessing of God to natural humanity. Nature remains God's blessing; thereby it is ordered toward the preservation of the creatures of God and is itself that ordering.[29]

---

[28] Quoted in D. Klemm, and W. Schweiker, *Religion and the Human Future: An Essay on Theological Humanism* (Malden, MA: Blackwell, 2008), p. 17.

[29] P. Scott, 'The Technological Factor: Redemption, Nature, and the Image of God', *Zygon* 35 (2000), p. 382. This essay was republished along with several other related essays in P. Scott, *Anti-Human Theology: Nature, Technology and the Postnatural* (London: SCM Press, 2010). This collection of essays argues that theology must forego its exclusive emphasis on humanity in favor of a political advocacy of the non-human and human alike.

Not only does spatiality remind us we are in a 'real, natural context', spatiality also reminds us that we live in the middle of history. For humans, then, spatiality further reinforces the social and temporal dimensions of our unique ways of being in the world. Human integrity is quite different from other species – human integrity is fundamentally different from the integrity of butterflies in intellectual, emotional, and physical ways. But our desire for human integrity pushes us toward a broader, more holistic theology that embraces life in all its forms. In other words, human integrity exists when our theology, on the one hand, maintains a systematic, constructive stance, while on the other, it is porous and accepting of the many ways that theological thinking can learn from other creatures through their different and unique modes of dwelling with integrity.

Dwelling, in sum, *extends our inhabitation into a gathered spiritual and moral realm*. It is a work that involves a new way of thinking in order to create a new way of being in the world. As Zimmerman writes about Heidegger's concept of dwelling, 'The argument is that in order for people to be heirs of a new way of thinking, more may be required than learning a new vocabulary. A paradigm shift does not occur by our reading books about it; nor does it happen when we set about to put into practice what we have heard preached'.[30] In like manner, the dwelling we are discussing suggests itself as a spiritual discipline that opens us to theological questions concerning the meaning of place and the integrity of the lives of other animal kinds. This places dwelling as a practice in what Klemm and Schweiker define as the 'true religion' that exists as a middle way between hypertheism and secular humanism: 'The spiritual struggle of life is thereby to inhabit one's religious identity for a good that exceeds that identity, namely, the integrity of life'.[31] Dwelling localizes the integrity of life.

If dwelling is the work of localizing the integrity of life, then it provides the site of *redemption* for the human and non-human alike. Within the Christian theological tradition, redemption has been conceived of narrowly as the reconciliation of the human soul to God. But we can use Denis Edwards' definition to suggest an alternative that sees '... the word redemption, like the word salvation, in the wide sense of transformation in Christ, rather than in the limited sense of forgiveness of human sin. ... As well as forgiveness, redemption/salvation involves healing, reconciliation, fulfilment, liberation

---

[30] M. Zimmerman, 'The Role of Spiritual Discipline in Learning to Dwell on Earth', *Dwelling, Place, and Environment: Toward a Phenomenology of Person and World* (D. Seamon, and R. Mugerauer (eds); New York: Columbia University Press, 1985), p. 248.

[31] Klemm and Schweiker, *Religion and the Human Future*, p. 161.

from death, resurrection life, transformation in Christ, and communion in the life of the Trinitarian God with all God's creation'.[32] Holmes Rolston likewise suggests a broader view of redemption:

> If redemption means being saved from the guilt of sin, then fauna, flora, rocks, and rivers have no guilt and cannot be redeemed. ... If redemption can also mean being rescued from harm (Latin: *redimo* to release, to buy back), then our inquiry is still open. If redemption can mean that value in one life is rescued and restored, or that the value in one life survives to contribute to lives beyond one's own, then our inquiry is promising. If redemption can mean that there is a transformation by which destruction of the old, lower life is not really destruction but renovation, the creation of newer, higher levels of life, then our inquiry is promising indeed.[33]

Finally, Rolston argues, nature itself is cruciform and allows for a larger sense of redemption in the midst of natural processes. Discussions by Celia Deane-Drummond and Christopher Southgate also suggest ways of incorporating non-human animals into a theological sense of redemption.[34] While these authors are not in complete agreement over the process of this Christic redemption of all creation, the implication of these discussions is that there is a need for an ecological dimension within Klemm and Schweiker's vision of the integrity of life.

Taking seriously the claims of thinkers such as Edwards and Rolston, there is theological promise in discussing integrity and the redemption of non-human animals. In their essay 'Will Animals be Redeemed?', Petroc and Eldred Willey begin with two statements:

> First, central to Christianity is a concern with redemption, both from death and from sin, from a destructive pattern of relationships with God, with one another, with ourselves, and with creation. Secondly, both scripture and tradition agree that the Christian understanding of redemption involves the whole of the created order – and therefore animals – in some sense.[35]

Redemption includes the here-and-now, not simply the hereafter; thus, we might say that a respectful and relational 'dwelling' is another name for 'building Heaven' among us.

---

[32] D. Edwards, 'The Redemption of Animals in Incarnational Theology', *Creaturely Theology* (C. Deane-Drummond, and D. Clough (eds); London: SCM Press, 2009), p. 81.

[33] H. Rolston, 'Does Nature Need to Be Redeemed?', *Zygon* 29 (1994), p. 211.

[34] C. Deane-Drummond, *Christ and Evolution: Wonder and Wisdom* (Minneapolis: Fortress, 2009); C. Southgate, *The Groaning of Creation: God, Evolution, and the Problem of Evil* (Louisville, KY: Westminster/John Knox, 2008).

[35] P. and E. Willey, 'Will Animals be Redeemed?', *Animals on the Agenda* (A. Linzey, and D. Yamamoto (eds); Urbana, IL: University of Illinois Press, 1998), p. 190.

For the Willeys, the redemption of animals can be modelled as either representative or non-representative. In representative models, creation is redeemed *through* human redemption, insofar as humans serve as representatives of the entirety of creation. In non-representative models, by contrast, creation is redeemed on its own behalf; it is unique and independent in the process of redemption. So, one of the important issues involved in what this redemption might mean relates to the question of whether animals have selves. Selfhood, the Willeys show, is important for redemption, but it has been debated whether animals have selves in any meaningful way. For representative models, there is no need for a unique animal self. In non-representational models, animals have selves that are unique. Thus, 'If the interiority and individuality of animals is such that they cannot be adequately represented in and through humankind then redemption will feature animals selves in their own right'.[36] The Willeys suggest agnosticism on this point, insofar as there is no definitive way of proving either model.

The idea of dwelling, however, offers a third way between the representational and non-representational models of the Willeys. This third way involves the promotion of a sense of self while acknowledging the interconnections of selfhood. As we have seen above, dwelling occurs only through a mediation of the self with the other; both human and non-human are defined through their situatedness in place. The possibility of a fullness of the self through dwelling thus connects dwelling and redemption. Denis Edwards writes, 'What we have in the Christian tradition is the resurrection: a promise that we are held in the faithful love of God, which is stronger than death; a promise that we along with all things will be transformed in Christ'.[37] Edwards' discussion focuses on communion and memory, and he concludes by saying, 'The diverse range of creatures that springs from the abundance of this divine communion finds redemption in being taken up eternally into this communion. Because God relates to each creature on its own terms, final fulfilment will fit the nature of each creature'.[38] The act of approaching each creature on its own terms, I argue, occurs only in light of our ability to inhabit a place – to dwell – with and for others. Evoking Robert Scharlemann's phrase, we might name the wholeness and flourishing of place as 'the being of God when God is not being God'.[39] Thus,

---

[36] Ibid., p. 198.
[37] D. Edwards, *Ecology at the Heart of Faith* (Maryknoll, NY: Orbis, 2006), p. 93.
[38] Ibid., p. 98.
[39] R. Scharlemann, *Inscriptions and Reflections* (Charlottesville, VA: University Press of Virginia, 1989), pp. 30–53.

when we truly dwell, we dwell with others, and this culminates in a detour of self and other that is completed in the wholeness of God, in the fulfilment of Christ, and in the communion of all in all.

Admittedly, the focus on dwelling is an unusual approach toward redemption. Several theologians rightly have seen the immediacy of suffering as a more traditional approach toward redemption, especially as suffering affects individuals, species, and ecosystems. For example, Holmes Rolston has noted that suffering is an inevitable part of the biotic world, even if non-human animals are unable to make fully moral choices.[40] Celia Deane-Drummond argues that the question of animal morality and the issue of suffering are necessary components for the discussion of atonement and redemption of non-human animals;[41] the shadow side of Sophia is present throughout creation, but is overcome through redemption and atonement. Michael Northcott goes even further to suggest dolphins, at least, are fully moral creatures and stand in need of redemption in a world of fragility and suffering.[42] Celia Deane-Drummond, in response to Northcott, questions whether animals such as dolphins can truly be said to sin – to turn away from God – but acknowledges that nonhuman morality and immorality connect with human sinfulness and thus stands in need of redemption.[43] Sigurd Bergmann reminds us of the importance of the concept of liberation in response to suffering when attempting to understand the 'opera of ecologic salvation'.[44] Finally, Christopher Southgate's important work, *The Groaning of Creation*, offers an 'evolutionary theodicy' that addresses the individual creature as well as creation. In Southgate's picture, suffering creates a number of issues for redemption. Redemption in the midst of suffering, therefore, must be worked out through both evolutionary theory and God's patterning of individual creatures through the Word. In contrast to this approach, my admittedly preliminary suggestion begins with a different set of concerns. I suggest that these explorations of redemption and suffering can illuminate the sense of how individuals and species inhabit particular locales, thereby further developing the sense of dwelling of each creature and the place itself. At the same time, the creation of place lends itself to see in new ways

---

[40] Rolston, 'Does Nature Need to Be Redeemed?', pp. 205–29.
[41] C. Deane-Drummond, 'Shadow Sophia in Christological Perspective: The Evolution of Sin and the Redemption of Nature', *Theology and Science* 6 (2008), pp. 13–32.
[42] M. Northcott, 'Do Dolphins Carry the Cross?: Biological Moral Realism and Theological Ethics', *New Blackfriars* 84 (2003), pp. 540–53.
[43] Deane-Drummond, *Christ and Evolution*, pp. 166–7.
[44] S. Bergmann, 'Trinitarian Cosmology in God's Liberating Movement: Exploring Some Signature Tunes in the Opera of Ecologic Salvation', *Worldviews* 14 (2010), pp. 185–205.

the depths of suffering and the possibility of an intersubjective integrity of life before God.

To conclude, then, we turn once more to humble, elusive butterflies. Butterflies offer us a ready-made symbol for transformation and redemption in Christianity. But, as I have suggested, the real question is not what they symbolize, but how they dwell. Individual butterflies dwell in place in fundamentally different and transformational ways; in so doing, they allow us to reflect on how we gather together the places and landscapes of our lives and become redeemed and transformed ourselves. That is to say, butterflies, in ever-changing ways, exist betwixt and between our human-centred lives, quietly changing the places in which we dwell. If such dwelling is a spiritual practice involved with redemption, butterflies dwell through transformation – a transformation of self and other, which is both a physical and a redemptive act. But we might then ask, how are *we* transforming place? Individual species of butterflies are threatened by climate change, habitat encroachment, and a myriad of other effects of human actions. How might human inhabitation be transformative, redeemed through the intersubjective experience of dwelling with butterflies?

Bibliography

Bekoff, M., 'Considering Animals – Not "Higher" Primates', *Zygon* 38 (2003), pp. 229–45.

—'The Evolution of Animal Play, Emotions, And Social Morality: On Science, Theology, Spirituality, Personhood, and Love', *Zygon* 36 (2001), pp. 615–55.

—'Minding Animals, Minding Earth: Old Brains, New Bottlenecks', *Zygon* 38 (2003), pp. 911–41.

Bergmann, S., 'Trinitarian Cosmology in God's Liberating Movement: Exploring Some Signature Tunes in the Opera of Ecologic Salvation', *Worldviews* 14 (2010), pp. 185–205.

Bonaventure, St., *The Soul's Journey into God/The Tree of Life/The Life of Saint Francis* (Ewert Cousins (trans.); New York: Paulist Press, 1978).

Callicott, J. B., 'Animal Liberation: A Triangular Affair', *Environmental Ethics* 2 (1980), pp. 311–38.

Clingerman, F., 'The Intimate Distance of Herons: Theological Travels Through Nature, Place, and Migration', *Ethics, Place & Environment: A Journal of Philosophy and Geography* 11 (2008), pp. 313–25.

Cunningham, D. S. 'The Way of All Flesh: Rethinking the Imago Dei', *Creaturely Theology: On God, Humans and Other Animals* (C. Deane-Drummond, and D. Clough (eds); London: SCM Press, 2009), pp. 100–17.

Deane-Drummond, C., *Christ and Evolution: Wonder and Wisdom* (Minneapolis: Fortress, 2009).

—'Shadow Sophia in Christological Perspective: The Evolution of Sin and the Redemption of Nature', *Theology and Science* 6 (2008), pp. 13–32.

Deane-Drummond, C., and D. Clough, 'Introduction', *Creaturely Theology: On God, Humans and Other Animals* (C. Deane-Drummond, and D. Clough (eds); London: SCM Press, 2009), pp. 1–18.

Douglas, M., *The Lives of Butterflies* (Ann Arbor: University of Michigan Press, 1986).

Edwards, D., *Ecology at the Heart of Faith* (Maryknoll, NY: Orbis, 2006).

—'The Redemption of Animals in Incarnational Theology', *Creaturely Theology: On God, Humans and Other Animals* (C. Deane-Drummond, and D. Clough (eds); London: SCM Press, 2009), pp. 81–99.

Gross, A., 'The Question of the Creature: Animals, Theology and Levinas' Dog', *Creaturely Theology: On God, Humans and Other Animals* (C. Deane-Drummond, and D. Clough (eds); London: SCM Press, 2009), pp. 121–37.

Heidegger, M., 'Building Dwelling Thinking', *Poetry, Language, Thought* (New York: Harper, 1971), pp. 143–61.

Hirst, D., *Superstition* (Beverly Hills: Gagosian Gallery, 2007).

Hobgood-Oster, L., *Holy Dogs & Asses: Animals in the Christian Tradition* (Urbana, IL: University of Illinois Press, 2008).

Huddleston, R. (ed.), *The Little Flowers of Saint Francis of Assisi* (Springfield, IL: Templegate, 1988).

Klemm, D., and W. Schweiker, *Religion and the Human Future: An Essay on Theological Humanism* (Malden, MA: Blackwell, 2008).

Linzey, A., *Animal Theology* (Urbana, IL: University of Illinois Press, 1995).

Mathews, F., 'Planetary Collapse Disorder: The Honeybee as Portent of the Limits of the Ethical', *Environmental Ethics* 32 (2010), pp. 353–67.

McDaniel, J., 'All Animals Matter: Marc Bekoff's Contribution to Constructive Christian Theology', *Zygon* 41 (2006), pp. 29–58.

—*Of God and Pelicans: A Theology of Reverence for Life* (Louisville, KY: Westminster/ John Knox Press, 1989).

Northcott, M., 'Do Dolphins Carry the Cross?: Biological Moral Realism and Theological Ethics', *New Blackfriars* 84 (2003), pp. 540–53.

Petersen, A., 'Recreate, Relate, Decenter: Environmental Ethics and Domestic Animals', *Placing Nature on the Borders of Religion, Philosophy and Ethics* (F. Clingerman, and M. H. Dixon (eds); Aldershot: Ashgate, 2011), pp. 165–82.

Pyle, R. M., *A Handbook for Butterfly Watchers* (New York: Scribner's, 1984).

Rolston, H., 'Does Nature Need to Be Redeemed?', *Zygon* 29 (1994), pp. 205–29.

Schappert, P., *A World for Butterflies* (Buffalo: Firefly Books, 2000).

Scharlemann, R., *Inscriptions and Reflections* (Charlottesville, VA: University Press of Virginia, 1989).

Scott, P. M., *Anti-Human Theology: Nature, Technology and the Postnatural* (London: SCM Press, 2010).

—'The Technological Factor: Redemption, Nature, and the Image of God', *Zygon* 35 (2000), pp. 371–84.

Southgate, C., *The Groaning of Creation: God, Evolution, and the Problem of Evil* (Louisville, KY: Westminster/John Knox, 2008).

Ward, B., (ed.), *The Lives of the Desert Fathers* (Kalamazoo, MI: Cistercian Publications, 1981).

Willey, P., and E. Willey, 'Will Animals be Redeemed?', *Animals on the Agenda* (A. Linzey, and D. Yamamoto (eds); Urbana, IL: University of Illinois Press, 1998), pp. 190–200.

Zimmerman, M., 'The Role of Spiritual Discipline in Learning to Dwell on Earth', *Dwelling, Place, and Environment: Toward a Phenomenology of Person and World* (D. Seamon, and Robert Mugerauer (eds); New York: Columbia University Press, 1985), pp. 247–56.

9

'Marvel at the Intelligence of Unthinking Creatures!': Contemplative Animals in Gregory of Nazianzus and Evagrius of Pontus

Eric Daryl Meyer

As with every bottomless gaze, as with the eyes of the other, the gaze called 'animal' offers to my sight the abyssal limit of the human: the inhuman or the ahuman, the ends of man, that is to say, the bordercrossing from which vantage man dares to announce himself to himself, thereby calling himself by the name that he believes he gives himself.[1]

In *The Animal that Therefore I Am,* Derrida queries what (or who) feeds at the limit between the human and the animal. What is it that is nourished by this distinction? Who stands to benefit from maintaining a single line, a clean cut between the human and the animal? By the end of the text he has come to the conclusion that the thinking subject (the *je suis* that both 'follows' the animal and recognizes itself by means of the encounter with the animal) must be something neither dead nor alive; the *je suis* is neither animal nor some *thing* that is added to the animal.[2] Subjectivity is a reflexive activity that produces itself precisely by cutting itself off from 'the animal', a disavowal that produces 'the human' as that being who goes by a different name. For Derrida, then, the creature named 'human' is an animal that doubles back on itself in order to theorize itself as something other, to 'announce himself to himself'. *The human is a process by which an animal disavows its animality.* But what is it that remains in this disavowal; and how should this remainder be figured theologically?

Following on Derrida's analysis of a great disavowal of animals in Western philosophical thinking about human subjectivity, this essay examines the

---

[1] J. Derrida, *The Animal that Therefore I Am* (M. Mallet (ed.); D. Wills (trans.); New York: Fordham University Press, 2008), p. 12; with occasional reference to the original French text, *L'Animal que donc je suis* (M. Mallet (ed.); Paris: Éditions Galilée, 2006).
[2] Derrida, *Animal,* pp. 87, 102.

contemplative subjectivity described by Gregory of Nazianzus and Evagrius of Pontus.[3] I argue that while both Gregory and Evagrius describe the *activity* of spiritual contemplation as humanity's transcending above animality, nevertheless, the *mode of subjectivity* that they describe in the human who perfectly contemplates God corresponds exactly to the mode of subjectivity attributed to animals guided by their instincts. The much-vaunted transcendence of humanity over animality, then, turns out to be an empty ideological disavowal, the announcement of the self to itself in a gesture that actually signals the isolation of humanity from God and fellow creatures. Thinking with venerable figures like Gregory and Evagrius helps to locate some of the perennially recurring fractures and short-circuits within Christian anthropological projects and to explore alternate resolutions to their conceptual stalemates – crossing or uncrossing different wires, moving down avenues of thought which they have opened, but not taken themselves.

The essay proceeds in two parts: first, a summary of Gregory and Evagrius' contemplative theological anthropology and an articulation of their conception of contemplation as the transcendence of humanity above animality; second, an exploration of the failed transcendence of humanity over animality within the terms of Gregory and Evagrius' arguments and an attempt to figure differently the relation of humanity, animality, and divinity.

I. Contemplative Theological Anthropology

Gregory of Nazianzus is routinely boggled that the human being should be a mixture of dirt and spirit. For the creature who is named as the apex and ruler of creation to be made in such a composite manner seems manifestly unwise to Gregory. Surely a pure and unmixed intelligence, not subject to mortality and corruption would have been far, far superior to this odd mixture of mud and soul! The mystery of human nature for Gregory is the conjunction of two natures in one being. On Gregory's reading of Genesis 1–2, God first

---

[3] I have chosen to write on Gregory and Evagrius because of striking similarities within their theological anthropologies. While the significant differences between the two should not be ignored, both projects are basically Origenian, tripartite, and emphasize the νοῦς as the loftiest aspect of human life. Both figures have also exerted tremendous influence on subsequent Christian tradition – Gregory on the East through his orations and Evagrius in the West through his spirituality (as mediated by John Cassian). Incidentally, they were also acquaintances in Cappadocia and Constantinople; see J. McGuckin, *Saint Gregory of Nazianzus: An Intellectual Biography* (Crestwood, NY: St. Vladimir's Seminary Press, 2001), pp. 276–8.

constructs an *intellectual-spiritual* creation followed by a *material* creation, placing humanity right at the boundary between the two, the sole creature to be fully an inhabitant of both the intellectual and the material order. The human being is 'another angel', a worshipper of God and bearer of divine and angelic light; yet at the same time a debased bodily creature, who – like the animals – is subject to decay and corruption.

> Then, gazing upon everything constructed and thinking,
> [God] was delighted by the conceptually unified works of a masterful Child,
> but, [God] sought someone acquainted with the wisdom of the Mother of all things (μητρὸς ἁπάντων),
> of those drawn from the soil, a God-fearing ruler (χθονίων βασιλῆα θεουδέα).
> So [God] said:
> 'Already, my pure and ever-living attendants
> have the breadth of heaven. Holy minds! Noble angels!
> Composers of hymns who never cease celebrating my praise in song and dance!
> Yet Earth still glories in thoughtless animals (ζώοισιν ἀγάλλεται ἀφραδέουσι).
> It is my pleasure to appoint a kind of mixture from both,
> an intelligent light (νοήμονα φῶτα) between the mortals and immortals;
> delighting in my works; a prudent initiate
> into heavenly matters; of those sprung from soil, a great power (μέγα κράτος);
> another angel;
> from the soil, a singer of my mind and intentions (ὑμνητῆρά τ' ἐμῶν μενέων τε νόου).'[4]

The paradox of the placement of the human at this limit is almost too much for Gregory to bear. But not only does the human being (alone of all the creatures) *straddle* the line between the intelligible and material creation, this limit also runs *interior* to every human being. The human being is a *microcosmos*, a mysterious conjunction that mirrors the mystery of the doubleness of creation.

---

[4] This, and all subsequent translations from the Greek are my own. Gregory of Nazianzus, 'In Praise of Virginity', ll. 78–95, PG 37:528–9; cf. ll. 30–55, PG 37:524–5: J. Migne (ed.), *Patrologiae Cursus Completus: Series Graece* (vol. 37; Paris: Migne, 1863), hereafter, PG; full translation: *On God and Man: The Theological Poetry of Gregory of Nazianzus* (P. Gilbert (trans.); Crestwood, NY: St. Vladimir's Seminary Press, 2001). Similar passages are often repeated in Gregory's oeuvre: Orat. 38.9–11, PG 35:320d–324b; Orat. 40.5, PG 36:364bc; Orat. 45.2, PG 36:624bc–625ab; Orat. 45.5–7, PG 36:629a–632b; 'On the Soul', ll. 65–80, PG 37:452. In keeping with common practice, I cite the Orations according to column numbers in PG; texts, however, are from: *Grégoire de Nazianze: Discours 27–31* (P. Gallay (ed. and trans.); Sources Chrétiennes, no. 250; Paris: Éditions du Cerf, 1978); and *Grégoire de Nazianze: Discours 38–41* (C. Moreschini (ed.); P. Gallay (trans.); Sources Chrétiennes, no. 358; Paris: Éditions du Cerf, 1990). Translations: *On God and Christ: The Five Theological Orations and Two Letters to Cledonius* (L. Wickham, and F. Williams (trans.); Crestwood, NY: Saint Vladimir's Seminary Press, 2002); and *Festal Orations* (N. V. Harrison (trans.); Crestwood, NY: Saint Vladimir's Seminary Press, 2008).

Following Origen, Gregory and Evagrius both conceive of the human being as composed of flesh/body (σάρξ/σῶμα), soul (ψυχή), and mind (νοῦς).[5] Humanity shares the flesh (σάρξ) and soul (ψυχή) with the animals, while mind (νοῦς) is the substance of both the human mind and angelic existence. But humanity's composite construction is not entirely stable and settled. Gregory feels his flesh and his mind pulling in opposite directions; the mind naturally gravitates toward contemplation and illumination, while the flesh is burdensome and opaque. While other theologians (including Evagrius) associate the animality of the human flesh and soul (σάρξ and ψυχή) primarily with uncontrolled energies and desires, for Gregory, human-animality represents the corporeal 'thickness' (παχύτης) which impedes and distracts from contemplation.[6] Animality figures only the 'lower' half of humanity, the flesh that the mind must master and direct. Thus, within a human being there is a division or caesura that marks the point at which humanity-as-such transcends human-animality. While animality opens up to its apex and summit in humanity, humanity is partially closed off to animality, laying exclusive claim to the realm of contemplation, knowledge of the heavens, and participation in the angelic intelligible creation. Humanity's calling to transformative contemplation of God thus inherently involves transcendence over (or beyond) human animality.[7]

Giorgio Agamben turns the perspective of Gregory's wonderment precisely upside down, so that it becomes a solution in search of a problem. Where

---

[5] Both Gregory and Evagrius differentiate the νοῦς from the ψυχή to a greater degree than Origen. For a detailed comparison of all three on this point see M. O'Laughlin, 'The Anthropology of Evagrius Ponticus and Its Sources', *Origen of Alexandria: His World and His Legacy*, (C. Kannengiesser, and W. Petersen (eds); Notre Dame, IN: Notre Dame University Press, 1988), pp. 357–73. See also, C. Beeley, *Gregory of Nazianzus on the Trinity and the Knowledge of God: In Your Light We Shall See Light* (New York: Oxford University Press, 2008), pp. 272–3; D. Bertrand, 'L'implication du Νοῦς dans la prière chez Origène et Évagre le Pontique', *Origeniana Septima* (Louvain: Leuven University Press, 1999); A. Louth, *The Origins of the Christian Mystical Tradition* (Oxford: Oxford University Press, 1981), p. 100.

[6] Gregory of Nazianzus, Orat. 39.8, PG 36:344a; cf. Orat. 28.12, PG 36:40d–41a; Orat. 28.13, PG 36:41cd–44a.

[7] Beeley (*Gregory of Nazianzus on the Trinity and the Knowledge of God*, pp. 79–83) is correct that the tension within Gregory's anthropology between σάρξ and νοῦς does not ultimately amount to a hatred and rejection of the body as such. Nevertheless, it is worth asking why the rigor of Gregory's κάθαρσις (purification) is frequently mistaken for such a rejection. There is a violent sort of separation that takes place through κάθαρσις, but rather than an escape of the νοῦς from the body, κάθαρσις effects the eradication of the body's animality. Gregory does not reject embodiment per se, so much as an ongoing essential continuity with other animals, so that the corporeal human who enjoys union with God has been stripped of his or her animality. For example, examine the relationship between κάθαρσις and animality in Orat. 28.2, PG 36:28a-d; Orat 28.15, PG 36:45bc; Orat. 39.6, PG 36:341a; Orat. 39.7, PG 36:341c. Beeley is answering the supposition of a mind-body dualism which he finds in A. Ellverson, *The Dual Nature of Man: A Study in the Theological Anthropology of Gregory of Nazianzus* (Stockholm: Uppsala University, 1981), pp. 28–32; and R. R. Ruether, *Gregory of Nazianzus: Rhetor and Philosopher* (Oxford: Clarendon Press, 1969), pp. 134–6, though he perhaps oversimplifies Ellverson's nuanced understanding of Gregory's paradoxical anthropology in order to heighten the difference with his own.

Gregory gapes at the human being as the *mysterium coniunctionis* – the strange conjunction of alien natures, Agamben puzzles at the widespread perception of internal tension that gives rise to the notion of the human being as a 'mixture' in the first place. Why does this creature, he asks, insist on everywhere and always picking itself apart in order to better discern itself? From where does this sense of internal tension come, this fractured self-understanding composed of two natures pulling in opposite directions? Agamben observes thinkers like Gregory theorizing one portion of their being as animal and another portion of their being as human, and marvels that no one should have asked yet why this careful dismantling is such a prevalent activity. The mystery of humanity is a *mysterium disuinctionis* – an inexplicable sense that human beings are internally complex, or composite.[8] He argues that coming to grips with this ceaseless activity whereby humanity parses itself out as a mixture of animal and angel and 'jamming' this 'anthropological machine' is a task more imperative than 'to take positions on the great issues, on so-called human rights and values'.[9] Agamben invokes a theological register in naming the goal of this project as a 'Shabbat of animal and man'.[10]

Agamben perceives two models of the anthropological machine, an ancient and a modern version.[11] The ancient model of the anthropological machine *incorporates* animality within humanity so that truly exceptional (and therefore distinctively human) traits may appear in greater relief. The ancient concern with centaurs, werewolves, and half-bred creatures (always placed in faraway lands, living among the barbarians who were themselves 'marginally' human) was a way of recognizing the continuities between humans and animals precisely in order to find – and emphasize – the discontinuities. Likewise, when animals are simultaneously denied moral agency and yet described with a negative moral valence as vile, reprehensible, or disgusting, it is the boundary between humanity and animality that is being limned. True humanity then, is that *part* of the human, which exceeds and transcends its own animality (and all other animals). The human contains both animality and a core of humanity-within-the-human. The purpose that drives the 'anthropological machine' forward is the production of a pure humanity, conceptually standing over-against human animality. Necessarily, however, the machine's operation also produces a concept

---

[8] G. Agamben, *The Open: Man and Animal* (K. Attell (trans.); Stanford, CA: Stanford University Press, 2004), pp. 13–16.
[9] Ibid., p. 16.
[10] Ibid., p. 92.
[11] Ibid., p. 37.

of pure animality.[12] So, for example, the thick, material density which hinders human contemplation is paradigmatically 'animal' for Gregory. Animality is that which must be strained out through κάθαρσις (purification) in order to safeguard the contemplative mind (νοῦς) as truly and authentically human as it draws near to God.[13] This division *within* the human being corresponds to a conception of animals (categorically) as spiritually blind, unthinking brutes too caught up in their corporeal concerns to be cognizant of God.

Agamben's anthropological machine is at work in the thought of Evagrius of Pontus as much as Gregory's. Evagrius accepts from Origen the (Stoic) notion that animals are moved to action by images that arise internally.[14] So, an ox lowers his head and takes a bite of grass when the image of grass arises within, motivating him to eat; the image of a predator incites the deer to flee. Humans, Evagrius believes, are no different on this score. Humans too are driven by the arising of internal images (νοήματα). But unlike animals, humans are equipped with a mind (νοῦς), a function of participating in the intelligible creation. The mind has the task of passing judgement on the images that arise, discerning which images are to be given attention and which are to be ignored.[15] The human alone has the ability to act freely relative to the images that arise internally, a freedom that comes from the rational function of the mind, which stands over and above the 'animal' level at which the images arise. Internal images are susceptible to demonic corruption. So, for example, a demon might take hold of the image of a woman within an ascetic and cause 'her' figure to move in sexually inviting ways, in order to lure the monk's mind into committing conceptual adultery with the image, joining the image in mental

---

[12] Though there are important differences between the two projects, I discern a fundamental affinity between Agamben and Derrida's analyses with regard to animality. Agamben's anthropological machine and Derrida's unveiling of the way that Western philosophy 'names the human' by means of the '*animot*' (*animaux* +*mot*) are clearly complementary. For both, the word/concept 'animal' functions as a single and indispensible point of contrast for constructing 'humanity', because it represents a (falsely) homogenous category that effaces the differences between millions of species. J. Derrida, *The Animal*, pp. 47–51; G. Agamben, *The Open*, p. 16.

[13] Gregory of Nazianzus, Orat. 28.2, PG 36:28a-d; Orat 28.15, PG 36:45bc; Orat. 39.6, PG 36:341a; Orat. 39.7, PG 36:341c; 'On the Cheapness of the Outward Man,' PG 37:766-78.

[14] Origen, *De principiis*, §3.1.2–3; translation: *On First Principles* (G. Butterworth (trans.); New York: Harper and Row, 1966).

[15] Evagrius, *On Thoughts*, §§2, 3, 16, 17 [text: Évagre le Pontique: Sur les pensées (P. Géhin, C. Guillaumont, and A. Guillaumont (eds); Sources Chrétienes, no. 438; Paris: Éditions du Cerf, 1998); translation: *Evagrius of Pontus: The Greek Ascetic Corpus* (R. Sinkewicz (trans.); Oxford: Oxford University Press, 2003)]; *Great Letter*, §§41, 42, 46 [text: G. Vitestam, *Seconde partie du traité qui passe sous le nom de 'La grande lettre d'Evagre le Pontique à Mélanie l' Ancienne', publiée et traduite d'après le manuscrit du British Museum Add. 17192* (Lund: Glerrup, 1964); translation: *Evagrius Ponticus* (A. Cassiday (trans.); New York: Routledge, 2006)]. See also E. Clark's discussion of the tasks of the ascetic mind, 'New Perspectives on the Origenist Controversy: Human Embodiment and Ascetic Strategies', *Church History* 59.2 (1990), pp. 151–4.

copulation.[16] In order to prevent this from happening, the mind must tirelessly work as a shepherd of the images, keeping them safely grouped together, secure and tame:

> The Lord handed over to the human the mental representations (Τὰ νοήματα) of this age just like sheep to a good shepherd. … It is necessary, therefore, for the anchorite to keep watch (φυλάττειν) over this flock by night and day, so that one of these mental representations does not get snatched by wild beasts or fall into the possession of thieves (θηριάλωτον ἢ λῃσταῖς περιπέσῃ). But if something like that happens down in the glen, then immediately he should tear it out from the mouth of the lion and the bear [cf. 1 Kg 17]. The mental representation of a brother (τὸ νόημα τὸ περὶ τοῦ ἀδελφοῦ) gets snatched by wild beasts if it is set to graze in us along with hatred (μίσους); the mental representation of a woman, if it is nurtured in us with base desire (αἰσχρᾶς ἐπιθυμίας); the mental representation of silver and gold, if it passes the night with avarice (πλεονεξίας); and the mental representation of holy gifts, if it is fed with conceited (κενοδοξίας) intentions. The other mental representations happen to be stolen by the passions in like manner.[17]

When the (animal) images get loose and go astray, they are devoured by demons, corrupted, and turned against the monk. The monk's task, then, is to keep all the images that reside in the irrational animal portion of his soul well-fed, well-groomed, and tame. Evagrius' spirituality approaches human animality with the logic of taming and slaughter. In Agamben's terms, 'humanity' is produced by means of control over internal animality. It is cultivated, preserved, and produced through the virtue of impassibility (ἀπάθεια), the virtue that names a continuous throttling of animal (and inhuman) agency.[18] Unlike other theologians who think of impassibility primarily as a divine attribute and distant goal of human spirituality, Evagrius considers impassibility to be an attainable precondition for genuine and undistracted contemplation.[19]

---

[16] Evagrius, *To Eulogios*, §18 (translation: R. Sinkewicz, *Evagrius*).

[17] Evagrius, *On Thoughts*, §17.

[18] 'Of the impure demons, there are some who tempt a human as a human (τὸν ἄνθρωπον ὡς ἄνθρωπον ἐκπειράζουσιν), and there are some who confound a human as an irrational animal (ζῷον ἄλογον ἐκταράσσουσι). Approaching, the first inflict upon us mental representations (νοήματα) of conceit (κενοδοξίας), arrogance (ὑπερηφανίας), envy (φθόνου), or fault-finding (κατηγορίας), for none of these touch the irrational animals (τῶν ἀλόγων). Drawing near, the second set desire or irascibility (θυμὸν ἢ ἐπιθυμίαν) in motion unnaturally (παρὰ φύσιν). For these passions are common to us and the irrational animals, though they are covered over in us by the rational nature (ὑπὸ τῆς λογικῆς καλυπτόμενα φύσεως)'. Evagrius, *On Thoughts*, §18; cf. *The Monk/Praktikos*, §§54–6 (text: Évagre le Pontique: Traité Practique ou Le Moine (A. Guillaumont, and C. Guillaumont (eds); Sources Chrétiennes, nos. 170–71; Paris: Éditions du Cerf, 1971); translation: R. Sinkewicz, *Evagrius*).

[19] E. Clark, 'New Perspectives', p. 154. For a detailed exposition of Evagrius' understanding of ἀπάθεια in relation to Origen's, see R. Somos, 'Origen, Evagrius Ponticus and the Ideal of Impassibility', *Origeniana Septima* (Louvain: Peeters, 1999), pp. 371–3.

Evagrius tells the story of a monk who had achieved impassibility (ἀπάθεια) and who stood outside his desert cell chanting through the psalter. In an attempt to distract this monk from prayer, a demon took the form of a lion and rushed at the monk, digging his claws into the monk's side. This monk, Evagrius boasts, continued to pray through the remainder of the psalter with the lion's claws embedded in his flesh, before dismissing the demon and walking away unharmed.[20] That the demon should take the form of a lion is no coincidence in Evagrius' cosmology because animals and demons have a special affinity.[21] In the *Kephelaia Gnostika* Evagrius names the elements and dispositions most prominent in all God's creatures, because discerning the composition (the inner λόγος) of creatures is an intermediary step on the way to theological contemplation.[22] Angels are characterized by fire and mind (νοῦς); humans by earth and desire (ἐπιθυμία); animals by earth and irascibility (θύμος); and demons by irascibility (θύμος) and air. The monk who understands that irascibility is a bond shared by the demons and the animals can employ his knowledge against the demons. When demons introduce lustful or greedy thoughts, it is right and proper for the monk to allow his irascible, animal part to arise in anger and drive the demons away, 'fighting fire with fire', as it were. Evagrius frequently employs the image of a guard dog who barks at the approach of an intruder in order to illustrate the spiritual use of irascibility (θύμος):

> 8. Irascibility (Θυμός) is a power of the soul, destructive of thoughts (φθαρτικὴ λογισμῶν).
>
> 9. The contemplative mind is like a dog (Κυνικός ἐστι νοῦς θεωρητικὸς) chasing away all the passion-ridden thoughts (ἐμπαθεῖς λογισμούς) through the movement of irascibility.
>
> 10. The practical mind is like a dog (Κυνικός ἐστι νοῦς πρακτικὸς) barking at all the unjust thoughts (ἀδικους … λογισμούς).[23]

Animal anger at the approach of the demons of lust and gluttony is good and natural. But this anger must always be under the control of the mind (νοῦς),

---

[20] Evagrius, *Chapters on Prayer*, §106 (text: *Philokalia*, vol. 1, also the text of questionable reliability in PG 79:1165–200; translation: R. Sinkewicz, *Evagrius*).

[21] Evagrius, *On Thoughts*, §§12, 15,16; *Chapters on Prayer*, §§50, 107–9.

[22] Evagrius, *Kephalaia Gnostika*, 1.68 [text: (Syriac) *Les six Centuries des 'Kephalaia Gnostica' d'Évagre le Pontique* (A. Guillaumont (ed. and trans.); Patrologia Orientalis 28.1, no. 134; Paris: Fermin-Didot, 1958); (and Syriac with Greek retroversion) *Evagrius Ponticus* (W. Frankenberg (ed. and trans.); Abhandlungen der königlichen Gesellschaft der Wissenschaften zu Göttingen, Philologisch-historische Klasse, Neue Folge, 13.2; Berlin: Weidmannsche Buchhandlung, 1912)]. The manuscript tradition of the *Kephelaia Gnostika* is particularly convoluted and unreliable. The vocabulary and concepts here are not at all atypical of Evagrius, and could be gleaned from a number of other texts.

[23] Evagrius, *Reflections*, §§8–10 (text: J. Muyldermans, 'Evagriana', *Muséon: Revue d'études orientales* 44 (1931), pp. 37–68, 369–83; translation: R. Sinkewicz, *Evagrius*).

the dog must be tame and obedient: for some especially nefarious demons will introduce lustful or gluttonous thoughts precisely in order to draw out an uncontrolled animal anger in the monk.[24] So, Evagrius cautions, the mind – that core of humanity within the human – must be hyper-vigilant to patrol the internal limit keeping control over the animals (the inhuman or ahuman desire and irascibility) that reside within.

Gregory and Evagrius both task humanity with contemplating the divine through understanding the true nature of created things (the λόγοι of creatures which reflect the creative Λόγος). Both argue that in order to do this, the human must cultivate a life of virtue and restraint. If someone gives herself over to the concerns of the animals, her faculties of rational contemplation will atrophy, and she will become more like an animal, blind to the intelligible world. Instead of feeding the inner animal, she must exercise her rational faculties, and feed the human-within-the-human on the λόγοι (reasons, principles) that structure creation and point to its creator. For both Gregory and Evagrius, the trajectory of virtue is a transformation whereby the human becomes less and less animal, and more and more angel. For Evagrius, this trajectory of transcendence takes place through the absolute control of the mind over tame and malleable desire and irascibility. For Gregory, this transcendence takes place through the purification (κάθαρσις) whereby the 'animal' flesh is rarefied so that it no longer impedes the contemplative illumination of the mind. The grace of the divine Λόγος initiates a journey in which the redeemed leave animality behind, abandoning the inhuman or ahuman other within.

II. False Transcendence and True Contemplation

In the remainder of this paper, however, I want to query and problematize this trajectory of spiritual departure from animality – not by arguing that it is altogether misguided (though it may be), but by demonstrating that Gregory and Evagrius' theological projects are both marked by a necessary failure on the terms of their own arguments. In fact, the particular conceptual slippage in their anthropological projects opens the possibility that animality may be the key to salvific transformation rather than its offscouring. Instead of either effacing the fractures to recover a 'more positive' Gregory and Evagrius, or blaming them anachronistically for shortsightedness concerning animality, I hope to

---

[24] Evagrius, *On Thoughts*, §§13, 16, 17; Evagrius, *The Monk/Praktikos*, §24.

demonstrate their inconsistencies in order to 'start over' from the anthropological cracks in these projects. This approach holds the possibility to change
the role of human-animality in our theological descriptions of contemplation
and salvation in a manner that continues in conversation with the tradition of
Gregory and Evagrius.

Nemesius of Emesa, a contemporary of Gregory and Evagrius, notes that
every species of animal is endowed with an 'image of skill and a shadow of
rationality' that guides its behaviour.[25] He adduces the cunning tricks of both
rabbits and wolves whereby they intelligently hunt and evade one another. The
intelligent behaviour among animals *appears* for all purposes to be rational, but
Nemesius disavows its rationality because *every* rabbit and wolf acts, so he says,
in the same manner as every other, while truly rational human behaviour varies
from individual to individual.

Alongside Nemesius' rabbits and wolves, other strains of pseudo-rational
creatures infest the textual tradition of Christian Late Antiquity; bees and ants
seem to swarm into every discussion of animality and rationality. It is Philo who
initiates the use of bees and ants for theological reflection, noting their complex
social structures and manifestly well-ordered homes as evidence that divine
providence has structured the world.[26] Nemesius too has recourse to ants and
bees as testimony to providential care over large communities.[27] For Origen,
the behaviour of bees and ants proves the superiority of rational beings over
irrational beings – for even irrational creatures imitate the rational![28] Evagrius

---

[25] 'Each kind of irrational animal (τῶν ἀλόγων) is moved by the drive proper to it (οἰκείαν ὁρμὴν),
which has come about from the beginning in relation to its requirements and activity, which,
in turn, it has in relation to its purposeful formation. The Maker did not abandon them totally
helpless, but into each nature that [the Maker] did not cast a rational intelligence, [the Maker] set
trickery (πανουργίας) – an image of [genuine] skill (τέχνης εἰκόνα) and a shadow of [genuine]
reason (σκιὰν λογικήν)' . Nemesius of Emesa, *On Human Nature* §2, Morani, *Nemesius*, p. 36 [text:
Nemesius: De natura hominis (M. Morani (ed.); Leipzig: BSB B.G. Teubner, 1987); translation:
Nemesius: On the Nature of Man (R. Sharples, and P. van der Eijk (trans.); Liverpool: Liverpool
University Press, 2008)].

[26] Philo of Alexandria, *De providentia*, 1.25 [text: *De Providentia: I et II* (M. Hadas-Lebel (ed.); Les
Oeuvres de Philon D' Alexandrie; Paris, Éditions du Cerf, 1973); translation: *The Works of Philo* (C.
Yonge (trans.); Peabody MA: Hendrickson, 1993)].

[27] Nemesius, *On Human Nature*, §43.

[28] 'Neither has [Celsus] observed the difference in these matters [the behaviour of bees and ants]
between things completed by reason and thought (τὰ ἀπὸ λογου καὶ λογισμοῦ) and things that
come about through irrational nature and basic constitution (ἀπ᾽ ἀλόγου φύσεως καὶ κατασκευῆς
ψιλῆς). Reason takes up responsibility for none of these [latter] realities in those who act, because
none of them possess reason! But the eldest, the Son of God, the Ruler of all who are subordinate,
has made the irrational nature as an irrational assistance to those who were not deemed worthy of
reason (φύσιν ἄλογον πεποίηκε, βοηθοῦσαν ὡς ἄλογον τοῖς οὐκ ἀξιωθεῖσι λόγου)'. Origen, *Contra
Celsum*, 4.81, cf. 4.81–5 [text: *Origène: Contre Celse* (M. Borret (ed.); Sources Chrétiennes, no.
136; Paris: Éditions du Cerf, 1968); translation: *Contra Celsum* (H. Chadwick (trans.); Cambridge:
Cambridge University Press, 1965)].

mentions bees and ants as 'skilled workers' and marvels at their craft,[29] Jerome's *Life of Malchus* turns to ants as exemplars of monastic love and virtue, models of a community in which each one serves the collective good.[30] Gregory too marvels at the quasi-rationality of ants and bees as evidence of God's Λόγος giving structure to the whole of creation.

> Where does the industry and artistry (φιλεργὸν καὶ φιλότεχνον) of bees and spiders come from? They fabricate and hold honeycombs together with hexagonal, alternating pipes, the stability of which is systematically worked out through partitioning walls and alternately interweaving the straight lines of the corners. And all of this in such dusky light that the formations of the beehive must be invisible! [Spiders] weave complex webs stretched in many shapes with threads so very fine and nearly aerial that these are invisible from the beginning. Of the same web they make worthy homes and hunting grounds where they enjoy weaker creatures as food. What Euclid could mimic these— contemplating lines (γραμμαῖς ἐμφιλοσοφῶν) without substance and struggling in their demonstration? … And I remain silent with regard to the well-known observations of the chambers and chamber-masters among the ants with food laid up in store perfectly measured for the season, and again with regard to their many roads, and leaders, and the good order of their projects.[31]

These authors, however, explain the 'rational' behaviour of ants, bees, and other animals by *externalizing* the reason that guides their behaviour. In other words, it is not animal reason at work, but a rationality mediated by the animal's *nature*, or finally divine rationality which instructs these creatures in the way that they should act. Much like Origen's claim about irrational mimesis of reason, Gregory exclaims (without, so far as I can tell, a sense of irony), 'I beg you, marvel at the intelligence of irrational nature and present your explanations! (Σὺ δὲ μοι θαύμασον καὶ ἀλόγον φυσικὴν σύνεσιν, καὶ τοὺς λόγους παράστησον.)'[32] The intelligence that is manifest in the lives of these creatures is not their own, but an intelligence which guides their lives from beyond. Ants and bees do not make plans and follow them through, they do not *respond* to the world around

---

[29] Evagrius, *On the Faith*, §39 [text: Jean Gribomont, '(Pseudo)Basil, "Epistula 8"', in *Basilio di Cesarea, Le Lettere* (M. Forlin-Patrucco (ed.); Torino: Società Editrice Internazionale, 1983); translation: A. Cassiday, *Evagrius Ponticus*], cf. *On the Eight Thoughts*, §11 (text: J. Muyldermans, 'Une nouvelle recension du *De octo spiritibus malitiae* de S. Nil', *Le Muséon: Revue d'études orientales* 52 (1939), pp. 235–74; translation: R. Sinkewicz, *Evagrius*).

[30] Jerome, *Life of Malchus*, §7 [text: *Jerome: Trois vies de moines: Paul, Malchus, Hilarion* (P. Leclerc, E. Morales, and A. de Vogüé (eds); Sources Chrétiennes, no. 508; Paris: Éditions du Cerf, 2007); translation: 'Life of Malchus', (M. Ewald (trans.); Fathers of the Church, no. 15; R. Deferrari (ed.); Washington, DC: Fathers of the Church Inc., 1952)].

[31] Gregory of Nazianzus, Orat. 28.25, PG 36:60cd–61b.

[32] Ibid., Orat. 28.25, PG 36:60c

them, but merely *react* on the basis of implanted instinct. There is no space for reflection; these creatures behave 'rationally' in accordance with God's will *precisely by lacking their own rationality*. Unthinkingly, they participate in the Λόγος of God implanted within them – and they are better for it.

Now, for Gregory and for Evagrius, the goal of ascetic contemplation is a more perfect participation in the divine Λόγος – whether in comprehending the manifold ways in which material creatures show forth the Λόγος of the intelligible creation or in the immortal joy of being drawn into the divine life. Being conformed to the divine Λόγος carries not only spiritual, but psychological, and physiological implications – it is the transformation of one's whole being.

For Evagrius, the truly virtuous person simply *reacts* in accord with the divine will because she has internalized the divine Λόγος to such a degree.

> 50. What is it to the demons that they wish to affect in us gluttony, sexual immorality, greed, wrath, grudges and the rest of the passions? It is so that the mind might be fattened upon them, and thus unable to pray as is necessary. For these passions – since they begin from the irrational animal part (τοῦ ἀλόγου μέρους πάθη ἄρξαντα) – do not permit the mind to be moved in a rational manner (λογικῶς) to seek after the Word of God (τὸν Θεοῦ Λόγον).
>
> 51. We pursue the virtues because of the reasons of beings (τοὺς λόγους τῶν γεγονότων), and [we pursue] these because of the Word who brings them to being, and this one most often appears in a prayerful condition.
>
> 52. A prayerful condition is the attainment of impassibility (ἀπαθὴς), for the most highly beloved, seized up to the intellectual height of philosophy and the spiritual mind (ὕψος νοητὸν ἁρπάζουσα τὸν φιλόσοφον, καὶ πνευματικὸν νοῦν).
>
> 53. To hasten to pray truly, it is necessary to master not only irascibility (θυμοῦ) and desire (ἐπιθυμίας), but also the passion-ridden mental representation (ἐμπαθοῦς νοήματος) that comes out of them.[33]

The perfected human is equal to the angels (ἰσάγγελος) in understanding the λόγοι of created things, an initiate into the deep knowledge (γνῶσις) of the divine life.[34] In order to attain such a state, the monk must attune his nature to God such that contrary thoughts (λογισμοί) do not even gain enough traction on the ascetic mind to require consideration and rejection. The monk who attains impassibility remains utterly unmoved by the wiles of the demons.

---

[33] Evagrius, *Chapters on Prayer*, §§50–3, following Sinkewicz's preference for a textual variant in 51, I have substituted Word (λόγον) for Lord (κύριον), the latter being the reading of PG, R. Sinkewicz, *Evagrius*, p. 302; cf. *The Monk/Praktikos*, §§2–4, 89; *Reflections*, §§1–5; *On Thoughts*, §19; *Great Letter*, §§8, 13–16, 21–2.

[34] Evagrius, *Chapters on Prayer*, §113.

Gregory describes contemplative participation in the divine life through the metaphor of *illumination*. Although illumination *is* fundamentally a metaphor about *knowledge* for Gregory, the knowledge that is gained through illumination and union with the divine is more experiential intimacy than discursive comprehension. Light expresses continuity between God and humanity that bridges the Creator/creature distinction without rendering God accessible/comprehensible. The apex of spiritual perfection for Gregory is complete illumination.

> By fear they are rectified, purified, and (so to speak) rarefied (λεπτυνομένους) in order to rise up to the heights. For where fear is, there is heeding of commands. Where heeding of commands is, there is purification of flesh (σαρκὸς κάθαρσις) – that cloud eclipsing the soul (τοῦ ἐπιπροσθοῦντος τῇ ψυχῇ νέφους), not allowing it to see the beam of divine light in purity. But where purification is, there is illumination (ἔλλαμψις), and illumination is the fulfillment of yearning (πόθου πλήρωσις) for those longing for great things, the greatest thing, or what lies beyond greatness.[35]

Furthermore, light is intimately bound up with λόγος within Gregory's theology. Thus, 'Indeed, the highest light is God – unapproachable, inexpressible, susceptible neither to being grasped by the mind nor defined by reason (οὔτε νῷ καταληπτὸν οὔτε λόγῳ ῥητόν), yet the illumination of every wholly rational nature (πάσης φωτιστικὸν λογικῆς φύσεως)'.[36] Paradoxically, the light of God illumines rational – or perhaps better, 'discursive' – creatures, yet can never be comprehended or encompassed in human discourse/rationality (λόγος). What is the nature of this gap between human λόγος and divine Λόγος – especially when animal behaviour is caught up so closely with divine wisdom?

For both Gregory and Evagrius, the 'gap' that currently separates the human from God and causes so much misery is overcome – not because the human overcomes the creature/Creator distinction, and emphatically *not* because the human mind is able to comprehend the divine essence in the terms of its own discursive thought (λόγος) – but because the human is conformed to God to such a degree that her instincts match God's intentions perfectly. Thus although the human mind with its λόγος is the aspect of human life most proximate to God, nevertheless, in perfect union with God, the mind is flooded with light such that God is never the stable object of a complete human discourse (λόγος), but the incomprehensible subject whose nearness changes the whole human

---

[35] Gregory of Nazianzus, Orat. 39.8, PG 36:344a.
[36] Ibid., Orat. 40.5, PG 36:364bc.

being endlessly and unimaginably. The redeemed human is outstripped and transformed by the ever-active Λόγος and Spirit (πνεῦμα) of God.

Where should the distinctively human λόγος so lauded by Gregory and Evagrius be situated relative to this utterly transparent suffusion of the redeemed creature in the Λόγος of God? For Gregory and Evagrius, human beings are rational and therefore do not merely *react* to the world, but are able to discern what is better and worse and *respond*. Rational vigilance distinguishes the human from the animal, who simply obeys unthinkingly the voice of instinct. Yet the space of independent *response* is also the space of resistance and rebellion to the divine Λόγος, and if the human being is going to be conformed more fully to the image of God, it may be the case that this space of response is precisely what is forfeited. Paradoxically, if one follows Gregory and Evagrius' conceptions of salvation through, it is precisely the space of pure humanity generated by the anthropological machine that *separates* the beings called human from God. With a view toward subjectivity and freedom, the total transparency of the redeemed human λόγος to the divine Λόγος remains completely indistinguishable from the deterministic instincts attributed to animals. Who (or what), then, is the paradigmatic religious subject? The saintliest humanity, in other words, may be found in the *moral* and *spiritual* animal, who – like the ants and the bees – participates in the order of justice, love, beauty, and humility instinctively, not because these are the products of her own reason, but because she is interpellated, subjectivized within an external rationality, the rationality of God. Once the anthropological machine is jammed and the compulsion to produce pure humanity is left in its tracks, Gregory and Evagrius might seem to suggest (inadvertently) that animals might be our best spiritual teachers, and that – were we quieted and tamed of our distinctive, discursive anthropological self-concern – our own animality might draw us further into communion with God.

The calling in which humanity is supposedly most differentiated from other animals – approaching God through disciplined contemplation – turns out to return human beings to a mode of subjectivity which is indistinguishable from that attributed to other animals. God's Λόγος becomes the perfected human being's most native and natural instinct so that her disposition, desire, and behaviour are completely aligned with God's effulgent life. What substantial difference can remain between this perfected religious subjectivity and the instinctual subjectivity of other animals? If none can be found, then it would seem that clinging to the gears of the cultural machine that generates a hermetically exclusive domain for 'humanity' simultaneously produces the alienation that divides humanity from God. Paradoxically, even though they both labour to set humanity off from animality in a categorical manner, following the spiritual wisdom of Gregory and Evagrius may entail a deeper attention to – and perhaps even emulation of – the religious subjectivity of fellow animals. To return to Derrida's question: What is it that feeds at the limit of the human and the animal? What is nourished by this boundary? What does the anthropological machine actually produce? Is it not a lifeless, inanimate, human λόγος – a non-animal suspended between life and death?

Bibliography

Agamben, G., *The Open: Man and Animal* (K. Attell (trans.); Stanford, CA: Stanford University Press, 2004).

Beeley, C., *Gregory of Nazianzus on the Trinity and the Knowledge of God: In Your Light We Shall See Light* (New York: Oxford University Press, 2008).

Bertrand, D., 'L'implication du Νοῦς dans la prière chez Origène et Évagre le Pontique', *Origeniana Septima* (Louvain: Leuven University Press, 1999), pp. 355–63.

Clark, E. A., 'New Perspectives on the Origenist Controversy: Human Embodiment and Ascetic Strategies', *Church History* 59.2 (1990), pp. 145–62.

Derrida, J., *L'Animal Que Donc Je Suis* (M. L. Mallet (ed.); Paris: Éditions Galilée, 2006).

—*The Animal That Therefore I Am* (M. L. Mallet (ed.); D. Wills (trans.); New York: Fordham University Press, 2008).

Ellverson, A. S., *The Dual Nature of Man: A Study in the Theological Anthropology of Gregory of Nazianzus* (Stockholm: Uppsala University, 1981).

Evagrius of Pontus, Évagre le Pontique: Sur les pensées (P. Géhin, C. Guillaumont, and A. Guillaumont (eds); Sources Chrétienes, no. 438; Paris: Éditions du Cerf, 1998).

—Évagre le Pontique: Traité Practique ou Le Moine (A. Guillaumont, and C. Guillaumont (eds); Sources Chrétiennes, nos. 170–71; Paris: Éditions du Cerf, 1971).

—*Evagrius of Pontus: The Greek Ascetic Corpus* (R. Sinkewicz (trans.); Oxford: Oxford University Press, 2003).

—*Evagrius Ponticus* (A. M. Cassiday (trans.); New York: Routledge, 2006).

—*Evagrius Ponticus* (W. Frankenberg (ed. and trans.); Abhandlungen der königlichen Gesellschaft der Wissenschaften zu Göttingen, Philolologisch-historische Klasse, Neue Folge, 13.2; Berlin: Weidmannsche Buchhandlung, 1912).

—*Les six Centuries des 'Kephalaia Gnostica' d'Évagre le Pontique* (A. Guillaumont (ed. and trans.); Patrologia Orientalis, 28.1, no. 134; Paris: Fermin-Didot, 1958).

—*Seconde partie du traité qui passe sous le nom de 'La grande lettre d'Evagre le Pontique à Mélanie l' Ancienne'*, publiée et traduite d'après le manuscript du British Museum Add. 17192 (G. Viestam (ed.); Lund: Glerrup, 1964).

Gregory of Nazianzus, *Festal Orations* (N. V. Harrison (trans.); Crestwood, NY: Saint Vladimir's Seminary Press, 2008).

—*Grégoire de Nazianze: Discours 27–31* (P. Gallay (ed. and trans.); Sources Chrétiennes, no. 250; Paris: Éditions du Cerf, 1978).

—*Grégoire de Nazianze: Discours 38–41* (C. Moreschini (ed.); P. Gallay (trans.); Sources Chrétiennes, no. 358; Paris: Éditions du Cerf, 1990).

—*On God and Christ: The Five Theological Orations and Two Letters to Cledonius* (L. Wickham, and F. Williams (trans.); Crestwood, NY: Saint Vladimir's Seminary Press, 2002).

—*On God and Man: The Theological Poetry of St. Gregory of Nazianzus* (P. Gilbert (trans.); Crestwood, NY: Saint Vladimir's Seminary Press, 2001).

Gribomont, J., '(Pseudo)Basil, "Epistula 8"', *Basilio di Cesarea, Le Lettere* (M. Forlin-Patrucco (ed.); Torino: Società Editrice Internazionale, 1983), pp. 84–112.

Jerome, *Jerome: Trois vies de moines: Paul, Malchus, Hilarion* (P. Leclerc, E. M. Morales, and A. de Vogüé (eds); Sources Chrétiennes, no. 508; Paris: Éditions du Cerf, 2007).

—'Life of Malchus', *Early Christian Biographies* (R. Deferrari (ed.); M. L. Ewald (trans.); Fathers of the Church, no. 15; Washington, DC: Fathers of the Church Inc., 1952), pp. 281–97.

Louth, A., *The Origins of the Christian Mystical Tradition* (Oxford: Oxford University Press, 1981).

McGuckin, J., *Saint Gregory of Nazianzus: An Intellectual Biography* (Crestwood, NY: St. Vladimir's Seminary Press, 2001).

Migne, J. P. (ed.), *Patrologiae Cursus Completus: Series Graece* (vol. 37; Paris: Migne, 1863).

Muyldermans, J., 'Evagriana', *Muséon: Revue d'études orientales* 44 (1931), pp. 37–68, 369–83.

—'Une nouvelle recension du *De octo spiritibus malitiae* de S. Nil', *Le Muséon: Revue d'études orientales* 52 (1939), pp. 235–74.

Nemesius of Emesa, *Nemesius: De natura hominis* (M. Morani (ed.); Leipzig: BSB B. G. Teubner, 1987).

—*Nemesius: On the Nature of Man* (R. W. Sharples, and P. J. van der Eijk (trans.); Translated Texts for Historians, vol. 49; Liverpool: Liverpool University Press, 2008).

O'Laughlin, M., 'The Anthropology of Evagrius Ponticus and Its Sources', *Origen of Alexandria: His World and His Legacy* (C. Kannengiesser and W. Petersen (eds); Notre Dame, IN: Notre Dame University Press, 1988), pp. 357–73.

Origen of Alexandria, *Contra Celsum* (H. Chadwick (trans.); Cambridge: Cambridge University Press, 1965).

—*On First Principles* (G. W. Butterworth (trans.); New York: Harper and Row, 1966).

—*Origène: Contre Celse* (M. Borret (ed.); Sources Chrétiennes, no. 136; Paris: Éditions du Cerf, 1968).

Philo of Alexandria, *De Providentia: I et II* (M. Hadas-Lebel (ed.); Les Oeuvres de Philon D' Alexandrie; Paris: Éditions du Cerf, 1973).

—*The Works of Philo* (C. D. Yonge (trans.); Peabody, MA: Hendrickson, 1993).

Ruether, R. R., *Gregory of Nazianzus: Rhetor and Philosopher* (Oxford: Clarendon Press, 1969).

Somos, R., 'Origen, Evagrius Ponticus and the Ideal of Impassibility', *Origeniana Septima* (Louvain: Peeters, 1999).

10

Putting Animals in Their Place:
On the Theological Classification of Animals

David Clough

I. Classifying Our Way Back to Eden

On the title page of the eleventh edition of Linnaeus's *Systema naturae* there is a remarkable picture (Figure 1).[1] Entitled *Numeros et Nomina* (Numbers and Names), the image presents a magnificent diversity of creaturely life surrounding a multi-breasted Diana representing nature's fecundity.[2] Two trees frame the picture to the left and right and are populated by a peacock, owl, spider, a bat, a squirrel, a parrot, a bat, a smiling monkey eating a banana, and beetles climbing the trunks. In the foreground are various plants and shells together with other ape-like creatures, butterflies, other insects, a lizard, a frog, a snake, and a hummingbird supping from a flower. Surrounding Diana are two majestic stags and a lion, nearby a turkey, a roosting hen, and a hedgehog. Behind them are grouped an elephant, a buffalo, a horse, a camel, a sheep, and a goat, joined by rabbits and perhaps a mouse. This group leads us to a beach where a crocodile ranges, and on the other side of the picture a walrus is joined by a lobster, a crab, a starfish, and perhaps a sea urchin, among other small sea creatures. In the sea we can see narwhals, a spouting whale, a ray, and possibly some diving sea birds. Beyond the sea are mountains and a cloudy sky filled with birds, some flying in a skein like geese, one long-necked like a heron.

---

[1] C. Linnaeus, *Systemae Naturae: Per Regna Tria Naturae: Secundum Classes, Ordines, Genera, Species, Cum Characteribus, Differentiis, Synonymis, Locis/Praefatus Est Ioannes Ioachimus Langius* (Halae Magdeburgicae: Typis et sumtibus Io. Iac. Curt, Ad editionem decimam reformatam Holmiensem ed. 1760).

[2] Linnaeus used the image of Diana in other publications, and Londa Schiebinger argues that it may have had particular significance for him given his innovative classification of mammals on the basis of their suckling milk from the breast (L. Schiebinger, 'Why Mammals Are Called Mammals: Gender Politics in Eighteenth-Century Natural History', *The American Historical Review* 98 (1993), pp. 382–411).

Figure 1: Linnaeus as a second Adam, from the 1760 edition of his *Systema naturae.*

Amid this scene, at the foot of the left-hand tree, sits a man, naked except for a cloth over his lap, writing in a book with a quill, looking across to the right and pointing, perhaps at the smiling and banana-eating monkey. The identity of the man is no mystery: next to him at the foot of the tree grows the plant *Linnea borealis*, the flower Linnaeus named after himself.[3]

The picture is a bold claim concerning the theological context in which Linnaeus saw his work. Peter Harrison notes that in 1746 his contemporary Albrecht von Haller accused Linnaeus of thinking of himself as a 'second Adam', assuming 'unbridled dominion' in categorizing animals without regard to his predecessors.[4] The publication of this image in 1760 makes clear that von Haller's criticism did not persuade Linnaeus to set aside his view of the significance of his work. This was in accordance with his view of botany as 'the divine science' and his own binomial system as 'a psalter for divine worship'; Linnaeus pictured himself as a reformer of natural science in the pattern of Martin Luther's reforms of Christianity.[5] He was not shy of claiming other biblical images as self-referential, likening himself elsewhere to Moses on the

[3] The image is discussed in P. Harrison, 'Linnaeus as a Second Adam? Taxonomy and the Religious Vocation', *Zygon* 44.4 (2009), pp. 879–93 (890); and J. Heilbron, 'The Measure of Enlightenment', *The Quantifying Spirit in the 18th Century* (T. Frangsmyr, J. Heilbron, and R. Rider (eds); Berkeley: University of California Press, 1990), pp. 207–43 (242).

[4] Harrison, 'Linnaeus as a Second Adam?', p. 879.

[5] Ibid., p. 890.

mountain, quoting 1 Kings 17.8 'and the word of the Lord came unto him' as a prophecy of his classificatory scheme, and seeing 2 Samuel 7.9 'And I... have cut off all thine enemies out of thy sight' as a prophecy of his victory over his rival Buffon.[6] While Linnaeus acknowledged that some of the genera and classes he proposed were artificial, he believed them to be substitutes for use only until the true natural categories could be discovered, with Adam's example used to demonstrate the possibility of the enterprise of true naming.[7]

Linnaeus's theological interpretation of the classificatory work of science was shared with Francis Bacon, who had argued that through science the effects of the Fall could be to some extent repaired.[8] For Bacon, the true end of knowledge is 'not the pleasure of curiosity, nor the quiet of resolution, nor the raising of the spirit, nor victory of wit, nor faculty of speech, nor lucre of profession, nor ambition of honour or fame, nor inablement for business' but instead 'a restitution and reinvesting (in great part) of man to the sovereignty and power (for whensoever he shall be able to call the creatures by their true names he shall again command them) which he had in his first state of creation'.[9] It is easy to see how Linnaeus could have become excited about the potential for his project in this Baconian perspective: to learn the true and natural way in which the creation was ordered seemed to have the potential to restore the human dominion over creation lost by Adam in the Fall. In his commentary on Genesis, Martin Luther had pictured the original dominion to mean that Adam could command lions with a single word, as we do with trained dogs, but Luther lamented that this dominion had been almost entirely lost after the Fall. He looked forward to the time it would be re-established and even enhanced beyond what Adam knew.[10] Where Luther was prepared to await the time when God would bring about this transformation, both Bacon and Linnaeus seem to wish to claim a vocation to remedy the fallen condition of humanity through science and technology. For them, grasping after such knowledge promises,

---

[6] K. Lisbet, 'Carl Linnaeus in His Time and Place', *Cultures of Natural History* (N. Jardine, J. Secord, and E. Spary (eds); Cambridge: Cambridge University Press, 1996), pp. 145–63 (155, 157); citing in relation to the 1 Kings reference S. Lindroth, 'Linné — Legend Och Verklighet', *Lychnos* (1965).

[7] P. Harrison, 'Linnaeus as a Second Adam?', p. 890. Harrison notes that John Webster (1611–82) had argued that Adam's naming must have been in agreement with the nature of the creatures named, and that Adam had possessed an encyclopaedic facility 'in the very language of nature' (p. 887).

[8] F. Bacon, *The New Organon* (L. Jardine, and M. Silverthorne (eds); Cambridge Texts in the History of Philosophy; Cambridge: Cambridge University Press, 2000), Bk II, aph. LII, p. 221.

[9] F. Bacon, 'Valerius Terminus (of the Interpretation of Nature)', *Collected Works of Francis Bacon* (J. Spedding, R. Ellis, and D. Heath (eds); vol. III; London: Routledge, 1996), pp. 215–52 (222). P. Harrison comments on this text in *The Fall of Man and the Foundations of Science* (Cambridge: Cambridge University Press, 2007), p. 27.

[10] M. Luther, *Lectures on Genesis, Chapters 1–5* (J. Pelikan (ed.); Luther's Works, vol. I; Saint Louis: Concordia, 1958), pp. 64–5.

ironically, to make possible a return to Eden, from which humanity was exiled precisely through a previous seeking after knowledge. It is easy to see why Bacon thought it necessary to defend such enquiry in a theological context; it is less easy to see how he could consider undoing God's punishment of human beings as a Christian enterprise.

We can already see, then, that Linnaeus's project of classifying creatures was by no means innocent. Instead, the goal of putting each creature in its place was at once an act of dominion over the other animals and the precondition for the desired restoration of this dominion. Coming to know the true names of the other animals would be to attain Adam's relationship with them, so that the giving of Latin binomial names to creatures was a way of establishing their subordinate place in a hierarchy of earthy creatures with humanity at the top. This non-innocent classificatory activity is not seeking out knowledge of the ordering of nature for its own sake, nor for the benefit of the creatures subjected to classification, but to capture them within classificatory schemes for human ends. Through this classificatory activity, Bacon and Linnaeus hope that humans will fight their way back past the flaming sword and cherubim that guard the east of Eden; the far-from-innocent Baconian-Linnaean project of putting other animals in their place is an attempt to regain the innocence lost in the Edenic exile.

Most other attempts to classify animals are not expressly motivated by the aim of dominion evident in Bacon and Linnaeus, but we should be chastened by their interpretation of the classificatory project, and therefore alert to the way in which classification is an activity which can never leave the relationship between the classifier and classified unchanged. Such interests in classification are many and various. The first appearance of other animals in human narratives that we are aware of is in Aesop's fables, where they were classified morally, rather than physically, in order to teach moral truths, launching a tradition that continued in the moral and spiritual descriptions of animals that continued in the *Physiologus* and the bestiaries.[11] It is notable that alongside Linnaeus's lofty theological ambitions were motivations that were more down to earth: in 1746 he explained to the Swedish Academy of Science that his desire to undertake voyages was based on the belief that 'Nature has arranged itself in such a way, that each country produces something especially useful; the task of economics is to collect [plants] from other places and cultivate such things that

---

[11] See Morus (R. Lewisohn), *Animals, Men and Myths: A History of the Influence of Animals on Civilization and Culture* (London: Victor Gollancz, 1954), p. 96; R. Grant, *Early Christians and Animals* (London: Routledge, 1999), pp. 44–72.

don't want to grow [at home] but can grow [there]'.[12] Perhaps the simplest and clearest example of the interest we have in classifying other animals is evident in an Augustinian critique of the Manichees. Augustine reports a Manichean argument against the goodness of the creator on the basis that a good creator would have had no cause to create animals unnecessary or pernicious to human beings. Augustine responds that animals can be divided into those that are 'useful to us, or pernicious or superfluous' and argues that the pernicious ones are 'either to punish us or to put us through our paces or to frighten us, so that instead of loving and desiring this life, subject to so many dangers and trials, we should set our hearts on another better one', and of the superfluous ones we should be thankful they do no harm rather than complaining that they are no use.[13] Human beings have human interests in classifying other animals in these cases – and in all others.

II. The Challenge of Classification

In reviewing attempts to classify animals and other creatures, however, what is immediately striking is not the motivation behind such activity, but its complexity and difficulty. Aristotle's account is astonishingly ambitious and influential, but even at the outset of his *Historia animalium*, the challenge of how to deal with the sheer diversity of animal life is clear:

> There are two ways of being water-animals. Some both live and feed in the water, take in water and emit it, and are unable to live if deprived of it: this is the case with many of the fishes. Others feed and live in the water; but what they take in is air, not water; and they breed away from the water. Many of these animals are footed: e.g., the otter, the beaver, the crocodile; many are winged, e.g., the shearwater and the plunger; many are footless, e.g., the water-snake. Some animals, although they get their food in the water and cannot live away from it, still take in neither water nor air: examples are the sea-anemones and shellfish. Again, some water-animals live in the sea, some in rivers, some in lakes, some in marshes (e.g., the frog and the newt).[14]

[12] C. Linnaeus, 'Letter to the Swedish Academy of Science, Uppsala, 10th January 1746', *Bref Och Skrifvelser Af Och Till Carl Von Linné* (T. Fries, and J. Hulth (eds); 2 vols; Stockholm and elsewhere, 1907), vol. I, p. 67, cited in Lisbet, 'Carl Linnaeus in His Time and Place', p. 151.

[13] Augustine, *On Genesis: On Genesis: A Refutation of the Manichees, Unfinished Literal Commentary on Genesis, the Literal Meaning of Genesis* (J. Rotelle (ed.); E. Hill (trans.); The Works of Saint Augustine: A Translation for the 21st Century; New York: New City Press, 2002), Bk. 1, ch. 16, §26.

[14] Aristotle, *Historia Animalium* (A. Peck (trans.); Loeb Classical Library; London and Cambridge, MA: William Heinemann Ltd. and Harvard University Press, 1965), 487a 14–28.

Aristotle next sets out various kinds of land animals, acknowledging the complexity of animals that live half their lives in water and half on land. He observes that animals differ in being stationary or moving about; gregarious or solitary; carnivorous, frugivorous, or omnivorous; building their own homes or not; nocturnal or diurnal; tame, wild, or tameable; capable of making noise or mute; prone to copulation or less prone; gentle or ferocious; intelligent and timid or mean and scheming; blooded or bloodless; two-footed or four-footed; viviparous, oviparous, larviparous in their mode of reproduction; living on land, swimming, or flying. Aristotle concludes the passage by indicating seven main groups of animals: birds, fishes, cetacea, shellfish, soft-shelled animals, 'softies' such as calamari and cuttlefish, and insects. In relation to the animals missing from this list: conspicuously including land animals, including human beings, Aristotle judges that there are no large groups.[15]

The absence of land animals from the groupings indicates that Aristotle's scheme does not seek to establish a comprehensive and definitive scheme for putting animals in their place, unlike the ambitions of Bacon and Linnaeus. Even within the limits of Aristotle's aims, however, it is clear that the range of difference he surveys presents a problem for classification: any one of the differences he lists could function as the basis of a classificatory scheme, and which one is chosen will depend on which differences are considered most important by the classifier. In the *Generation of Animals,* Aristotle judges that the mode of reproduction is the most basic category, because it represents a scale of perfection, with viviparous animals the most perfect, larviparous animals the least and oviparous animals occupying an intermediate category. He notes, however, the complex interrelationship between this category and even a single alternative:

> Bipeds are not all viviparous (birds are oviparous) nor all oviparous (man is viviparous); quadrupeds are not all oviparous (the horse and ox and heaps of others are viviparous), nor all viviparous (lizards and crocodiles and many others are oviparous). Nor does the difference lie even in having or not having feet: some footless animals are viviparous (as vipers, and the Selachia), some are oviparous (as the class of fishes, and the rest of the serpents); and of the footed animals many are oviparous, many viviparous (e.g., the quadrupeds already mentioned). There are footed animals which are internally viviparous (as man), and footless ones also (as the whale and the dolphin). So we find no means

---

[15] Aristotle, *Historia Animalium*, 487a–490b.

here for making a division: the cause of this difference does not lie in any of the organs of locomotion.[16]

Were we to attempt to map the twelve other differences between animals noted from Aristotle above, the complexity would be many orders of magnitude worse.

Thomas Aquinas follows Aristotle in judging that the mode of reproduction of animals is useful to order animals, judging that land animals are more perfect than birds or fishes because of the distinctness of their limbs and their 'higher manner of breeding'.[17] He recognizes, however, that a scale based on the mode of reproduction does not correspond to one based on intelligence, since 'imperfect' animals, such as ants and bees, are more intelligent in certain ways. Aquinas runs into his own classificatory complexities when he attempts to make sense of the different categories of animals discussed in Genesis 1. He argues that Genesis 1.24 appropriately describes the earth bringing forth 'living souls' (*animam viventem*), excluding the fish called 'creeping creatures having life' (*reptile animæ viventis*), since fish are 'bodies having some kind of soul in them' (*corpora habentia aliquid animæ*), while land animals have a higher perfection and are 'living souls' (*animam viventem*).[18] Aquinas next responds to the objection that the same verse makes a mistake in listing 'cattle', 'beasts', and 'quadrupeds' as parallel categories. He explains that 'cattle' means domestic animals, i.e., those which are of service to human beings in any way, 'beasts' means 'wild animals, e.g., bears and lions', and 'creeping things' means those animals who have no feet or whose feet are too short to lift them far from the ground, such as lizards and turtles. Aquinas argues that it is necessary to add 'quadrupeds' either because some animals, such as deer and goats, fall into none of these classes, or otherwise because 'quadruped' is used first as the genus and then followed by a number of terms referring to species.[19]

One attempt to impose a more coherent ordering on creation was the Neo-Platonic idea of a great chain linking all that exists, stretching between God at its utmost height, through spiritual beings, humans as both spiritual and material, other material animals, plants, rocks, and so on, to the most insignificant aspects of materiality. Central to the scheme of this Great Chain of Being

---

[16] Aristotle, *Generation of Animals* (A. Peck (trans.); Loeb Classical Library; London and Cambridge, MA: William Heinemann Ltd. and Harvard University Press, 1943), 732b 19–28.
[17] Thomas Aquinas, *Summa Theologica* (Fathers of the English Dominican Province (trans.); London: Blackfriars, 1963), I.72 *ad*. 1.
[18] Ibid.
[19] Ibid.

was the idea every creature had an essential and non-substitutable place in this chain: in the words of Alexander Pope's seventeenth-century 'Essay on Man',

> On superior pow'rs
> Were we to press, inferior might on ours;
> Or in the full creation might leave a void,
> Where, one step broken, the great scale's destroyed;
> From Nature's chain whatever link you strike,
> Tenth, or ten thousandth, breaks the chain alike.[20]

This mode of ordering creatures is attractive in describing a coherent position for each aspect of creation, but it is implausible in the context of evolutionary theory because, as Arthur Lovejoy notes, it cannot accommodate change in creaturely kinds. It requires every place in the chain to be filled, so if there is change, either the chain was not complete before, or it is not complete afterwards.[21] There are also theological objections to such a scheme, since God is in danger of having to create the Universe exactly as it actually exists, so that creation becomes a necessary act. It is therefore clear that the ultimate scheme of classification, with a place in line for every creature, is not theologically adequate or theoretically viable.

The difficulties with the Great Chain of Being do not mean that the idea does not remain influential in our thinking about our place in the universe and that of other creatures. The basic patterning of humanity ranked above all other animals, primates ranked above other mammals, mammals above other animals, animals above plants, plants above rocks and streams, and so on is hard to escape as a default mapping of life. In place of a Neo-Platonic metaphysics to sustain such an ordering, we have substituted rationality, intelligence, self-consciousness, degree of evolvedness, and many other criteria representing attributes we value in our humanity. All can clearly be seen to fail as a way of ordering creatures on the grounds of plausibility – criteria for assessing intelligence are radically contested even within human populations, so reliable cross-species criteria seem wholly implausible – and on the grounds of arbitrariness – why pick on intelligence, rather than speed, loudness, size, ability to fly, and so on? Just as with Aristotle's decision about mode of reproduction, whatever characteristic we select merely identifies one point of difference among creatures with any number of other interesting differences.

---

[20] A. Pope, 'Essay on Man', VIII, cited in A. O. Lovejoy, *The Great Chain of Being: A Study of the History of an Idea* (Cambridge, MA: Harvard University Press, 1942), p. 60.

[21] Lovejoy, *The Great Chain of Being*, p. 329.

It is tempting to think that post-Linnaean biological schemes of classification solve these difficulties of incoherence and arbitrariness, but it turns out that this is not the case. John Dupré argues that Darwinism disposes of the idea 'that an organism has an essence that determines its necessary place in a unique nested hierarchy of kinds' and this points towards the possibility of 'a variety of different classificatory schemes, suited to a variety of purposes, some scientific and some not, that may criss-cross and overlap one another in various ways'.[22] Even within biology, Dupré argues, different schemes must be kept in play because classification by evolutionary descent, which makes excellent sense in many contexts, would make the task of classification in many areas impossible, as well as leading to unexpected and implausible associations.[23] In a particularly striking example, he notes that the received modern wisdom that whales are not fish masks a dispute between two incompatible classificatory schemes. The term 'fish' in the classification of ordinary language, he notes, corresponds to no category in a scientific taxonomy, and 'whale' similarly fails to correspond to any particular class or genus. Biologists might be able to say that all whales in their scheme are mammals, and no fish are mammals, but Dupré notes that biologists have no grounds to object to the possibility that whales could be both fish according to ordinary language classification *and* mammals, according to scientific taxonomy.[24] Biology, therefore, will not free us from the inescapable plurality and complexity of classificatory schemes.

III. Uncontainable Animals

The illustrations of the difficulty of classification in the previous section lead us to the starting point of Michel Foucault's reflections on classification. He identifies the origin of his 1966 work *Les Mots et les Choses*, published in English as *The Order of Things*, with his laughter at the passage Jorge Luis Borges claims to quote from an ancient Chinese encyclopaedia:

> On those remote pages it is written that animals are divided into (a) those that belong to the Emperor, (b) embalmed ones, (c) those that are trained, (d) suckling pigs, (e) mermaids, (f) fabulous ones, (g) stray dogs, (h) those that are included in this classification, (i) those that tremble as if they were mad, (j)

---

[22] J. Dupré, *Humans and Other Animals* (Oxford: Clarendon, 2002), p. 4.
[23] Ibid., pp. 38–9.
[24] Ibid., pp. 27, 46.

innumerable ones, (k) those drawn with very fine camel's hair brush, (l) others, (m) those that have just broken a flower vase, (n) those that resemble flies from a distance.[25]

For Foucault, the laughter provoked by this impossible scheme of classification shattered all the familiar landmarks of thought, 'breaking up all the ordered surfaces and all the planes with which we are accustomed to tame the wild profusion of existing things'.[26] He is led to contrast *utopias*, in which things could be placed, arranged, and unfolded in an untroubled way, with *hetero-topias*, which 'make it impossible to name this *and* that, because they shatter or tangle common names', 'dessicate speech', and 'stop words in their tracks'.[27] This vision of an untameable profusion of things that prevents the operation of the classificatory enterprise is reminiscent of Giorgio Agamben's finding resources in the work of Walter Benjamin to bring the anthropological machine that produces the difference between human and animal to a standstill.[28] Agamben's *The Open: Man and Animal* uncovers the deeply troubling consequences of the way in which human beings have sought to identify the boundary between the human and non-human: Agamben argues that *Homo sapiens* names 'neither a clearly defined species nor a substance', but 'a machine or device for producing the recognition of the human'.[29] The operation of this machine is devastating in its creation of a zone of exception between the human and the animal that contains: 'only a life that is separated and excluded from itself—only a bare life'.[30] Various entities considered marginal to understandings of humanity have been assigned in this space at different times, such as pygmies, orang-utans, satyrs, sphinxes, cynocephali, ape-men, wild men, and – Agamben notes chillingly – the Jew, so that concentration camps themselves are a form of the anthropo-logical machine, 'a monstrous attempt to decide between the human and the inhuman'.[31] Agamben suggests that the terms 'human' and 'animal' cannot be overcome, but that we might deploy Walter Benjamin's concept of the 'saved night' to escape the theological logic of revelation and redemption so that nature

---

[25] J. L. Borges, *Other Inquisitions, 1937–52* (Austin, TX: University of Texas Press, 1964), p. 103, cited in M. Foucault, *The Order of Things: An Archaeology of the Human Sciences* (London: New York: Routledge, 2002), p. xvi.

[26] M. Foucault, *The Order of Things*, p. xvi.

[27] Ibid., p. xix.

[28] G. Agamben, *The Open: Man and Animal* (K. Attell (trans.); Stanford, CA: Stanford University Press, 2004), p. 83. I am grateful to Aaron Gross and Chris Baker for invaluable discussions of this text.

[29] Ibid., p. 26.

[30] Ibid., p. 38.

[31] Ibid., pp. 22, 25, 37.

can be 'given back to itself' instead of overcome in a history of redemption.[32] We could then give up on the search for articulations of what separates the human from the animal, but 'risk ourselves in this emptiness: the suspension of the suspension, Shabbat of both animal and man'.[33]

Agamben's vision of what will be necessary to bring the anthropological machine to a standstill clearly represents a challenge to theological accounts seeking to attend to the problems he identifies, since the way he sketches to bring the machine to a stop seems to require giving up on the narratives of redemption that Christianity has espoused and many theologians – including myself – would see it necessary to retain. It seems to me, however, that Benjamin's 'saved night' is not the only alternative to the frightening operation of the anthropological machine: we could instead envisage God's redemption of creation in a manner that draws all things into the triune life and gives nature back to itself in this very different mode. Such a vision could draw on the hope of the gathering up of all things in Christ proclaimed at the opening of the letter to the Ephesians and the restitution of all things envisaged in the Patristic doctrine of *apokatastasis*.[34] While Christian accounts of redemption have very frequently been used to establish separation between creatures – usually on an intra-human basis – there is a salvific counter-narrative with a broader vision that could be used to interrupt rather than enable the anthropological machine. For a theological approach to play this role, however, it seems clear to me that it must escape the classificatory zeal of Bacon, Linnaeus, and many of the other philosophical and theological voices surveyed in this chapter. Instead of seeking to put other animals in their place in this way, and secure the unique place of the human in God's purposes, a theological account with the potential to support Agamben's project would need to risk the challenge to human identity that a peaceable Sabbath between non-human and human animals would require. This would mean that theologians attend to the lives of other animals not to restore dominion over them, but instead because they seek the delight of appreciating their part in the magnificent diversity of God's creative purposes, no longer concerned to put other animals in their place, but rather to celebrate the place and mode of life in which their Creator had established for them. In this

---

[32] Ibid., pp. 81–2.
[33] Ibid., p. 91.
[34] See my exploration of accounts of redemption inclusive of humans and other animals in chapters 6 and 7 of D. Clough, *On Animals: I. Systematic Theology* (London: T&T Clark/Continuum, 2012), on *apokatastasis* in particular, pp. 149–51. I explore related issues in D. Clough, 'The Problem With Human Equality: Towards a Non-Exclusive Account of the Moral Value of Creatures in the Company of Martha Nussbaum', *Transforming Exclusion: Engaging Faith Perspectives* (H. Bacon, W. Morris, and S. Knowles (eds.); London; New York: T&T Clark International, 2011), pp. 83–94.

context, the complexity of the classificatory enterprise evident in the preceding section becomes a blessing, rather than a curse: it is an inescapable reminder that the diversity of creation will defeat human attempts to contain it.

If we doubt that theologians would be able or interested in such a role in relation to other creatures, it seems to me that one compelling example of just such a project is Basil of Caesarea's *Hexaemeron*. The work is a series of sermons, preached over several days and treating the days of creation. Basil's enthusiasm for his subject matter is everywhere apparent, portraying a world devised 'to the great advantage of all beings'.[35] When he reaches the creation of animals his delight in their variety is clearly evident. In terms clearly indebted to Aristotle, though possibly at some remove,[36] he lists testaceans, 'such as mussels, scallops, sea snails, conchs, and numberless varieties of bivalves', crustaceans such as 'crayfish, crabs, and all similar to them', 'soft fish', such as polyps and cuttlefish, among which there are 'innumerable varieties':

> In fact, there are weevers, and lampreys, and eels, which are produced in the muddy rivers and swamps, and which resemble in their nature venomous animals more than fish. Another class is that of ovipara, and another, that of vivipara. The sharks and the dogfish and, in general, the cartilaginous fish are vivipara. And of the cetaceans the majority are vivipara, as dolphins and seals; these are said to readmit and hide in their belly the cubs, while still young, whenever they have for some reason or other been startled.[37]

He goes on, and on, discussing the trickery of the octopus and his personal observation of wondrous fish migrations, before finally concluding the evening homily because of the weakness of his body and the lateness of the hour, in regret for the many wonders he is thereby forced to leave out.[38] The following morning he begins to consider the land animals, before stopping because he realizes he has left out the birds. Again, he is impressed by their 'numberless variations' in size, form, and colour, as well as with respect to their lives, actions, and customs.[39] He is impressed by the wisdom of the honeybee, the sentry-keeping of cranes, the alliance between storks and crows and the inventiveness of swallows, and much, much more.[40] Again, he stops because he perceives that

---

[35] Basil, 'On the Hexaemeron', *Exegetic Homilies* (Washington, DC: Catholic University of America, 1963), Homily 1, §6.
[36] On Basil's sources for the *Hexaemeron*, see Grant, *Early Christians and Animals*, p. 77; and D. Runia, *Philo in Early Christian Literature* (Assen; Minneapolis: Van Gorcum; Fortress, 1993).
[37] Basil, 'On the Hexaemeron', Homily 7, §2.
[38] Ibid., Homily 7, §6.
[39] Ibid., Homily 8, §3.
[40] Ibid., Homily 8, §§4–8.

his speech 'is going beyond due limits' but in concluding he observes, 'I have not even begun my explanation'.[41] Returning to the land animals in the ninth homily, he treats the virtues and vices of the ox, ass, horse, wolf, fox, deer, ant, dog, lion, leopard, bear, and others,[42] and marvels at the wondrous design of many more animals. Once more he has to restrain himself, stating that he can almost hear his audience clamouring for a discussion of the human. He squeezes in a few comments about the creation of humanity at the end of the homily, but with such brevity that his brother, Gregory of Nyssa, introduced his treatise 'On the Making of Man' with the rationale that the consideration of humanity was lacking in Basil's work.[43]

What we have, therefore, in Basil's *Hexaemeron* is a theologian who has been so far carried away with excitement about the innumerable variety of God's creatures that he goes on for too long, has no time to fit them all in, and cannot make space even for the discussion of the human, which he acknowledges his listeners are craving. Here is a theological project that is focused on celebration rather than classification, that seeks not to put other animals in their place, but is drawn by them beyond reasonable limits. Unlike Linnaeus, Basil does not picture himself as Adam in Eden, capable of the universal grasp of animal life that is the secret of human power over it. Instead, Basil's discourse is unable to contain and comprehend the variety of creaturely life about which he is so enthusiastic: rather than focusing on classification, he is seized by the unfathomable diversity of creaturely life and piles example upon example in its illustration. We could therefore understand Basil's work in terms of Agamben's vision of the interruption of the anthropological machine: an account that has left behind the division between human and animal even at the risk of failing to secure human identity. Where others have attempted to tame the variety of creatures, Basil revels in it; the classificatory dominion to which Bacon and Linnaeus aspire is here not thinkable even as a possibility. In Basil's account it is not humans putting other animals in their place but entirely the other way around: like Job, Basil is taken beyond himself, enabled to glimpse the wondrous and excessive expanse of God's dealings with creation, and placed by that vision into the midst of God's creatures, worshipping with them the God who alone comprehends the life of each and all.

---

[41] Ibid., Homily 8, §8.
[42] Ibid., Homily 9, §3.
[43] Gregory of Nyssa, 'On the Making of Man', *A Select Library of Nicene and Post-Nicene Fathers of the Christian Church. Second Series* (P. Schaff (ed.); vol. 5; Edinburgh: T&T Clark, 1997).

Bibliography

Agamben, G., *The Open: Man and Animal* (K. Attell (trans.); Stanford, CA: Stanford University Press, 2004).

Aquinas, Thomas, *Summa Theologica* (Fathers of the English Dominican Province (trans.); London: Blackfriars, 1963).

Aristotle, *Generation of Animals* (A. L. Peck (trans.); Loeb Classical Library; London and Cambridge, MA: William Heinemann Ltd. and Harvard University Press, 1943).

—*Historia Animalium* (A. L. Peck (trans.); Loeb Classical Library; London and Cambridge, MA: William Heinemann Ltd. and Harvard University Press, 1965).

Augustine, *On Genesis: On Genesis: A Refutation of the Manichees, Unfinished Literal Commentary on Genesis, the Literal Meaning of Genesis* (J. E. Rotelle (ed.); E. Hill (trans.); The Works of Saint Augustine: A Translation for the 21st Century; New York: New City Press, 2002).

Bacon, F., *The New Organon* (L. Jardine, and M. Silverthorne (eds); Cambridge Texts in the History of Philosophy; Cambridge: Cambridge University Press, 2000).

—'Valerius Terminus (of the Interpretation of Nature)', *Collected Works of Francis Bacon* (J. Spedding, R. L. Ellis, and D. D. Heath (eds); vol. III; London: Routledge, 1996), pp. 215–52.

Basil, 'On the Hexaemeron', *Exegetic Homilies* (Washington, DC: Catholic University of America, 1963), pp. 3–150.

Borges, J. L., *Other Inquisitions, 1937–52* (Austin, TX: University of Texas Press, 1964).

Clough, D., *On Animals: I. Systematic Theology* (London: T&T Clark/Continuum, 2012).

Dupré, J., *Humans and Other Animals* (Oxford: Clarendon, 2002).

Foucault, M., *The Order of Things: An Archaeology of the Human Sciences* (London and New York: Routledge, 2002).

Grant, R. M., *Early Christians and Animals* (London: Routledge, 1999).

Gregory of Nyssa, 'On the Making of Man', *A Select Library of Nicene and Post-Nicene Fathers of the Christian Church. Second Series* (P. Schaff (ed.); vol. 5; Edinburgh: T&T Clark, 1997).

Harrison, P., *The Fall of Man and the Foundations of Science* (Cambridge: Cambridge University Press, 2007).

—'Linnaeus as a Second Adam? Taxonomy and the Religious Vocation', *Zygon* 44.4 (2009), pp. 879–93.

Heilbron, J. L., 'The Measure of Enlightenment', *The Quantifying Spirit in the 18th Century* (T. Frangsmyr, J. L. Heilbron, and R. E. Rider (eds); Berkeley: University of California Press, 1990), pp. 207–43.

Lindroth, S., 'Linné — Legend Och Verklighet', *Lychnos* (1965), pp. 56–122.

Linnaeus, C., *Systemae Naturae: Per Regna Tria Naturae: Secundum Classes, Ordines, Genera, Species, Cum Characteribus, Differentiis, Synonymis, Locis/Praefatus Est*

Ioannes Ioachimus Langius (Halae Magdeburgicae: Typis et sumtibus Io. Iac. Curt, Ad editionem decimam reformatam Holmiensem ed. 1760).

—Fries, T. M., and J. M. Hulth (eds.), *Bref Och Skrifvelser Af Och Till Carl Von Linné* (Stockholm and elsewhere: 1907).

Lisbet, K., 'Carl Linnaeus in His Time and Place', *Cultures of Natural History* (N. Jardine, J. A. Secord, and E. C. Spary (eds); Cambridge: Cambridge University Press, 1996), pp. 145–63.

Lovejoy, A. O., *The Great Chain of Being: A Study of the History of an Idea* (Cambridge, MA: Harvard University Press, 1942).

Luther, M., *Lectures on Genesis, Chapters 1–5* (Jaroslav Pelikan (ed.); Luther's Works, vol. I; Saint Louis: Concordia, 1958), pp. 64–5.

Morus (R. Lewisohn), *Animals, Men and Myths: A History of the Influence of Animals on Civilization and Culture* (London: Victor Gollancz, 1954).

Runia, D., *Philo in Early Christian Literature* (Assen and Minneapolis: Van Gorcum and Fortress, 1993).

Part Four

Animals as Subjects of
Religious Ethics

11

'Your Wives, Your Children, and Your Livestock': Domesticated Beings as Religious Objects in the Book of Deuteronomy[1]

Raymond F. Person, Jr.

The book of Deuteronomy envisions its world from a privileged position of the urban literati of ancient Israel, a perspective that is clearly both anthropocentric and androcentric as is clear in the dichotomy between the implied audience of males addressed in the book and their wives, children, and livestock.[2] In order to present this ideological construction more fully, I will briefly discuss the background – that is, the dichotomy of 'land' versus 'wilderness' found in Deuteronomy, and the family household as the most basic social unit in ancient Israel. I will explore the dichotomy of men versus wives, children, and livestock – that is, the patriarchal reinterpretation of the family household found in Deuteronomy – and then examine how animals (and to some degree plants) are treated in the Deuteronomic legal material concerning worship as representatives of this patriarchal reinterpretation. After describing the anthropocentric and androcentric character of Deuteronomy, I will conclude with a critique of this position. The critique will begin with a discussion of the book of Jonah, a work that is widely understood as satirizing the Deuteronomic understanding of prophecy. We will also see that the book of Jonah satirically criticizes the duality of men and women-children-livestock in the Deuteronomic worldview and, in fact, places all of creation (including, the fish, the *qiqiyon* plant, and the

---

[1] This essay is closely related to my forthcoming commentary on Deuteronomy in the Earth Bible Commentary series published by Sheffield Phoenix Press. The Earth Bible Commentary series itself arises from the Earth Bible project. For introductions to the approach taken in these series, see N. Habel, 'Introducing the Earth Bible', *Readings from the Perspective of Earth* (N. Habel (ed.); Earth Bible, vol. 1; Sheffield: Sheffield Academic Press, 2000), pp. 25–37; The Earth Bible Team, 'Guiding Ecojustice Principles', *Readings from the Perspective of Earth*, pp. 38–53; and N. Habel, 'Introducing Ecological Hermeneutics', *Exploring Ecological Hermeneutics* (N. Habel (ed.); Symposium 46; Atlanta: Society of Biblical Literature, 2008), pp. 1–8.

[2] For my discussion of the urban setting of the Deuteronomic literati, see R. F. Person, Jr., *The Deuteronomic School: History, Social Setting, and Literature* (Studies in Biblical Literature, vol. 2; Atlanta: Society of Biblical Literature, 2002), especially pp. 56–63, 79–81.

Ninevite livestock) on a par with humans as active subjects who can obey God's commands. The critique will then end with some reflections on how modern people of faith might adopt a critical reading of Deuteronomy's understanding of household as an appropriate aid to developing a more holistic approach to the environmental crisis.

I. 'Land' Versus 'Wilderness'

Our human predilection for creating dichotomies of 'us' and 'them' is evident in the rhetoric of Deuteronomy, including its construction of the dichotomy of 'land' versus 'wilderness'.[3] We will see that 'land' and 'wilderness' are both topographical and theological constructs that are used in the Deuteronomic construction of legal materials that limit human behaviour within their ideologically built environments.

In Deuteronomy, 'land' (אֶרֶץ) refers to habitable and hospitable land that God has given to humans. In fact, the 'land' is not only habitable but inhabited: 'the land of Moab' (1.5), 'the land of the Canaanites' (1.7), 'the land of Egypt' (1.27), 'a land of the Rephaim' (2.20), 'King Sihon the Amorite of Heshbon and his land' (2.24), and so forth.[4] God parcels out 'land' to humans: 'When the Most High apportioned the nations, when he divided humankind, he fixed the boundaries of the peoples according to the number of the gods' (32.8). These decisions are not permanent. God can choose to dispossess some in order to give 'land' to others, and this not only applies on behalf of the people of Israel: God dispossessed the Horim, so that the descendants of Esau had 'land' (2.12, 22), and the Rephaim, so that the Ammonites had 'land' (2.21). Of course, the central displacement in the narrative was God dispossessing 'the Hittites, the Girgashites, the Amorites, the Canaanites, the Perizzites, the Hivites, and the Jebusites, seven nations' (7.1) of their 'land', so that the people of Israel would have a 'good land'.

Although God has given other peoples hospitable 'land' as their home, the phrase 'the good land' (1.25, 35; 3.25; 4.21, 22; 6.18; 8.7, 10; 9.6; 11.17) is reserved for the 'land' God swore to Abraham, Isaac, and Jacob (1.8).

> For the Lord your God is bringing you into a good land, a land with flowing
> streams, with springs and underground waters welling up in valleys and hills, a

---

[3] For a brief discussion and rejection of 'Western dualism' and its negative effects on Earth and women, see The Earth Bible Team, 'Guiding Ecojustice Principles', pp. 40–2.
[4] I have consistently used the NRSV translation, except where otherwise noted.

land of wheat and barley, of vines and fig trees and pomegranates, a land of olive trees and honey, a land where you may eat bread without scarcity, where you will lack nothing, a land whose stones are iron and from whose hills you may mine copper. You shall eat your fill and bless the Lord your God for the good land that he has given you. (8.7–10)

… a land flowing with milk and honey. For the land that you are about to enter to occupy is not like the land of Egypt, from which you have come, where you sow your seed and irrigate by foot like a vegetable garden. But the land that you are crossing over to occupy is a land of hills and valleys, watered by rain from the sky, a land that the Lord your God looks after. (11.9b–12a)

This 'good land' 'is not like the land of Egypt' because this 'land' is God's homeland that God tends and cares for, thereby minimizing for God's people the labour of irrigation.[5] Thus, this 'good land' is, in the words of Norman Habel, 'a divinely sanctioned and legal land grant'.[6]

In contrast, the 'wilderness' (מדבר) is inhospitable to humans and, as such, is uninhabited. The space between Horeb and the land of the Amorites is described as 'that great and terrible wilderness' (1.19). When Moses sings of their history, he describes the 'wilderness' as 'a desert, … a howling wilderness waste' (32.10), where one would normally experience 'wasting hunger, burning consumption, bitter pestilence' (32.24), where one must avoid 'the teeth of beasts' and 'the venom of things crawling in the dust' (32.24).

The people of Israel spend forty years wandering in this 'wilderness'. God, however, provides for their survival. 'He sustained him [that is, Jacob] in a desert land, in a howling wilderness waste; he shielded him, cared for him, guarded him as the apple of his eye' (32.10). The 'wilderness' was a place of punishment and cleansing and the place in which God revealed his law (1.6; 4.9–14). The people wandered in the 'wilderness' as a punishment for their disobedience of the law. This punishment would cleanse the people by the 'evil generation' dying out in the 'wilderness' (1.34–5; 4.21–2) so as to prevent the pollution of the 'good land'. The giving of the law in the wilderness is certainly an important event in this cleansing as preparation for entering the 'good land'.

---

[5] Note, however, that the 'good land' is clearly distinguishable because of the crops and livestock that humans had domesticated (for example, wheat and barley, cattle and goats), thereby betraying the anthropocentric bias of the construct 'good land'.

[6] N. Habel, *The Land is Mine: Six Biblical Land Ideologies* (Overtures to Biblical Theology; Minneapolis: Fortress Press, 1995), p. 52. See his entire chapter on Deuteronomy, 'Land as Conditional Grant', pp. 36–53.

Moses instructs the people that, in order to enter the 'good land' and to remain there, the people must obey the law.

> If you will only heed his every commandment that I am commanding you today – loving the Lord your God, and serving him with all your heart and with all your soul – then he will give the rain for your land in its season, the early rain and the later rain, and you will gather in your grain, your wine, and your oil, and he will give grass in your fields for your livestock, and you will eat your fill. Take care, or you will be seduced into turning away, serving other gods and worshipping them, for then the anger of the Lord will be kindled against you and he will shut up the heavens, so that there will be no rain and the land will yield no fruit; then you will perish quickly off the good land that the Lord is giving you. (11.13–17)

That is, because the earth belongs to God, the 'good land' can become 'wilderness', if God's anger is kindled.[7]

The 'good land' and the 'wilderness' are theological constructs that are defined in opposition to each other. At first glance, this opposition appears to be primarily topographical – the 'good land' is in 'the land of Canaan' and the 'wilderness' is elsewhere, 'beyond the Jordan'. However, a closer look at the text clearly indicates that the dichotomy is really theological. When the people wandered in the 'wilderness', they 'lacked nothing' for God was with them (2.7); it was as if they were living in a 'good land'.[8] Despite the 'wilderness' being a God-forsaken place, the people of Israel survived their 'wilderness' experience because of God's unusual mercy and promise to Abraham, Isaac, and Jacob. When the people move out of the 'wilderness' into the 'good land', they must reflect on what they learned in the 'wilderness' and obey God's law that was given to them there. If they disobey, they will find themselves in the 'wilderness' again, even if it requires God's changing the 'good land' into 'wilderness'.

This constructed dichotomy underlies much of the law – that is, the particular construction of 'land' versus 'wilderness' influences the construction of human activity as defined by the law. Obedience to the law brings with it certain blessings.

---

[7] Although I am emphasizing the dichotomy of a 'good land' and the 'wilderness' in Deuteronomy *and* I am confident that this dichotomy is an emphasis within the text itself, I am also aware that this dichotomy is undermined somewhat within Deuteronomy. First, Deut. 10.14 asserts that 'heaven and the heaven of heavens belong to the Lord your God, the earth with all that is in it', so both the 'good land' and the 'wilderness' belong to God. Second, the place where Moses stands is described both as 'beyond the Jordan – in the wilderness' (1.1) and 'the land beyond the Jordan' (3.8). This 'land' is 'the land of King Sihon of the Amorites ... the land of King Og of Bashan' (4.46–7), which becomes 'land' and 'territory' of the tribes of Reuben, Gad, and Manasseh (3.12–13).

[8] On this theme, see W. Brueggemann, *Land* (Philadelphia: Fortress Press, 1977), chapter 3.

If you will only obey the Lord your God, ... Blessed shall you be in the city, and blessed shall you be in the field. Blessed shall be the fruit of your womb, the fruit of your ground, and the fruit of your livestock, both the increase of your cattle and the issue of your flock. Blessed shall be your basket and your kneading bowl. Blessed shall you be when you come in, and blessed shall you be when you go out. (28.1, 3–6)

Because God will so richly bless those who obey the law, there are special laws that relate to these blessings. In recognition of the bounty coming from God, the people of Israel must present their first fruits as thanksgiving offerings to God (26.1–11). Also, the bounteous harvest is so great that a portion must be left for 'the alien, the orphan, and the widow' to glean (24.19–22).

The law requires that the 'good land' be protected from human defilement. The latrine must be 'outside the camp' (23.12–14). The location is symbolically not in the 'good land'; rather, it is out of sight in the 'wilderness'. Those who commit evil acts must also be purged, because they threaten the 'good land' (13.5; 17.7, 12; 19.13, 19; 21.9, 21; 22.21, 22, 24; 24.7). This purging refers to capital punishment that must be carried out outside the city gates (17.5; 22.23–4). Once again, symbolically, the guilty are removed from the 'good land' and killed in the 'wilderness', where their blood and corpses cannot pollute the 'good land'. However, in the case of an unknown homicide in 'open country', the boundaries between the 'good land' and the 'wilderness' shift again (21.1–9). The bloodguilt that has polluted the 'good land' must be satisfied and the elders of the nearest town must sacrifice a heifer for this purpose.

The law concerning how the Israelites relate to those of other lands is also informed by this dichotomy. Although the law forbids charging interest to an Israelite, interest can be charged to a 'foreigner' – namely, someone who does not belong in the 'good land' because he should be elsewhere in his own 'land' (23.19–20). The law concerning war differs for those enemies who live outside the 'good land' and those 'unclean' peoples who must be annihilated from the 'good land' (20.1–20).

This quick review has demonstrated how the boundaries between the 'good land' and the 'wilderness' shift, how the boundaries are both topographical and theological. The 'good land' can be understood as the entire promised land that must be taken from the other peoples, including the open country as well as the towns and cities. God blesses the entire land of Israel so that the bounteous harvest provides for all, including the poorest, and from this plenty the people give of their first fruits to God. However, the 'good land' can also be understood as being within the town walls so that defiling acts (for example, defecation and capital punishment) can occur in the nearby 'wilderness' outside the walls, thereby not requiring a major journey out of the country. Therefore, the theological 'wilderness' can be found within the topographical 'good land', when it is practically necessary, but it is also outside the topographical 'good land', that is 'beyond the Jordan'.

II. The Family Household[9]

The basic social unit in ancient Israel was called the *bet ab* (בֵּת אָב), in English most literally the 'house of the father'. This term does not simply refer to the dwelling, but also to the humans, animals, plants, and land that together make up the basic socio-economic unit. As such, the common translations are 'the household of the father' or the 'patriarchal household'; however, following the arguments of Carol Meyers, I prefer to use the translation 'family household' to refer to *bet ab* as the social reality behind the text. Meyers has made an excellent argument that the typical *bet ab* in early ancient Israel may not have been as patriarchal as the biblical literature suggests. Based on her reading of the biblical text, archaeological evidence, and comparative anthropological studies, such a household in an agrarian economy may have had strictly defined gender roles; nevertheless, the gender roles may have been valued equally in that the survival of the household required all household members to contribute significantly to the household's economy, including having important decision-making authority over the various gendered household tasks. Therefore, 'patriarchal household' may carry unnecessary negative connotations for describing the historical reality of the *bet ab*, so much so that 'family household' may be preferable. Below, I will elaborate more on Meyers' reconstruction of the *bet ab* in ancient Israel.

The social unit that played the most significant role in family identity – that is, the group with which individuals most clearly self-identified – was the village,

---

[9] This section is based primarily on C. Meyers, 'The Family in Early Israel', *Families in Ancient Israel* (L. Perdue, J. Blenkinsopp, J. Collins, C. Meyers (eds); Louisville: Westminster John Knox Press, 1997), pp. 1–47. Although Meyers' essay specifically concerns the family in premonarchical Israel, the other contributors to the volume *Families in Ancient Israel* argue that the *bet ab* continues into the later periods, including into the rabbinic period, as the basic social unit. Therefore, although the basic social unit of family may have been redefined significantly in urban areas during the later periods, the *bet ab* as described by Meyers nevertheless continued as the basic social unit throughout ancient Israel in the agrarian based economies of the villages. See J. Blenkinsopp, 'The Family in First Temple Israel', *Families in Ancient Israel*, pp. 48, 51; J. Collins, 'Marriage, Divorce, and Family in Second Temple Judaism', *Families in Ancient Israel*, pp. 105–6; and L. Perdue, 'The Israelite and Early Jewish Family: Summary and Conclusions', *Families in Ancient Israel*, pp. 179, 192.

mispahah (מִשְׁפָּחָה), which was characterized by 'its sense of being bound by a common heritage, by kinship ties, and by shared subsistence concerns'.[10] These villages were home to probably 50–150 persons from the various interrelated *bet abot*, each of which would have rarely exceeded 15 persons in each household.[11] Each family household would have 'included a set of related people as well as the residential buildings, outbuildings, tools, equipment, fields, livestock, and orchards; it sometimes also included household members who were not kin, such as "sojourners", war captives, and servants'.[12] The pillared house typical of Israelite architecture not only included living quarters for the humans on the second floor, but the ground level included housing for some of the livestock and rooms for the preparation and storage of agricultural products for food.[13]

Due to its remarkable geographical diversity, various ecological niches exist within Israel and the change from one to another can occur rapidly within a short distance. Nevertheless, the general agricultural subsistence strategy throughout ancient Israel remained within the 'Mediterranean agricultural pattern' that produced the major crops of grain, wine, and oil so often referred to in the biblical text, as well as a variety of legumes, fruits, nuts, herbs, and vegetables in addition to the food provided by the herding of goats and sheep.[14] Because of the tremendous diversity of ecological niches in ancient Israel and the resulting wide range of adaptations necessary for subsistence strategies in these niches, 'virtually every family household experienced a different set of challenges in establishing a productive subsistence strategy'.[15] According to Meyers, it was the necessity of insuring that the land, and the knowledge about how the subsistence strategies connected to the specific ecological limitations of that land, remain within the family that led to the patrilineal and patrilocal traditions of ancient Israel, including levirate marriage (Deut. 25.5–6) – that is, descent is traced through male ancestors (patrilineal) and at marriage the newlyweds join the husband's family household (patrilocal). Because of such ecological connections to the household's land and the patrilineal and patrilocal

---

[10] Meyers, 'The Family in Early Israel', p. 37.

[11] Ibid., pp. 12, 19.

[12] Ibid., p. 14.

[13] Ibid., pp. 14–15. See also O. Borowitz, *Daily Life in Ancient Israel* (Archaeology and Biblical Studies, vol. 5; Atlanta: Society of Biblical Literature, 2003), p. 19.

[14] Meyers, 'The Family in Early Israel', pp. 10–11. For a fuller discussion of the natural history of ancient Israel and the different subsistence strategies within the different natural domains, see D. Hillel, *The Natural History of the Bible: An Environmental Exploration of the Hebrew Scriptures* (New York: Columbia University Press, 2006). Although he too quickly accepted the historical reliability of the biblical text, his description of the geography of ancient Israel and the resulting subsistence strategies remains helpful.

[15] Meyers, 'The Family in Early Israel', pp. 19–20.

traditions, '[t]he identity of any family unit was thus inseparable from its land, which was the material basis of its survival'.[16]

The *bet ab* depended on maximizing the labour of the entire family for its very survival and this was differentiated to some degree according to both age and gender.[17] Some seasonal tasks, such as the harvesting and storage of the main crops, required all able-bodied members of the family household to assist; some ongoing tasks such as tending orchards and vineyards or milking the animals may have been shared by all. However, other tasks were probably differentiated between men, women, and children. The men were primarily responsible for the growing of the field crops and the 'start-up' operations, such as clearing fields, building terraces, constructing homes, making and repairing tools. The women were primarily responsible for childcare, tending the gardens and livestock near the home, textile production, and food preservation and production. The children helped out with many of the light, time-consuming household tasks under the guidance of the women until they reached the age when they could take on their own roles with the men or women. This division of labour along gender lines meant that, on the one hand, the ecological knowledge necessary for growing the field crops was primarily male knowledge; on the other hand, the technological knowledge of food preparation and textile production was primarily female knowledge. Thus, a patrilineal and patrilocal system strengthened both gendered realms of knowledge: male knowledge, which was necessarily connected to the household's specific ecological niche, continued *in situ*; female knowledge, which depended less on the geographical factors, was transported to other households, thereby sharing any newfound strategies with other households. Both of these gendered realms of knowledge were closely interconnected (for example, the male knowledge that produced the grains in the field and the female knowledge that could store and prepare it for food) and both were valued highly since the family's survival depended on them both. Thus, Meyers concluded as follows:

> The high level of gender interdependence in early Israelite farm families, along with the important managerial role of senior females in the life activities of the household, may mean that the biblical term for the complex family unit – *bet ab* – refers to the descent reckoning among male lines but not necessarily to male dominance in household functioning.[18]

[16] Ibid., p. 21.
[17] Ibid., pp. 22–32.
[18] Ibid., p. 34.

Although Meyers has made an excellent argument that the typical *bet ab* in early ancient Israel may not have been as patriarchal as biblical literature suggests, the book of Deuteronomy certainly portrays the gender relations in the *bet ab* in a patriarchal manner. Such an androcentric portrayal may more accurately reflect the hierarchical structure of the urban literati and their families removed from an agrarian context in contrast to the patriarchal households in the rural villages.[19] Thus, my discussion below of the language in Deuteronomy may more accurately reflect an urban elite's misunderstanding of their contemporary agrarian economy than households within the agrarian economy itself. Nevertheless (and here in relationship to the Deuteronomic vision I think that the translation of *bet ab* as 'patriarchal household' with its negative connotations is most appropriate), the patriarchal household as envisioned by Deuteronomy significantly influenced the legal code of Deuteronomy and, in turn, is influenced by the legal code, at least when it could be enforced in the rural villages. That is, the patriarchal dichotomy between, on the one hand, the adult males addressed in the book and, on the other, the women, children, and livestock underlies much of the legal material in Deuteronomy.

III. 'Wives', 'Children', and 'Livestock' in Deuteronomy

The title of this chapter is based primarily on Deut. 3.19: 'Only your wives, your children, and your livestock – I know that you have much livestock – shall stay behind in the towns that I have given to you'. This verse comes from the section of Deuteronomy in which Moses is relaying God's instructions to the people in the 'wilderness' concerning their upcoming conquest of the 'land'. Although the men are being commanded to cross over the Jordan River to conquer the promised land, their wives, children, and livestock – that is, the rest of their household – must remain safely in the towns in the Transjordan already controlled by the Israelites.

This androcentric grouping of women, children, and livestock is found in other passages in Deuteronomy as well, including legal material concerning the spoils of war and the language of blessing and cursing that depends on Israel's obedience to God's law. The divine command for genocide against the inhabitants of the land, the Canaanites, contains this grouping: 'You shall put the inhabitants of that town to the sword, utterly destroying it and everything in

---

[19] Blenkinsopp, 'The Family in First Temple Israel', p. 48.

it – even putting its livestock to the sword' (Deut. 13.15). Here the inhabitants of the land are identified as both humans and livestock. However, when warring against other peoples not in the promised land – that is, non-Canaanites – they become spoil for the men of Israel: 'You may, however, take as your booty the women, the children, livestock, and everything else in the town, all its spoil. You may enjoy the spoil of your enemies, which the LORD your God has given you' (Deut. 20.14). The blessing and cursing language not only includes references to women, children, and livestock, but also includes references to the plants culti-vated by the household. If they obey God's law, they will be blessed in the land: 'Blessed shall be the fruit of your womb, the fruit of your ground, and the fruit of your livestock, both the increase of your cattle and the issue of your flock' (Deut. 28.4; see also 28.11). If they disobey, they will be cursed: 'Cursed shall be the fruit of your womb, the fruit of your ground, the increase of your cattle and the issue of your flock' (Deut. 28.18). The commandment against coveting puts it all together, giving a fuller picture of the patriarchal household: 'Neither shall you covet your neighbour's wife. Neither shall you desire your neighbour's house, or field, or male or female slave, or ox, or donkey, or anything that belongs to your neighbour' (Deut. 5.21).

Even from this quick review of selected passages, we can see that the legal material in Deuteronomy is written not only from an anthropocentric perspective, but also a patriarchal perspective that often places all of the mammalian members of the household, other than the free Israelite adult males, into the same category of domesticated beings – that is, those beings viewed as subservient to the interests of male humans.

IV. Legal Material Relating to Animals (and Plants) in Worship

As seen above in the quote from Deut. 28.4, the members of a thriving Israelite household, including livestock, are considered a blessing from God in the 'good land'. The legal material in Deuteronomy relating to animals begins with the assumption that livestock are blessings from God and, as with all such blessings, a certain portion should be devoted to God in the midst of worship. We will see this in a brief discussion of two representative passages: Deut. 14.22–6 concerning tithes, and Deut. 15.19–23 concerning the sacrifice of first-born livestock.

> Set apart a tithe of all the yield of your seed that is brought in yearly from the field. In the presence of the Lord your God, in the place that he will choose as a

dwelling for his name, you shall eat the tithe of your grain, your wine, and your oil, as well as the firstlings of your herd and flock, so that you may learn to fear the Lord your God always. But if, when the Lord your God has blessed you, the distance is so great that you are unable to transport it, because the place where the Lord your God will choose to set his name is too far away from you, then you may turn it into money. With the money secure in hand, go to the place that the Lord your God will choose; spend the money for whatever you wish – oxen, sheep, wine, strong drink, or whatever you desire. And you shall eat there in the presence of the Lord your God, you and your household rejoicing together. (Deut. 14.22–6)

This practice of tithing had some practical economic consequences; for example, some of the tithes were used to support Levites and other temple personnel as well as the poor. However, in this passage we see the religious motivation expressed as 'learning to fear the Lord your God' – that is, remaining ever conscious of God as the giver of all blessings and, therefore, giving thanks to God for one's blessings. Since both grain and livestock come from the patriarchal household and its land, they truly represent the patriarchal household as a whole. Thus, this practice seems to be a religious expression of acknowledging the blessings of the patriarchal household as a whole by returning a portion of these blessings – the portable assets of food – to give thanks to God. Of course, even these portable assets of the patriarchal household may become burdensome when traveling great distances with them, so that provision is made to convert the grains and livestock into money to purchase similar offerings upon arrival in Jerusalem, a practice that would have benefited significantly both the temple cult personnel and nearby farmers.

Closely connected with the practice of tithing is the law concerning the sacrifice of the first-born male livestock. The sacrifice of the firstling is the animal equivalent of the tithe for grains and other plant-based products. Although one could easily determine, for example, what a tenth of the grain harvest was, some other mechanism was necessary for determining what the tithe was for livestock. The sacrifice of the firstling male seems to serve this purpose.

Every firstling male born of your herd and flock you shall consecrate to the Lord your God; you shall not do work with your firstling ox nor shear the firstling of your flock. You shall eat it, you together with your household, in the presence of the Lord your God year by year at the place that the Lord will choose. But if it has any defect – any serious defect, such as lameness or blindness – you shall not sacrifice it to the Lord your God; within your towns you may eat it, the unclean and the clean alike, as you would a gazelle or deer. Its blood, however, you must not eat; you shall pour it out on the ground like water. (Deut. 15.19–23)

Since the firstling sacrifice is also mentioned in Deuteronomy 14.22–6, the religious motivation for this sacrifice must also be 'learning to fear the Lord your God' (Deut. 14.23) by remembering the divine source of all blessings.

V. Conclusion Concerning Deuteronomy

The book of Deuteronomy envisions the thriving family household, reinterpreted within its patriarchal worldview, as a blessing from God for God's people who obey God's law in the 'good land'. The hierarchy within the household is free male Israelites, their women and children, and then the livestock. This hierarchy is reflected in various legal materials as well as the language of God's blessings or curses based on obedience or disobedience of God's law. Despite the hierarchy that places the women and children above the livestock in some contexts, Deuteronomy also envisions the members of the patriarchal household in two groups, the free male Israelites, on the one hand, and the women, children, and livestock, on the other, especially in contexts concerning the (primary) male activity of warfare.

One of the requirements of God's law is remembering the divine source of the blessings of the patriarchal household in the practice of providing tithes and the sacrifice of the firstborn male livestock. Thus, animal sacrifice is understood as an essential element of maintaining the divine blessings provided from the 'good land' in the patriarchal household.

Since the family household was the most basic social unit in ancient Israel, Deuteronomy reinterprets the world from its own ideological perspective of the patriarchal household – that is, in a way that is clearly both anthropocentric and androcentric.

VI. The Book of Jonah as Critique of Deuteronomic Thought

The Book of Jonah is widely understood as a satire targeting the common dichotomy found in the prophetic literature of the Israelites: God's chosen people versus all other ethnic groups, 'the nations'.[20] Above, we have seen how this dichotomy informs Deuteronomy concerning the conduct of war and what spoils are permitted: genocide is commanded for all the ethnic groups inhabiting the promised land, but, in contrast, the women, children, and livestock of those enemies not inhabiting the promised land may be taken as war booty. I have argued elsewhere that, although the ethnocentric and satiric interpretation of the Jonah narrative is accurate, it is sorrowfully inadequate because this interpretation misses the observation that the book is also a satire of the anthropocentrism present in much of the prophetic literature associated with Deuteronomic thought, including the books of Samuel, Kings, and Jeremiah.[21] In this section, I will briefly review my argument for why Jonah is a satire targeting both the ethnocentrism and anthropocentrism found in Deuteronomic literature in order to show that even within the biblical text itself a strong critique exists rejecting the specific anthropocentric view of animals and other members of the Earth community in the book of Deuteronomy.

Within the Jonah narrative all of the characters fear God, and thus eventually obey God's commands, including the human and non-human characters. As soon as they understand what God requires, the pagan sailors and the people of Nineveh obey God's commands. Immediately the non-human characters – the wind, the storm, the fish, the plant, the worm, the sun, and the Ninevite livestock – obey God's commands. The only character who is really placed in a bad light in relationship to God is the prophet Jonah, who clearly wanted nothing to do with warning the Ninevites of their possible destruction. In Jonah's mind, the so-called 'evil' enemy of Israel, the Ninevites, deserved destruction. Thus, the narrative sets up a sharp contrast between disobedient Jonah, who must be forced into his prophetic role, and all of the other human and non-human characters, who immediately obey God's command once they understand it. Jonah is portrayed as a petty ethnocentric prophet, while the rest of creation is portrayed as obedient to God's will.

Moreover, the non-human characters are often portrayed as active subjects within the narrative. For example, in Jon. 1.15 the narrative reads 'the sea ceased its raging' rather than 'the Lord calmed the sea'. At times the language used to

---

[20] For my fuller discussion of the satirical tone in Jonah, see R. F. Person, Jr., *In Conversation with Jonah: Conversation Analysis, Literary Criticism, and the Book of Jonah* (Journal for the Study of the Old Testament Supplements Series 220; Sheffield: Sheffield Academic Press, 1996), especially pp. 83–8, 153–7. The English translation of Jonah given below is consistently my own as found in this volume.

[21] R. F. Person, Jr., 'The Role of Non-Human Characters in Jonah', *Exploring Ecological Hermeneutics* (N. Habel, and P. Trudinger (eds); Symposium 46; Atlanta: Society of Biblical Literature, 2008), pp. 85–90.

describe this active role is explicitly anthropomorphic, possibly as a way of emphasizing how all creation, not just humans, has a role to play in God's plan. For example, in Jon. 1.4 the narrative most literally reads 'the ship thought to break up'. The narrative also uses language that implies that God has conversations with non-human characters in much the same way he communicates with Jonah; for example, Jon. 2.11 reads, 'Then the Lord spoke to the fish and it vomited Jonah upon dry land'. God also 'appoints' the fish to swallow Jonah (2.1), the plant to shade Jonah (4.6), the worm to kill the plant (4.7), and the wind to destroy Jonah's booth (4.8).

The Jonah narrative ends with God's challenging question to Jonah, which is also the question that the readers of Jonah must struggle with:

> Yet I should not have compassion on Nineveh, that large city, which has in it more than one hundred and twenty thousand people, who do not know their right hand from their left hand, and many cattle as well? (Jon. 4.11)

Unfortunately, many modern readers have missed the anti-anthropocentric critique of the satire in Jonah, for example, dismissing all of the Ninevite livestock wearing sackcloth and ashes as part of the ridiculousness of satire in general. However, I am convinced that, upon closer examination of the text, this dismissal reflects the modern interpreters' own anthropocentrism and, therefore, misses the satirical criticism being levelled at the anthropocentrism within the tradition as is evident in Deuteronomy.

VII. Conclusion

Although it is quite probable that the *bet ab* in early ancient Israel was not as patriarchal as described, Deuteronomy unquestionably envisions the world through androcentric and anthropocentric lenses, including its understanding of the patriarchal household. The household is a hierarchy, beginning with God and then continuing in order to men, women, children, and finally livestock. Various dichotomies operate within the Deuteronomic worldview, but, for our present purposes, the most important is the dyad of free Israelite men, on the one hand, and their wives, children, and livestock, on the other.

This dichotomy must be challenged on gender grounds. However, the fact that the Deuteronomic worldview envisions the patriarchal household as including both human and non-human members of the Earth community holds some promise as a correction of our modern Western dichotomies of human versus nature. The legal material in Deuteronomy clearly defines what the relationships between humans, livestock, plants, and land should be within the patriarchal household. Although we certainly should question the androcentric and anthropocentric presuppositions underlying how these relationships are defined, the legal material in Deuteronomy nevertheless asserts that we too should struggle to understand better how the members of the household are related to one another, and that the success of the household requires some measure of cooperation and mutuality among its various members, human and non-human.

Lest we think that we moderns are the only ones to entertain a critique of the androcentric and anthropocentric presuppositions underlying the Deuteronomic legal material, it is important to note that this critique existed within ancient Israel itself. Jonah satirically criticizes the ethnocentrism and anthropocentrism found in Deuteronomy and other Deuteronomic literature. The non-human characters in Jonah are active subjects, fulfilling their role in God's plan. Furthermore, God's rhetorical question at the end of the book clearly suggests that God's compassion is not only for God's chosen people, the people of Israel, but also includes the Ninevite people as well as their livestock. Thus, the main character, Jonah, himself a free Israelite male who represents the head of the patriarchal household according to Deuteronomic understanding, is corrected in that his ethnocentricism and his anthropocentrism are rejected. Countering his narrow-minded ideology is a vision of the world in which even so-called 'evil' pagans and non-human beings, such as worms, fish, and wind, are active members of God's community. In other words, even those who are excluded from Deuteronomy's definition of the patriarchal household and who live outside the 'land' are re-imagined as within the realm of God's compassion, breaking down some of the problematic dichotomies found in Deuteronomy.

The family household in early Israel may provide a helpful model for us as we struggle to address the global problems we face today. If 'the Israelite household functions were dynamically interlocked and interdependent,'[22] and if the household included not only humans but also land, animals, and plants, we too should re-imagine our household and, therefore, re-build it so that all of the members of the household – lands, humans, non-human animals, plants, and other members of the Earth community – are understood as interlocked and interdependent within our household. And given what we now know about the global village, we must re-imagine our household as all of the Earth community,

---

[22] Meyers, 'The Family in Early Israel', p. 23.

as all of God's household, not just those we find within the walls of our houses or our towns or even within the boundaries of our countries or our continents.

Bibliography

Blenkinsopp, J., 'The Family in First Temple Israel', *Families in Ancient Israel* (L. G. Perdue, J. Blenkinsopp, J. J. Collins, and C. Meyers (eds); Louisville: Westminster John Knox Press, 1997), pp. 48–103.

Borowitz, O., *Daily Life in Ancient Israel* (Archaeology and Biblical Studies, vol. 5; Atlanta: Society of Biblical Literature, 2003).

Brueggemann, W., *Land* (Philadelphia: Fortress Press, 1977).

Collins, J. J., 'Marriage, Divorce, and Family in Second Temple Judaism', *Families in Ancient Israel* (L. G. Perdue, J. Blenkinsopp, J. J. Collins, C. Meyers (eds); Louisville: Westminster John Knox Press, 1997), pp. 104–62.

The Earth Bible Team, 'Guiding Ecojustice Principles', *Readings from the Perspective of Earth* (N. Habel (ed.); Earth Bible, vol. 1; Sheffield: Sheffield Academic Press, 2000), pp. 38–53.

Habel, N., 'Introducing Ecological Hermeneutics', *Exploring Ecological Hermeneutics* (N. Habel (ed.); Symposium 46; Atlanta: Society of Biblical Literature, 2008), pp. 1–8.

—'Introducing the Earth Bible', *Readings from the Perspective of Earth* (N. Habel (ed.); Earth Bible, vol. 1; Sheffield: Sheffield Academic Press, 2000), pp. 25–37.

—*The Land is Mine: Six Biblical Land Ideologies* (Overtures to Biblical Theology; Minneapolis: Fortress Press, 1995).

Hillel, D., *The Natural History of the Bible: An Environmental Exploration of the Hebrew Scriptures* (New York: Columbia University Press, 2006).

Meyers, C. L., 'The Family in Early Israel', *Families in Ancient Israel* (L. G. Perdue, J. Blenkinsopp, J. J. Collins, C. Meyers (eds); Louisville: Westminster John Knox Press, 1997), pp. 1–47.

Perdue, L. G., 'The Israelite and Early Jewish Family: Summary and Conclusions', *Families in Ancient Israel* (L. G. Perdue, J. Blenkinsopp, J. J. Collins, C. Meyers (eds); Louisville: Westminster John Knox Press, 1997), pp. 163–222.

Person, R. F., Jr., *The Deuteronomic School: History, Social Setting, and Literature* (Studies in Biblical Literature, vol. 2; Atlanta: Society of Biblical Literature, 2002).

—*In Conversation with Jonah: Conversation Analysis, Literary Criticism, and the Book of Jonah* (Journal for the Study of the Old Testament Supplements Series 220; Sheffield: Sheffield Academic Press, 1996).

—'The Role of Non-Human Characters in Jonah', *Exploring Ecological Hermeneutics* (N. Habel, and P. Trudinger (eds); Symposium 46; Atlanta: Society of Biblical Literature, 2008), pp. 85–90.

12

Transgenic Animals and Ethics: Recognizing an Appropriate Dignity[1]

Robert Song

In 2011 the Academy of Medical Sciences published a thorough review of the ethical and regulatory aspects of research involving animal embryos and 'animals containing human material'.[2] The report was occasioned by an awareness of the increasingly urgent need for a public discussion of the growing use in medical research of animals that contain sequences of human DNA or mixtures of animal and human cells and tissues. Some forms of research which involve animal-human mixtures are long established: hybrid cells, for example, which are formed through the fusion of cells from two different species but which could never grow into animals, have been a staple of cell biology for nearly half a century. But others are much more recent: these include, for example, mice into whose livers human liver cells have been implanted in order to help understanding of human liver disease or to provide animal models for testing drugs. Others still are not just versions of xenotransplantation (i.e. the transplantation of organs or tissues between species) but are genuinely transgenic: that is, they contain material at the genetic or chromosomal level that has been imported from another species. For example, sheep, cows, or goats can be modified so that they produce human proteins in their milk such as insulin or antithrombin; mice have been developed that contain an extra human chromosome 21, which may help the scientific understanding of Down's syndrome; and monkeys have been produced which have the version of the human gene that causes Huntington's disease. A further possibility is a combination of xenotransplantation and transgenic technologies: a human liver might be grown inside a pig for transplanting

[1] I am grateful to David Albert Jones for discussion on these themes and to Celia Deane-Drummond for her comments on an earlier draft of this chapter.
[2] The Academy of Medical Sciences, *Animals Containing Human Material* (London: Academy of Medical Sciences, 2011).

into a human recipient, but the pig might be genetically modified in order to avoid rejection of the liver by the patient's immune system.

These developments raise moral questions that surpass the standard concerns about the use of animals in scientific research. Animals, of course, have been used in medical (and indeed non-medical) research for a very long time, but my interest in this chapter is not the theology or ethics of medical research on animals, as such. Rather my concern, regardless of the conclusions of that discussion, is whether a special wrong or an additional harm is done in creating animals that contain human material and in using them for the purposes of research. For those who think that research on animals can be justified in certain circumstances, there remains a further question whether it makes a difference if those animals are transgenic. Equally, for those who think that no research on animals can be justified, although genetically modifying animals is scarcely likely to make the case for research on them more attractive, an analysis of the issue is still likely to illuminate our understanding of animals overall.

I will approach these questions through a discussion of two Roman Catholic contributions: the first a discussion paper on xenotransplantation by the Pontifical Academy for Life issued in 2001,[3] and the second a response to it published in 2006 by a group of respected Australian bioethicists.[4] Although the Pontifical Academy document addresses the xenotransplantation of organs from animals to human beings, rather than the modification of animals, as such, it does seek to provide a framework for answering the question of what may be done to animals for the sake of human benefit. The bioethicists' response to it is more specifically oriented to transgenic animals; it argues (problematically, I will suggest) that creating them is morally unacceptable on the grounds that it is a threat to human dignity.

My own understanding of the issues is an elaboration of the idea that in these procedures there are two parties involved and not just one: the human being into whom the xenografted organ will be transplanted and the animal from which it is taken; the human being who will receive the benefit from the research and the animal that will make the sacrifice. The mere recognition that there is an element of reciprocity here suggests that we need a rather different

---

[3] Pontifical Academy for Life, *Prospects for Xenotransplantation: Scientific Aspects and Ethical Considerations*, http://www.vatican.va/roman_curia/pontifical_academies/acdlife/documents/rc_pa_acdlife_doc_20010926_xenotrapianti_en.html (accessed 13 August 2012).

[4] N. Tonti-Filippini, J. Fleming, G. Pike, and R. Campbell, 'Ethics and Human-Animal Transgenesis', *National Catholic Bioethics Quarterly* 6 (2006), pp. 689–704. Although I choose these two pieces to discuss, I make no claims that either of them is representative of the Roman Catholic tradition as a whole, nor do I take a view on the status of the Pontifical Academy for Life's document as an authoritative statement of the Church's teaching. My interest in them is as representative of an influential mode of thinking within Western Christianity, not in their official status (or lack of it).

understanding of the relationship between human and nonhuman animals, one that evokes a sense of shared origins and a shared destiny. I begin to address this through an account of the notion of 'appropriate dignity', a conception that is intended to refuse the categorization of animals in terms of their capacity (or lack of capacity) for sentience or suffering or rationality, all of which implicitly model animals on human beings, and thereby fail to recognize their otherness or to constitute them as subjects in their own right. Only if we have some such notion will we be able to begin to address the ethical questions of xenotransplantation and transgenesis with any effectiveness.

The Pontifical Academy for Life's document takes as its theme the science and ethics of interspecies organ and tissue transplantation. In line with some dicta by both Pope Pius XII and Pope John Paul II, it concludes that with some important conditions xenotransplantation from animals to human beings is in principle morally licit. Although, theologically, animals have their own specific value that must be respected, nevertheless they are placed 'at the service of man, so that man could achieve his overall development through them'. Xenotransplantation is, they declare, one application of the service of animals to humankind, a 'further opportunity for *creative responsibility* in making reasonable use of the power that God has given' to human beings.[5]

The Pontifical Academy reach this conclusion through a discussion of the doctrine of creation and the proper nature of human intervention in the created order. Humankind is made in the image of God and is at the summit of all creation: all that exists is intended for human beings, and they 'have the task of co-operating with the Creator in leading creation to its final perfection'. This does not imply 'arbitrarily "lording it over" the other creatures, reducing them to humiliating and destructive slavery in order to satisfy any whim [man] may have, but to guide, through his responsible work, the life of the creation towards the authentic and integral good of man'.[6] But nor does it mean that animals and human beings have equal dignity, or that there is something mistaken in asserting the superior dignity of humankind. Human beings have a '*unique* and *higher* dignity', by virtue of which they may sacrifice animals for their benefit, albeit answering to the Creator for the manner in which they do so. Thus, there are ethical constraints in the use of animals: 'unnecessary animal suffering must be prevented; criteria of real necessity and reasonableness must be respected;

---

[5] Pontifical Academy for Life, *Prospects for Xenotransplantation*, para 8 (italics original).

[6] Ibid., para 7. For further comment on the way the image of God could be discussed in relation to other creatures from a Roman Catholic perspective, see Charles Camosy's chapter this volume.

genetic modifications that could significantly alter the biodiversity and the balance of the species in the animal world must be avoided.[7]

Although xenotransplantation can therefore be defended in principle, there are limits to it. These limits relate to the human identity of the person who receives a xenografted organ. Personal identity, the Pontifical Academy maintain, has both ontological and psychological dimensions. It comprises both an individual's 'unrepeatability and essential core' as the ontological basis of identity, but also the subjective *feeling* that he or she is a person, both of which are mediated through the body. On these are grounded the person's moral value and the rights and duties that pertain to him or her.[8] However, even if identity is mediated through the body, 'it should be observed that not all organs of the human body are in equal measure an expression of the unrepeatable identity of the person'.[9] While some are purely functional and have no specific relation to a person's identity, others are inextricably related to that identity. These latter include notably the brain and the reproductive organs, which are crucial to the psychological and genetic make-up of an individual. And this distinction has moral implications: while those organs which are not crucial to a person's identity may in principle be subject to transplantation, and indeed to xenotransplantation, transplantation of the brain or the reproductive organs can never be justified 'because of the inevitable objective consequences that they would produce in the recipient or in his descendants'.[10]

The Pontifical Academy lists various other pertinent ethical issues – health risks, informed consent, allocation of resources, patenting, and so on – which I will not attend to here since my current concern is primarily the intrinsic moral issues of transferring tissue between humans and animals. However, before we proceed to consider their views on transgenic animals, we should note some features of their understanding of animals.

First, there is some tension in their description of the goals of creation. 'Man,' they assert, 'created "in the image and likeness of God", is placed at the centre and at the summit of the created order, not only because everything that exists is intended for him, but also because woman and man have the task of

---

[7] Ibid., para 9 (italics original).
[8] Ibid., para 10.
[9] Ibid., para 11.
[10] Ibid. Interestingly these exceptions to the principle of xenotransplantation parallel two of the three areas of public concern about animals containing human materials that were listed in a public attitudes survey carried out in conjunction with the Academy of Medical Sciences report. The third area of concern noted in the survey relates to any modification that might humanise the appearance of an animal. See Academy of Medical Sciences, *Animals Containing Human Material* (London: Academy of Medical Sciences, 2011), pp. 6, 79–80.

co-operating with the Creator in leading creation to its final perfection'.[11] On the one hand, everything that exists is intended for human beings; on the other hand, human beings are also called to work with God in leading creation to its eschatological fulfilment. Evidently they seem to see no problems of inconsistency with this language, but it does leave a question hovering awkwardly in the background: do animals together with the rest of creation reach their eschatological perfection solely through human mediation, or is there any sense in which they have their own place in the final perfection of creation independently of their relationship to humankind?

Second, a similar tension is displayed when in supporting this theological analysis they appeal to a 'purely rational basis' that is independent of any theological reasoning. They assert 'the ontological superiority of mankind over the other beings of the earth', which is 'founded on the very nature of the human person, whose rational and spiritual dimensions place man at the centre of the universe'.[12] However, in support of this ontological conclusion they appeal to what appears to be an empirical claim:

> A simple look at humanity's long presence on the earth is sufficient to show an irrefutable fact clearly: it is man who has always directed the realities of the world, controlling the other living and non-living beings according to determined purposes.[13]

All existing realities, they continue, find a 'universal harmonic and orderly design' in their relationship to human beings. But, one might ask, even if a version of the ontological-anthropological conclusion is arguable, it is scarcely supported by the apparently empirical claim, which far from being an 'irrefutable fact' derivable from a 'simple look', as they suppose, seems obviously false. In what sense are the hydrogen-sulphide dependent bacteria that cluster around deep-sea volcanic vents controlled according to humanly directed purposes? In what sense were the lumbering monsters of the Jurassic or Cretaceous controlled by human design? The ontological claim about human dignity and even in some sense the superiority of humankind to other creatures may be justifiable in other terms, but it does not require that all other creatures are oriented to their own destiny through their relationship with human beings. Nor, needless to say, does it justify the history of abuse and cruelty with which human beings have too often directed the realities of animals' worlds.

---

[11] Pontifical Academy for Life, *Prospects for Xenotransplantation*, para 7.
[12] Ibid.
[13] Ibid., para 8.

In addition to these apparent tensions in their understanding of creation and the role of human beings and animals in it, we should note, third, that although some animal welfare guidelines are explicit and clearly laid down, and although animals are to find their fulfilment through human beings, the orientation to human benefit remains paramount in the Pontifical Academy's mind: at no point in their report is it ever made clear how nonhuman animals might actively benefit from all these arrangements with regard to xenotransplantation. The outworking of this theologically informed philosophical cosmology, in which human beings have a special place in creation and are called to co-operate in leading the rest of creation to its fulfilment, is one which in practice is attentive to the fulfilment of human beings but forgetful of the fulfilment of animals.

Prospects for Xenotransplantation does include a paragraph on transgenic animals, and this leads us into the central focus of the present chapter. The general principle they lay down in relation to genetically altered animals is that 'the possibility of working out such genetic modifications, using genes of human origin as well, is morally acceptable when done in respect for the animal and for biodiversity, and with a view to bringing significant benefit to man himself'.[14] In principle transgenesis is permissible so long as it 'does not compromise the overall genetic identity of the mutated animal or its species',[15] and it is performed with recollection of human responsibility towards the created order and towards the improvement of human health. A number of further ethical conditions are laid down:

1   Concern for the well-being of genetically modified animals should be guaranteed so that the effect of the transgene's expression, possible modification of the anatomical, physiological and/or behavioural aspects of the animal may be assessed, all the while limiting the levels of stress and pain, suffering and anxiety experienced by the animal;

2   The effects on the offspring and possible repercussions for the environment should be considered;

3   Such animals should be kept under tight control and should not be released into the general environment;

4   The number of animals used in experiments should be kept to a bare minimum;

---

[14] Ibid., para 15.
[15] Ibid. The text reads 'while recognizing that transgenesis does not compromise the overall genetic identity of the mutated animal or its species', which does not serve the argument well: therefore, I understand 'recognizing that' to mean 'on condition that'.

5   The removal of organs and/or tissues must take place during a single surgical operation;

6   Every experimental protocol on animals must be evaluated by a competent ethics committee.[16]

But the general conclusion remains that in principle the genetic modification of animals for the purposes of furthering human health is morally acceptable.

It is this conclusion on genetic modified animals that Nicholas Tonti-Filippini and colleagues contest in their response to the Pontifical Academy's document.[17] They appear to be broadly accepting of its conclusions on xenotransplantation of organs into adult human beings. By contrast, they argue that the insertion of human genetic material into animal genomes at the embryonic stage is not justified on the grounds that it is an offence against human dignity. At first blush this stance appears to benefit animals, since the result of their recommendations would be that no animals would be harmed (or for that matter enhanced – if that is different) through possessing a partly human genome. However, as I shall argue, their appeal to *human* dignity rather than to *animal* dignity ironically leads to the effacement of nonhuman animals.

Their argument can be reconstructed in stages. First, they discuss, without using the term, the case of cytoplasmic hybrid embryos (or cybrids) in which the DNA from a human cell nucleus is inserted into an animal egg from which the nucleus has been removed. These, they argue, should be given the benefit of the doubt as to their moral status and should be treated as having the dignity of human embryos on the grounds that 'as a matter of science, the genome is determinative of the nature and capacity of the zygote'.[18] But even if we can resolve the question of the moral standing of human-animal cybrids in this way, they argue further that it would be wrong to create cybrids in the first place. This is in good part 'because of the confusion of the identity and status of the being' that was created: it would create perplexity, not just of a moral and practical kind about how the cybrid should be treated, but of a more fundamental ontological kind, of what kind of being it is. And the same reasoning applies, they argue, in the case of a human/nonhuman animal created through cross-species genetic modification: the nature of the being created is *intrinsically* a source of perplexity.

Now it is easy to see this perplexity in the case of 'true hybrids', that is embryos formed from the fusion of gametes of different species: a human being crossed with

---

[16]   Ibid.
[17]   Tonti-Filippini, Fleming, Pike, and Campbell, 'Ethics and Human-Animal Transgenesis'.
[18]   Ibid., p. 693. The phrasing incidentally suggests a somewhat crude understanding of embryonic development as shaped purely by genetic code.

a mouse, for instance. We can also recognize the perplexity in the case of cybrids in which human nuclear DNA has been inserted into an enucleated animal egg, or of human admixed embryos in which non-human animal DNA is inserted into a human embryo. And we can agree on how the practical moral perplexity ought to be resolved, namely by giving these entities the benefit of the doubt (the doubt that is intimated in the very use of the term 'entities'). But it is much less clear what we should think about examples of animal embryos (and therefore of grown animals) to which a very small human genetic complement has been added. Think of the case of growing a human liver inside a pig where a human gene might need to be added to a pig zygote in order to inhibit subsequent rejection by the human immune system after transplantation of the liver back to a human patient.

'Our view', they state in response to this question, 'is that the confusion of identity arises as soon as any human genes become formative of the new being'.[19] The presence of a single human gene is sufficient to create perplexity, even if visibly, phenomenally, behaviourally, the transgenic pig is indistinguishable from the unmodified pig. But why should such an apparently small change be regarded as having such momentous consequences? We can easily imagine at one extreme plenty of hypothetical examples of human-animal mixing which would undoubtedly produce such confusion of identity. Take for example the 'humanzee' cross between human beings and chimpanzees which Soviet scientists attempted to create in the 1920s. As David Jones asks,

> How would the newborn 'humanzee' be regarded? Would he be a child or a nonhuman animal? Should he go to special school? Should he be reared in a human environment? … If he were subject to experimentation or brought up in a laboratory environment (as might be the case if he were created deliberately by scientists) would this be an injustice? If there were a dilemma in which it were possible to save either the humanzee or a human child, but not both, would it ever be right to choose to save the humanzee and let a human child die?[20]

Equally at the other extreme we could accept with Tonti-Filippini and his colleagues that there are examples of human crossing with non-humans that clearly do not create much perplexity, if any at all. They instance the practice, standard in biomedical research, of inserting human genes into bacteria, which is to say into unicellular organisms that are incapable of embryogenesis or of forming more complex organisms with differentiated cellular structures, let alone

---

[19] Ibid.
[20] D. Jones, 'Is the Creation of Admixed Embryos "An Offense against Human Dignity"?', *Human Reproduction and Genetic Ethics* 16.1 (2010), pp. 87–114 (106).

of forming organisms with integrated autonomous activity. Transferring human DNA into bacteria does seem closer, as they say, to altering the genome of somatic cells in culture; such cells can never grow into complex or autonomous organisms, and the procedure is not obviously intrinsically morally problematic.[21]

The cases which are more like those we are concerned with – the pig with the human liver, say, or the sheep that produces human insulin in its milk – seem to lie somewhere between humanzees and hybrid cells but at first sight do not obviously create perplexity about their identity or status. To understand Tonti-Filippini's concerns better, we need to appreciate that behind their worries about perplexity lies a fundamental anxiety about the threat which transgenic animals, even ones with apparently relatively minor human genetic additions, pose to human dignity. Their concern is that the creation of transgenic animals would undermine, as they put it, 'that very notion of human dignity and sacredness which determines the moral status of every human being'.[22] Or again,

> If we deliberately create beings that have DNA from both human and animal sources, then we violate the sacredness of all human beings. The distinction between human and animal identity, so vital for the protection of basic human rights, would be blurred.[23]

One might wonder why adding a solitary human gene to a pig zygote would undermine *human* dignity. The dignity of the pig might perhaps be at stake, it might be thought, but less obviously that of 'all human beings'. In defence of their claim Tonti-Filippini and colleagues provide a number of arguments, of which I will present three.

The first argument is that genetically modifying a pig or chimpanzee with human genes might make it display characteristically human functions such as rationality. But they claim that this would infringe a sacred boundary that surrounds humankind by blurring the distinction between human and nonhuman animals, and the reason it would blur this boundary is that both would share in rationality, which is in some sense a uniquely human possession. We might call this the 'sacred boundary of rationality' argument.[24]

---

[21] Tonti-Filippini, Fleming, Pike, and Campbell, 'Ethics and Human-Animal Transgenesis', p. 697.
[22] Ibid.
[23] Ibid., p. 698.
[24] A full statement of the argument would need considerable nuancing, inasmuch as a lot depends on the relevant understanding of rationality: many non-human animals display forms of reasoning, and chimpanzees and orang-utans evidence cognitive capacities in some domains that are not incomparable to those of two-year-old children. Moreover, rationality is an enormously complex capacity (or group of capacities) that is not the simple product of genetic manipulation. These considerations are however not decisive for the current argument.

The second argument draws on the same concern about nonhuman animals displaying the rationality that is characteristic of human beings but reworks it in terms of a fear that genetically modifying animals might give credence to Lockean views of personhood. This family of approaches to personhood prominent in the bioethics literature, evaluates dignity and moral standing in terms of an individual's capacity for rationality or sentience (for example), and therefore tends to render higher primates and perhaps some other animals more deserving of the title of persons than newborn babies, and to relegate those who have severe cognitive impairments, say, or who are in late-stage dementia, to a lesser status than chimpanzees. Such arguments, they fear, 'might well be enhanced when the chimpanzee or pig in question has a genome that is, in part, human'.[25] By creating transgenic pigs or chimpanzees, one might add plausibility to the argument that it is not species membership that is decisive for moral standing but capacity. We might call this the '(not) giving credence to Peter Singer' argument.

This second argument is not, as such, a philosophical argument about the merits of Lockean views of personhood, but rather a causal slippery slope argument drawing on a sociology-of-knowledge claim that the creation of such beings is likely to make such styles of thinking more culturally plausible. For those of us who share the authors' views and who fear the dehumanizing implications of criterion-based accounts of personhood, this is, of course, not a negligible point. But equally, speculation about future trends in culturally prevalent modes of thought provides no *philosophical* ground for thinking that human dignity, as such, necessarily is undermined by transgenic animals. Moreover it should be noted that inserting small amounts of relatively marginal genetic material (genes for inhibiting immune reaction, for instance) would afford no increased public plausibility at all to Lockean styles of thinking about personhood, since by supposition functions as complex as sentience or rationality would not have been affected. Genes, such as those for immune protection, are relatively marginal, and therefore their transfer is arguably less morally suspect precisely because they do not have an effect on the higher functions. Of course, it may not be an easy matter to determine whether particular genes have a bearing on those capacities, since genes typically have complex effects and are involved in a variety of phenotypic traits. But in general, if no genes are transferred which are connected with cognitive capacities, the credence-giving effect is likely to be negligible.

---

[25] Ibid., p. 697.

It is hard not to think that this second argument is driven in part by an unexpressed anxiety rooted in the assumption that there must be two exclusive alternatives: *either* human dignity is based on species membership, *or* it is based on capacity. In the background there seems to lurk a belief that moral standing must be based either on membership of the human race, in which case it can only be attributed to human beings, and not to any other animals; or it must be attributed in accordance with a criterion-based measure, in which case it is liable to be ascribed to all creatures, human or not, which make the criterion but none (including at least some human beings) that do not. However, it is not at all obvious that this strong disjunction is justified: rather than assuming a logic of exclusion, we might equally opt for a logic of inclusion, which makes clear both that all members of the human species are included, whatever their age or level of health or intelligence, and grants that other species should not be excluded from an appropriate dignity. That is, we could endorse an alternative norm that asserted that 'every member of any species which characteristically exhibits a certain level of rationality is entitled to an appropriate dignity'. Note the phrase 'every member': if adult chimpanzees are entitled to analogous protection to human beings, then so are unborn chimpanzees and chimpanzee embryos.[26]

All of this also serves as a response to the first argument that human uniqueness should be protected by the sacred boundary of rationality and should not be blurred by letting non-human animals too close to the perimeter. Why should levelling up animals be a reason for thinking that human dignity would be undermined? We might equally appeal to a notion of a dignity appropriate to particular kinds and suggest that genetically modified animals would be deserving of what we might term an 'appropriate dignity'. To propose this is not to advocate a programme of genetic enhancement of animal intelligence, of course, but rather to emphasize a claim about the relative status of human beings and animals. We do not have to think of dignity as a limited resource, its distribution a zero-sum game. Nor do we need to think of dignity as the exclusive preserve of human beings. Instead, we might think in terms of gradations

---

[26] Or, as Robert Spaemann suggests, all porpoises, which is the example he uses to illustrate his general claim that 'if there exist within the universe other natural species of living beings possessing an inner life of sentience, whose adult members usually command rationality and self-awareness, we would have to acknowledge *not only those instances but all instances* of that species to be persons' (*Persons: The Difference Between 'Someone' and 'Something'* (O. O'Donovan (trans.); Oxford: Oxford University Press, 2006), p. 248 (italics original). For another critical account of the Roman Catholic tradition's attitudes towards animals compared with its attitude towards the human embryo, see C. Deane-Drummond, 'Animal Ethics: Where Do We Go from Here?', *Moral Theology for the Twenty-First Century: Essays in Celebration of Kevin Kelly* (J. Clague, B. Hoose, and G. Mannion (eds); London: Continuum, 2008), pp. 155–63.

of dignity, each species having a dignity proper to its kind. Precisely what appropriate dignity would obtain in any particular instance and what practical consequences would follow would be a matter for detailed and finely grained casuistical argument in relation to many different issues and many different animals. But, to give one example concerning the relation of human beings and chimpanzees, the force of the notion of appropriate dignity might be that, on the one hand, one could not morally perform experiments on chimpanzees that one could not also perform on human children, but on the other hand, that if one were faced with the choice of saving either the chimpanzee or the human child, one should choose the human child. Appropriate dignity is not equal dignity; there is no reason to think that the unique dignity of human beings would be compromised by attributing an appropriate dignity to non-human primates, or indeed to any other creatures.

This leaves Tonti-Filippini's third argument for thinking that transferring even a small amount of human genetic material would be an offence against human dignity. The argument goes (and it is only a single sentence): 'Given that as human beings we are a psychosomatic unity, we cannot make satisfactory distinctions between which genes are thus acceptably added and which are not'.[27] Not only are human beings indissoluble unities of body and soul, the argument seems to be, they are also indissoluble unities at a chromosomal and genetic level, which implies that no line can be drawn between those human genes that might be acceptably spliced into an animal genome and those that might not.

It is worth distinguishing the major and minor premises of this argument. The major premise is roughly: if there is no discernible difference between acceptable and unacceptable genes, then we should not insert any human genes into animal genomes. The minor premise asserts that there is in fact no discernible difference between genes that are acceptable and unacceptable for transfer. Now the major premise seems to me to be correct: if we have no way of distinguishing, we should create no transgenic embryos at all. But the minor premise seems less certain and surely not certain enough that it can be assumed not to require further justification. It seems at least as reasonable to argue, together with the Pontifical Academy, that transgenesis need not compromise the essential integrity either of the mutated animal or of the human being from whom the gene was taken, and that some functions are sufficiently trivial that they do not compromise the basic integrity of either partner in the procedure.

---

[27] Tonti-Filippini, Fleming, Pike, and Campbell, 'Ethics and Human-Animal Transgenesis', p. 698.

While the argument needs further development, it could be compatible with a variety of conceptions of the genome. For example, it could be based on an appeal to an understanding of the genome as built out of a series of separable building blocks – genes – which are stretched out along chromosomes. On this understanding individual genes are understood as relatively detachable. But this has precisely the implication that isolating them and inserting them in an animal does not necessarily involve an ontological compromise of human integrity. Alternatively, one might observe that the genome is intricate and remarkably internally organized, and that the 'building block' understanding of the genome is based on a failure to recognize both the integrated way in which the genome operates and the complex nature of the manner in which human DNA sequences are related to the phenotypic human organism (think of the role of epigenetic modifications or the relation between control regions and coding sequences). But this understanding need not carry the implication that separating single gene sequences out from the genome as a whole is destructive of human integrity and dignity. On the contrary the genome's very integration might be an argument for questioning the extent to which one can talk of a 'human gene' – even of a gene that is human-lineage specific and not found outside of human beings – outside of its context of the whole human genome. Individual human genes are not microcosms; they do not each contain or reveal the whole of human identity.

The drift of these considerations is towards scepticism about arguments about transgenic animals, which appeal to the idea that their creation would somehow be harmful towards human dignity. However, I should make clear, none of this is said as a defence of human-gene-modified animals, rather the opposite: it is precisely because these appeals to human dignity are either unsuccessful or, at best, inconclusively successful that we need to find other ways to protect animals. We need to recognize animals as possessors of a particular dignity that is valuable in its own right and is not dependent on or derived from human dignity or human desires. Animals need to be shielded from the human colonization of the nonhuman and from all the processes by which nonhuman animals are not merely subjugated to human purpose through instrumental rationality, but are also deprived of even being recognized as authentically other because of the absorption of the natural world into the metabolism of human subjectivity.

The two pieces I have discussed are representatives of a style of thinking that shows little interest in conceiving nonhuman animals as having an independent integrity in their own right. They display only a vestigial awareness that animals are created as objects of the divine blessing in their own right and as oriented to their own eschatological fulfilment independently of any service they may perform for human beings. Perhaps the most striking evidence of this failure of thought and imagination is that there is never any sense of how nonhuman animals might themselves benefit from all this experimentation. The question of how animal health might be improved as a result of xenotransplantation or transgenic research is never broached. The issue of animal-human mixing is always asked in medical terms, never in terms of benefit to animals. Of course, in raising this concern about animal benefit, we are asking not merely after veterinary benefit, if by that is meant benefit to the animal production industry, but rather benefit to animals in and for themselves independent of any implicit or ultimate benefit to human beings. And if we begin to see animals in these terms, we will also begin to find it inadequate to treat them merely as the objects of welfare, rather than as themselves subjects with an appropriate dignity.

How might we begin to see animals as subjects in their own right and possessors of an appropriate dignity? First, theologically, we need to recall both the Genesis vision of creation, in which each creature is created according to its kind, and the eschatological vision of harmony between animal and animal, between human and non-human animal: the lion eating straw like an ox, the child fearless of the snake's nest. Human action is called to be a symbolic witness to these realities. Creation will be healed in a way that is wholly unthinkable to us now, inasmuch as everything we know scientifically about all living entities is indexed in relation to their evolved nature: we cannot biologically conceive of a lion that is not constituted to pursue and devour living animals – though, importantly, we can and do conceive of such lions in our dreams and children's storybooks. Because the creation healed of carnivorous predation is absolutely unthinkable, we can never directly target it in our action, though we can symbolically point towards it in acts of eschatological witness that simultaneously indicate and embody that which they indicate. Shepherding pods of pilot whales in danger of stranding themselves on distant beaches is an act not just of compassion, but also of witness. Similarly, if we were finally to judge it permissible under certain circumstances for human beings to benefit from xenografts or from genetically modified animals, it would be only reasonable that we find real, albeit no doubt small-scale, ways of ensuring that nonhuman animals benefit from such research in return.

Elaborating the notion of appropriate dignity also requires a revision of some long-standing philosophical commitments. Here we might draw on the work of Robert Spaemann, much of whose work has been devoted to uprooting the nature-person dualism which has bedevilled philosophical thought on animals, the traces of which lie in the two works I have been discussing in this chapter.[28] Spaemann notes that, according to the theory of recognition found in German idealism, we owe recognition only to those who are themselves capable of recognizing. Thus, for Kant rational nature alone has absolute and unconditional value: while rational agents have duties *to* other rational agents, they only have duties *regarding* non-rational nature, including animals. On such a view we can only recognize those who are themselves equally capable of recognition; rational beings can never recognize any other beings that do not satisfy prior criteria of rationality. But 'if I recognize them only qua rational beings then what I recognize are not actually other subjects, but only my own criterion of rationality which I find instantiated in those subjects'.[29] In consequence, we can never give recognition to animals or pre-sentient unborn children. By contrast, classical accounts of nature also implied a theory of recognition, but this was a theory that recognized other beings as possessing their own selfhood and telos on the basis of which human beings could live alongside them in a shared community. Recalling this would allow us to recognize the value of all creatures as also possessing their own organic and lived unity, their own inner teleology, each in their own kind. Human beings share this with all creatures differing from animals only in their ability consciously to heed the command as a command. They alone can demonstrate that their nature exceeds nature, since they alone are capable of obeying imperatives of practical reason. But those imperatives need to be rewritten in a manner that refuses the opposition of person and nature. 'Act in such a way', Spaemann suggests, 'that you always treat *nature*, whether in your own person *or in every other natural being*, never simply as a means, but always at the same time as an end'.[30] Animals, we might say, have a dignity and not just a price.

Bibliography

Academy of Medical Sciences, *Animals Containing Human Material* (London: Academy of Medical Sciences, 2011).

Deane-Drummond, C., 'Animal Ethics: Where Do We Go from Here?', *Moral Theology for the Twenty-First Century: Essays in Celebration of Kevin Kelly* (J. Clague, B. Hoose, and G. Mannion (eds); London: Continuum, 2008), pp. 155–63.

---

[28] R. Spaemann, *Essays in Anthropology: Variations on a Theme* (G. de Graaff, and J. Mumford (trans.); Eugene, OR: Wipf and Stock, 2010).

[29] Ibid., p. 92.

[30] Ibid., p. 93 (emphasis original).

Jones, D. A., 'Is the Creation of Admixed Embryos "An Offense against Human Dignity"?', *Human Reproduction and Genetic Ethics* 16.1 (2010), pp. 87–114.

Pontifical Academy for Life, *Prospects for Xenotransplantation: Scientific Aspects and Ethical Considerations*, http://www.vatican.va/roman_curia/pontifical_academies/acdlife/documents/rc_pa_acdlife_doc_20010926_xenotrapianti_en.html (accessed 13 August 2012).

Spaemann, R., *Essays in Anthropology: Variations on a Theme* (G. de Graaff, and J. Mumford (trans.); Eugene, OR: Wipf and Stock, 2010).

—*Persons: The Difference Between 'Someone' and 'Something'* (O. O'Donovan (trans.); Oxford: Oxford University Press, 2006).

Tonti-Filippini, N., J. I. Fleming, G. K. Pike, and R. Campbell, 'Ethics and Human-Animal Transgenesis', *National Catholic Bioethics Quarterly* 6 (2006), pp. 689–704.

13

Other Animals as Persons? – A Roman Catholic Inquiry

Charles Camosy

I. Introduction

Secular utilitarians like Princeton philosopher Peter Singer, often in defence of the ethical treatment of other animals, sometimes criticize a traditional Catholic Christian ethic as 'speciesist'. Thomas Aquinas, in particular, has been singled out as an important part of the unjustified privileging of the species *Homo sapiens*. But this essay, which focuses specifically on claims about moral status and personhood, argues that the narrative generally offered in support of this view is inadequate. Roman Catholic theology, and Thomas Aquinas in particular, understands personhood to exist outside the species *Homo sapiens* (with respect to angels, for example), and this leaves an important opening to talk about a very high moral status for non-human animals. I will argue that one can use a Thomistic approach to show that both the image and likeness of God subsist in various human and non-human creatures along a spectrum related to their ability to know and to love. This tradition not only avoids arbitrarily putting human beings at the top of a hierarchy of moral value (angels far exceed humans), but it also clears the conceptual space for exploring whether any non-human animals have a moral status similar to that of human beings. The essay will also attempt to address an important challenge derived from the latest work of Celia Deane-Drummond on this topic[1] – one which asks important critical questions of strategies which invoke the personhood of other animals.

My method in writing this essay is that of a Catholic Christian theologian, and therefore I will disproportionately cite documents and ideas from Thomas

---

[1] C. Deane-Drummond, 'In God's Image and Likeness: From Reason to Revelation in Humans and Other Animals', in Lieven Boeve, Yves de Maeseneer and Ellen van Stichel (eds), *Image of God, Image of Humanity? Perspectives on Theological Anthropology for the 21st Century* (New York: Fordham University Press, in press).

Aquinas and other figures working out of this tradition. But because Roman Catholic teaching on this topic is very much in the process of being formed, much of what will constitute 'the tradition' will not be doctrinal – but rather part of the exciting growing edge of the Church's reflection. When I refer to 'the Church', though I hope it will be clear from the context, I will most often mean the Roman Catholic Church. Some readers might find this problematic, but I use this merely as a shorthand way of referring to a particular approach to Christian ethics, and not as part of a larger argument that, say, other Christian churches do not count as real churches or that other Christians do not count as real Christians. Indeed, as important figures like Andrew Linzey, David Clough, and several others have demonstrated, Protestant Christians generally have been significantly ahead of Catholic Christians on issues related to animal ethics.[2]

II. Singer's Narrative

In order for a Roman Catholic ethic to be taken seriously as one which could support the dignity of other animals, some conceptual space may need to be cleared. The Church focuses on the sanctity of human life, and many who have concern for other animals are understandably worried that such an ethic is actually harmful to, and certainly not helpful for, those of us who attempt to foster such concern. Peter Singer offers the following well-worn narrative:

> Western attitudes to animals have roots in two traditions: Judaism and Greek antiquity. These roots unite in Christianity, and it is through Christianity that they came to prevail in Europe. A more enlightened view of our relations with animals emerges only gradually, as thinkers begin to take positions that are relatively independent of the Church; and in fundamental respects we still have not broken free of the attitudes that were unquestionably accepted in Europe until the eighteenth century.[3]

He cites Genesis 9.3 – where God gives explicit permission to eat other animals and even says that the relationship between human and non-human animals

---

[2] One important exception is the Roman Catholic ethicist John Berkman who has written 'Prophetically Pro-Life: John Paul II's Gospel of Life and Evangelical Concern for Animals', *Josephinum Journal of Theology* 6 (1999), pp. 43–59, and 'A Trinitarian Theology of the 'Chief End' of 'All Flesh'', *Good News For Animals?* (J. McDaniel, and C. Pinches (eds); New York: Orbis, 1992). I do not think, however, that Protestant thought puts it in any better position than Catholic thought on these issues. Indeed, this essay is arguing that a Catholic moral anthropology puts it in a very interesting and important position to deal with complex problems related to animal ethics.
[3] P. Singer, *Animal Liberation* (New York: Avon Books, 1990), p. 186.

will be one of fear and dread – as particularly problematic. In addition, he claims that the New Testament is 'completely lacking in any injunction against cruelty to animals, or any recommendation to consider their interests'.[4] And he saves particular distain for what he considers to be the speciesist views of Thomas Aquinas, the great Christian theologian of the Middle Ages, and on whose work much of Catholic theology rests.[5] When asking whether the prohibition on killing applies to creatures other than human beings, for instance, Thomas answers by saying the following in II:II 64:1 of the *Summa Theologica*:[6]

> There is no sin in using a thing for the purpose for which it is. Now the order of things is such that the imperfect are for the perfect, even as in the process of generation nature proceeds from imperfection to perfection. Hence it is that just as in the generation of a man there is first a living thing, then an animal, and lastly a man, so too things, like the plants, which merely have life, are all alike for animals, and all animals are for man. Wherefore it is not unlawful if man use plants for the good of animals, and animals for the good of man, as the Philosopher states (Polit. i, 3). Now the most necessary use would seem to consist in the fact that animals use plants, and men use animals, for food, and this cannot be done unless these be deprived of life: wherefore it is lawful both to take life from plants for the use of animals, and from animals for the use of men. In fact this is in keeping with the commandment of God Himself: for it is written (Gen. 1:29–30): "Behold I have given you every herb ... and all trees ... to be your meat, and to all beasts of the earth": and again (Gen. 9:3): "Everything that moveth and liveth shall be meat to you".

In response to Thomas' claim that eating animals is justified based on our rational capacity to conform to the order of justice described above, rather than savagery and brutality, Singer responds with dismissive incredulity: 'Human beings, of course, would not kill for food unless they had first considered the justice of so doing!'[7]

But perhaps, though eating animals is permitted, at least the *suffering* of such creatures is an evil? Thomas cannot say this, according to Singer, because he has no room for wrongs of this kind in his moral schema, given that they are divided

---

[4] Ibid., p. 191.
[5] Much of what follows in the discussion of Singer and Thomas Aquinas is taken from my own work *Peter Singer and Christian Ethics: Beyond Polarization* (Cambridge: Cambridge University Press, 2012), chapter three.
[6] It should be noted that this article of the *Summa* was specifically asking the question about whether killing animals involved a particular kind of injustice, which violates the commandment against murder. Whether non-human animals have any moral claim on us at all is a different question.
[7] Singer, *Animal Liberation*, p. 194.

into sins against God, self, and neighbour.[8] But perhaps, Singer asks, it is at least charitable to be kind to other animals? Thomas, at least as Singer understands him, does not appear to allow for this either:

> Charity, he says, does not extend to irrational creatures for three reasons: they are "not competent, properly speaking, to possess good, this being proper to rational creatures"; we have no fellow feeling with them; and, finally "charity is based on the fellowship of everlasting happiness, to which the irrational creatures cannot attain." It is only possible to love these creatures, we are told, "if we regard them as the good things that we desire for others," that is "to God's honor and man's use."[9]

Singer playfully tries to get Thomas off the hook by wondering if perhaps he, like some other philosophers, held the 'absurd' view that non-human animals did not actually suffer. For this 'would at least excuse him on the charge of indifference to suffering'.[10] But Singer closes off this possible escape route with Thomas' own words when, in attempting to explain why our pity is aroused by non-human animals, he says that even irrational animals are sensible to pain. And such pity according to Aquinas is not good for the sake of its object – the animal – but rather because it helps create a similar concern for human beings. 'No argument', says Singer, 'could reveal the essence of speciesism more clearly'.[11]

Though he is willing to admit the Christian tradition is becoming more complex on these issues, Singer's narrative nevertheless insists that his interpretation of Thomas Aquinas' approach with regard to non-human animals is still the dominant one for Christianity and particularly for Roman Catholicism. But I argue that Singer is missing an important part of the Christian tradition on non-human animals. Not only is this tradition not the enemy but also Singer should see a Christian understanding of non-human animals as an ally.

III. A Counter-Narrative

In responding to Singer's narrative, we must first be more precise about the history of our species with regard to the issue at hand. Whether it was non-human animals – or even certain human beings (slaves, women, etc.)

---

8   Ibid.
9   Ibid., pp. 194–5.
10 Ibid., p. 195.
11 Ibid., p. 196.

– powerful people have been dominating the weak from as far back as history allows us to peer. It was simply because some human beings *could* dominate other beings that they *did* come to dominate them. There was nothing about the triumph of the Judeo-Christian tradition that made this more likely to happen.[12] Indeed, it was the eventual triumph of the secular Enlightenment – particularly with its emphasis on industry, profit, consumerism, and the priority of the rational – which took the cruel domination of other animals to levels that were previously unimaginable. These Enlightenment values are at the heart of what drives the widespread intensive factory farming of non-human animals – a practice that has institutionalized cruelty on an absolutely massive scale.

But given my goals stated above, it is not enough to point out that the Church's tradition is not the source of the problem: I need to show that it can be part of the solution. It goes beyond the scope of this essay to make an adequate response to Singer's criticism of the Biblical tradition on other animals,[13] but a few quick points are in order. Genesis 9.3 provides an account of our relationship with other animals in light of sin, but the relationship for which those who are convinced by the Judeo-Christian tradition (and in particular of the non-violent preference for the most vulnerable exemplified by Jesus) should strive is a far different reality. Indeed, Genesis 1 and 2 confirm that other animals are created 'good' independent of human beings, that God intends non-human animals to be our companions, and that God gives all animals green plants (and not other animals) to eat. Perhaps most importantly, the Bible is clear that our current relationship with other animals is not the moral ideal and, indeed, is only a temporary state of affairs.[14] The prophets Isaiah, Ezekiel, and Hosea all predict a return to the non-violence of Eden. And the way Isaiah describes the 'Peaceable Kingdom' in chapter 11.6–9 is, in my opinion, the most beautiful part of the Bible:

The wolf will live with the lamb,
the leopard will lie down with the goat,

---

[12] And from the perspective of vulnerable and weak human beings, at least, the triumph of this tradition was a great boon – having laid the foundations for thinking about the equal dignity of all human beings (all being made in the image and likeness of God). Not to mention the specific Christological example of having a particular focus on the weak and vulnerable.

[13] Chapter three of Camosy, *Peter Singer and Christian Ethics* has more details on this and on the discussion below.

[14] And even in this fallen and sinful world the Bible has restrictions, which nevertheless uphold the dignity of non-human animals. Consider that animals rest on the Sabbath along with human beings. A human being is enjoined to help free not only one's own animals, but also those of one's enemy, from a crushing burden. There are even specifications for the sharpness of the slaughtering knife to ensure the animal gets a quick death. Proverbs 12.10 says that, '[t]he righteous care for the needs of their animals, but the kindest acts of the wicked are cruel'.

the calf and the lion and the yearling together;
and a little child will lead them.
The cow will feed with the bear,
their young will lie down together,
and the lion will eat straw like the ox.
The infant will play near the hole of the cobra,
and the young child put his hand into the viper's nest.
They will neither harm nor destroy
on all my holy mountain,
for the earth will be full of the knowledge of the LORD
as the waters cover the sea.

God's will from the beginning, and even now going forward, is peace and non-violence for all creation. Furthermore, Jesus is clear that God cares for non-human animals (in Mt. 6.25–27 and Lk. 12.6–7 we learn, for instance, that even the lowly sparrow cannot escape God's notice and concern), and Paul is convinced that all of creation will be recapitulated and made new at the end of time (Eph. 1.9–10).

Furthermore, there is important evidence that the person most responsible for promoting the contemporary Catholic tradition also shares this Biblical understanding of the relationship between human and non-human animals. Though it is not an argument all by itself, it certainly does not hurt that Benedict XVI is well-known for being an animal lover.[15] He has to be reminded that he cannot take in stray cats from the surrounding Roman streets, and throughout his life he has often been given pets as Christmas presents. He has even publically questioned the morality of factory farming. PETA has even heralded his words in their advertisements. One that got a significant amount of public attention focused on his answer to the following question asked by German journalist Peter Seewald not long before he became Pope, and during which time he was the doctrinal watchdog for the entire Church: 'Are we allowed to make use of animals, and even to eat them?' Here is his answer:

> That is a very serious question. At any rate, we can see that they are given into our care, that we cannot just do whatever we want with them. Animals, too, are God's creatures. Certainly, a sort of industrial use of creatures, so that geese are fed in such a way as to produce as large a liver as possible, or hens live so packed

---

[15] He is also well-known for his ecological concern more generally, and in some places is being called 'the Green Pope'. Under his watch, the Vatican has won awards from secular organization for its Green Practices, and his latest encyclical, *Caritas in Veritate*, had a special ecological concern – even going so far as to say that God has a *covenant* with creation.

together that they become just caricatures of birds, this degrading of living creatures to a commodity seems to me in fact to contradict the relationship of mutuality that comes across in the Bible.[16]

Unsurprisingly, the Church's official teaching – that humanity's dominion is limited by the fact that all creation has its own integrity and that God surrounds animals with his providential care – is consistent with this claim. According to *The Catechism of the Catholic Church*, we owe animals kindness and it is immoral to cause them to suffer and die needlessly.[17]

But aside from scripture, what of Thomas Aquinas? Is he really the speciesist that Singer thinks he is? Though the passages to which Singer points are indeed problematic, it should be noted at the outset (perhaps with some surprise[18]) that Aquinas never has a sustained, particular focus on non-human animals anywhere in his huge corpus. However, as John Berkman points out, we should put non-human animals in the context of Aquinas' larger picture of

the entire physical universe (for example plants, birds, non-human and human animals) ordered toward 'ultimate perfection', which is in turn ordered to God, and by its perfection gives glory to the goodness of God. Each creature manifests the goodness of God by living according to its own *telos*... In other words, Aquinas' view is that '[t]he perfection of the universe is marked essentially by the diversity of natures, by which the diverse grades of goodness are filled up'. Thus, for Aquinas, God's plan in creation, while hierarchical, is by no means anthropocentric.[19]

For Thomas, the highest good after God

among the created things, is the good of the order of the whole universe, since every particular good of this or that thing is ordered to it as to an end ... and so, each part is found to be for the sake of its whole. Thus, among created things, what God cares for most is the order of the universe.[20]

In some ways, a Thomistic teleological approach actually has *more* room for understanding the moral value of other animals than theories of most ethicists

---

[16] J. Ratzinger, *God and the World: A Conversation with Peter Seewald* (San Francisco: Ignatius Press, 2002), pp. 78–9.

[17] *Catechism of the Roman Catholic Church* (United States Catholic Conference; vol. Citta del Vaticano; Washington, DC: United States Catholic Conference, 2nd edn, 2000), #2415, #2416, and #2418.

[18] Especially given the massive amount of material that Thomas covered in his enormous corpus, and that his teacher, Albert the Great, was arguably the greatest zoologist of the medieval period, it seems odd that he does not deal with these issues in more detail.

[19] C. Deane-Drummond, and D. Clough (eds), *Creaturely Theology* (London: SCM Press, 2009), p. 24.

[20] Thomas Aquinas, *Summa Contra Gentiles* (A. Pegis (trans.); Notre Dame, IN: University of Notre Dame Press, 2005), Book III, 1, 64, paragraph 10.

concerned about other animals. Because he is a preference utilitarian, someone like Peter Singer, for instance, finds it difficult to condemn the wanton slaughter of certain animals (for pleasure, sport, etc.) in a way that does not violate their preferences.[21] A Thomistic ethic can appeal to the intrinsic goodness of non-human animals apart from human beings and the *telos* of all members of the created order and, unlike a utilitarian ethic, can talk about the morally problematic nature of the (often vicious and violent) act of snuffing out a non-human animal's life 'before its time'.

But what of the view that human beings are the highest form of creation? Whatever we can say about the advantages of a Thomistic teleological approach, surely the claim that the human organism is the pinnacle of creation is speciesist, isn't it? When investigating this claim it is important to remember that, for Thomas (and the broad Christian tradition all the way back to at least Boethius), human persons are not ultimately valuable in light of their being *Homo sapiens,* but rather based on what being *Homo sapiens* indicates: being a *substance with a rational nature* (that is, a person). Humans are not the only examples of such substances, however, and Thomas actually considers us to be the *lowest* of those with rational natures – ranking far below angels. So, for Thomas, not only are there persons who are not human beings, but human beings are also the most limited kind of persons.

This provides an important opening to flesh out Catholic Christian thought in yet another non-speciesist direction: might there be some non-human animals who should be considered persons? Many medieval Christian thinkers took seriously the idea from certain ancient authors that there were *homines* in unknown parts of the earth who were biologically different from humans, and they saw no contradiction between this belief and their other theological commitments. Often citing St. Augustine as their source, there was a particular focus on 'cynocephali': creatures, otherwise human, who had the heads of dogs. Also consider that the Vatican Observatory and the Pontifical Academy of Sciences recently hosted its second conference on *astrobiology*. The director of the Observatory, Fr. Jose Funes, S.J, began his remarks by answering the question:

> "Why is the Vatican involved in astrobiology?" Fr. Funes stated that despite the field's newness, "the questions of life's origins and of whether life exists elsewhere in the universe are very interesting and deserve serious consideration."[22]

---

[21] This could be done by painlessly killing of a non-self-aware creature with no capacity to have an interest in continuing to live, for example.

[22] 'Vatican Observatory examines theological implications of finding alien life', *Catholic News Agency*, http://www.catholicnewsagency.com/news/vatican_observatory_examines_theological_implications_of_finding_alien_life/ (accessed 3 August 2012).

One of the issues discussed was the possibility of rational creatures existing on other worlds:

> The possibility raises a difficult theological question concerning redemption from the original sin, which by Christian tradition occurred in the Garden of Eden when Adam and Eve ate the forbidden fruit of a particular tree. Funes told the Osservatore Romano: "If other intelligent beings exist, it's not certain that they need redemption."[23]

Given what has been shown above, the question should not be, '*Could* Catholics accept that some non-human animals are persons?' The answer to that question is now obviously in the affirmative. Instead we should ask, 'Are some non-human animals, in fact, substances of a rational nature?' Of course, much about this answer depends on what one means by 'rational' – and we will explore this question in some detail below – but there is ample evidence to think that there are such animals. Many can think abstractly and symbolically and solve problems systematically, and some are even self-aware. Consider, for instance, that other primates can use tools, understand numbers, and recognize themselves in a mirror. They can also show evidence of third-order reflection by engaging in deliberately deceptive behaviour. Indeed, it appears that many different kinds of animals have several of the traits mentioned above to a greater or lesser extent along a graded scale. Several non-human animals (other primates and dolphins would be good candidates) have them to such a degree that they even appear to fit into the moral and legal category of 'person' – though, much like our relationship to angels, their capacities put them lower on the scale in relationship to human beings. All of this should be hardly surprising if we take the (less exaggerated[24]) claims of contemporary sociobiology seriously – after all, evolution has produced many of these traits in various species over time, with an increasing level of complexity.

IV. A Christian Understanding of Personhood

But one might argue that the discussion of personhood so far has a distinctly Enlightenment flavour to it. A concept of rationality so strongly connected to

---

[23] American Foreign Press, 'Vatican searches for extra-terrestrial life', *Google*, http://www.google.com/hostednews/afp/article/ALeqM5iXaUKFhkbVieQAqtllc-sCKsba9w (accessed 3 August 2012).
[24] Celia Deane-Drummond, while not denying that many 'complex tasks' in human communities have evolutionary origins, nevertheless challenges contemporary sociobiology for drawing too close a connection between the most sophisticated traits of *Homo sapiens* (morally speaking) and similar or primordial traits in other species. See Deane-Drummond, 'In God's Image and Likeness'.

self-awareness, third-order reflection, abstract thinking, and problem-solving, may capture or point toward something in the Christian tradition, but it has an undue focus on the individualistic and abstract. Turning again to the views of Thomas Aquinas is one way to avoid using a concept of rationality that has not been borrowed from the secular Enlightenment. Unsurprisingly, Thomas has a lot to say about rationality, but to understand what he means when he claims that human beings are substances of a rational nature we must first understand what he means when he claims that human beings are made in the image of God. He says that while 'in all creatures there is some kind of likeness to God, in the rational creature alone we find a likeness of "image" as we have explained above (1,2)'.[25] This kind of rational capacity is very different from the Enlightenment concept described above:

> Thus the image of God is found in the soul according as the soul turns to God, or possesses a nature that enables it to turn to God... The meritorious knowledge and love of God can be in us only by grace. Yet there is a certain natural knowledge and love as seen above (12, 12; 56, 3; 60, 5). This, too, is natural that the mind, in order to understand God, can make use of reason, in which sense we have already said that the image of God abides ever in the soul; "whether this image of God be so obsolete," as it were clouded, "as almost to amount to nothing," as in those who have not the use of reason; "or obscured and disfigured," as in sinners; or "clear and beautiful," as in the just; as Augustine says (De Trin. xiv, 6).[26]

Therefore, what Thomas means when he says that human beings are substances of a rational nature is that we are the kinds of things that have *the capacity to know and love God*. This, quite clearly, is an understanding that goes beyond a kind of thinking to engaging in a particular kind of *relationship*.

Could non-human animals ever engage in this kind of relationship? Could (or do) non-human animals ever know and love God? As Celia Deane-Drummond points out, while Thomas believed that non-human animals are *like* God in various ways, he ultimately rejects the idea that any non-human animal even approaches that which 'marks out human beings' as bearers of the *image* of God.[27] Thomas argues:

> Not every likeness, not even what is copied from something else, is sufficient to make an image; for if the likeness be only generic, or existing by virtue of some

---

[25] *Summa Theologica*, Book I, 93, 6.
[26] Ibid., Book I, 93, 8.
[27] Deane-Drummond, 'In God's Image and Likeness'.

common accident, this does not suffice for one thing to be the image of another. For instance, a worm, though from man it may originate, cannot be called man's image, merely because of the generic likeness. Nor, if anything is made white like something else, can we say that it is the image of that thing; for whiteness is an accident belonging to many species. But the nature of an image requires likeness in species; thus the image of the king exists in his son: or, at least, in some specific accident, and chiefly in the shape; thus, we speak of a man's image in copper.[28]

So even though some non-human animals 'know and understand', the knowing and understanding of which substances of a rational nature are capable (that which allows them to know and love God) so far surpasses those of non-human animals that it puts them in a different ontological category. Consequently, as we saw above, Thomas therefore thinks very differently about their moral status.

But Thomas does not rule out the possibility *a priori* that other animals image God, and especially because he does not spend significant time wrestling with this topic, it is quite possible that he would have changed his mind if he had had access to the results of contemporary biology – especially if he thought about it in conjunction with the Church's development of doctrine with regard to how non-Christians can come to be saved. Consider this remarkable claim from the *Dogmatic Constitution on the Church*:

> Those also can attain to salvation who through no fault of their own do not know the Gospel of Christ or His Church, yet sincerely seek God and moved by grace strive by their deeds to do His will as it is known to them through the dictates of conscience.[29]

Could non-human animals strive by their deeds to do God's will by following their conscience? Though it may sound strange to say so, I think there is good reason to think that the answer is yes.

As we will see in more detail below, Deane-Drummond's latest work has cooled on approaches that emphasize non-human animals as specifically bearing the image of God, but in other places she has marshalled some impressive evidence in support of the claim that many other animals 'seem capable of showing care, even when there seems to be no advantage to them. Companionships between blind animals (including humans) and other animals

---

[28] *Summa Theologica.* Book I, 93, 2.
[29] Pope Paul VI, 'Dogmatic Constitution on the Church – *Lumen Gentium*', Vatican: the Holy See, http://www.vatican.va/archive/hist_councils/ii_vatican_council/documents/vat-ii_const_19641121_lumen-gentium_en.html (accessed 3 August 2012), 16.

abound, including some unusual liaisons such as that between a one-year-old hippopotamus and a century-old tortoise'.[30] Or consider this stunning relationship between Bella the dog and Tarra the elephant:

> "When it's time to eat they both eat together. They drink together. They sleep together. They play together," Buckley says.
>
> Tarra and Bella have been close for years – but no one really knew how close they were until recently. A few months ago Bella suffered a spinal cord injury. She couldn't move her legs, couldn't even wag her tail. For three weeks the dog lay motionless up in the sanctuary office.
>
> And for *three weeks* [emphasis added] the elephant held vigil: 2,700 acres to roam free, and Tarra just stood in the corner, beside a gate, right outside that sanctuary office.
>
> "She just stood outside the balcony – just stood there and waited," says Buckley. "She was concerned about her friend."[31]

Deane-Drummond makes the important point that several 'social animals show a degree of acceptance toward those in their social group that are injured or born with difficulties, as shown by examples of tolerance of, for example, a mentally retarded monkey in a group of rhesus macaques'.[32] Recent studies of primates have also shown both a remarkable awareness of death and of empathy for their companions going through the grieving process.[33]

Empathy may be important (and even serve as a foundation for other morally significant capacities), but seeing evidence of what we would call 'moral behaviour' is more convincing if we want to talk about other animals following their conscience. *Are* some non-human animals moral? On this question, Deane-Drummond cites the fascinating research of Marc Bekoff, who

> has observed play behaviour among canids. Dogs, coyotes, and wolves all learn quickly to play in a way that is fair according to the rules set up by the particular species. Those that fail to engage in fair play become more isolated and drift

---

[30] Deane-Drummond, and Clough, *Creaturely Theology*, p. 196.

[31] S. Hartman, 'On Elephant Sanctuary, Unlikely Friends', *CBS News* (8 November 2010) http://www.cbsnews.com/stories/2009/01/02/assignment_america/main4696340.shtml?tag=currentVideoInfo; videoMetaInfo (accessed 3 August 2012).

[32] Deane-Drummond, and Clough, *Creaturely Theology*, p. 194.

[33] 'Chimps may be aware of others' deaths', *ScienceNews* 177.11 (22 May 2010), www.sciencenews.org/view/generic/id/58652/title/Chimps_may_be_aware_of_others'_deaths (accessed 3 August 2012); and R. Alleyne, 'Chimpanzees grieve for loved ones', *The Telegraph* (26 April 2010), http://www.telegraph.co.uk/science/science-news/7634918/Chimpanzees-grieve-for-loved-ones.html (accessed 3 August 2012).

away from the group… Particular 'rules' for fair play include invitation signals, variations in sequence of actions, self-handicapping, and role-reversing.[34]

Oliver Putz also cites Bekoff, but in a similar kind of study on great apes:

In the game juvenile bonobos cover their eyes with either an object or their hand and then stumble around the climbing frame some 15 feet in the air. This play requires individuals to agree to play by the rules – not look unless one loses one's balance—and also the understanding that others can see and judge whether or not one is truly covering one's eyes. [35]

Putz claims that the presence of traits previously mentioned should lead one to conclude that the fairness and rule-following in the bonobo games 'can result from moral decision making'.[36] Deane-Drummond, though a bit more hesitant, nevertheless makes a similar interpretation. Especially because Bekoff cites examples of the game's rule-breakers feeling shame or embarrassment, something she thinks could be the evolutionary primordia of a moral conscience, Deane-Drummond claims that this is evidence of morality 'of some sort'. And while she does not equate it with the 'universal reasoning' of which human persons are capable, the difference, importantly, 'seems to be one of degree, rather than absolute distinction'.[37]

Could some non-human animals, then, strive by their deeds to do God's will by following their conscience? At the very least, many kinds of non-human animals bear the likeness of God in this way at a very high level. They can be rational, self-aware, empathetic, and have a sense of fairness. Even if we refused to say that such creatures had the moral status equivalent to that of human persons, we should not take a binary approach in which personhood is an either/or proposition. We should rather extend the hierarchy of persons on a graded scale down from angels and humans and then to several kinds of non-human animals. Indeed, I can find no reason to deny sophisticated primates and dolphins a moral status similar to that of human persons. For if there is some evidence which suggests that *in some limited sense* non-human animals like primates and dolphins can know and love God by following their conscience, they should be considered persons.

---

[34] Ibid., p. 195.
[35] O. Putz, 'Moral Apes, Human Uniqueness, and the Image of God', *Zygon* 44.3 (September 2009), p. 619.
[36] Ibid.
[37] Deane-Drummond, and Clough, *Creaturely Theology*, p. 207.

V. Focusing on Personhood: Some Concerns

As mentioned above, Deane-Drummond has recently offered an important argument for not taking an approach that causes the dignity of non-human animals 'to be absorbed into the human world'.[38] While this approach may seem attractive at first because it is designed to protect some non-human animals, she worries that 'the special place of other creatures in their relationship with God both within their own worlds and in communion with human subjects may become compromised, as greater attention is paid to those creatures that are most like us'. For Deane-Drummond, my approach of trying to locate the image of God and personhood[39] in other animals may have 'anthropocentric overtones' in that it might not allow other forms of reflecting divinity to be sufficiently recognized. If non-human animals are to be thought of as only weakly bearing the image of God, it still seems to put them 'on the same hierarchical *scale* as humans, and they are then found wanting'.[40] Deane-Drummond's suggestion is to instead

> retain the idea of human distinctiveness in divine image bearing, but now interpret it in an active way that presents the particular *task* of humanity as one that recognizes a divine vocation to serve God and exist in respectful communion with other creatures. In this case such a theological anthropology is still prepared to restrict the theological language of divine image bearing to humans, but now understands it to make most sense within a communal understanding of shared creaturely being, and also in the light of the particular *religious* vocation of humankind.[41]

This approach, maintains Deane-Drummond, understands human dignity in a way that does not set it over and against the dignity of other animals in some kind of zero-sum game. The fact that human beings bear the image of God is not so much about ontology or even relationality, but rather 'a religious goal to be achieved, an active performance receptive to the grace of God, a means of building community with other creaturely kinds, instead of a means for separation and assumption of superiority'.[42]

This is an important worry and argument. In focusing on the personhood of some non-human animals, one certainly does not want to ignore or marginalize

---

[38] Deane-Drummond, 'In God's Image and Likeness'.
[39] She does not mention *personhood* specifically, but at least in the Christian tradition, personhood seems to be linked to the image of God. Certainly Aquinas seems to understand it this way.
[40] Ibid.
[41] Ibid.
[42] Ibid.

the value of animals who are not persons. If one gets stuck in a simplistic person/non-person binary (which tends to see value as the zero-sum game which Deane-Drummond wishes to avoid), then this is a very real danger. But especially if we take Thomas' teleological approach to the universal common good seriously, and apply it consistently, then we can avoid making the false choice between recognizing the important and non-instrumental value of non-personal creatures, and the even greater value of persons. This does not mean that, in each and every circumstance, any good of a person necessarily trumps any good of a non-person. Just as there is a hierarchy of moral value and status, there is a hierarchy of goods. Some persons (like former American NFL quarterback Michael Vick) get the goods of pleasure and financial resources from running dog-fighting rings, but the more valuable good of dogs not being torn apart in vicious fights trumps the shallow goods – even when they are goods proper to persons. To give a more common example, many persons also get the goods of pleasure and (saving) financial resources by eating cheap chicken flesh grown in intensive factory farms, but the more valuable good of chickens not being tortured in such farms also trumps the goods at stake for persons.

But some animal activists, especially when concerns about power relationships are involved, are going to reject any kind of hierarchy altogether. Different kinds of animals may flourish by realizing their *telos* in different ways, but this, they might argue, gives us no good reason to claim that one has a higher moral value or status than another. After all, isn't it precisely this kind of hierarchical thinking that got us into the mess of human animals treating non-human animals so poorly? Haven't we learned our lesson?

While I understand what is behind the worry here as well, I believe there are at least three reasons it is bad for animal ethics – particularly from a Christian perspective – to reject hierarchy in this way. First, it just seems undeniable that some creatures mirror their creator more perfectly than do others. A rock, for instance, exists and therefore mirrors God in that weak sense. Some rocks (though certainly not all) might be beautiful, and some might be solid and steadfast, etc., and these kinds of things mirror God in slightly more important ways. A dandelion might mirror God on a higher level, given that it is alive and it can produce life. But a person – capable of knowledge and engaging in loving relationships – bears God's image in a way that is qualitatively different from that of the rock or dandelion. And this insight is not limited to those who share the Christian theological story. Even Peter Singer says that it 'seems obvious' that a universe with persons is better than one without persons. A peopled universe, after all, contains beings who lead rich and full lives, experiencing the joys of love and friendship, of fulfilling and meaningful work, and of bringing up children. They seek knowledge, successfully adding to their understanding of themselves and the universe they inhabit. They respond to the beauties of nature, cherish the forests and animals that pre-date their own existence, and create literature and music on and par with the works of Shakespeare and Mozart.[43]

And when we do have a situation where there is actually a zero-sum game being played, the hierarchy becomes even more clear. Suppose a ten-year-old girl (who is not my child) is starving and near death, and I can either choose to kill a wild pig so that she can eat his flesh, or I can let her starve to death. Those who see no hierarchy of moral value will, I suppose, be forced to flip a coin when deciding who should live and who should die in this scenario, but those of us with a hierarchy of moral value will be able to choose to save the human child.[44]

Another reason that it is a bad idea for animal ethics to reject hierarchies of status and value is because, rightly understood, they *promote* the ethical treatment of the vulnerable. In response to my vegetarianism, I'm often greeted with the following objection, "But don't animals eat each other? Then why can't we eat them too?" A good rejoinder, of course, is to explain that we are a *different kind of animal* – one which has the power to reflect on our source of ultimate concern and the values associated with it, and then act accordingly. If these values lead us to conclude that we are to treat others with kindness and not allow them to suffer and die needlessly, then we should. Non-human animals who do not have this capacity to love cannot be held to the same standard. Ought implies can. But now we can see how hierarchy, thus understood, can avoid the critique described above. As Deane-Drummond suggests, the power and dominion that human persons have over other animals is one that enjoins upon us the ethical responsibility of love, care, and stewardship. A Christian understanding of leadership and power always has a preference of concern for the most vulnerable, and is therefore a kind of *servant leadership*. Jesus, for example, insisted that he needed to engage in the lowly (and often disgusting) act of washing his disciples' feet. Pope St. Leo the Great furthered

---

[43] P. Singer, *Practical Ethics* (Cambridge: Cambridge University Press, 2011), pp. 116–17. Singer might get himself off the hook here by saying that the preferences of persons are stronger, but perhaps he does not say this because it just is not clear that the preference of a person to listen to music is stronger than the preference of, say, a non-human animal to satisfy her hunger.

[44] Notice, however, this conclusion is obvious only because what is being compared is 'life' vs. 'life'. If it was 'life' vs. 'the pleasure of eating bacon', then finding in favour of the child would certainly not be the obvious conclusion, and is likely not the correct one.

this understanding by insisting that the papacy was filled by the 'servant of the servants of God'.

A final reason to refuse to let go of the hierarchy focuses on the harm done to creatures of more value vs. the harm that is done to those of less value. Caging a self-aware gorilla for a medical experiment, for instance, might be quite different from caging a mouse for a similar experiment. A gorilla's *telos* and flourishing is intrinsically connected to social interaction, and she has enough sense of her own existence to become severely mentally disturbed by a mindless existence in a cage, but (perhaps) a mouse is not social or self-aware enough to be harmed (at the same level) in this way. Surely caging a gorilla is worse (all other things being equal) than caging a mouse, but there is no way to undergird this intuition without invoking a hierarchy. And it is precisely this kind of hierarchy that can serve as an essential tool when attempting to protect gorillas (and similar animals) via a change of public policy. One can make public arguments highlighting the fact that the traits of primates are very similar to those of human persons, and this can go a long way to eventually protecting the value of similar animals with the force of law.

VI. Conclusion

In this essay I have tried to show that, especially from the perspective of Catholic Christianity, we should consider seriously the possibility that some non-human animals are persons. This is a theocentric rather than an anthropocentric approach.[45] The image of God is what makes personhood a meaningful concept, and human beings are just one example of several kinds of persons in the created order. Angels, as mentioned above, more perfectly image God than do human beings – but because some non-human animals also appear to also be on a spectrum of various substances of rational nature, we should consider them persons as well. For if there is evidence which suggests that non-human animals, such as primates, elephants, and dolphins, in some sense, can know and love, they can and should be categorized (morally and legally) as persons.

This is no mere ivory-tower, abstract, merely intellectual argument: multiple countries (including Britain, New Zealand, and, most recently, Spain) have moved toward legally supporting something like the Great Ape Project, 'which

---

[45] Indeed, the very concepts of theological and moral 'anthropology' might need to be rethought. Perhaps we should speak rather of the study of persons and call it theological and moral 'personology'?

argues that three essential human rights – life, liberty and freedom from physical and psychological torture – should be extended to our closest hominid relatives'.[46] As shown above, acknowledgement and protection of these limited rights of some other animals is not only compatible with a Christian approach, but ought to be something toward which Christians should be directing significant energies – especially if we are truly committed to consistently nonviolent stewardship of God's creation.

Bibliography

Abend, L., 'In Spain, Human Rights for Apes', *TIME.com*, http://www.time.com/time/world/article/0,8599,1824206,00.html (accessed 3 August 2012).

Alleyne, R., 'Chimpanzees grieve for loved ones', *The Telegraph* (26 April 2010), http://www.telegraph.co.uk/science/science-news/7634918/Chimpanzees-grieve-for-loved-ones.html (accessed 3 August 2012).

American Foreign Press, 'Vatican searches for extra-terrestrial life', *Google News*, http://www.google.com/hostednews/afp/article/ALeqM5iXaUKFhkbVieQAqtllc-sCKsba9w (accessed 3 August 2012).

Aquinas, Saint Thomas, *Summa Contra Gentiles* (A. C. Pegis (trans.); Notre Dame, IN: University of Notre Dame Press, 2005).

Berkman, J., 'Prophetically Pro-Life: John Paul II's Gospel of Life and Evangelical Concern for Animals', *Josephinum Journal of Theology* 6.1 (Winter/Spring 1999), pp. 43–59.

—'A Trinitarian Theology of the "Chief End" of "All Flesh"', *Good News For Animals?* (J. McDaniel, and C. Pinches (eds); New York: Orbis, 1992), pp. 62–74.

Bettenson, H. (trans.), *Concerning the City of God Against the Pagans* (New York: Penguin Books, 2003). Camosy, C., *Peter Singer and Christian Ethics: Beyond Polarization* (Cambridge: Cambridge University Press, 2012).

Catechism of the Catholic Church (United States Catholic Conference; vol. Citta del Vaticano; Washington, DC: United States Catholic Conference, 2nd edn, 2000).

'Chimps may be aware of others' deaths', *ScienceNews* 177.11 (22 May 2010), www.sciencenews.org/view/generic/id/58652/title/Chimps_may_be_aware_of_others'_deaths (accessed 3 August 2012).

Deane-Drummond, C., 'In God's Image and Likeness: From Reason to Revelation in Humans and Other Animals', In Lieven Boeve, Yves de Maeseneer and Ellen van Stichel (eds), *Image of God, Image of Humanity? Perspectives on Theological Anthropology for the 21st Century* (New York: Fordham University Press, in press 2014).

---

[46] L. Abend, 'In Spain, Human Rights for Apes' *TIME.com*, http://www.time.com/time/world/article/0,8599,1824206,00.html (accessed 3 August 2012).

Deane-Drummond, C., and D. Clough (eds), *Creaturely Theology* (London: SCM Press, 2009).

Hartman, S., 'On Elephant Sanctuary, Unlikely Friends', *CBS News* (8 November 2010), http://www.cbsnews.com/stories/2009/01/02/assignment_america/main4696340.shtml?tag=currentVideoInfo;videoMetaInfo (accessed 3 August 2012).

Paul VI, Pope., "Dogmatic Constitution on the Church – *Lumen Gentium*", *Vatican: the Holy See*, http://www.vatican.va/archive/hist_councils/ii_vatican_council/documents/vat-ii_const_19641121_lumen-gentium_en.html (accessed 3 August 2012).

Putz, O., 'Moral Apes, Human Uniqueness, and the Image of God', *Zygon* 44.3 (September 2009), pp. 613–24.

Ratzinger, J. C., *God and the World: A Conversation with Peter Seewald* (San Francisco: Ignatius Press, 2002).

Singer, P., *Animal Liberation* (New York: Avon Books, 1990).

—*Practical Ethics* (Cambridge: Cambridge University Press, 2011).

'Vatican Observatory examines theological implications of finding alien life', *Catholic News Agency*, http://www.catholicnewsagency.com/news/vatican_observatory_examines_theological_implications_of_finding_alien_life/ (accessed 3 August 2012).

Bibliography

Abend, L., 'In Spain, Human Rights for Apes', *TIME.com*, http://www.time.com/time/world/article/0,8599,1824206,00.html (accessed 3 August 2012).

Abram, D., *The Spell of the Sensuous: Perception and Language in a More-than-Human World* (New York: Pantheon Books, 1996).

Academy of Medical Sciences, *Animals Containing Human Material* (London: Academy of Medical Sciences, 2011).

Acta Philippi, textus (F. Bovon, B. Bouvier, and F. Amsler (eds); Turnhout: Brepols, 1999).

Les Actes de Paul et ses lettres apocryphes (Introduction, texts, traduction, and commentary by Léon Vouaux; Paris: Libraire Letouzey et ané, 1913).

The Acts of the Christian Martyrs (H. Musurillo (trans.); Oxford: Clarendon Press, 1972).

Adams, C., and J. Donovan (eds), *Animals and Women: Feminist Theological Explorations* (Durham, NC: Duke University Press, 1995).

Agamben, G., *The Open: Man and Animal* (K. Attell (trans.); Stanford, CA: Stanford University Press, 2004).

Albrecht of Scharfenberg, *Der Jüngere Titurel* (W. Wolf, and K. Nyholm (ed.); 4 vols; Berlin: Akademie-Verlag, 1955–1995).

Alexander, J., *Durkheimian Sociology: Cultural Studies* (Cambridge: Cambridge University Press, 1988).

Alleyne, R., 'Chimpanzees grieve for loved ones', *The Telegraph* (26 April 2010), http://www.telegraph.co.uk/science/science-news/7634918/Chimpanzees-grieve-for-loved-ones.html (accessed 3 August 2012).

Alsdorf, L., *The History of Vegetarianism and Cow-Veneration in India* (W. Bollée (ed.); B. Patil (trans.); revised by N. Hayton; London and New York: Routledge, 2010).

Alvar, J., *Romanising Oriental Gods: Myths, Salvation and Ethics in the Cults of Cybele, Isis and Mithras* (R. Gordon (ed. and trans.); Religion in the Graeco-Roman World; Leiden: Brill, 2008).

American Foreign Press, 'Vatican searches for extra-terrestrial life', *Google News*, http://www.google.com/hostednews/afp/article/ALeqM5iXaUKFhkbVieQAqtllc-sCKsba9w (accessed 3 August 2012).

Ammianus Marcellinus, *The History* (J. Rolfe (trans.); Loeb Classical Library, 3 vols; London: Heinemann, 1963–64).

Aquinas, *Summa Contra Gentiles* (A. Pegis (trans.); Notre Dame, IN: University of Notre Dame Press, 2005).

—*Summa Theologica* (Fathers of the English Dominican Province (trans.); London: Blackfriars, 1963).

Aristotle, *Generation of Animals* (A. Peck (trans.); Loeb Classical Library; London and Cambridge, MA: William Heinemann Ltd. and Harvard University Press, 1943).

—*Historia Animalium* (A. Peck (trans.); Loeb Classical Library; London and Cambridge, MA: William Heinemann Ltd. and Harvard University Press, 1965).

—*Metaphysics*.

—*Nicomachean Ethics*.

—*De Partibus Animalium*.

Assman, J., *Moses the Egyptian* (Cambridge: Harvard University Press, 1997).

Athanasius, *Vie d´Antoine* (Introduction, texte critique, traduction, notes et index par G. Bartelink; Sources Chrétiennes, 400; Paris: Cerf, 1994).

Augustine, *On Genesis: On Genesis: A Refutation of the Manichees, Unfinished Literal Commentary on Genesis, the Literal Meaning of Genesis* (J. Rotelle (ed.); E. Hill (trans.); The Works of Saint Augustine: A Translation for the 21st Century; New York: New City Press, 2002).

—*The Manichean Debate* (Introduction and notes by R. Teske; Works of Saint Augustine: A Translation for the 21st Century, I/19; Hyde Park: New City Press, 2006).

Avramescu, C., *An Intellectual History of Cannibalism* (A. Blyth (trans.); Princeton and Oxford: Princeton University Press, 2009).

Bacon, F., *The Great Instauration: The Plan of the Work: Works of Francis Bacon, Baron of Verulam, Viscount St. Alban and Lord High Chancellor of England, Vol. IV* (J. Spedding, R. Ellis, and D. Heath (eds); London: Spottiswoode, 1858), pp. 22–33.

—*The New Organon* (L. Jardine., and M. Silverthorne (eds); Cambridge Texts in the History of Philosophy; Cambridge: Cambridge University Press, 2000).

—'Valerius Terminus (of the Interpretation of Nature)', *Collected Works of Francis Bacon* (J. Spedding, R. Ellis, and D. Heath (eds); vol. III; London: Routledge, 1996), pp. 215–52.

Basil, 'On the Hexaemeron', *Exegetic Homilies* (Washington, DC: Catholic University of America, 1963), pp. 3–150.

—*The Hexaemeron* (P. Schaff, and H. Wace (ed.); B. Jackson (trans.); The Nicene and Post-Nicene Fathers, vol. 8; Edinburgh: T&T Clark, 1989).

Batra, S., 'The Sacredness of the Cow in India', *Social Compass* 33.2–3 (1986), pp. 163–75.

Beck, B., 'The Goddess and the Demon. A Local South Indian Festival and its Wider Context', *Autour de la Déesse Hindoue* (M. Biardeau (ed.); Paris: Éditions de l'École des Hautes Études en Sciences Sociales, 1981), pp. 83–136.

BeDuhn, J., *The Manichaean Body: In Discipline and Ritual* (Baltimore and London: The John Hopkins University Press, 2008).

Beeley, C., *Gregory of Nazianzus on the Trinity and the Knowledge of God: In Your Light We Shall See Light* (New York: Oxford University Press, 2008).

Bekoff, M., 'Considering Animals—Not "Higher" Primates', *Zygon* 38 (2003), pp. 229–45.

—'The Evolution of Animal Play, Emotions, And Social Morality: On Science, Theology, Spirituality, Personhood, and Love', *Zygon* 36 (2001), pp. 615–55.

—'Minding Animals, Minding Earth: Old Brains, New Bottlenecks', *Zygon* 38 (2003), pp. 911–41.

Bellah, R., *Religion in Human Evolution: From the Paleolithic to the Axial Age* (Cambridge, MA: Belknap Press of Harvard University Press, 2011).

Benfey, O., 'August Kekulé and the Birth of the Structural Theory of Organic Chemistry in 1858', *Journal of Chemical Education* 35.1 (1958), pp. 21–23.

Berger, P., *The Sacred Canopy: Elements of a Sociological Theory of Religion* (New York: Anchor Books, 1990).

Bergmann, S., 'Trinitarian Cosmology in God's Liberating Movement: Exploring Some Signature Tunes in the Opera of Ecologic Salvation', *Worldviews* 14 (2010), pp. 185–205.

Berkman, J., 'Prophetically Pro-Life: John Paul II's Gospel of Life and Evangelical Concern for Animals', *Josephinum Journal of Theology* 6.1 (Winter/Spring 1999), pp. 43–59.

—'A Trinitarian Theology of the "Chief End" of "All Flesh"', *Good News For Animals?* (J. McDaniel, and C. Pinches (eds); New York: Orbis, 1992), pp. 62–74.

Berkson, C., *The Divine and Demoniac: Mahisa's Heroic Struggle with Durga* (Delhi: Oxford University Press, 1997).

Bertrand, D., 'L'implication du Νοῦς dans la prière chez Origène et Évagre le Pontique', *Origeniana Septima* (Louvain: Leuven University Press, 1999), pp. 355–63.

Bettenson, H. (trans.), *Concerning the City of God Against the Pagans* (New York: Penguin Books, 2003).

Biblia Sacra iuxta Vulgatam versionem (R. Weber et al., (ed.); Stuttgart: Deutsche Bibelgesellschaft, 1983).

Blake, W., 'The Marriage of Heaven and Hell', *Complete Writings* (G. Keynes (ed.); Oxford: Oxford University Press, 1966).

—'A Vision of the Last Judgement', *Complete Writings* (G. Keynes (ed.); Oxford: Oxford University Press, 1966).

Blenkinsopp, J., 'The Family in First Temple Israel', *Families in Ancient Israel* (L. Perdue, J. Blenkinsopp, J. Collins, and C. Meyers (eds); Louisville: Westminster John Knox Press, 1997), pp. 48–103.

Böhland, D., 'Integrative Funktion durch exotische Distanz. Zur Cundrie-Figur in Wolframs *Parzival*', *Böse Frauen – gute Frauen. Darstellungskonventionen in Texten und Bildern des Mittelalters und der Frühen Neuzeit* (U. Gaebel, and E. Kartschoke (eds); Trier: Wissenschaftlicher Verlag, 2001), pp. 45–58.

Bonaventure, St., *Major Life of St. Francis*.

—*The Soul's Journey into God/The Tree of Life/The Life of Saint Francis* (E. Cousins (trans.); New York: Paulist Press, 1978).

Bono, J., *The Word of God and the Languages of Man: Interpreting Nature in Early Modern Science and Medicine* (Madison, WI: University of Wisconsin Press, 1995).

Borges, J., *Other Inquisitions, 1937–52* (Austin, TX: University of Texas Press, 1964).

Borowitz, O., *Daily Life in Ancient Israel* (Archaeology and Biblical Studies, vol. 5; Atlanta: Society of Biblical Literature, 2003).

Børresen, B., 'Menneskets medfødte forutsetninger som vertskap for produksjonsdyr', *Dyreetikk* (A. Føllesdal (ed.); Oslo: Fagbokforlaget, 2000), pp. 16–39.

Bosch, L. van den, 'Yama, the God on the Black Buffalo', *Visible Religion: Annual for Religious Iconography, Vol. 1, Commemorative Figures* (H. Kippenberg (ed.); Leiden: Brill, 1982), pp. 21–64.

Bown, N., *Fairies in Nineteenth-Century Art and Literature* (Cambridge: Cambridge University Press, 2001).

Boyer, P., 'Being Human: Religion: Bound to Believe?', *Nature* 455 (23 October 2008), pp. 1038–9.

—'Functional Origins of Religious Concepts: Ontological and Strategic Selection in Evolved Minds', *Journal of the Royal Anthropological Institute* 6.2 (2000), pp. 195–214.

—*Religion Explained: The Human Instincts That Fashion Gods, Spirits and Ancestors* (London: Heinemann, 2001).

Brooke, R., 'Heaven', *Collected Poems* (vol. 4; New York: John Lane, 1916).

Brown, C., *The Triumph of the Goddess: The Canonical Models and Theological Visions of the Devī-Bhāgavata Purāṇa* (Delhi: Sri Satguru Publications, 1992).

Brueggemann, W., *Land* (Philadelphia: Fortress Press, 1977).

Brummack, J., *Die Darstellung des Orients in den deutschen Alexandergeschichten des Mittelalters* (Berlin: Erich Schmidt, 1966).

Burkert, W., *Creation of the Sacred: Tracks of Biology in Early Religions* (Cambridge: Harvard University Press, 1996).

Caillois, R., 'Mimicry and Legendary Psychasthenia', *October* 31 (1984) (J. Shepley (trans.)), pp. 16–32.

—'The Praying Mantis: From Biology to Psychoanalysis', *The Edge of Surrealism: A Roger Caillois Reader* (C. Frank (ed.); Durham and London: Duke University Press, 2003), pp. 69–81.

Calarco, M., *Zoographies: The Question of the Animal from Heidegger to Derrida* (New York: Columbia University Press, 2008).

Callicott, J., 'Animal Liberation: A Triangular Affair', *Environmental Ethics* 2 (1980), pp. 311–38.

Camosy, C., *Peter Singer and Christian Ethics: Beyond Polarization* (Cambridge: Cambridge University Press, 2012).

Carroll, N., *The Philosophy of Horror; or, Paradoxes of the Heart* (New York: Routledge, 1990).

Carruthers, M., *The Book of Memory: A Study of Memory in Medieval Culture* (Cambridge: Cambridge University Press, 1990).

—*The Craft of Thought: Meditation, Rhetoric and the Making of Images, 400–1200* (Cambridge: Cambridge University Press, 1998).

Catechism of the Catholic Church (United States Catholic Conference; vol. Citta del Vaticano; Washington, DC: United States Catholic Conference, 2nd edn, 2000).

Cato, *On Agriculture* (W. Hooper (trans.); Loeb Classical Library; London: Heinemann, 1967).

Certeau, M. de, *The Practice of Everyday Life* (S. Rendall (trans.); Berkeley, CA: University of California Press, 1984).

Chakravarti, M., *The Concept of Rudra-Śiva through the Ages* (Delhi: Motilal Banarsidass, 1994).

Chesterton, G. K., *The Everlasting Man* (London: Hodder & Stoughton, 1925).

—'Skepticism and *Spiritualism*', *Illustrated London News* (14 April 1906).

'Chimps may be aware of others' deaths', *ScienceNews* 177.11 (22 May 2010), www.sciencenews.org/view/generic/id/58652/title/Chimps_may_be_aware_of_others'_deaths (accessed 3 August 2012).

Cicero, *De finibus bonorum et malorum* (H. Rackham (trans.); Loeb Classical Library; London: Heinemann, 1914).

Clark, E., 'New Perspectives on the Origenist Controversy: Human Embodiment and Ascetic Strategies', *Church History* 59.2 (1990), pp. 145–62.

Clark, S. R. L., *The Nature of the Beast* (Oxford: Oxford University Press, 1982).

Clingerman, F., 'The Intimate Distance of Herons: Theological Travels Through Nature, Place, and Migration', *Ethics, Place & Environment: A Journal of Philosophy and Geography* 11 (2008), pp. 313–25.

—'Reading the Book of Nature: A Hermeneutical Account of Nature for Philosophical Theology', *Worldviews: Global Religions, Culture, Ecology* 13.1 (2009), pp. 72–91.

Clough, D., *On Animals: I. Systematic Theology* (London: T&T Clark/Continuum, 2012).

Coburn, T., 'Devī. The Great Goddess', *Devī. Goddesses of India* (J. Hawley, J. Stratton, and D. Wulff (eds); Berkeley and Los Angeles: California University Press, 1996), pp. 31–48.

—*Devī-Māhātmya: The Crystallisation of The Goddess Tradition* (Delhi: Motilal Banarsidass, 1988).

—*Encountering the Goddess: A Translation of the Devī-Māhātmya and A Study of Its Interpretation* (Delhi: Sri Satguru Publications, 1992).

Coleman, K., 'Fatal Charades: Roman Executions Staged as Mythological Enactments', *The Journal of Roman Studies* 80 (1990), pp. 44–73.

Collins, J., 'Marriage, Divorce, and Family in Second Temple Judaism', *Families in Ancient Israel* (L. Perdue, J. Blenkinsopp, J. Collins, C. Meyers (eds); Louisville: Westminster John Knox Press, 1997), pp. 104–62.

Columella, *On Agriculture* (H. Ash, E. Forester, and E. Heffner (trans.); Loeb Classical Library, 3 vols; London: Heinemann, 1955).

Cooper, K., 'The Voice of the Victim: Martyrdom and the Subversion of Roman Power in late Antiquity', Lecture at the Theological Faculty, The University of Oslo, 25 April 2003.

Craddock, E., 'Reconstructing the Split Goddess as Śakti in a Tamil Village', *Seeking Mahādevī: Constructing Identities of the Hindu Great Goddess* (T. Pintchman (ed.); Albany: Albany University Press, 2001), pp. 145–98.

Crist, E., *Images of Animals: Anthropomorphism and Animal Mind* (Philadelphia: Temple University Press, 1999).

Cunningham, D., 'The Way of All Flesh: Rethinking the Imago Dei', *Creaturely Theology: On God, Humans and Other Animals* (C. Deane-Drummond, and D. Clough (eds); London: SCM Press, 2009), pp. 100–17.

Curley, M., *Physiologus: A Medieval Book of Nature Lore* (Chicago: University of Chicago Press, 2009).

Deane-Drummond, C., 'Animal Ethics: Where Do We Go from Here?', *Moral Theology for the Twenty-First Century: Essays in Celebration of Kevin Kelly* (J. Clague, B. Hoose, and G. Mannion (eds); London: Continuum, 2008), pp. 155–63.

—*Christ and Evolution: Wonder and Wisdom* (Minneapolis: Fortress, 2009).

—'In God's Image and Likeness: From Reason to Revelation in Humans and Other Animals', in Lieven Boeve, Yves de Maeseneer and Ellen van Stichel (eds), *Image of God, Image of Humanity? Perspectives on Theological Anthropology for the 21st Century* (New York: Fordham University Press, in press 2014).

—'Shadow Sophia in Christological Perspective: The Evolution of Sin and the Redemption of Nature', *Theology and Science* 6 (2008), pp. 13–32.

Deane-Drummond, C., and D. Clough (eds), *Creaturely Theology: On God, Humans and Other Animals* (London: SCM Press, 2009).

Derrida, J., *L'Animal Que Donc Je Suis* (M. Mallet (ed.); Paris: Éditions Galilée, 2006).

—*The Animal That Therefore I Am* (M. Mallet (ed.); D. Wills (trans.); Perspectives in Continental Philosophy; New York: Fordham University Press, 2008).

—'"Eating Well," or the Calculation of the Subject', *Points... Interviews, 1974–1994* (E. Weber (ed.); Stanford, CA: Stanford University Press, 1995).

—*Of Spirit: Heidegger and the Question* (G. Bennington, and R. Bowlby (trans.); Chicago and London: University of Chicago Press, 1989).

Detienne, M., 'Culinary Practices and the Spirit of Sacrifice', *The Cuisine of Sacrifice Among the Greeks* (M. Detienne, and J. Vernant (eds); Chicago and London: University of Chicago Press, 1989), pp. 1–20.

The Digest of Justinian (T. Mommsen, and P. Krueger (eds); A. Watson (trans.); vol. 1–4; Philadelphia: University of Pennsylvania Press, 1985).

Dio Chrysostom, *Works* (J. Cohoon, and H. Lamar (trans.); Loeb Classical Library, 5 vols; London: Heinemann, 1932–1951).

Diogenes Laertius, Epicurus (R. Hicks (trans.); Loeb Classical Library, 2 vols; London: Heinemann, 1965).

—*Lives of the Eminent Philosophers* (R. Hicks (trans.); Loeb Classical Library; London: Heinemann, 1925).

Douglas, M., *The Lives of Butterflies* (Ann Arbor: University of Michigan Press, 1986).

Downing, F., *Cynics and Christian Origins* (London: Routledge, 1992).

Dupré, J., *Humans and Other Animals* (Oxford: Clarendon, 2002).

During Caspers, E., 'Rituals and Belief Systems in the Indus Valley Civilisation', *Ritual, State and History in South Asia: Essays in Honour of J. C. Heesterman* (A. Van den Hoeck, D. Kolff, and M. Oort (eds); Leiden: Brill, 1992), pp. 102–27.

Durkheim, E., *The Elementary Forms of the Religious Life* (J. Swain (trans.); London: Allen & Unwin, 1915); (K. Fields (trans.); New York: Free Press, 1995).

Durkheim, E., and M. Mauss, *Primitive Classification* (Chicago: University of Chicago Press, 1963).

The Earth Bible Team, 'Guiding Ecojustice Principles', *Readings from the Perspective of Earth* (N. Habel (ed.); Earth Bible, vol. 1; Sheffield: Sheffield Academic Press, 2000), pp. 38–53.

Edwards, D., *Ecology at the Heart of Faith* (Maryknoll, NY: Orbis, 2006).

—'The Redemption of Animals in Incarnational Theology', *Creaturely Theology: On God, Humans and Other Animals* (C. Deane-Drummond, and D. Clough (eds); London: SCM Press, 2009), pp. 81–99.

Eliade, M., *A History of Religious Ideas, Volume 1: From the Stone Age to the Eleusinian Mysteries* (W. Trask (trans.); 3 vols; Chicago: University of Chicago Press, 1981).

Ellverson, A., *The Dual Nature of Man: A Study in the Theological Anthropology of Gregory of Nazianzus* (Stockholm: Uppsala University, 1981).

Epiphanius, *The Panarion of Epiphanius of Salamis* (F. Williams (trans.); Nag Hammadi Studies, 35; Leiden: Brill, 1987–1994).

Epistles of the Brethren of Purity: The Case of the Animals versus Man Before the King of the Jinn: An Arabic Critical Edition and English translation of Epistle 22 (L. Goodman, and R. McGregor (eds); New York: Oxford University Press, 2010).

Evagrius of Pontus, *Évagre le Pontique: Sur les pensées* (P. Géhin, C. Guillaumont, and A. Guillaumont (eds); Sources Chrétienes, no. 438; Paris: Éditions du Cerf, 1998).

—*Évagre le Pontique: Traité Practique ou Le Moine* (A. Guillaumont, and C. Guillaumont (eds); Sources Chrétiennes, nos. 170–71; Paris: Éditions du Cerf, 1971).

—*Evagrius of Pontus: The Greek Ascetic Corpus* (R. Sinkewicz (trans.); Oxford: Oxford University Press, 2003).

—*Evagrius Ponticus* (A. Cassiday (trans.); New York: Routledge, 2006).

—*Evagrius Ponticus* (W. Frankenberg (ed. and trans.); Abhandlungen der königlichen Gesellschaft der Wissenschaften zu Göttingen, Philolologisch-historische Klasse, Neue Folge, 13.2; Berlin: Weidmannsche Buchhandlung, 1912).

—*Les six Centuries des 'Kephalaia Gnostica' d'Évagre le Pontique* (A. Guillaumont (ed. and trans.); Patrologia Orientalis, 28.1, no. 134; Paris: Fermin-Didot, 1958).

—*Seconde partie du traité qui passe sous le nom de 'La grande lettre d'Evagre le Pontique à Mélanie l' Ancienne', publiée et traduite d'après le manuscript du British Museum Add. 17192* (G. Vitestam (ed.); Lund: Glerrup, 1964).

Evans-Pritchard, E., *Theories of Primitive Religion* (Oxford: Clarendon Press,1965).

Fabre, J., *Social Life in the Insect World* (B. Miall (trans.); London: T. Fisher Unwin, 1912).

Fasbender, C., '"Willehalm" als Programmschrift gegen die "Kreuzzugsideologie" und "Dokument der Menschlichkeit"', *Zeitschrift für deutsche Philologie* 116 (1997), pp. 16–31.

Fernández-Armesto, F., *So You Think You're Human? A Brief History of Humankind* (Oxford: Oxford University Press, 2004).

Fischer, S., *The Dream in the Middle High German Epic: Introduction to the Study of the Dream as a Literary Device to the Younger Contemporaries of Gottfried and Wolfram* (Bern, Frankfurt am Main, and Las Vegas: Lang, 1978).

Foucault, M., *The Order of Things: An Archaeology of the Human Sciences* (London and New York: Routledge, 2002).

Frankfurter, D., 'Egyptian Religion and the Problem of the Category "Sacrifice"', *Ancient Mediterranean Sacrifice* (J. Knust, and Z. Várhelyi (eds); Oxford: Oxford University Press, 2011), pp. 75–93.

Friedman, J., *The Monstrous Races in Medieval Art and Thought* (Cambridge, MA and London: Harvard University Press, 1981).

Friedrich, U., *Menschentier und Tiermensch. Diskurse der Grenzziehung und Grenzüberschreitung im Mittelalter* (Göttingen: Vandenhoeck & Ruprecht, 2009).

—'Der Ritter und sein Pferd. Semantisierungsstrategien einer Mensch-Tier-Verbindung im Mittelalter', *Text und Kultur. Mittelalterliche Literatur 1150–1450* (U. Peters (ed.); Stuttgart and Weimar: Metzler, 2001), pp. 245–67.

Galilei, G., *Discoveries and Opinions of Galileo* (S. Drake (trans.); Garden City, NY: Doubleday Anchor, 1957).

Garnsey, P., *Food and Society in Classical Antiquity* (Cambridge: Cambridge University Press, 1999).

Gasparro, G., *Soteriology and Mystic Aspects in the Cult of Cybele and Attis* (Leiden: Brill, 1985).

Geith, K.-E., 'Die Träume im *Rolandslied* des Pfaffen Konrad und in Strickers Karl', *Träume im Mittelalter. Ikonologische Studien* (A. Bagliani, and G. Stabile (eds); Stuttgart, Zürich: Belser, 1989), pp. 227–40.

Gerhardt, C., 'Wolframs Adlerbild ("Willehalm", 189, 2–24)', *Zeitschrift für deutsches Altertum* 99 (1970), pp. 213–22.

Gieser, T., 'Embodiment, Emotion and Empathy: A Phenomenological Approach to Apprenticeship Learning', *Anthropological Theory* 8.3 (2008), pp. 299–318.

Gilhus, I., *Animals, Gods and Humans: Changing Attitudes to Animals in Greek, Roman and Early Christian Ideas* (London and New York: Routledge, 2006).

Goodall, J., *In the Shadow of Man* (New York: Houghton Mifflin, 1971).

Gordon, R., 'Magical Lessons in Natural History: Unique Animals in Graeco-Roman Natural Magic', *Myths, Martyrs, and Modernity: Studies in the History of Religions in Honour of Jan N. Bremmer* (J. Dijkstra, J. Kroesen, and Y. Kuiper (eds); Leiden and Boston: Brill, 2010), pp. 249–69.

Grandin, T., and C. Johnson, *Animals Make Us Human* (Orlando: Houghton Mifflin, 2009).

Grant, M., *The Antonines: Roman Empire in Transition* (London and New York: Routledge, 1996).

Grant, R., *Early Christians and Animals* (London: Routledge, 1999).

Gregory of Nazianzus, *Festal Orations* (N. Harrison (trans.); Crestwood, NY: Saint Vladimir's Seminary Press, 2008).

—*Grégoire de Nazianze: Discours 27–31* (P. Gallay (ed. and trans.); Sources Chrétiennes, no. 250; Paris: Éditions du Cerf, 1978).

—*Grégoire de Nazianze: Discours 38–41* (C. Moreschini (ed.); P. Gallay (trans.); Sources Chrétiennes, no. 358; Paris: Éditions du Cerf, 1990).

—*On God and Christ: The Five Theological Orations and Two Letters to Cledonius* (L. Wickham, and F. Williams (trans.); Crestwood, NY: Saint Vladimir's Seminary Press, 2002).

—*On God and Man: The Theological Poetry of St. Gregory of Nazianzus* (P. Gilbert (trans.); Crestwood, NY: Saint Vladimir's Seminary Press, 2001).

Gregory of Nyssa, 'On the Making of Man', *A Select Library of Nicene and Post-Nicene Fathers of the Christian Church. Second Series* (P. Schaff (ed.); vol. 5; Edinburgh: T&TClark, 1997).

Gribomont, J., '(Pseudo)Basil, "Epistula 8"', *Basilio di Cesarea, Le Lettere* (M. Forlin-Patrucco (ed.); Torino: Società Editrice Internazionale, 1983), pp. 84–112.

Groos, A., 'Cundrie's Announcement ("Parzival" 781–782)', *Beiträge zur Geschichte der deutschen Sprache und Literatur* 113 (1991), pp. 384–414.

Gross, A., 'Jewish Animal Ethics', *Oxford Handbook of Jewish Ethics and Morality* (E. Dorff, and J. Crane (eds); Oxford: Oxford University Press, 2012), p. 422–9.

—*The Question of the Animal and Religion* (New York: Columbia University Press, fothcoming 2013).

—'The Question of the Creature: Animals, Theology and Levinas' Dog', *Creaturely Theology: On God, Humans and Other Animals* (C. Deane-Drummond, and D. Clough (eds); London: SCM Press, 2009), pp. 121–37.

Habel, N., 'Introducing Ecological Hermeneutics', *Exploring Ecological Hermeneutics* (N. Habel (ed.); Symposium 46; Atlanta: Society of Biblical Literature, 2008), pp. 1–8.

—'Introducing the Earth Bible', *Readings from the Perspective of Earth* (N. Habel (ed.); Earth Bible, vol. 1; Sheffield: Sheffield Academic Press, 2000), pp. 25–37.

—*The Land is Mine: Six Biblical Land Ideologies* (Overtures to Biblical Theology; Minneapolis: Fortress Press, 1995).

Habermehl, P., *Perpetua und der Ägypter* (Berlin: Akademie Verlag, 1992).

Hallowell, A., 'Ojibwa Ontology, Behavior and World View', *Culture in History: Essays in Honor of Paul Radin* (S. Diamond (ed.); New York: Columbia University Press, 1960), pp. 19–52.

—'The Role of Dreams in Ojibwa Culture', *Contributions to Anthropology: Selected Papers of A. Irving Hallowell* (R. Fogelson, F. Eggan, M. Spiro, G. Stocking, A. Wallace, and W. Washburn (eds); Chicago: University of Chicago Press), pp. 449–74.

Hardy, A., *The Living Stream: A Restatement of Evolution Theory and Its Relation to the Spirit of Man* (London: Collins, 1965).

Harris, N., 'Animal, Vegetable, Mineral. Some Observations on the Presentation and Function of Natural Phenomena in Willehalm and in the Old French Aliscans', *Wolfram's 'Willehalm'. Fifteen Essays* (M. Jones, and T. McFarland (eds); Columbia, SC: Camden House, 2002), pp. 211–29.

Harrison, P., *The Fall of Man and the Foundations of Science* (Cambridge: Cambridge University Press, 2007).

—'Linnaeus as a Second Adam? Taxonomy and the Religious Vocation', *Zygon* 44.4 (2009), pp. 879–93.

Hartman, S., 'On Elephant Sanctuary, Unlikely Friends', *CBS News* (8 November 2010), http://www.cbsnews.com/stories/2009/01/02/assignment_america/main4696340. shtml?tag=currentVideoInfo;videoMetaInfo (accessed 3 August 2012).

Haug, W., 'Parzivals *zwivel* und Willehalms *zorn*. Zu Wolframs Wende vom höfischen Roman zur chanson de geste', *Strukturen als Schlüssel zur Welt. Kleine Schriften zur Erzählliteratur des Mittelalters* (Tübingen: Niemeyer, 1989), pp. 529–40.

Haussleiter, J., *Der Vegetarianismus in der Antike* (Berlin: Verlag von Alfred Töpelmann, 1935).

Heathcote-James, E., *Psychic Pets: How Animal Intuition and Perception Has Changed Human Lives* (London: John Blake, 2007).

Heidegger, M., 'Building Dwelling Thinking', *Poetry, Language, Thought* (New York: Harper, 1971), pp. 143–61.

Heilbron, J., 'The Measure of Enlightenment', *The Quantifying Spirit in the 18th Century* (T. Frangsmyr, J. Heilbron, and R. Rider (eds); Berkeley: University of California Press, 1990), pp. 207–43.

Heinzle, J., 'Die Heiden als Kinder Gottes. Notiz zum "Willehalm"', *Zeitschrift für deutsches Altertum* 123 (1994), pp. 301–8.

—'Noch einmal: Die Heiden als Kinder Gottes in Wolframs "Willehalm"', *Zeitschrift für deutsche Philologie* 117 (1998), pp. 75–80.

Hennecke, E., and W. Schneemelcher, *New Testament Apocrypha, I-II* (London: SCM Press, 1973–5).

Herodotus, *The Histories* (A. Godley (trans.); Loeb Classical Library, 4 vols; London: Heinemann, 1966).

Hesiod, *Theogony and Works and Days* (M. West (trans.); Oxford: Oxford University Press, 2008).

Heston, A., 'An Approach to the Sacred Cow of India', *Current Anthropology* 12.2 (1971), pp. 191–209.

Heyman, G., *The Power of Sacrifice: Roman & Christian Discourses in Conflict* (Oxford: Oxford University Press, 2007).

Hillel, D., *The Natural History of the Bible: An Environmental Exploration of the Hebrew Scriptures* (New York: Columbia University Press, 2006).

Hiltebeitel, A., 'The Indus Valley "Proto-Śiva", Reexamined through Reflections on the Goddess, the Buffalo, and the Symbolism of Vāhana', *Anthropos* 73.5–6 (1978), pp. 767–97.

—'Rāma and Gilgamesh: The Sacrifices of the Water Buffalo and the Bull of Heaven', *History of Religions* 19.3 (1980), pp. 187–223.

Hirst, D., *Superstition* (Beverly Hills, CA: Gagosian Gallery, 2007).

Ho, M.-W., 'The Role of Action in Evolution: Evolution by Process and the Ecological Approach to Perception', *Cultural Dynamics* 4.3 (1991), pp. 336–54.

Hobgood-Oster, L., *Holy Dogs & Asses: Animals in the Christian Tradition* (Urbana, IL: University of Illinois Press, 2008).

Hogue, C., 'The Bugfolk', *Terra* 17.4 (1979), pp. 36–8.

Holdrege, C., 'Doing Goethean Science', *Janus Head* 8.1 (2005), pp. 27–52.

Hopkins, G., 'God's Grandeur', *Poems* (W. Gardner, and N. Mackenzie (eds); Oxford: Oxford University Press, 1967).

Houston, W., 'What was the Meaning of Classifying Animals as Clean or Unclean?', *Animals on the Agenda* (A. Linzey, and D. Yamamoto (eds); London: SCM Press, 1998), pp. 18–24.

Howe, N., 'The Cultural Construction of Reading in Anglo-Saxon England', *The Ethnography of Reading* (J. Boyarin (ed.); Berkeley, CA: University of California Press, 1992).

Huddleston, R. (ed.), *The Little Flowers of Saint Francis of Assisi* (Springfield, IL: Templegate, 1988).

Hume, D., *Enquiry Concerning the Principles of Morals* (J. Schneewind (eds); Indianapolis: Hackett, 1983).

Ingold, T., *Being Alive: Essays on Movement, Knowledge and Description* (London: Routledge, 2011).

—'From Trust to Domination: An Alternative History of Human-Animals Relations', *The Perception of the Environment: Essays in Livelihood, Dwelling and Skill* (T. Ingold (ed.); London: Routledge, 2008), pp. 61–76.

—'Hunting and Gathering as Ways of Perceiving the Environment', *Animals and the Human Imagination* (A. Gross, and A. Vallely (eds); New York: Columbia University Press, 2012), pp. 31–54.

—'Life Beyond the Edge of Nature? Or, the Mirage of Society', *The Mark of the Social* (J. Greenwood (ed.); Lanham, MD: Rowman and Littlefield, 1997), pp. 231–52.

—*Lines: A Brief History* (London: Routledge, 2007).

—*The Perception of the Environment: Essays on Livelihood, Dwelling & Skill* (London and New York: Routledge, 2008).

—(ed.), *What is an Animal?* (London: Routledge, 1988).

Jacobs, D., *Secret Life: Firsthand Documented Accounts of UFO Abductions* (New York: Fireside/Simon and Schuster, 1992).

Jacobsen, K., 'The Institutionalization of the Ethics of 'Non-Injury towards All Beings in Ancient India', *Environmental Ethics* 16.3 (1994), pp. 287–302.

—'Sacred Animals', *Brill's Encyclopedia of Hinduism, Vol. 1: Regions, Pilgrimage, Deities* (K. Jacobsen (ed.); Leiden: Brill, 2009), pp. 711–18.

Jerome, *Jerome: Trois vies de moines: Paul, Malchus, Hilarion* (P. Leclerc, E. Morales, and A. de Vogüé (eds); Sources Chrétiennes, no. 508; Paris: Éditions du Cerf, 2007).

—'Life of Malchus', *Early Christian Biographies* (R. Deferrari (ed.); M. Ewald (trans.); Fathers of the Church, no. 15; Washington, DC: Fathers of the Church Inc., 1952), pp. 281–97.

Jha, D., *The Myth of the Holy Cow* (London: Verso, 2002).

Jones, D., 'Is the Creation of Admixed Embryos "An Offense against Human Dignity"?', *Human Reproduction and Genetic Ethics* 16.1 (2010), pp. 87–114.

Jung, C., *Letters* (G. Adler (ed.); vol. 1; Princeton: Princeton University Press, 1975).

—*Visions: Notes of the Seminar Given in 1930–1934* (C. Douglas (ed.); Princeton, NJ: Princeton University Press, 1997).

—*Zarathustra Seminar* (J. Jarrett (ed.); Princeton: Princeton University Press, 1988).

Kant, I., *Kant's Political Writings* (H. Reiss (ed.); Cambridge University Press: Cambridge, 1970).

Kartschoke, D., 'Commentary', *Das Rolandslied des Pfaffen Konrad* (D. Kartschoke (ed., trans., and comm.); Stuttgart: Reclam, 1993), pp. 627–750.

Kasten, I., 'Häßliche Frauenfiguren in der Literatur des Mittelalters', *Auf der Suche nach der Frau im Mittelalter* (B. Lundt (ed.); München: Wilhelm Fink, 1991), pp. 255–76.

Kelley-Romano, S., 'Mythmaking in Alien Abduction Narratives', *Communication Quarterly* 54.3 (2006), pp. 383–406.

Kent, J., *There's No Such Thing as a Dragon* (New York: Random House Children's Books, 2009).

Keul, I., *Hanuman, der Gott in Affengestalt. Entwicklung und Erscheinungsformen seiner Verehrung* (Berlin and New York: De Gruyter, 2002).

Kirby, W., and W. Spence, *An Introduction to Entomology: or Elements of the Natural History of Insects* (vol. 1, London: Longman, Hurst, Rees, Orme and Brown, 3rd edn., 1818).

Kirk, G., J. Raven, and M. Schofield, *The Presocratic Philosophers: A Critical History with a Selection of Texts* (Cambridge: Cambridge University Press, 2nd edn, 1983).

Klemm, D., and W. Schweiker, *Religion and the Human Future: An Essay on Theological Humanism* (Malden, MA: Blackwell, 2008).

Klenk, N., 'Listening to the Birds: A Pragmatic Proposal for Forestry', *Environmental Values* 17.3 (2008), pp. 331–51.

Knapp, F., 'Die Heiden und ihr Vater in den Versen 307, 27f. des "Willehalm"', *Zeitschrift für deutsches Altertum* 122 (1993), pp. 202–7.

—'Und noch einmal: Die Heiden als Kinder Gottes', *Zeitschrift für deutsches Altertum* 129 (2000), pp. 296–302.

Knust. J., and Z. Várhelyi (eds), *Ancient Mediterranean Sacrifice* (Oxford: Oxford University Press, 2011).

Konrad, *Rolandslied* (C. Wesle, and P. Wapneswki (eds); Tübingen: Niemeyer, 1985).

Korom, F., 'Holy Cow! The Apotheosis of Zebu, or Why the Cow Is Sacred in Hinduism', *Asian Folklore Studies* 59.2 (2000), pp. 181–203.

Kowalski, G., *The Souls of Animals* (Walpole, NH: Stillpoint Publishing, 1991).

Krishna, N., *Sacred Animals of India* (Delhi and London: Penguin Books, 2010).

Lash, N., *The Beginning and the End of 'Religion'* (Cambridge: Cambridge University Press, 1996).

Leclercq, J., *The Love of Learning and the Desire for God* (C. Misrahi (trans.); New York: Fordham University Press, 1961).

Lecouteux, C., *Les monstres dans la literature allemande du moyen âge* (3 vols; Göppingen: Kümmerle, 1982).

Leemans, P. de, and M. Klemm, 'Animals and Anthropology in Medieval Philosophy', *A Cultural History of Animals in the Medieval Age* (B. Resl (ed.); Oxford and New York: Berg, 2007), pp. 153–77.

Legros, G. V., *Fabre, Poet of Science* (B. Miall (trans.); London: T. Fisher Unwin, 1913).

Lévi-Strauss, C., *Totemism* (R. Needham (trans.); Boston: Beacon Press, 1963).

Lewels, J., *The God Hypothesis: Extraterrestrial Life and its Implications for Science and Religion* (Mill Spring, NC: Wildflower Press, 1997).

Lindroth, S., 'Linné — Legend Och Verklighet', *Lychnos* (1965), pp. 56–122.

Linnaeus, C., *Bref Och Skrifvelser Af Och Till Carl Von Linné* (Fries, T., and J. Hulth (eds); Stockholm: 1907).

—*Systemae Naturae: Per Regna Tria Naturae : Secundum Classes, Ordines, Genera, Species, Cum Characteribus, Differentiis, Synonymis, Locis / Praefatus Est Ioannes Ioachimus Langius* (Halae Magdeburgicae: Typis et sumtibus Io. Iac. Curt, Ad editionem decimam reformatam Holmiensem ed. 1760).

Linzey, A., *Animal Theology* (Urbana, IL: University of Illinois Press, 1995).

Lisbet, K., 'Carl Linnaeus in His Time and Place', *Cultures of Natural History* (N. Jardine, J. Secord, and E. Spary (eds); Cambridge: Cambridge University Press, 1996), pp. 145–63.

Lloyd, G., *Science, Religion and Ideology* (Cambridge: Cambridge University Press, 1983).

Loovers, J., '"*You Have to Live It*": Pedagogy and Literacy with Tweetl'it Gwich'in' (PhD thesis, University of Aberdeen, 2010).

Louth, A., *The Origins of the Christian Mystical Tradition* (Oxford: Oxford University Press, 1981).

Lovejoy, A., *The Great Chain of Being: A Study of the History of an Idea* (Cambridge, MA: Harvard University Press, 1942).

Lutgendorf, P., *Hanuman's Tale: The Messages of a Divine Monkey* (New York and Oxford: Oxford University Press, 2006).

Luther, M., *Lectures on Genesis, Chapters 1–5* (J. Pelikan (ed.); Luther's Works, vol. I; Saint Louis: Concordia, 1958), pp. 64–5.

MacIntyre, A., *God, Philosophy, Universities: A History of the Catholic Philosophical Tradition* (London: Rowman & Littlefield, 2009).

Mack, J., *Abduction: Human Encounters with Aliens* (London: Simon and Schuster, 1995).

The Mahābhārata (J. van Biutenen (ed. and trans.); Chicago: University of Chicago Press, 1973–1978).

Maimonides, M., *The Guide of the Perplexed* (J. Guttmann (ed.); C. Rabin (trans.); Indianapolis: Hackett, 1995).

Mallebrein, C., 'When the Buffalo Becomes a Pumpkin: The Animal Sacrifice Contested', *Periphery and Centre: Studies in Orissan History, Religion and Anthropology* (G. Pfeffer (ed.); Delhi: Manohar, 2007), pp. 443–72.

Markus, R., 'Surrealism's Praying Mantis and Castrating Woman', *Woman's Art Journal* 21.1 (2000), pp. 33–9.

Martial, *On the Spectacles, in Epigrams* (W. Ker (trans.); Loeb Classical Library, 2 vols; London: Heinemann, 1961).

The Martyrdom of Saints Perpetua and Felicitas, in *The Acts of the Christian Martyrs* (H. Musurillo (trans.); Oxford: Oxford University Press, 1972), pp. 106–31.

Marx, K., 'Introduction', *The Critique of Hegel's Philosophy of Right* (J. O'Malley (ed.); first published 1843–4; Cambridge: Cambridge University Press, 1970).

Masson, J., and S. McCarthy, *When Elephants Weep: The Emotional Lives of Animals* (London: Vintage, 2nd edn, 1996).

Mathews, F., 'Planetary Collapse Disorder: The Honeybee as Portent of the Limits of the Ethical', *Environmental Ethics* 32 (2010), pp. 353–67.

McClymond, K., *Beyond Sacred Violence: A Comparative Study of Sacrifice* (Baltimore: The John Hopkins University Press, 2008).

McDaniel, J., 'All Animals Matter: Marc Bekoff's Contribution to Constructive Christian Theology', *Zygon* 41 (2006), pp. 29–58.

—*Of God and Pelicans: A Theology of Reverence for Life* (Louisville, KY: Westminster/John Knox Press, 1989).

McGuckin, J., *Saint Gregory of Nazianzus: An Intellectual Biography* (Crestwood, NY: St. Vladimir's Seminary Press, 2001).

McLain, K., 'Holy Superheroine: A Comic Book Interpretation of the Hindu Devī Māhātmya Scripture', *Bulletin of SOAS* 71.2 (2008), pp. 297–322.

McLean, S., 'Stories and Cosmogonies: Imagining Creativity Beyond "Nature" and "Culture"', *Cultural Anthropology* 24.2 (2009), pp. 213–45.

Meyers, C., 'The Family in Early Israel', *Families in Ancient Israel* (L. Perdue, J. Blenkinsopp, J. Collins, C. Meyers (eds); Louisville: Westminster John Knox Press, 1997), pp. 1–47.

Michaels, A., 'Blutopfer in Nepal', *Mythen des Blutes* (C. von Braun, and C. Wulf (eds); Frankfurt/Main: Campus, 2007), pp. 91–107.

—'Notions of Nature in Traditional Hinduism', *Environment Across Cultures* (E. Ehlers, and C. Gethmann (eds); Berlin-Heidelberg: Springer, 2003), pp. 111–22.

Michel, P., *Formosa deformitas. Bewältigungsformen des Häßlichen in mittelalterlicher Literatur* (Bonn: Bouvier, 1976).

Migne, J. (ed.), *Patrologiae Cursus Completus: Series Graece* (vol. 37; Paris: Migne, 1863).

Miller, P., 'Jane Goodall', *National Geographic* 188.6 (1995), pp. 102–28.

Miquel, D., *Dictionnaire symbolique des animaux. Zoologie mystique* (Paris: Le Léopard d'Or, 1992).

Montaigne, M. de, *Apology for Raymond Sebond* (R. Ariew, and M. Grene (trans.); Indianapolis: Hackett, 2003).

Morus (R. Lewisohn), *Animals, Men and Myths: A History of the Influence of Animals on Civilization and Culture* (London: Victor Gollancz, 1954).

Muffet, T., *The Theater of Insects*: E. Topsell, *The History of Four-footed Beasts and Serpents* (London, 1658).

Murdoch, I., *The Sovereignty of Good* (London: Routledge & Kegan Paul, 1970).

Muyldermans, J., 'Evagriana', *Muséon: Revue d'études orientales* 44 (1931), pp. 37–68, 369–83.

—'Une nouvelle recension du *De octo spiritibus malitiae* de S. Nil', *Le Muséon: Revue d'études orientales* 52 (1939), pp. 235–74.

Nagar, S., *Mahishasuramardini in Indian Art* (New Delhi: Aditya Prakashan, 1988).

Narain, A., 'Gaṇeśa: A Protohistory of the Idea and the Icon', *Ganesh: Studies of an Asian God* (R. Brown (ed.); Albany: State University of New York, 1991), pp. 19–48.

Nemesius of Emesa, *De natura hominis* (M. Morani (ed.); Leipzig: BSB B. G. Teubner, 1987).

—*On the Nature of Man* (R. Sharples, and P. van der Eijk (trans.); Translated Texts for Historians, vol. 49; Liverpool: Liverpool University Press, 2008).

Newmyer, S., *Animals, Rights and Reason in Plutarch and Modern Ethics* (Oxford and New York: Oxford University Press, 2006).

Nicholls, A., *Goethe's Concept of the Daemonic: After the Ancients* (Rochester, NY: Camden House, 2006).

Northcott, M., 'Do Dolphins Carry the Cross?: Biological Moral Realism and Theological Ethics', *New Blackfriars* 84 (2003), pp. 540–53.

Obermaier, S., 'Antike Irrtümer und ihre mittelalterlichen Folgen: Das Flusspferd', *Antike Naturwissenschaft und ihre Rezeption* 21 (2011), pp. 135–79.

O'Flaherty, W., *Women, Androgynes, and Other Mythical Beasts* (Chicago and London: Chicago University Press, 1980).

O'Laughlin, M., 'The Anthropology of Evagrius Ponticus and Its Sources', *Origen of Alexandria: His World and His Legacy* (C. Kannengiesser and W. Petersen (eds); Notre Dame, IN: Notre Dame University Press, 1988), pp. 357–73.

Olson, D., *The World on Paper: The Conceptual and Cognitive Implications of Writing and Reading* (Cambridge: Cambridge University Press, 1994).

Origen, *Contre Celse* (Introduction, texte critique, traduction, et notes par M. Borret; Sources Chrétiennes, 132, 136, 147, 150, 227; Paris: Cerf, 1967–6).

—*Contra Celsum* (H. Chadwick (trans.); Cambridge: Cambridge University Press, 1965, 1980).

—*On First Principles* (G. Butterworth (trans.); New York: Harper and Row, 1966).

Otto, R., *The Idea of the Holy: An Inquiry into the Non-Rational Factor in the Idea of the Divine and its Relation to the Rational* (J. Harvey (trans.); Oxford: Oxford University Press, 1936).

Padmapurāṇa (N. Deshpande (ed. and trans.); Delhi: Motilal Banarsidass, 2009).

Patterson, C., *Eternal Treblinka: Our Treatment of Animals and the Holocaust* (New York: Lantern Books, 2002).

Patton, K., ' "Caught with Ourselves in the Net of Life and Time": Traditional Views of Animals in Religion', *A Communion of Subjects: Animals in Religion, Science, and Ethics* (P. Waldau, and K. Patton (eds); New York: Columbia University Press, 2006).

—' "He Who Sits in the Heavens Laughs": Recovering Animal Theology in the Abrahamic Traditions', *Harvard Theological Review* 93.4 (2000), pp. 401–34.

Paul VI, Pope, 'Dogmatic Constitution on the Church – *Lumen Gentium*', *Vatican: the Holy See*, http://www.vatican.va/archive/hist_councils/ii_vatican_council/documents/vat-ii_const_19641121_lumen-gentium_en.html (accessed 3 August 2012).

Pedersen, N., *Studies in The Sermon of the Great War: Investigations of a Manichean-Coptic Text from the Fourth Century* (Århus: Århus University Press, 1996).

Perdue, L., 'The Israelite and Early Jewish Family: Summary and Conclusions', *Families in Ancient Israel* (L. Perdue, J. Blenkinsopp, J. Collins, and C. Meyers (eds); Louisville: Westminster John Knox Press, 1997), pp. 163–222.

Perkins, J., *The Suffering Self: Pain and Narrative Representations in the Early Christian Era* (London and New York: Routledge, 1995).

Person, R., Jr., *In Conversation with Jonah: Conversation Analysis, Literary Criticism, and the Book of Jonah* (Journal for the Study of the Old Testament Supplements Series 220; Sheffield: Sheffield Academic Press, 1996).

—*The Deuteronomic School: History, Social Setting, and Literature* (Studies in Biblical Literature, vol. 2; Atlanta: Society of Biblical Literature, 2002).

—'The Role of Non-Human Characters in Jonah', *Exploring Ecological Hermeneutics* (N. Habel, and P. Trudinger (eds); Symposium 46; Atlanta: Society of Biblical Literature, 2008), pp. 85–90.

Peschel-Rentsch, D., 'Pferdemänner. Kleine Studie zum Selbstbewußtsein eines Ritters', *Pferdemänner. Sieben Essays über Sozialisation und ihre Wirkungen in mittelalterlicher Literatur* (D. Peschel-Rentsch (ed.); Erlangen and Jena: Palm & Enke, 1998), pp. 12–47.

Petersen, A., 'Recreate, Relate, Decenter: Environmental Ethics and Domestic Animals', *Placing Nature on the Borders of Religion, Philosophy and Ethics* (F. Clingerman, and M. Dixon (eds); Aldershot: Ashgate, 2011), pp. 165–82.

Petropoulou, M.-Z., *Animal Sacrifice in Ancient Greek Religion, Judaism, and Christianity, 100 BC to AD 200* (Oxford Classical Monographs; Oxford: Oxford University Press, 2008).

Philo of Alexandria, *Philonis Alexandrini de Animalibus* (A. Terian (ed. and trans.); Studies in Hellenistic Judaism; Chico, CA: Scholars Press, 1981).

—*De Providentia: I et II* (M. Hadas-Lebel (ed.); Les Oeuvres de Philon D' Alexandrie; Paris: Éditions du Cerf, 1973).

—*The Works of Philo* (C. Yonge (trans.); Peabody, MA: Hendrickson, 1993).

Philostratus, *The Life of Apollonius of Tyana* (F. Conybeare (trans.); Loeb Classical Library, 2 vols; London: Heinemann, 1989–2000).

Pinchbeck, D., *Breaking Open the Head: A Psychedelic Journey into the Heart of Contemporary Shamanism* (New York: Broadway Books, 2003).

Pliny, *Natural History* (H. Rackham (trans.); Loeb Classical Library, 10 vols; London: Heinemann, 1962–7).

Plotinus, *Ennead*, in *Enneads* (A. Armstrong (trans.); Loeb Classical Library, vol. 6 and 7; London: Heinemann, 1988).

Pluskowski, A., *Wolves and the Wilderness in the Middle Ages* (Woodbridge, Suffolk: Boydell Press, 2006).

Plutarch, *(Gryllus) Beasts are Rational* (H. Cherniss, and W. Helmbold (trans.); Loeb Classical Library; London: Heinemann, 1968).

—*De Iside et Osiride* (J. Griffiths (ed. and trans.); Cambridge: University of Wales Press, 1970).

—'On Isis and Osiris', *Moralia* (F. Babbitt (trans.); Loeb Classical Library, vol. 5; London: Heinemann, 1936).

—'On Love to One's Offspring', *Plutarch's Morals* (A. Shilleto (trans.); Bibliolife: Charleston 2009).

—'On the Cleverness of Animals* (H. Cherniss, and W. Helmbold (trans.); Loeb Classical Library; London: Heinemann, 1968).

—*On the Eating of Flesh* (H. Cherniss, and W. Helmbold (trans.); Loeb Classical Library; London: Heinemann, 1968).

Pontifical Academy for Life, *Prospects for Xenotransplantation: Scientific Aspects and Ethical Considerations*, http://www.vatican.va/roman_curia/pontifical_academies/acdlife/documents/rc_pa_acdlife_doc_20010926_xenotrapianti_en.html (accessed 13 August 2012).

Porphyry, *De l`abstinence* (J. Bouffartigue, M. Patillon, A. Segonds, and L. Brison (trans.); Budí series, 3 vols; Paris: Societe d´Edition "Les Belles Lettres", 1977–1995).

—*Life of Plotinus*, in *The Enneads* (A. Armstrong (trans.); Loeb Classical Library, vol. 1; London: Heinemann, 1966).

—*On Abstinence from Killing Animals* (G. Clark (trans.); London: Duckworth, 2000).

Pressly, W., 'The Praying Mantis in Surrealist Art', *The Art Bulletin* 55.4 (1973), pp. 600–15.

Prete, F., and M. Wolfe, 'Religious Supplicant, Seductive Cannibal, or Reflex Machine? In Search of the Praying Mantis', *Journal of the History of Biology* 21.1 (1992), pp. 91–136.

Putz, O., 'Moral Apes, Human Uniqueness, and the Image of God', *Zygon* 44.3 (2009), pp. 613–24.

Pyle, R., *A Handbook for Butterfly Watchers* (New York: Scribner's, 1984).

The Ramayan of Valmiki (R. Griffith (ed. and trans.); Benares: E. J. Lazarus, 1895).

Ratzinger, J., *God and the World: A Conversation with Peter Seewald* (San Francisco: Ignatius Press, 2002).

Richter, H., *Kommentar zum Rolandslied des Pfaffen Konrad* (Teil I; Bern and Frankfurt: Herbert Lang & Cie, 1972).

Der Rig-Veda. Aus dem Sanskrit ins Deutsche übersetzt und mit einem laufenden Kommentar versehen von Karl Friedrich Geldner (Cambridge: Harvard University Press, 2003).

Rives, J., 'The Theology of Animal Sacrifice in the Ancient Greek World: Origins and Developments', *Ancient Mediterranean Sacrifice* (J. Knust, and Z. Várhelyi (eds); Oxford: Oxford University Press, 2011), pp. 187–201.

Roberts, R., *Serendipity: Accidental Discoveries in Science* (New York: Wiley, 1989).

Robinson, C., and D. Cush, 'The Sacred Cow: Hinduism and Ecology', *Journal of Beliefs & Values* 18.1 (1997), pp. 25–37, http://dx.doi.org/10.1080/1361767970180104 (accessed 1 July 2012).

Rodrigues, H., *Ritual Worship of the Great Goddess: The Liturgy of the Durga Puja with Interpretations* (Albany: Suny Press, 2003).

Rolston, H., 'Does Nature Need to Be Redeemed?', *Zygon* 29 (1994), pp. 205–29.

Ruether, R., *Gregory of Nazianzus: Rhetor and Philosopher* (Oxford: Clarendon Press, 1969).

Runia, D., *Philo in Early Christian Literature* (Assen and Minneapolis: Van Gorcum and Fortress, 1993).

Rüpke, J., 'Hellenistic and Roman Empires and Euro-Mediterranean Religion', *Journal of Religion in Europe* 3 (2010), pp. 197–214.

Sabini, M. (ed.), *The Earth Has a Soul: The Nature Writings of C. G. Jung* (Berkeley, CA: North Atlantic Books, 2005).

Saenger, P., 'Silent Reading: Its Impact on Late Medieval Script and Society', *Viator* 13 (1982), pp. 367–414.

Sax, B., *The Mythical Zoo: An Encyclopaedia of Animals in World Myth, Legend and Literature* (Santa Barbara, CA: ABC-Clio, 2001).

Schappert, P., *A World for Butterflies* (Buffalo: Firefly Books, 2000).

Scharlemann, R., *Inscriptions and Reflections* (Charlottesville, VA: University Press of Virginia, 1989).

Schenda, R., 'Hund', *Enzyklopädie des Märchens* 6 (1990), col. 1317–1340.

Schiebinger, L., 'Why Mammals Are Called Mammals: Gender Politics in Eighteenth-Century Natural History', *The American Historical Review* 98 (1993), pp. 382–411.

Scott, P., *Anti-Human Theology: Nature, Technology and the Postnatural* (London: SCM Press, 2010).

—'The Technological Factor: Redemption, Nature, and the Image of God', *Zygon* 35 (2000), pp. 371–84.

Seneca, *Letters*, in *The Hellenistic Philosophers* (A. Long, and D. Sedley (eds); vol. 1; Cambridge: Cambridge University Press, 1987).

Shaw, B., 'Body/Power/Identity: Passions of the Martyrs', *Journal of Early Christian Studies* 4.3 (1996), pp. 269–312.

Shaw, G., *Theurgy and the Soul: The Neoplatonism of Iamblichus* (University Park, PA: The Pennsylvania State University Press, 1995).

—'Theurgy: Rituals of Unification in the Neoplatonism of Iamblichus', *Traditio* 41 (1985), pp. 1–28.

Shelton, J.-A., 'Lucretius on the Use and Abuse of Animals', *Eranos* 94 (1996), pp. 48–64.

Shepardson, D., 'Bugs, Butterflies, and Spiders: Children's Understandings about Insects', *International Journal of Science Education* 24 (2002), pp. 627–43.

Silver, C., *Strange and Secret Peoples: Fairies and Victorian Consciousness* (Oxford: Oxford University Press, 1999).

Simoons, F., S. Batra, A. Chakravarti, P. Diener, G. Eichinger Ferro-Luzzi, M. Harris, A. Heston, R. Hoffpauir, D. Lodrick, S. Malik, W. Mey, S. Mishra, S. Odend'hal, R. Palmieri, D. Pimentel, E. Robkin, C. Schwabe, J. Schwartzberg, M. Suryanarayana, and P. Wagner, 'Questions in the Sacred-Cow Controversy [and Comments and Reply]', *Current Anthropology* 20.3 (1979), pp. 467–93.

Singer, P., *Animal Liberation* (New York: Avon Books, 1990).

—*Practical Ethics* (Cambridge: Cambridge University Press, 2011).

Śivapurāṇa (J. Shastri (ed. and trans.); Delhi: Motilal Banarsidass, 1995).

Skandapurāṇa (G. Tagare (ed. and trans.); Delhi: Motilal Banarsidass, 2007).

Smelik, K., and E. Hemelrijk, ' "Who knows not what monsters demented Egypt worships?" Opinions on Egyptian Animal Worship in Antiquity as Part of the Ancient Conception of Egypt', *Aufstieg und Niedergang der Römischen Welt* 17.4 (Berlin and New York: Walter de Gruyter, 1984), pp. 1852–2357.

Smith, J. Z., *Imagining Religion: From Babylon to Jonestown* (Chicago Studies in the History of Judaism; Chicago: University of Chicago Press, 1988).

—*Map Is Not Territory: Studies in the History of Religions* (Chicago: University of Chicago Press, 1993).

Sobol, P., 'The Shadow of Reason', *The Medieval World of Nature. A Book of Essays* (J. Salisbury (ed.); New York and London: Garland Publishing, 1993), pp. 109–28.

Somos, R., 'Origen, Evagrius Ponticus and the Ideal of Impassibility', *Origeniana Septima* (Louvain: Peeters, 1999).

Sontheimer, G.-D., *Pastoral Deities in Western India* (A. Feldhaus (trans.); New York and Oxford: Oxford University Press, 1989).

Sorabji, R., *Animal Minds and Human Morals: The Origins of the Western Debate* (London: Duckworth, 1993).

Southgate, C., *The Groaning of Creation: God, Evolution, and the Problem of Evil* (Louisville, KY: Westminster/John Knox, 2008).

Spaemann, R., *Essays in Anthropology: Variations on a Theme* (G. de Graaff, and J. Mumford (trans.); Eugene, OR: Wipf and Stock, 2010).

—*Persons: The Difference Between 'Someone' and 'Something'* (O. O'Donovan (trans.); Oxford: Oxford University Press, 2006).

Speckenbach, K., 'Der Eber in der deutschen Literatur des Mittelalters', *Verbum et signum. Friedrich Ohly zum 60. Geburtstag überreicht* (H. Fromm (ed.); 2 vols; München: Fink, 1975), vol. 1, pp. 425–76.

Spengler, O., *Decline of the West: Form and Actuality* (C. Atkinson (trans.); vol. 1; New York: Albert A. Knopf, 1926).

—*The Decline of the West: Perspectives of World History* (C. Atkinson (trans.); vol. 2; New York: Alfred A. Knopf, 1928).

Srinivasan, D., 'The So-called Proto-Śiva Seal from Mohenjo-Daro: An Iconological Assessment', *Archives of Indian Art* 29 (1975–6), pp. 47–58.

—'Unhinging Śiva from the Indus Civilization', *Journal of the Royal Asiatic Society of Great Britain and Ireland* (1984), pp. 77–89.

Staal, F., *Rules without Meaning: Ritual, Mantras, and the Human Sciences* (Toronto Studies in Religion, vol. 4; New York: P. Lang, 1990).

Stewart, S., *On Longing: Narratives of the Miniature, the Gigantic, the Souvenir, the Collection* (Durham, NC: Duke University Press, 1993).

Strassman, R., *DMT: The Spirit Molecule* (Rochester, VT: Park Street Press, 2001).

Strassman, R., S. Wojtowicz, L. Eduardo, and E. Frecska, *Inner Paths to Outer Space: Journeys to Alien Worlds through Psychedelics and Other Spiritual Technologies* (Rochester, VT: Park Street Press, 2008).

Straten, F. van, *Hiera Kala: Images of Animal Sacrifice in Archaic and Classical Greece* (Leiden: Brill, 1995).

The Stricker, *Karl der Große* (K. Bartsch (ed.); Berlin: de Gruyter, 1965).

Strieber, W., *Communion: A True Story* (New York: Avon, 1987).

Taves, A., 'No Field Is an Island: Fostering Collaboration between the Academic Study of Religion and the Sciences', *Method and Theory in the Study of Religion* 22 (2010), pp. 170–88.

—*Religious Experience Reconsidered: A Building Block Approach to the Study of Religion and Other Special Things* (Princeton, NJ: Princeton University Press, 2009).

Thomas, E., *The Hidden Life of Dogs* (Boston: Houghton Mifflin, 1993).

Tiger, L., 'Can Animals be Religious?', *Big Think* (20 May 2010), http://bigthink.com/ideas/20164 (accessed 24 July 2012).

Tiger, L., and M. McGuire, *God's Brain* (New York: Prometheus Books, 2010).

Tonti-Filippini, N., J. Fleming, G. Pike, and R. Campbell, 'Ethics and Human-Animal Transgenesis', *National Catholic Bioethics Quarterly* 6 (2006), pp. 689–704.

Tsai, J., 'Entomology in the People's Republic of China', *Journal of the New York Entomological Society* 90.3 (1982), pp. 186–212.

Ullucci, D., *The Christian Rejection of Animal Sacrifice* (Oxford: Oxford University Press, 2012).

—'Contesting the Meaning of Animal Sacrifice', *Ancient Mediterranean Sacrifice* (J. Knust, and Z. Várhelyi (eds); Oxford: Oxford University Press, 2011), pp. 57–74.

Ulrich of Etzenbach, *Alexander* (W. Toischer (ed.); Reprint Stuttgart/Tübingen: Bibliothek des Litterarischen Vereins, 1888; Hildesheim: Olms, 1974).

'Unthinkable? Faster than light', *The Guardian* (24 September 2011), http://www. guardian.co.uk/commentisfree/2011/sep/23/unthinkable-faster-than-light-editorial (accessed 9 August 2012).

Uther, H.-J., 'Schwein', *Enzyklopädie des Märchens* 12 (2007), col. 393–8.

Varro, *On Agriculture* (W. Hooper (trans.); Loeb Classical Library; London: Heinemann, 1967).

'Vatican Observatory examines theological implications of finding alien life', *Catholic News Agency*, http://www.catholicnewsagency.com/news/vatican_observatory_ examines_theological_implications_of_finding_alien_life/ (accessed 3 August 2012).

Vernant, J., *Mortals and Immortals: Collected Essays* (Princeton, NJ: Princeton University Press, 1991).

Vogel, S., 'The Silence of Nature', *Environmental Values* 15.2 (2006), pp. 145–71.

Vorderstemann, J., 'NEITUN und MUNTUNZEL. Zu "Willehalm" 425,25–426,30', Kritische Bewahrung. Beiträge zur deutschen Philologie. Festschrift für Werner Schröder zum 60. Geburtstag (E.-J. Schmidt (ed.); Berlin: Erich Schmidt, 1974), pp. 328–34.

Waldau, P., 'Religion and Other Animals', *Sightings* (29 May 2008), http://divinity. uchicago.edu/martycenter/publications/sightings/archive_2008/0529.shtml (accessed 24 July 2012).

—'Seeing the Terrain We Walk: Features of the Contemporary Landscape of "Religion and Animals"', *A Communion of Subjects: Animals in Religion, Science, and Ethics* (P. Waldau, and K. Patton (eds); New York: Columbia University Press, 2006).

—*The Specter of Speciesism: Buddhist and Christian Views of Animals* (Oxford: Oxford University Press, 2002).

Waldau, P., and K. Patton (eds), *A Communion of Subjects: Animals in Religion, Science, and Ethics* (New York: Columbia University Press, 2006).

Ward, B. (ed.), *The Lives of the Desert Fathers* (Kalamazoo, MI: Cistercian Publications, 1981).

Werness, H., *The Continuum Encyclopedia of Animal Symbolism in Art* (New York and London: Continuum, 2006).

West, M. (ed. and trans.), 'Homeric Hymn to Aphrodite', *Homeric Hymns. Homeric Apocrypha. Lives of Homer* (Loeb Classical Library; London: Heinemann, 2003).

Wiedemann, T., *Emperors and Gladiators* (New York/London: Routledge, 1995).

Willey, P., and E. Willey, 'Will Animals be Redeemed?', *Animals on the Agenda* (A. Linzey, and D. Yamamoto (eds); Urbana, IL: University of Illinois Press, 1998), pp. 190–200.

Wisbey, R., 'Wunder des Ostens in der "Wiener Genesis" und in Wolframs "Parzival", *Studien zur frühmittelhochdeutschen Literatur. Cambridger Colloquium 1971* (L. Johnson, H.-H. Steinhoff, and R. Wisbey (eds); Berlin: Erich Schmidt, 1974), pp. 180–214.

Wittkower, R., 'Marvels of the East. A Study in the History of Monsters', *Journal of the Warburg and Courtauld Institutes* 5 (1942), pp. 159–97.

Wolfram of Eschenbach, *Parzival* (K. Lachmann, and B. Schirok (eds); Berlin: de Gruyter, 1998).

—*Willehalm* (A. Leitzmann (ed.); Tübingen: Niemeyer, 1963).

Yeats, W., 'Supernatural Songs VIII', *Collected Poems* (London: Wordsworth Editions, 1994).

Zeiler, X., 'Transformations in the Textual Tradition of Dhūmāvatī. Changes of the Tantric Mahāvidyā Goddess in Concept, Ritual, Function and Iconography', *Transformations and Transfer of Tantra in Asia and Beyond* (I. Keul (ed.); Berlin and New York: De Gruyter, 2012), pp. 165–94.

Zimmerman, M., 'The Role of Spiritual Discipline in Learning to Dwell on Earth', *Dwelling, Place, and Environment: Toward a Phenomenology of Person and World* (D. Seamon, and R. Mugerauer (eds); New York: Columbia University Press, 1985), pp. 247–56.

Zuntz, G., *Persephone: Three Essays on Religion and Thought in Magna Graecia* (Oxford: Clarendon Press, 1971).

Index of Scripture References

Index of Subjects

Index of Names